Geo. W. Bethune

MEMOIR

OF

REV. GEO. W. BETHUNE, D. D.

BY

REV. A. R. VAN NEST, D. D.

NEW YORK:
SHELDON AND COMPANY.
498 BROADWAY.
1867.

J. E. FARWELL & CO.,
Stereotypers and Printers,
37 Congress Street,
Boston.

CONTENTS.

CHAPTER I.

PAGE

Early Life. 1

CHAPTER II.

Turning to God. 19

CHAPTER III.

Seminary.—Visit to the South. 41

CHAPTER IV.

Rhinebeck Ministry. 70

CHAPTER V.

Ministry in Utica. 84

CHAPTER VI.

Settling in Philadelphia.—Wanderings in Europe. . 122

CHAPTER VII.

Success in Philadelphia. 153

CHAPTER VIII.

Art of Angling.—Forest Life. 199

CHAPTER IX.

Literary and Public Labors. 226

CHAPTER X.

New Church at Brooklyn.—Goes Abroad. . . . 249

CHAPTER XI.

PLATFORM ORATORY. 273

CHAPTER XII.

ANONYMOUS ATTACK. 319

CHAPTER XIII.

PATRIOTISM.—UNION SPEECH. 352

CHAPTER XIV.

DEPARTURE FROM BROOKLYN.—RESIDENCE IN NEW YORK.—
RETURN TO EUROPE. 376

CHAPTER XV.

CLOSING SCENES. 407

CHAPTER XVI.

PERSONAL REMINISCENCES. 424

PREFACE.

The compiler of this volume presents the results of his labor to the public with modesty. This does not arise from any want of interest or importance in the subject, but because it has been found difficult to present the portrait of a person so varied in gifts and rich in culture. He prefers therefore to call it a Memoir, as an instrument to preserve Dr. Bethune in memory, rather than a life which could assume to give a full and perfect representation. If there is any deficiency it is not caused by any lack of loving assistants in the good endeavor. Seldom has a book been written in which so many willing hands have borne a part. First and foremost stands Mrs. Bethune, who, with untiring fidelity, has collected her husband's correspondence and has contributed many precious associations Mr. George Trott of Philadelphia, frequently known in the subsequent pages as "the Major," has filled up many blanks. J. B. Brown Esq., formerly consul at Florence, Italy, has been useful in collecting letters, and his facile pen has supplied many connecting sentences. Finally, when pastoral duty compels the editor to leave the country, Rev. Dr. W. J. R. Taylor, of the American Bible Society, has promised to see the book safely through the press. The names of other generous assistants will appear as the work proceeds, and to them our readers will owe a debt of gratitude. Specimens of Dr. Bethune's sermonizing would have been given were it not contemplated to produce at least two volumes of his popular lectures and choice discourses. That there must be difference of opinion as to the positions taken by a man of such strong character on great questions is certain, but the aim of the biographer has been to take his view from the stand-point of his subject, and not to justify his course. Let those opposed exercise the grace of charity.

The Memoir has been delayed by the collection of material, in fact the work was not fully put in our care until a little more than a year since. If the result shall be to revive the love that any felt for this "radiant messenger of God," if it shall justify him in the sight of any who have misunderstood his theories; above all, if it shall be the means of winning any to that Saviour whom it was the sincere and single desire of Dr. Bethune to proclaim, the writer will not have labored in vain: Salvete Omnes.

DR. BETHUNE IN STUDY DRESS.

MEMOIR OF

GEO. W. BETHUNE, D. D.

CHAPTER I.

EARLY LIFE.

WHEN a person has gained a distinguished position, and made a marked impression upon the men of his time, it becomes interesting to observe the method or training by which such power has been acquired. It must be confessed that the subject of our memoir stood eminent amongst his own countrymen, and while much of his success was due to natural gifts, vastly more must be attributed to early culture and divine grace. George W. Bethune was descended from a long line of honored and pious ancestry. On the paternal side he sprang from the French Huguenots. In Picardy a large town bears the family name, and his house could boast of relation to the Duke of Sully, the friend of King Henry IV. *

Persecution compelled them to join in the exodus from their native country, and they found a new home in Scot-

* The name "Bethune" holds an illustrious place in French history. The family were Counts of Flanders, and one of them, Robert de Bethune, signalized himself by taking La Roche Vandais where the rebel Marcel had retired. Another of the same name in Sicily killed Maufnoy, the tyrant, an act which Charles of Anjou rewarded by the gift of his daughter Catherine as wife. In later times they formed the highest social connections, even contracting royal alliances.—*Memoirs of the Duke of Sully.*

land. From Rosshire in that land, Divie Bethune, the father of Dr. B., emigrated in early life first to Tobago, West Indies, and afterwards to the United States, locating in New York. His motive for the latter change seems to have been a religious one, as is evident from his first introduction to notice by Mrs. Graham: —

"There is a young man here of the name of Bethune (pronounced Beaton), who was in Tobago, and has told me of his steadiness in nonconformity to the world even there, and his strict adherence to his profession, though he stood one of two who made any. This young man became alarmed even there, and though his prospects of rising in life were confined to that place, he finally took the resolution to leave it and seek a Christian land; he engaged here as a clerk in a wholesale store, and wandered about from church to church for some time, at last our John nailed him, by the blessing of God, and last Sabbath he became a hopeful communicant. He is a lad of sense, has had a liberal education, and John thinks him a double acquisition."

His early promise was not disappointed. He soon became one of the most prominent and successful merchants of the city, around whom the younger would gather for advice. His piety increased with his years, and he was ready for every good and generous enterprise; in fact there was little in the way of Christian benevolence in which he was not a leader or a vigorous assistant.

"He printed the first religious tract long before the Tract Printing House, he imported Bibles for distribution long before the Bible Society was opened, was a foreign director of the London Missionary Society long before any Missionary Society existed here, was one of the founders of the American Colonization Society, and amongst the very earliest movers in the cause of Seamen, long before the Seamen's Friend Society."

He was one of the founders of the Princeton Theological Seminary. When most successful in business, this good man had an inclination to abandon his brilliant prospects and enter Princeton Seminary, that he might be fitted to become a missionary to the destitute parts of the country, and then he exults at the thought of his entire family being "Witnesses for Christ."

About this period he became acquainted with Miss Joanna Graham, who was a member of the Scotch Presbyterian Church, with which he connected himself, under the pastorate of Dr. John Mason; she, like him (Mr. B.,) was earnestly devoted to Christ, and sympathized in all his benevolent ideas; she was born in America, but her family were also from Scotland, and their faith, eminent through successive generations, brought down to her a rich inheritance of covenant promises. Her mother was Mrs. Isabella Graham, whose life of shining goodness has given her a high place in Christian biography. The father and mother of this lady, Mr. and Mrs. John Marshall, were both pious, and her grandfather was one of the Elders who quitted the Established Church with the Rev. Ralph and Ebenezer Erskine. She married Dr. John Graham, who, becoming a surgeon in the British army, was ordered to Canada, and thus the family fixed its future abode in the New World. The father having died, Mrs. Graham who had a finished education, was induced to open a school for young ladies in New York, in the management of which she was assisted by her daughters. This school soon became very flourishing, and a source of blessing to many ladies of the highest social position. To one of these daughters, Miss Joanna, Mr. Bethune professed his love, and after much serious reflection and prayer, a marriage was consummated. The union of such godly persons, well grounded in the doctrine of Christ, full of zeal in his cause, was very happily consummated; all their children were converted in their youth, and their only son became the useful minister concerning whom we write. He was born March 18, 1805, at Greenwich, then a small village, but long since absorbed in the magnificent growth of New York City. He was peculiarly a child of prayer; devout intercession was made before his birth, and the event is thus acknowledged in his father's diary.

"Lord, O Lord! how shall I praise thee for the mercies of this day. Truly it may be said of me and mine, what hath God wrought. Thou art our trust. Blessed be the Lord for a living mother and a living child. Oh! remember my request this morning. Receive my dedication of my son. Thou knowest all along what I have asked of my God, that if he gave me a son, he might be sanctified from the womb, and be made a faithful, honoured and zealous minister of the everlasting gospel. Lord, hear us in this thing. O! let this son be chosen of thee to declare to the Gentiles the unsearchable riches of Christ. Give to his dear mother and myself grace and wisdom for bringing him up in the nurture and admonition of the Lord. Let him be a Samuel to the Lord. 1 Sam. 1:27, 28."

A similar act of dedication occurred at his baptism on April 14, 1805:

"This afternoon my dear infant son George was baptized by Mr. Forrest. I hope I can say, that with full purpose of heart he was devoted to the Lord by both his dear mother and myself. Mr. F. preached from Gen. 1:27, and after sermon came home with us, and prayed fervently for our infant and other children. O my God! thou hast seen my exercises this day; the strong, simple faith I exercised in the promises thou hast made me to fasten upon, for my dear infant George this day devoted to thee. Lord, honour this faith of thine own operation. Let a blessing always attend the means of grace and instruction to this man child, whom thou hast given us. Open his understanding early to understand the Scriptures. Affect his heart even in infancy to love the precious Saviour, and to adore his covenant Jehovah. Instruct his mother and me to instruct him. Direct to proper teachers. Teach the teachers to teach and bless their labours to him. Fortify his young heart against the temptations, the false pleasures, the alluring vanities, the contaminating examples of an evil world. May he seek thee early and find thee. Endow him richly with spiritual gifts. Give him the learning of the world, and the divine wisdom to use his learning and his abilities for the noblest purposes, the illustration of thy love, thy will, thy grace to sinners of mankind. Make him a faithful minister of Jesus Christ, humble, holy and self denying. Give him a contented mind, a thankful heart. May he declare the whole counsel of God, and while he is faithful and sound in his doctrine, do thou grant him to be eloquent, animated, impressive and acceptable. I ask all this, for thou art able to grant all I can ask. I ask it now, young as he is, knowing that thou art God. Life is thy gift, life spiritual and divine is thy work in the soul of man, all the gifts and graces of the Holy Spirit are thine to bestow, power to make the preacher's word successful is of God, thou canst guide through life, conduct through death, and minister an abundant entrance into glory. To whom then shall I go? To whom would I go? My God! unto thee, and thee alone. Hear my supplications this day. Behold the promises I have taken." Isaiah 44: 3, 5. 65 : 23, 24, 59 : 21."

Most remarkable prayer and how wonderful the fulfilment. God granted to this man of faith, the very things he sought for. The entire diary of Mr. Bethune might be published to show the atmosphere which hallowed the home of this young Samuel, and as a pattern for Christian parents. Every important step in his life was sanctified by believing prayer. Only a few months passed, when he was brought very low by an attack of scarlet fever. This stroke came very heavily upon the parents, as they had lately been called to part with a beloved daughter, and now God seemed about to take away their only son. It was a time "of great searchings of heart," of deep humiliation and earnest wrestling with God, in that pious family. The good man prays, but he asks according to the rule of faith, "Lord, let this dispensation have a blessed effect, let us search our hearts and see, may we search them as with the candle of the Lord." As the case grows more alarming:

"O my God! it appears to be thy will to ask of us the surrender of our dear George, also. Lovely babe! How proud we were of him. But who gave him? Who made him such? None but thou, my God. Therefore, however dear to our hearts, however consoling to our pride, this precious gift may have been, it is our duty to resign him to thy call. O! make it a willing duty on our part. Let grace reign in our hearts to humble, to sanctify and to resign. To do this must be thy work. * * * But yet, low as he appears, it is still in thy power to save his life, and to restore him to us. Lord, if it be lawful for us to urge this request, we do urge it. What people is so great as thy people? Who have God so nigh unto them as the Lord our God is to us in all things that we call upon him for? Lord, if it be really thy purpose to take from me my George, O, receive him to thyself. May I yet meet my babe in heaven, and there hear him sing to all eternity glory to our God."

When in answer to this effectual, fervent prayer of a righteous man, health was restored, the voice of thanksgiving went up from that habitation, and the child was more than ever dedicated unto the Lord.

"Oh how thankful should I be! My babe, I trust, will not be raised for nothing. He will be the Lord's! Oh my gracious God, who hast so far consented to our prayers, do thou crown thy mercy by sanctifying this child from his infancy, and qualifying him by thy Spirit for being an eminently pious, able, useful, humble herald of thy gospel. Oh, my precious Saviour, thy goodness to me is overflowing goodness; my beloved son George, so providentially spared; so humbly but zealously set apart for thy special service, not only by me, but seemingly by pious Mr. Forrest and others; my confidence in thy protection through all my trials, all, all these rich mercies of my covenant God."

When the child was a little more than two years old, chastisement became necessary, which was attended with the same spirit of prayer. Sept. 27, 1807.

"This morning I had to use the rod of correction very severely, on my darling George, who discovers a most violent temper. And now, oh my God! enable me to plead for my George. He is a child of

Adam. Bless to his young heart the rod of correction. Oh, my God, my God, suffer me to surrender this charge to thee. Oh, undertake thou for me. Subdue thou his corruptions, and mould him early, even in infancy to thy will."

The same fault is mentioned in the fifth year of his age 1809. "Grant early and great grace to our dear George, who discovers so much of a high temper." "Behold his strong corruptions and headstrong manner. Teach him by thy grace, and oh, teach us to bring him up for thee."

This was a marked feature in the youth, at one time leading to the injury of a young companion, when his emotion was as intense in penitence, as it had before been in wrath. He suffered more than the one he wounded, and going upon his knees besought forgiveness. These prayers run on in the same spirit,day after day, and year after year. It would have been strange indeed, it would have argued against the truth of God's promises, if such faithful, loving entreaty, had not been followed by a great and abundant blessing. When we consider the future greatness of the man, we must recall the foundation of prayer on which his education was built.

The family residence at this time, was a pleasant villa on the banks of the Hudson, which the good man named in his Diary, "Mount Ebenezer." Dr. Bethune alludes to it in later years, in a poem to his mother:

I've lived through foreign lands to roam,
And gazed on many a classic scene,
Yet would the thoughts of that dear home
Which once was ours oft intervene,
And bid me close again my weary eye
To think of thee and those sweet days gone by.

That pleasant home of fruits and flowers,
Where by the Hudson's verdant side

My sisters wove their jasmine bowers,
 And he we loved, at eventide,
Would hastening come from distant toil to bless
Thine and his children's radiant happiness.

Alas the change! the rattling car
 On flint paved streets profanes the spot,
Where o'er the sod we sowed the Star
 Of Bethlehem and Forget-me-not.
Oh! woe to Mammon's desolating reign,
We ne'er shall find on earth a home again!

Divie Bethune being one of the foremost merchants of the city, it must have been a home of luxury and taste, and being prominent in every scheme of Christian benevolence, it must have been the constant resort of the great and the good; there too were found distinguished ministers, well-known missionaries and leaders in social life.

"Well do I remember," says one who was afterwards tenderly associated with the subject of this memoir, "our gambols on the green lawn which sloped to the river, and the glee with which we laved our hands in the grand Hudson. I have a sweet recollection of the happy family, the genial smile with which I was welcomed by his sainted father; kind words from his mother and sisters as we admired the new roses, and heard the history and specialty of each. She had named the pleasant home 'Rose Bank,' from its great variety of roses. The English cook too, who had come into the family when George was a few months old, and the Hindoo servant* who had been found by Mr. Bethune, stretched on his master's grave to die, and taken home to live and be a faithful servant for forty years, all ready and anxious to contribute to my happiness."

In the large hall of this mansion the village children assembled for Sabbath instruction, and when a grand occa-

* Known afterwards as Richard.

sion offered, as for instance a marriage, the orphans were recipients of the good cheer.

There were two sisters, the elder, Jessie, married Rev. Dr. McCartee of New York; the younger, Isabella, united to Rev. Dr. Duffield of Detroit, Mich. both of them gifted women, who with their brother, were early taught the practice of good works. He was a Sunday School teacher at the age of thirteen.

For several years his education was conducted entirely by his mother, who as we have seen, was a teacher of some experience, admirably adapted to develop the gifts of her son. To this maternal care he was indebted for many of the graces which adorned his future career, especially for his accomplishments as an orator, and intimate acquaintance with English Classics. Instruction was commenced early and by most easy and natural methods. When two years old his letters were learned from the walks at their villa, his mother drawing them upon the gravel. Grammar was taught by chairs, and arithmetic computed by marbles and balls. There was a remarkable development of talent, but it was difficult to subject to discipline. Causality was early prominent, for he was found one day struggling with the old cat, to bury her in the ground that she might grow kittens. The school system of that day was but little adapted to his disposition. The trial was not attempted until he had attained some years, but upon the very day of his introduction to school, seeing a companion who received undeserved punishment, he could not endure the wrong. Young as he was, he attacked the teacher and was summarily dismissed from the school. Later he was placed with Dr. Nelson, the blind teacher, whose severity was traditional amongst the older New York families, and a similar cause led to his removal.

When reading his Latin lesson, for every mistake in which a blow might be expected, he became so enraged that he seized the rod from the teacher's hand and applied it vigorously to his shoulders. Faulty as were these extravagances of temper, and much anxiety as they must have awakened; yet, it is to be observed, that it was this same impetuous, violent disposition which, when sanctified by Divine grace, made him such a resolute and intrepid defender of righteousness.

But over that display of depravity the godly father mourned, and it was the occasion of new and more earnest appeals to the throne of grace for Divine direction. These entries occur in his diary

Dec. 17, 1815.

"My dear and only son George gives me much uneasiness from his carelessness and seeming indifference to religious exercises." Feb. 4, 1816. "My poor young and only son George continues to exhibit a great degree of insensibility. Oh Lord have mercy upon him. His heart is hard and cold to religion. With man it is impossible to heal him, but with God all things are possible." April 14, 1816. "I am now at a loss to whose care I shall commit my dear son George, and am deeply exercised respecting his spiritual conviction. Oh Lord, my God, thou seest the deep and pungent exercises of my soul with regard to my beloved son, whom thou hast given me, whose life thou hast preserved. What shall I do with him? To whose care shall I commit him? I feel helpless as an infant in this work. Oh God, my Saviour, undertake for me. * * * I know that he lies at mercy, and my inmost soul rejoices that he lies at *thy mercy*. * * Make him thy chosen vessel consecrated to the Gospel Ministry. Every thing now seems to deny this hope, yet I would commend him to thee, and hope against hope." May 19, 1816. Blessed be thy name for giving us a prospect of placing him with thy servant, Dr. Proudfit. I trust it is from thee. Oh prepare his way before him."

Thus light dawned upon the path, the youth was placed

with Rev. Alex. Proudfit, D. D. of Salem, Washington Co., N. Y., pursuing his studies at the Academy under the care of Rev. Joel Nott. This school was the nursery of many ministers, Drs. Jas. M. Mathews, Wm. R. Dewitt, James Beattie, John Proudfit, and Messrs. J. B. Steele, and William Williams; most of them older than Bethune. It is feared that he did not advance rapidly in study at this place; but there were great advantages attending the change. He was, at a most impressible age, removed from the temptations of town life, and brought into contact with the simplicity of country manners. His physical nature was strengthened by manly sports of horsemanship and angling. Here he made acquaintance with Fisher Billy. Dr. Prime of the Observer, writes: —

"I asked Dr. Bethune where he, city born and bred, acquired his taste and skill in fishing. He said 'that when a boy, at the Academy in Salem, Washington County, N. Y., he fell in with a man called Fisher Billy who gave him lessons and showed him how.' 'What, Fisher Billy from Cambridge?' I asked, with some surprise, 'how came he there with you?' 'The same man,' the Dr. replied; 'he was often in debt and obliged to go to Salem on the limits; but the limits included a fine trout stream, and there he practised the vocation that had tempted him to neglect his business and lose his property.'"

Here, too, was cultivated that love of nature which was such a notable feature of Dr. Bethune, amidst some of its most lovely scenery, whilst gathering wild flowers upon the hills, or whipping the trout streams at the base of the Green Mountains. Neither was study entirely neglected. He writes playfully to his mother: —

"Dec. 1817.

My hat is a little too large; however if I stuff a little more Latin and Greek into my saphead, I shall be able to fill it. I have been studying hard, and think I shall be able to enter the Sophomore Class of Union College in the Spring."

At Salem, was formed an intimacy with Miss Mary Williams, the daughter of Colonel Williams, a beautiful maiden of his own age, which afterwards ripened into most devoted affection, an affection that increased with advancing years, which was the joy and beauty of his future life, which always had the warmth of youthful love and was not chilled even by death, which, sanctified as it was, will bloom fair and sweet in the morning of eternity. When she was about leaving her happy home for boarding-school, it was his part to cheer up her first great grief while the stars were shining in the sky, and with his merry and witty rhymes change the sighs of regret into shouts of laughter. He had some skill in music and often amused himself with the flute, on which he became a finished performer, beguiling away the hours and pains of sickness, in at least one instance, with his sweet melodies. He was quite an adept in the art of boxing, an exercise for which to the day of his death he expressed respect; which, if report speaks truly, was again called into exercise in behalf of injured innocence in the person of his young companion, John Williams, who suffered from the irritable temper of their tutor. His genial nature made him a great favorite with the young, and while the old people shook their heads and called him the mischievous New Yorker, they were not the less charmed with his humor, and many enjoyed the benefits of his bounties which he scattered with a lavish hand. Even at this early period he shone as a member of a literary club, known as the "Washington Adelphi Society," and in the youthful gatherings he was leader of the fun and frolic. The religious atmosphere of the place was not without its salutary influence. It is thus noted by his father: —

"Both of Dr. Proudfit's sons are under serious impressions. My dear son seems to understand much of the system of truth, with a secret hope of being brought to its saving knowledge, but his vivacity of manner and activity as yet prevent the hope of serious convictions." Again, "I have visited my son much to my satisfaction in Dr. Proudfit's family. I trust that Jehovah, who mercifully provided such a situation for my beloved son, will be graciously pleased to sanctify it to him. Oh may he live consecrated to God."

Thus peacefully and with much profit passed two of the happiest years of his life, when he was called to New York to be placed under a tutor's care in view of a better preparation for College. In this prospect, as in every important change, the pious father was diligent in seeking divine direction. At Salem young Bethune had formed a close friendship with William Williams, a little older than himself, "a truly pious boy, humble minded, intelligent and pleasant in his deportment, exercised in faith and unto godliness." The two young men were "like David and Jonathan." This latter was now invited to enter Mr. Bethune's family, doubtless with the purpose of improvement from his religious influence, and shortly after the father rejoices "that his dear son is at home with us, blessed with a pious youth for his companion and satisfied with him, both studying closely under a pious tutor," and was deeply impressed with the responsibility and honor of training these young men for the Lord's service. In the days of his son's greatest insensibility this purpose of the man of faith never faltered. When George was fourteen years of age they entered Columbia College, N. Y., in the fall of 1819. In the routine of academical studies he attracted no special interest. He held a moderate position, neither rising high in the scale of merit nor falling below respectability; but, as before, he was distinguished in all the exhibitions of eloquence, and was an ornament of the Philolexian Society. Upon leaving college his friends wrote:

"Your society will be mourning your loss in dust and ashes." "The exhibition (of the Society) was superior, but this did not happen without forcibly reminding me of my good old crony George, who afforded me so much pleasure in the recitation of the 'Prisoner of Chillon,' nor was I the only one in whom it excited the recollection of past pleasure. Many were heard to say, 'Do you recollect how well George recited.'"

Here was exerted that peculiar influence over his young companions, which in after years was described as a magical charm that he possessed of attaching others to himself. Perhaps a friend of his youth (Dr. Smith Pyne, of Washington, D. C,) has given the explanation of this power:

"I sympathize sincerely in your happiness, but my very dear friend, I think it is hardly possible for you to be unhappy anywhere. The strength of your understanding, and the buoyancy of your spirits fortify you against all the lesser, but most annoying ills of life, and you have that open-heartedness and fascination of manner, which must make friends for you wherever you may be. I do not believe, George, I ever met with a person whose countenance was so perfect an index of his feelings as yourself, and the quality which I love you most for, is that blunt honesty with which you will tell a friend his faults, and the single-heartedness and affectionate pleasure with which you praise his good qualities."

His humor and love of sport led him to practise on the dullness of a classmate who requested aid in the preparation of essays, by inditing the most extravagant and pedantic papers which the young gentleman would recite with all the sobriety of a Nestor, to the great amusement of all the college except the victim. In fact the life of young Bethune at this time was a joyous, rollicking one. Songs were continually upon his lips, smiles beamed on his face and play and fun occupied his whole heart. Another of his amusements at this period, which absorbed much of his time, was the game of billiards. An early acquaintance, who was requested to furnish materials for this memoir, said, "I was only intimate with him during his college days, and my associations are not such as you would care to put in the record of a gospel minister." Another classmate thus recalls old memories :

"At one time, I imagine myself in the window-seats of Columbia College cracking jokes with my old crony George, and I almost answer to the imaginary voice of old ——, 'Mr. Bethune and Mr. —— you are continually diverting my attention;' at another time I detect myself in the act of beating my own sides under the impression that I am the black stud's back, and endeavouring to cast the dust of the avenue in the eyes of C——'s mare. Then again I well imagine that I am in the Society room, listening with deep attention to your eloquence, or my lively imagination carries me forth to the cricket ground, where I view your weighty corpus in the fruitless contests for superiority of agility with the shadowy form of J. Y. and there also I hear your expostulations with old Turvey for the extravagant price and base qualities of his beer."

The same friend gives him a full account of the Long Island races and bets which he and other friends had made, and assumes that they both will be equally interested in the success of the great "Eclipse." But while thus occupied in a career of gayety and worldliness, it is not to be supposed that he sank into any of the baser forms of dissipation; he was frolicsome and this led him into mischief; he was impetuous and this caused many quarrels; but he was always devoted to refined female society, and this, combined with the sanctified influences of home, preserved him from the haunts of vice. A companion who was with him on an excursion, which had much of extravagance, says, that he reminded Dr. B. of it in after life, when he replied, "I remember it well and have deeply repented of it; from that text I have preached fifty sermons." As this made so deep an impression, we conclude that such occasions could not have been frequent even in his wild days. About this period, while engaged in cricket play upon the battery, his leg was dislocated by a young companion. With much self command he desired his friends to send for Dr. Post, an eminent surgeon. The Doctor ordered the attendants to pull off the boot, the operation being painful, the youth cried, "Cut the boot," when the Doctor interfered, saying, "Young man, when you earn the money to pay for boots, you may order them to be cut to pieces."—The good doctor's design was quickly evident, for in the hard pull upon the member it had been restored to its normal condition. This accident was the cause of a long and trying confinement, during which numerous friends came to visit him, among whom was the eloquent and saintly Methodist preacher, Summerfield, who had just commenced his ministry in New York. He talked seriously, although he said, the conversation of gay companions was now more acceptable; yet he felt sure that some day Bethune would not only delight in religion, but that he (Mr. S.) would hear him proclaim the Saviour's love with power to dying sinners. This hope was realized, for although it pleased the Lord to remove this good man from his labors before the youth had finished his theological studies, still Summerfield was privileged to hear him urge the cause of missions, pleading for the love of Jesus. At last he was restored to his full powers, but alas! neither the trying providence, nor all the pious addresses, nor the frequent prayers made in his behalf had produced any marked effect; he rose from his sick bed the same careless worldly youth; not that he was entirely destitute of religious impressions, such could scarcely be the case, considering the pious surroundings of his home. His father, who watched anxiously every hopeful sign, thus wrote in his diary:

"My dear George is now singing hymns. I hear his dear voice; it is a pleasant sound. O! my God, put life in his soul that there may be life in his praise."

Again: "Read with George and Williams three verses alternately, making afterwards suitable remarks, partly offered by myself, and partly elicited from them by the eighth chapter of Mark. I thought George appeared raised to more spiritual concern in the discussion of this important chapter than I have seen him for a long time."

But whatever signs of good there might have been, this was a period of deepest solicitude to the godly parent, and most earnestly did he betake himself to the throne of grace.

"Lord, bless my son. Thou seest how very cold and careless he is. Lord, do in this matter as in other things; when thou hast shown me my utter inefficiency towards effecting any good work in him, do thou be pleased to step in with majesty and grace to make him willing in the day of thy power." "Yesterday was the birthday of our beloved son, on which he completed his fifteenth year. Blessed, ever blessed be my God, who hath preserved him so long to his fond parents. Oh make his whole soul one flame of fire to Thee — his whole life a hymn of praise to Thee. Hasten it in its time. Oh, Lord God, strengthen my faith to wait for it; believing that though it tarry, I shall wait for it because it will surely come; it will not tarry; the just shall live by faith."

What strong, persevering faith was that which believed when appearances were so dark, and could hopefully say, "I seem to feel as if the conversion of our dear son George would be given to us." Neither was it all faith, but he joined works to faith. It has been noted with how much care he selected his school and tutor, sought out for him companions, supplied him with suitable religious books, directed him to such preaching and places as were specially favored by the Holy Ghost, and neither of his parents wearied in personal addresses on the subject. The following extract is a specimen of their soul-stirring appeals:

"Can I be easy, my beloved George, until I see you escaped from the snares of Satan, and delivered from the inward dominion of sin, the agent of Satan in the hearts of men. You have only to pray fervently to God for his Holy Spirit, and confessing your weakness, your ignorance and your danger, to cast yourself on the covenant mercy of God, ensured by his precious promises to them who ask the one and plead the other with sincerity of heart. Now, my dear George, retire to your room and pour out your heart before God, and examine the Scriptures, and plead the promises which I have set down for you; here are some texts marked. Were you to die in your present state, or to continue thoughtlessly in sin, until your heart became hardened through the deceitfulness of sin; alas! how awful would your end and your eternity be, and how heart-rending the affliction of your dear mother and myself for the eternal ruin of our only and dear son. My dear son, no other good is worth pursuing, until you have secured the chief good, and having once obtained the favour of God and the hope of eternal life, you could then pursue all other studies with cheerfulness, diligence and effect. You will therefore allow the love of a father to be importunate for the welfare of a dear son, and as you love me who love you so truly, I lay it upon you to think seriously on the subject, to occupy your mind with truth, and to devote a part of every day in retirement, to supplicate the blessing of God on your soul and your life."

During his youth he was subject to several attacks of sickness, often assuming a character of much severity. Although surrounded with so many good influences, addressed by so many tender appeals, warned by God's providences, Satan still had the mastery; the hard, natural heart resisted the means of grace, and George remained a worldling.

CHAPTER II.

TURNING TO GOD.

The mode of life we have described could not have been pleasing to godly parents and the position is thus given:

"My soul is afflicted by the thoughtless state of my dear son's mind. He has a hurried order of spirit which impels him to pursue with eagerness any object that suddenly gains his attention. At college he is exposed to companions and conversation unsuitable to the general tenor of my instructions to him. The young men rouse his pride and his jealousy by accounts of routs and plays and parties, and now before his education is finished, he is thirsting for enjoyments, which, by anticipating, he may never be able comfortably to possess. Whilst his heart is diverted from a love of religious duties and hardening against self-denying courses, whilst his deadness to spiritual things gives no sign of his becoming a minister of the gospel; his indolent, gay disposition, if indulged, will unfit him for those business habits so essential to a commercial life. My soul is sometimes harrowed within me."

At another time we read: — "Almighty God, I would now come before thee, and ask wisdom as to the course of conduct I should pursue with respect to my son. He is of an impetuous, assimilating temper, and much exposed to temptations at the college, with so many thoughtless companions, and no adequate benefit derived from the risk. He is in the way of idle, speculative views and habits, and is now getting a relish for company. He will be learning to spend largely, without being at all fitted to make anything. Would it not be better to place him at once with a merchant to learn his business, and to acquire habits of industry and diligence, as well as skill of goods? I beseech thee, oh my heavenly Father, to instruct and direct me in this important movement; teach me in this trying situation of my poor son."

He was now seventeen years old. It was indeed a time for the deepest parental solicitude. Were all those hopes of ministerial usefulness to be blasted? were all those consecrations, all those prayers and all those entreaties to be worthless? was that father to sit still and see his son laboring and toiling under the horrible yoke of the infernal one and wretchedly choosing the things of this world through the dominion of sin and unbelief in his soul? It could not be! And now light arose in the darkness, Christian prudence demanded that these associations which, though not sinful, were unfavorable to piety, should be sundered, and a most inviting prospect opened before them.

Rev. Dr. John M. Mason, a ripe scholar and the most eloquent pulpit orator of his country, and perhaps of his age, had been called to preside over Dickinson College at Carlisle, Pa. The faculty was small, but could scarcely have been more perfect, consisting of Prof. Vethake, a thorough mathematician, and Dr. Alexander McClelland, who as an educator of youth was without a parallel. This institution so admirably furnished, presented great attractions to the young and opened a door of hope to the praying father. Dr. Mason had long been a pastor and friend of Mr. Bethune's family, and Mr. Duffield, the son-in-law, was now pastor of the Presbyterian Church at Carlisle. In September 1822, young Bethune and his companion Williams, entered this college to complete the studies of the senior year, a change which in the providence of God proved of the greatest importance to his eternal welfare. Directly after his arrival, we find him speaking of the change with gratification. The professors at Columbia College were not popular with students, and we conclude that there had been quite an exodus from his class, part going to Carlisle and others to Yale. We find him writing of his new associations with pleasure, and giving the highest praise to Dr. McClelland and his lectures. Of Dr. Mason, however, he says: "I was too young to know him in his palmy days of strength and power. I did not come closely under his influence until 1822, which was some years after the shock which affected irreparably his mighty intellect:" although he speaks of Dr. Mason's "profound and elegant erudition," displayed in "his Comments on the Art of Poetry, by Horace, and the Treatise on the Sublime, by Longinus." We have no account of his standing at college, although we find him at once engaged in the Belles Lettres Society. At this time his father wrote to him as to a warm friend of Summerfield, who would take an interest in his health which was now rapidly failing, and speaks of young Willett who was one of Summerfield's converts and a great delight to his heart, seeing that, when he was dead, Willett could preach. He takes occasion to excite his pride in sustaining the credit of the college; hinting that there had been disorders of late and that this report had done much harm to its prospects. He concludes with an appeal on the great topic:

"I left you with strong emotions. Oh, that I could see you safe within the covenant. The eternal God is thy refuge. Can you choose a better? The contest is for heaven. You must begin the inward conflict, the battle with yourself, sooner or later, or your soul is *lost forever!!!* Begin at once. Ask the Lord for a new heart. Be not cheated out of your soul by a thoughtless impetuosity that gives way to outward temptations. Rouse, my son, and put a heavenly courage on. A crown of glory is the prize. Eternity against Time, holiness against pollution. Linger not, the Lord calls. Let your soul obey."

He had been located at Carlisle only a little more than a month when God visited the college in a very solemn manner by the death of one of their young companions, James H. Mason, the son of the President, and a very promising young man of great piety of character, who was carried off by typhus fever. The family were already in mourning from the recent death of his sister, Mrs. Van Vechten, and this second blow brought desolation indeed. Dr. Mason entertained a strong prejudice against funeral services, on the ground that they were apt to become occasions for eulogizing the dead. Upon this occasion, Mr. McCartee, who for the time supplied the pulpit of Mr. Duffield, was requested to beg that an address should be made at the grave for the sake of the young men in the College. He did so. Dr. Mason replied, "No, these things are so often abused." As the young men who served as pall-bearers lifted the coffin, the afflicted father exclaimed in solemn tones, which those who were present can never forget, "Young men, tread lightly! ye bear a temple of the Holy Ghost," then overcome by his feelings, he dropped his head upon his friend's shoulder and said, "Dear McCartee, say something which God may bless to his young friends." The scene in the graveyard is described as one of deep impressiveness. There was the grand old patriarch bowed to the ground under the weight of sorrow, with the youth of the college who felt that a brother had been stricken, and round about were mourning relatives and sympathizing towns-people. Mr. McCartee, who had a warm heart and whom sudden emotion would often raise to the highest eloquence, spoke as if by inspiration a lesson suited to the occasion; many people remarked that they had never seen such a graveyard, and all seemed in tears and many in agony. The address was wonderfully blessed of God. A revival powerful and precious in its fruits began in the college and town. In this revival young Bethune, had a share, but it may be imagined that such a strong and earnest nature as his would not yield without a struggle. While vice had not possession of him, yet the claims of pride and affection bound him to the world and he had undergone a hardening process, when resisting for years all the calls of Divine grace. Seldom had a young man been so surrounded with holy influences or resisted so many loving entreaties. Aware that from his earliest infancy he had been dedicated to the Lord, early taught to pray and love Jesus; on every proper occasion addressed upon the subject by father and mother; taken to hear the most eloquent preachers, addressed privately by Summerfield, Ward, young Edward Kirk, and others; again and again laid upon the bed of sickness, to give space for reflection; yet he had been able to resist all the strivings of the spirit, and although young in years, yet by custom he had become very hardened in his heart, and it was not without a fierce contest that the rebellious nature could be conquered even by the Saviour's love. But the history of an event so important in our memoir can be best gathered from anxious eye witnesses, Mrs. Bethune and Mr. Duffield:

"Our dear son," says his mother, "had been three years at Columbia College, N. Y. We placed him there, because he could still reside under the parental roof, and be under our own eye; that he might have a suitable companion, we educated a young man with him, and we fondly hoped that the Lord would accept the dedication of our son, which we had made to him in baptism, and fit him to serve him in the gospel ministry. Every affliction He visited him with, (and he has been often laid on the bed of sickness,) we hoped was the means to bring him home to himself, and although he often seemed serious and alarmed at the thoughts of death, yet whenever he got well he became as thoughtless as ever. When the college at Carlisle was revived, and our dear friend, Dr. Mason became its principal, our son and several other students of Columbia College became anxious to spend their last year of study under his care. We felt almost afraid to part with our son, yet seeing his great desire to go, and knowing that he would be under the kind and watchful eye of his dear brother Duffield, we consented. Little did we think of the blessing God was preparing for us in his providence, by directing the dear youth to this step. He entered upon study in September, 1822. I followed in October, and Mr. Mc Cartee arrived in Carlisle on the fifteenth of November, when James Hall Mason, son of our dear friends Dr. and Mrs. Mason, lay at the point of death in a bilious fever. Mr. Duffield, being obliged to administer the communion to a vacant congregation, was necessarily absent. Mr. Mc Cartee providentially arrived to administer consolation to our afflicted friends. James was delirious during the whole of his illness, but his conversation, although incoherent, showed that his mind dwelt on serious things. To Mr. Duffield, who sat up with him one night, he said, 'If you knew what a sinner I have been, you would not be so kind to me. I once thought that I had experienced the love of God shed abroad in my heart, and endeavoured to walk in the right way, but when I became a professor, I thought I must be a gentleman, and turned aside from the right way.' The morning of his death reason seemed to return, he knew those around him and uttered plainly these words, 'My son give me thy heart.' He departed about one, P. M., Saturday, the 16th. Mr. McCartee did not come out to dinner, and my son George, who never would believe that James would die, was fretting and fuming because he could not get his dinner and go out riding on horseback. I was shocked at his seeming indifference, and told him I was sure that James was dying, and that was what detained Mr. Mc Cartee. He ate his dinner and started for town. I went to my knees to plead for my poor boy, begging the Lord, for his name's sake, to have compassion on the poor youth whom nothing seemed to affect. I felt wretched, and said to his sister, that I deeply regretted we had let him come to Carlisle, he showed such violence of temper, and so much self-sufficiency that I trembled for the time when I should leave him from under parental authority. 'Lord help me,' was my cry. I had no comfort but trusting in a sovereign God. The youth seemed to scorn my advice, and would none of my reproof. God only could change his heart. I often told him that I never expected to see him curb his temper, till he began to pray. He seemed sorry after he had been in a passion, but for the merest trifle would again give way to his temper. When he returned in the evening, I asked him 'What he thought of himself, to be so concerned about his dinner, when his friend was passing from time to eternity?' He said 'Oh mother, don't talk about dinner, when poor James Mason is dead.' I endeavoured to improve this dispensation to him. He seemed to feel deeply; but it was only his sorrow for his friend that made him weep."

We continue the narrative as given by Mr. Duffield:

"The solemn scene at the interment of Mr. Duncan left upon the minds of many an apparently greater seriousness and attention to the means of grace than had before been observed. The communion season which followed was unusually solemn. Several of the young men in the college were very deeply impressed by the services of that day, and one or two sought for Christian instruction. The death of poor James Mason struck a peculiar awe upon the youth in college. Brother Mc Cartee's address at the grave was remarkably owned, and the hearts of many quaked at the thought of death. On the following Tuesday, eight of the students met with us under deep and anxious concern about the state of their souls. The number was increased to fourteen on Thursday after, of every one of whom we now entertain hopes. There are yet four or five more, deeply impressed, known to be so, but how many more it is impossible to conjecture. The church was crowded yesterday, and the audience as solemn as the grave. I never saw in any place such deep and fixed attention, and such evident struggling with feeling. What may be the present extent of the impression we know not, but that it is not confined to the college, the appearance of the congregation yesterday showed. I have no doubt that the Lord has commenced a good and gracious work among us, which will only be stopped by the unbelief and stumbling stocks which Christian professors may cast in the way.

The change in my dear brother George has filled our house with songs of triumph and praise. I know how anxiously you watched and prayed for him, so that anything relative to the great change will be peculiarly interesting. The Lord is a Sovereign, and he acts in such a sovereign manner, as to laugh all our wisdom to scorn. I think you will feel as we all do, that He was determined to let us see that it was only and altogether His own work. On Monday last, it was whispered among the pious students that there were several of their fellow collegiates distressed in their minds. On Tuesday, an invitation was given to brother McC. and myself to meet with them. George heard of it that day, and that Mr. Codwise was among the number of inquirers. He wrote a note to him, desiring him to come out here, but received a reply that he could not in consequence of the perturbed state of his mind. We met that evening and found that dear youth among the number and most deeply affected. Samuel McCoskry also was there, but he had obtained a hope. All George's friends were either there or reported to be deeply impressed. On our return home we began to state that we had seen some of the young men, and detailed their exercises, particularly of Codwise and McCoskry, and afterwards had family worship; when brother McC., William, and myself left the chamber for the parlor. "His mother writes, 'I felt confounded. I ought to have rejoiced, but I could not. My son is not amongst them,' burst from my lips; 'nothing seems to affect him.'

"I asked him," says Mr. Duffield, "if he had heard that so many of his young friends were inquiring. He seemed surprised, and got almost angry, said, How could it be? He had seen them within a day or two, and they were not serious then. I told him God was not like man. He could convince and convert in a short time. His great concern was, lest his dear friends should not know what they were doing, and by and by when the impression wore off, they would be branded as backsliders. He left his sister's room, and coming down to the parlour, walked in great agitation, accusing us of being instrumental in promoting religious calumny, of endangering the reputation of his friends, and manifested great warmth and violence of feeling. The first thing that was said, which appeared to calm him was, that we were as tenacious of the reputation of Codwise as he was, and loved him dearly. He then stated more calmly his own opinion upon the nature of their excited feelings, and said he thought it strange that a change should have taken place in his friends and he not know it; that it should be done so speedily, and that they should not acquaint him with it, from whom they had never concealed anything. He protested however, that he could not be duped, and that no man should know the state of his mind, until it had undergone a thorough change. Yet, in five minutes after, so rapidly did he cool down, that he told us he would rejoice if his friends were changed indeed, and that as for himself, he would do anything that might change his heart. He saw himself to be left alone and forsaken by his friends, and resolved to see them the next day and hear it from themselves before he could be satisfied.

"'I am all alone, what shall I do?' was his cry that night before he went to bed. I pressed him to pray, he said 'he could not.' I warned him now, while the Spirit was striving with him, that it would be dangerous not to attempt it. It was late at night; he hung to us, felt loth to part, and dropped a tear as I bid him good-night and begged of him to pray before he went to bed. I thought it prudent to let his own mind pursue its reflections until he should see Codwise and McCoskry.*

*Mr. Hamilton Codwise and Bishop McCoskry of the Episcopal church in Michigan.

On Wednesday they came to Mr. Duffield's study, who begged them to deal faithfully with George when he should call upon them that evening. He knew that they were with the minister but took no notice of them. His mother could discover nothing more than common in him, but was pleased to hear him say that he would go to lecture that evening, if Mr. McC. would make the first prayer. When he returned from college he looked solemn. In the evening he saw his friends, and went with them to lecture. He returned directly home, but said little; told his companion, Williams, 'that he believed every one of his friends and acquaintances were either Christians or seriously exercised, and that he could not find one, if he was so disposed, to carry on and sport with as before.' His mother mentioned that she had written to his father of the interest, but had given no names. He thanked her and said, 'It will not be secret long.' She asked 'If he thought them sincere.' 'Oh yes.' 'Don't they want you to go with them?' His heart was too full to answer. When his brothers and Williams returned from lecture they went straight to the study, and I heard them wrestling in prayer together. George seemed very solemn at family worship, but his mother thought it was only because others were so. The next morning he was still solemn and tender, and would allow himself to be spoken to, though none said anything to him but his mother, and that but little. He took no supper the evening before, nor did he breakfast the next morning. That day, Thursday, he again saw Codwise and McCoskry, and they were faithful to him. He did not come home till after dinner, then refused to eat. He had been weeping and went to his own room much agitated. His mother followed to restore his Bible and saw him sitting with a countenance like a condemned criminal. He remained by himself till near five o'clock when he had to attend college prayers. McCartee saw him wandering alone, and wanted him to go and drink tea at Prof. McClellan's; he declined. He then begged him to go to the Doctor's (Mason), but he still refused. 'That evening,' Mr. Duffield says, 'I was surprised to find him at the place appointed for meeting anxious persons. I addressed myself to him, when he fell into my arms and poured forth torrents of tears. His mind was pressed down with anxiety, but free from terror. After conversing with him in a smothered tone some time, it appeared as if a gleam of hope darted across his mind. I stated the numerous encouragements that he had to seek the God of Jacob. His feelings gushed forth in an expression of confidence, though but faint, and it thrilled as with an electric shock through the whole room. The tempest of his mind, he said, had been somewhat lulled to rest. We walked home together, talking about his views and feelings all the way, and when we came to the door, I proposed that we should quickly have worship and retire to rest, and that he should occupy my study. He told me that he had met a passage in Joel 2: 12, 13, which encouraged him, and he was determined to seek till he got the blessing. As late as one o'clock that night we heard him wrestling over our heads. As he lifted his voice in prayer, that passage crossed my mind, and I felt a confidence that he would not seek in vain, 'Surely thou hast not said unto the seed of Jacob, seek ye my face in vain.'

All hearts were deeply engaged for him, and he had been made the subject of special prayer, the evening before, by the serious young men in college. The next morning, Friday, he still continued solemn, and weeping frequently. His mother pressed his dear face to her bosom and asked, 'If he felt no better.' He answered 'Not much better.' 'What is the difficulty?' 'He feared that he would not be accepted.' She told him she expected that would be the case. He had resisted the Spirit on former occasions, and now the Lord was trying him; but she encouraged him to persevere, assuring him of victory.

He ate no breakfast and passed to college. Having now been without food for nearly two days, he was persuaded to take a little nourishment. Immediately after he opened the Bible and pointed, says Mr. Duffield, to the passage in Joel which encouraged him, and in a low tone began to converse with me about his feelings. I turned up several different passages in the Scriptures, but particularly Isa. 43: 22–26. I observed, these charges God makes against you; this is your character, but look at the grace, v. 25. Behold your duty and privilege, v. 26. A shower of tears fell instantly, and wetting his Bible soiled the page. Precious memorial! I asked him to retire to my study. For an hour we conversed about his exercises, until being crowded down with evidences in his favour, he could no longer doubt the work of God. I led him to the throne of grace, and poured out my heart in thankfulness to God. His heart seemed ready to break. As I rose from my knees I told him of necessary business, and though it was painful to my feelings to leave him, yet I must go. He then caught me by the hand and said, 'Oh no, my dear brother George, you must not go till I, too, return thanks to God.' He then bowed and prayed, and his heart was led forth in the strongest and most vivid exercises of faith. 'Thou wilt hear me, O God, when I cry unto thee. Thou hast said, Ask and ye shall receive. Lord, I have done so and I claim thy promise. Thou hast the price of my soul, the blood of thy Son, and thou delightest in judgment over mercy. It is thy darling attribute, for before mercy could be manifested, justice must be satisfied. I therefore claim the pardon of my sins, not for mine own sake, but for the sake of thy dear Son.'

Such were some of his expressions of faith. He continued in the same strain for some time, and then made a full dedication of himself to God, prayed to be furnished with the armor of God, to be perfected, strengthened, stablished; to be made a devoted servant of Christ; to be employed and made eminently successful in winning souls to Christ; to be enabled to endure all the fatigue and toils of the way and receive, at last, a crown of glory. His heart too, was earnest in prayer, for the work of God among us, for the conversion of sinners; especially that God would bless brother McC. and myself, for the work to which we had been called, and make us successful and reward us richly for our labours of love. One of his expressions of faith struck me with great force. He addressed God as 'the God of his father, the God of his mother, the God of his sisters, the God of his brothers, the God of all his friends, and claimed him as his own God and Redeemer.' His prayer carried with it to my mind the most overpowering evidence of being wrought in his heart by the Spirit of God. When we rose from our knees, we could neither of us speak, but fell into one another's arms and embraced as *brothers in Christ.* It seemed as if we could not part. Oh, it was a moment of exquisite joy. Heaven let fall upon us some of its own bliss, and our hearts exulted in the Lord our God. From that time, he has manifested the most striking change. It is literally true, 'old things have passed away and all things have become new.' Who can refuse to give all the glory to God, and acknowledge his work."

Thus terminated a glorious victory of Almighty grace. Mr. Duffield's house had been named "Happy Retreat" and it was now happy indeed. He hastened to Mrs. Bethune's room, his face bathed in tears of joy and cried, "Oh! dear mother, George is a new-born soul." Angels carried the good news to heaven on the 22d November, 1822.

It is impossible to describe the emotions which filled those praying and anxious, though long baffled and disappointed, yet never wearied nor hopeless, and now successful parents. Mrs. Bethune writes :

"And now O Lord, what can we, his parents, say. For thy servants' sake, and according to thine own heart hast thou done all this greatness in making known all these great things. O Lord God, there is none like unto thee, neither is there any God beside thee, according to all that we have heard with our ears. And what one nation in the earth is like thy people, like Israel whom God went to redeem to be his own people. And now, O Lord God, let the thing that thou hast spoken concerning thy servants and concerning their house, be established forever, and do as thou hast said. Now, therefore, let it please thee to bless the house of thy servants that it may be before thee forever, for thou blessest, O Lord, and it shall be blessed forever. Amen and Amen."

A story has been current amongst Dr. Bethune's friends, that this interesting event occurred while both his parents were absent from him, and that they were engaged in bemoaning his hopeless condition and their unanswered prayers, when the postman's knock was heard, bringing the joyful news of his conversion. The above narrative will show that it has no foundation in truth, as his mother was all the time at Carlisle, an attentive and careful observer of her son's progress. Neither was his father at all despondent, but with that wise forecast of faith which is often so remarkable, thus wrote on September 29 : " My mind has been exercised for the salvation of my dear son. At times I feel such nearness to the throne of grace with this petition, and such an assurance of hope, that it would seem as if the blessing were nigh at hand." Again, on November 25, when he has received the news of young Mason's death and that there is a little religious interest, and while his whole heart is engaged that his son may be a partaker of the hoped-for grace, he records :

"I have had of late, at times, amid all my fears for George, some sweet and secret intimations of expected mercy from my gracious God." And thus he was encouraged to plead more closely, more believingly, more perseveringly, and more fervently that a new heart might be given.

The new convert, having obtained a calmer state, penned the following to his father: —

"CARLISLE, *Nov.* 26, 1822.

It was my intention to have written you sooner, but the duties which devolved upon me at the death of my dear friend, James Mason, and subsequently to that, the anxiety I felt to attain to that state in which I could meet death with resignation and hope, have so occupied my time and disturbed my mind that I could not bring my thoughts sufficiently together. But now, having, I trust, found a sure foothold of faith in the blood of my Saviour, and having obtained the consequent joy and peace of mind, I feel as if it was my duty to write you, not only as a father in the flesh, but as one who is a joint heir with me in the salvation of Christ. You will no doubt wish to know what occasioned the thoughtless and wicked son you left, to have turned his thoughts on such subjects. I will give you an account of its beginning and progress. On Saturday, James Mason died. In the evening we met in the Belles Lettres Hall to form some resolutions as a tribute of respect to his memory. Then I felt sad and solemn at our loss. On Sabbath morning, McCartee preached an excellent sermon, but it reached not my hard heart, though bowed down, as it were, with grief. Sabbath afternoon, we followed him to his long home, and in the graveyard, though sobbing and weeping, I felt not the address which the solemn scene presented to my mind. Monday passed as usual, and Tuesday, until the evening when brother George and McC. came home and told me that Codwise, McCoskry, Cahoone, Gregg, A. Labagh, Samuel Boyd, and some others were seeking the way to salvation. First, I felt mad that they should be so foolish, as I thought. But it gave way to a deeper feeling of wonder, and then my love to Codwise made me think he must be sincere. And that night found me, for the first time of my life, as I can recollect, praying fervently. I felt as if my friends were going, and that I could not and should not stay behind. The next day I bridled my feelings until evening, when I went to lecture, and after lecture Codwise walked with me and advised, and that night again found me earnestly engaged for the salvation of my soul. Thursday evening, I went to the room where the inquirers met, and I went out lighter and seemingly more happy than when I entered. That night I wrestled hard, and said that I would wrestle like Jacob until the break of day, and that God should not go until he blessed me. But ah! I became fatigued, and went to sleep. But God did not forget his part of the engagement, he did bless me. On Friday evening I was rejoicing in the love of the Son of God. Oh, how dear does that blood appear to me now, which I have so often trampled under foot. It seems as if I would suffer anything to promote the glory of Christ's kingdom, and the interests of his church. It seems to me that the four years which must intervene before I can proclaim that gospel to sinners which has saved my soul, is a very long time. Temptations afflict me, doubts still harass me, but the love of Christ, like the sun among clouds, disperses all the darkness. I think I can rely firmly and steadfastly for salvation on the Saviour's atonement. I believe, I can never be cast out. His promises are very comfortable, especially those which speak of God's being the God of his people's children. The verse, however, which gave the most comfort in my darkest hours, is in the second chapter of Joel. 'Turn unto me with all your heart,' &c. I complied with the letter and spirit, I trust, and hoped God would do his part, and I was not deceived. He received me into his fold and nursed me, weak and trembling, in his arms. And I trust he will keep me in his fold, and if I should stray, that he will pursue me and constrain me to come back. Pray for me, my dear father, that I enter not into temptation, and if the devil should tempt, that I say to him, 'Get thee behind me.' Lindsey is, I hope, coming out clear and sure. Codwise and McCoskry like old Christians, Cahoone hoping and comforted, and your own son rejoicing with fear.

Your son and brother I trust, in Christ,

GEO. W. BETHUNE."

An interesting coincidence was, that about the same time Miss Mary Williams, to whom during the last summer, he had frequently read the Word of God when she lay upon a bed of sickness, gave her heart to God and made public confession of faith. This occurred without any concert of action between them, and was not discovered till years later.

His father makes this grateful comment:

"Thus the dear youth who was dedicated by his parents to the sacred office, in humble faith in God's promise and power, at the season of his natural birth, was enabled to dedicate himself also, at the hour of his spiritual birth. Amazing grace! unmerited goodness! Blessed word on which our blessed God has caused us to hope. He is faithful that promised, He also will do it. Thine be all the glory. Amen!"

Indeed it was an occasion of thanksgiving to many; the youth had a great power of attaching friends, and letters came from every quarter rejoicing over his happiness. The Rev. Dr. McCauley informed his mother that her son had often been a subject of prayer with him, and she writes: "Bacon, Ward, Sommerfield, Romeyn,* Caldwell, your dear grandmother, and still dearer father, all that praying breath spent for you; it will be difficult for you to tell who is your spiritual father, so many have been interested in you."

It will be seen that his warm, grateful nature was burning with desire to carry out his father's dedication and do something for Jesus, and that it was a great trial that years of preparation were demanded before he could proclaim the riches of Christ. As far as he had opportunity he commenced to plead for his Saviour, addressing some of his old companions at Columbia College. His epistles called forth a remonstrance from his friend, Smith Pyne, whose heart had experienced a change about the same time, but who thought that Bethune acted with indiscretion. Here the young professor finds himself beset by different religious theories in the person of his young friends, Pyne and Kirk. Pyne

* The family during his minority attended the Church under the care of Dr. J. B Romeyn, in Cedar Street.

considers it obtrusive thus to address his friends, asking them to turn from their evil ways. He puts him on his guard, and warns Bethune against enthusiasm. He does not mean that elevated love of God which every true Christian feels, but that impatience of human frailty and exclusive attention to particulars which degenerates into fanaticism. "Nothing," he says, "is more attractive than unaffected and unobtrusive piety, nothing more repulsive than a gloomy, pragmatical spirit which would deprive man of the innocent enjoyments with which God has surrounded him. For my part I never enjoyed society, conversation, plays and parties so much as I do now, but now I take them all in moderation. I surfeited myself formerly, I made them my first object, now merely as occasional relaxations from more weighty pursuits." Mr. Kirk writes, "Be faithful to the souls of sinners. Remember the pit from whence you were digged ; all sinners are as you once were, they need your prayers and your warnings. It is in the performance of this duty I have found the most encouragement. There has been a reaction upon my soul. You have entered upon a new life ; your companions, your pursuits, and your amusements are all changed. The Christian should always have his taste elevated so far above the beggarly elements of the world that they will be as bitter herbs in his mouth ;" and then adds severe views of Christian duty. Thus at the commencement of his religious life were presented the two extreme views of practice, from friends equally attached and sincere. It was his duty to choose that part, to which he adhered through life, the happy *mean*. He could not be conformed to the world, neither could his Christianity assume the form of asceticism.

It is fair to state that both friends were equally rejoiced at his religious change while each offered different views of practice. But whatever might be exterior influences, he went steadily on in the course of Christian duty. His sister wrote, "Dear George keeps very steady; we hear no more of 'Old King Cole;' but last night he was singing 'what think ye of Christ!' His father, whom he visited during the holidays, says:

"He has delighted the hearts of his dear mother and myself by the solemnity, devotion and sincerity of his demeanor. He manifests indeed the power of our God in the new creation of his soul. Last evening we had a meeting of several parents of sons awakened at Carlisle to declare unitedly one thanksgiving to the Lord, and to supplicate his continued grace. George Bethune, Samuel Boyd, Jr, and George Lindsay Campbell were present, three youthful representatives of the converts at Carlisle. On being questioned, they acknowledged the happiness they enjoyed by their change of state, and in the privilege of pouring out their hearts to God in prayer, that Christ was precious to their souls."

Again. "Yesterday morning our beloved son left us. Delightful indeed was his visit. Everybody in the house remarked the happy change he has undergone; no anxiety now about food or dress, no fretfulness, no empty wishes, no murmurings, no vain boastings, all seemed joy and peace in believing, his soul thirsting for the love of God."

"He was steadily attendant on prayer-meetings, and though so young a Christian, he was so solicited to pray as to make the concluding prayer at Mr. Morse's school-room at the Thursday evening meeting.. It is said to have been simple, fervent and unaffected. It produced much feeling and interest, being so manifest a proof of the power of God in turning a heart of stone to a heart of prayer. I was not present, or I would probably have prevented his being called upon to pray."

"Your conduct," said his mother, "I have reason to believe was blessed to all under our roof, even poor Richard has never been absent from worship since." Thus went on the young convert, his heart all alive in the Lord's service, instant in prayer, seeking his young companions, his room melodious with psalms and spiritual songs, and gentle and loving towards all. He followed his mother's advice! "I do not say you ought not to be cheerful, nay, you may even indulge in a little fun, provided you do not descend to buffoonery or romping." He was a cheerful, and yet an earnest Christian. About this time he published in the Religious Miscellany the following expression of his faith and love, not so bad for a lad of eighteen: —

Full many a star of purest light
Beams on the midnight wanderer's sight,
When winter howls not through the air
Nor tempests veil them with despair.
But oh! there is a brighter gem,
The lovely star of Bethlehem;
In vain the storm winds wildly roll,
Its heavenly light will cheer my soul,
Will pierce the veil of deep despair,
And bid me trust my Pilot's care.

Full many a flower of beauty blooms
And fills the air with sweet perfumes,
And smiles upon us as we stray
Along our devious, doubtful way,
But when the sunbeams scorch our plain
They wither ne'er to bloom again;
But vain the beauties these disclose
To those which shine on Sharon's rose;
It blooms, though blasting sunbeams glow
Or winter sheds his fleecy snow,
And cheers the weary pilgrim's eye
While other flowers in darkness lie.

When pale affliction's fainting child
In sadness roams the desert wild,

When thirsts have bound his parched tongue,
And e'en forbade the cheering song,
With joy he views the fountain flow,
Whose waters can assuage his woe.
But summer's heat, with scorching beam,
May dry the waters of the stream ;
And thus the Pilgrim's anxious eye
Finds but the channel dark and dry.

But there 's a fountain pure and bright
Which always flows in living light,
Which, drawn from Jesus' blessed veins,
Can quench our thirst and cleanse our stains.
Yes, Saviour! in thyself, divine,
These heavenly beauties, graces, shine,
Thou art our staff, our help, our joy,
Our hope, which time can ne 'er destroy.
May I within thy covenant dwell
Forever, great Immanuel!

JUBAL.

"Amen! my beloved son," responds his rejoicing father, but then he acts the critic, "I like Jubal very well. Like yourself, however, I think he has now and then a line or two needlessly long for the other lines, which, unless read with 'a quickstep,' will mar the smoothness of the poetry. Tell Jubal, therefore, to adjust the chords of his lyre more studiously, and the sweetness and strength of its sounds will be heard together."

Having become established in the faith of Jesus, and having given evidence of sincerity in a consistent life, he now proposed to make public confession, and unite with the Church in holy communion, which was done on the 9th of February, 1823, in the Presbyterian church of Carlisle, amidst a goodly company of new converts. On the same day his parents were communing at their own Zion. "No tongue can tell the joy of his mother's heart and mine on our communion Sabbath, realizing, as we did, that it was dear George's communion Sabbath also at Carlisle, when for the first time he professed his love to the dear Redeemer." In the college an opposition to the revival had grown up, and some of those who had been interested went back to the world. This awakened anxiety for his welfare, and called forth the liveliest exhortations from his mother. Having urged him to constant and fervent prayer, she adds: —

"Remember that many eyes will be upon you, some anxiously looking for the fruits of the revival at Carlisle, in your spiritual mindedness, circumspect walk and conversation; others will watch for your halting; not only the world, but some professors of religion, and who I believe are on the foundation, but who are jealous of revivals, and say, 'We will see, if these young converts hold on.' Oh my beloved son, wound not the dear Saviour, and Christians, by your untender walk and conversation."

An exhortation follows upon the extravagant use of money. From this, and similar advice of his father, it would appear that the young Christian had not yet learned the value of money, or did not feel the responsibility of treasuring this talent for the Lord's service. His father had just assumed much additional labor and care, that he might have the means to assist those of his family who were called to labor in word and doctrine.

The remainder of his Senior Year passed without any event of special interest. He graduated in the ensuing summer, and the Commencement gave opportunity to indulge the muse in a poem on the "Power of Fancy," an effort not wanting in strength or melody. Opening with its praises, he then depicts its sadder side, quoting Chatterton and his lines, "My broken lyre," and thus proceeds: —

"And yet who would not be thine ardent child
Fancy! high dame, with eye and aspect wild?
Who would not follow thee, tho' on his youthful head
Life's wrathful vials all their vengeance shed?
What tho' the thorn oft overspreads thy path,
And the rude tempest shades it with its wrath;
Yet there are flowers so sweet, so beautiful,
T 'were worth an age of woe, one wreath to cull.
What tho' the world, while still it loves the swell
Of his wild numbers, leave the bard to dwell
In silent loneliness, and plodding schools
Despise the eccentric wanderer from their rules;
He needs their friendship not, his lip is curl'd
In proud contempt of an ungrateful world;
He seeks his friends among the mountains high,
And the bright jewels of the azure sky."

His lyrical capacity was already acknowledged; Mr. Kirk requests copies of his poetical effusions, as pledges of his future usefulness to the Church of God, in aiding the flow of religious feeling and exalting the standard of sacred poetry. The Rev. Wm. Thorn of England, publishing a book on the Sabbath, affixed one of Mr. G. Bethune's hymns at the end. About this time was commenced a correspondence with the Rev. Mr. Prust, an independent clergyman of Bristol, England, which was the basis of a long friendship. During the summer he was a frequent visitor and great comforter to Miss Cornelia Brackenridge, a cultivated young person, skilful in music, who died in early life. Thus his father addressed him on his eighteenth birthday:

"I love to see you searching the Word of God, and leaning on that; it is the only source of wisdom, humility, comfort, reproof and establishment of heart. I would wish my beloved son to save himself much of my trouble by a close examination of the Word of God, and by a firm, unwavering grasp of the covenant of God in early life, that he may find them to be a lamp to his feet, and a light to his path. My chief safety amidst the storms of life has been owing to my firm faith in the Word of God, casting myself unreservedly on its promises, and pleading them fervently at the throne of grace, in the name of my blessed Lord and Saviour. I have had many answers to prayer, which I have regarded with astonishment, yet not often in the time and way I had looked for them, but in a much better way and time, so that often the heart has, as it were, cried out in response to the gracious declaration of God, 'O Israel thou hast destroyed thyself, but in me is thy help.'"

CHAPTER III.

SEMINARY.—VISIT TO THE SOUTH.

THE Commencement of Dickinson College, while it brought its joys and opened its brilliant hopes, still had a trial. The young men, who had taken sweet counsel together and been united so tenderly in the love of Jesus, were now to separate. They belonged to different denominations and would select various places for theological study. Mr. Codwise, the most intimate friend of young Bethune, was attached to the Episcopal Church, and this, with the added influence of Mr. Pyne and other associates at Columbia, would incline him in a similar direction. But his father's wish was law with him, and it was determined that he should enter the Seminary at Princeton. A season of relaxation from study was granted which was spent, in part, among the pleasant scenes at Salem, where he read Paley's Philosophy, Watts on the Mind, the works of Lord Kames, and various poets. He was much pleased with the writings of Dr. Alex. Proudfit, and purposed to make his Practical Godliness a frequent companion in future. These books had been seen before, but had never been read as they deserved. The student now develops and seeks to recover wasted opportunities. He was appointed to declaim at the Washington Adelphi Forum. Later, he accompanied his father, whose health was impaired, on a tour through Pennsylvania. Soon the time for labor returned and his father makes the following record:

"On the 5th of November I went with my beloved son George (early, frequently, and fervently devoted to the service and glory of my God), and five of his pious, youthful companions, in order to place them in the Theological Seminary at Princeton, New Jersey, where Dr. Alexander, Dr. Miller, and the Rev. Mr. Hodge are the able, faithful and pious teachers and professors. In a period like the present, when gaiety and fashionable amusements fascinate the youth of our city, my dear son had his share of example and temptation to plunge into these courses. My mind felt deep anxieties lest he should shrink from the closer studies of the Theological School, and the corresponding exercises of serious and thoughtful piety which attach to this manner of life. The Lord, who knows every heart, is my witness that all my conduct towards him, according to my limited capacity and slender stock of wisdom, has been directed to lead him, imperceptibly by him, in such a way as to preserve him from worldly temptations, and to cherish and keep alive in him, the holy impressions of love to God, and consecration to his service. The journey to Carlisle, undertaken with this view as to him, has had, I trust, a happy effect. The scenes of his first feelings of spiritual joy seemed to re-animate his soul; his communion with his dear youthful companions, converts with himself to righteousness in the sweet revival at Carlisle, refreshed his spirit; the solemn and awakening circumstances of the death of so many of his acquaintances, and more especially the sudden decease of his lively young friend Ellen Mc Kinney, of Harrisburg, were calculated to make a deep impression on his warm and youthful feelings, and to exalt, in his view, the importance and value of the religion of Jesus Christ, which purifies and sanctifies enjoyment in this life, and insures eternal happiness in that which is to come. Trembling, hoping, leaning upon the divine power, kindness and faithfulness of my covenant, Almighty God, I went with my boy to the school of the prophets, and blessed be His glorious name, He was not unmindful of His promises. I was truly astonished to see with what calmness, decision and sobriety of mind he entered the sacred place. The chaste solemnity of his manner, during the many religious exercises in which we were engaged for the five days I stayed with him, delighted my heart, and I could, at times, think that the shining of his countenance improved by the settled inward devotion of the heart. He seemed, when we parted, affected to tears by my tender care of him, (I being the only parent who went to the spot to settle their sons in the college rooms, which were to be furnished for three years,) but I was most pleased with his remarks that he trusted, above all, in a higher than an earthly parent, to his Father in heaven, for all that he stood in need of for life and duty. Rich were my parental feelings on that occasion, and rich were his filial feelings also. I thank my heavenly Father for this encouraging commencement, this first movement to lend my child to the Lord. I will praise Jehovah for all that is past, and praise him for all that is to come."

His experience in the Seminary does not prove very satisfactory. Dr. Miller's lectures are very interesting (on Chronology); and the Sunday conference is interesting and instructive, discussing, What are the best means of rendering our intercourse and communion profitable to each other? But the Hebrew is dull. His letters to friends are full of lamentations over this study. One replies, Hebrew presents "one parallax" after another, if not in name, in nature, at least in one respect, difficulty; the same report comes from the Episcopal Seminary. This should not be held as a proof of distaste for study, but is to be attributed to the imperfect manner in which the language was taught, very few of the theologians of that day being good Hebrew scholars. A disagreeable feature in the Seminary was an extreme censoriousness and captiousness; and "some of those men whom we understand to be quite lax and moderate abroad, turn out to be the most pious, consistent and devoted Christians among us." The mode of life was displeasing to one who had always enjoyed the comforts of a refined home. "Where can I, a poor desolate stranger, find a kind female to use a needle for me. My splendid needle and thread housewife, if well stocked, would be useful to me." His letters remind us of the scene pictured in his address before the University of Pennsylvania:

"How different is the commons table, often ill served, from the pleasing family board with its natural courtesies and confiding interchange of thought! No lady's eye overlooks them as they scramble like boors for the hasty meal. No woman's tidy hand has arranged their wardrobes, and no approving smile rewards and encourages decency of dress and carriage. A college student's wardrobe! What a collection it is of toeless stockings, buttonless wristbands, and uncared-for rents, some mothers can tell who have examined the trunks they saw packed so neatly a few months before. A college student's room, shared perchance, with one to whom neatness is an unknown quality; its littered, unscrubbed, uncarpeted floor; its confused and broken furniture; its close atmosphere, heated by a greasy stove, and redolent of tobacco; its bed a lounging place by day, whose pillows have never been shaken or sheets smoothed by other than the college porter, who intermitted for such ministry the carrying of wood, or the blacking of boots; its dim panes festooned with ancient cobwebs, through which the noonday sun looks yellow as through a London fog; it is indescribable as chaos. Wo to him whom sickness seizes in such an abode! Kind nurses he may have; but how rough! With what heavy tread and strange notions of the *materia medica!* Vainly does the fevered eye look around for mother, sister, or time-honored servant! Vainly does the fevered thirst crave the grateful drink their hands once pressed to his lips, when he was sick at home! There is none to sprinkle the fragrant spirit on his brow, or after bathing his feet in the attempered water, to wipe them dry and wrap them warm. Alas! poor youth; he has a mother, he has sisters, he has a home, where kindness might have made sickness a luxury, but they have sent him away to suffer among strangers."

Doubtless this picture was drawn from sad experience; and in answer to complaints, his prudent father wrote:

"My hopes of the stability of your future character are strong. As the boy departs and the man approaches, your judgment, which I have generally found radically good, will become more decisive in itself, more operative on your outward actions, and a more steady regulator of your inward thoughts and temper of mind. Growth in grace will assist the improvement of this excellent quality; and secret prayer, with a practical study of the Word of God, will soon ripen it to maturity. A steady exercise of a sound judgment will calm the feelings, subdue restlessness, and those constant cravings of the unsettled mind, which form its secret scorpion lash of irritations and restlessnesses. In moulding our own character, the first obstacles to be overcome are our own besetting sins. Watch your own heart, my son, as your worst enemy; learn to trace its windings to deceive. Resolve to be contented to act with judgment, under present inconveniences; and very soon you will find a steady peace, a holy triumph, with a happy consciousness you are fighting the good fight of faith with success, a comfort far beyond what change of situation would afford you."

However good the advice, the youth was never at rest until he had exchanged the rough fare and many annoyances of the Commons, for the comfort of a pleasant and respectable family; and surely no sensible man can blame him.

Books are sought for: Jahn's Archæology, Gerard's Institutes, Dr. Marsh's Lectures, Macknight on the Epistles, Stapferi Theologia.

Jan. 1824. At the holidays he returned home and "was greatly improved already, by his short stay at the Seminary. His parents were truly delighted by his conversation."

Having formed closer habits of study, he found it necessary to observe carefully rules of diet, living upon milk and vegetables and eating little meat. In the same view he took rapid exercise on horseback, so that far from being a fast liver, his habits were carefully formed to guard against the corpulency that was natural to him.

In Feb. 1824 he had "just begun the study of Theology; the studies in which he had been engaged were merely preparatory, and is glad in feeling that he is actually entering on the grand study." He was more impressed with the value of prayer. Speaking of the gifts of Mr. Wilberforce to the Seminary, he adds :—

"What a blessing we inherit in the prayers of so many good saints! If the effectual fervent prayer of 'one made righteous' availeth much, I rejoice to hear of good people praying. Oh, that we might be more engaged in prayer. We cannot weary our God, why then should we become weary? His arm is not shortened, why then should we fear to trust it? O! for the faith of Jacob to wrestle and prevail! O! for the faith of the apostles! 'I know that my Redeemer liveth' cannot be so earnestly asserted, even in these days of light, as in the time of Job.—Well may we beg now, 'Lord teach us to pray.' I find my warmth in prayer increase in a ratio to the attention, with which I perform it and all other religious duties, and I think I can feel my warmth increase as I am more engaged in prayer. Prayer seems to bend God down to us and to elevate us to Him."

And then in devout gratitude he makes this donation to his parents, praying that they might be strengthened for the responsible station they held in society; praying for them who had so often prayed for him. His fondest thoughts gathered about home, he pictures the happy family, once more in the social circle, enjoying themselves in the recollections of "Auld Lang Syne" and thinks "if that vacant chair were filled, the cheerful laugh might be swelled still louder and Richard sent still oftener for buttered toast."

About this time, the quiet of Princeton was invaded by a young Episcopal friend who was "so high, so very high church, why Dr. ——, hanging to St. John's steeple is nothing to this fellow, who has got on the weathercock and stood on tiptoe." But while there was the closest intimacy between him and the young Presbyterian, heart often beating against heart, undoubtedly theology was the occasion of much grave debate, and each polemic was of his own opinion still.

Before the year is half over an appetite for study awakens; and, strange to tell, for the Hebrew. He hopes for a time of reviving :—

"The increasing earnestness of prayer, and the reviving of Christian graces, seem like the slight rustling before the storm. I feel as if I was better in my religious feelings than I have been. Not that I improve as I ought in Christian grace, but I feel more love for the duties of the closet; more desire for close communion with that God from whose paths I have long shamefully and ungratefully wandered. The world, though it still has deep hold on my affections, I think I can reject with more firmness than formerly. But oh! my mother, what a heart I have! How prone to wander! So enthusiastic in literature, in music, in patriotism, and yet so cold and so dead to Him who should be to me, the chiefest among ten thousand and the one altogether lovely. When called to serve an earthly friend, I have been active and earnest; but called to follow Him who sticketh closer than a brother, I have sneaked to a distance so that it can be scarcely said whether I follow Him or not. O, that the Lord would descend and take possession of my heart. It is not a fit dwelling for the Lord of Hosts, so defiled with sin and evil thoughts; but the blood of Jesus cleanseth from all sin. O, that he would cleanse it for himself, that he would root out all uncleanliness and help me to tear the dearest idol from my heart and give it to him alone. I think I feel more of sense of duty in study than formerly. I regarded it then as a mere worldly requirement, now I think I may be sowing the seed of a harvest which may add to the granary of heaven, through the blessing of God attending my labours in the ministry.—Pray for me, my dear mother, pray. I need prayers. Prayers from a faithful spirit will avail much. Prayer opens heaven, the poet says. Oh, what a blessed privilege."

Up to this period he may have amused himself in literature, and have gone through the college recitations; even his father complained of his indolent habits, and a young friend fancies him, "A fat laughing youth, seated in a big cushioned chair with feet cocked up over a rousing fire, segar in his mouth, and hands in the breeches pockets," the picture of comfort and merry enjoyment; but from this date there is a change.

All his letters speak of pleasure in study; he wrote, "during the whole of this week, not a single evening is without its appropriate Society;" and it was his constant cultivation of such reunions, that ripened his powers of extempore speaking. He prepared theological essays on one of the most difficult metaphysical subjects; while Hebrew is still a bug-bear, it suffers from the assaults of violence. He says, "I never sat down to work with so much zest;" and there are records of immensely hard days' study. He became a contributor to a monthly magazine, published in Philadelphia under the signature of "ORION."

But in August, 1824, a great trial drew near him:

"I have been waiting with intense anxiety for news of my dear father. Often does my prayer ascend to heaven for him, and often my bed is wakeful with my thoughts of him. Never did I feel him, however dear as he was before, so dear as now; all his kindness, patience and forbearance with me rise to my view. Now I think I see him as he was once, healthful and vigorous; then weak and fatigued, yet always with the sweet smile so peculiarly his own. In my college days, I have often written with all the romantic fervour of youth of a father's affection and filial love, but now those descriptions however high wrought fall short of the reality, which is felt, not merely imagined. Yet what a glorious and soul comforting thought, 'Like as a father pitieth his children, so the Lord pitieth them that fear him.' How sweet to think that we are in his hand and that his ear is always open to our cry. But then though these are sweet and encouraging thoughts, I feel myself apt to forget my God and my duty, and almost murmur against his righteous judgments, and have to breathe the prayer of the sweet Milman,

'Hear all our prayer, hear not our murmurs, Lord,
And though our lips rebel, still make thyself adored.'"

Alas! that valuable diary which has been quoted so often, has been closed for some months; the father has written that he can do no more in correspondence than send the necessary money; he has sought health and strength from different sources in vain, and God has determined to take his faithful servant to himself. Never did son have more reason to love and thank a parent, and seldom was the debt of gratitude better repaid. The father had been a pleasant companion; although with him, religion was the chief concern, and he had aimed first of all to lead him to Jesus, yet he was a man of letters and paid his court to the Muse, so that he could sympathize in literary progress and the domestic conversations were adorned with tasteful and witty discussions. Crying, "Let me go home, let me go to my Saviour my race is run; my work is done, let me go," his wish was granted on the 18th of September, 1824. He had filled a larger sphere of usefulness than is often alloted to laymen. One who observed him in active business said, "he looked all the time as sereno as if he was sitting on down." Mrs. Graham wrote, "Divie Bethune stands in my mind, in temper, conduct and conversation, the nearest to the gospel standard of any man or woman I ever knew as intimately. Devoted to his God, to his church, to his family, to all to whom he may have the opportunity of doing good, duty is his governing principle." Friends in England wrote that a sweet savor attaches to the name of Bethune. His dying words to his son were: "Preach the gospel, my son, tell dying sinners of a Saviour, mind nothing else; it is all folly." Blessed be God for such an honorable, honored parent. How much was due to his example, his faith and his prayers. The following epitaph presents his son's ideal:

In memory of Divie Bethune,

BORN AT DINGWALL, ROSSSHIRE, SCOTLAND,

Died, Sept. 18, 1824, Aged, 53.

Thirty years of which he lived in the City of New York an honorable merchant, a faithful citizen, a hospitable gentleman, and a devout elder of Christ's Church. He spent his life in serving God, and, for God's sake, his fellow-men.

"Oh that men would praise the Lord for His goodness."

This event brought upon him a new burden of responsibility. The correspondents of his father desired him to carry on the business, and as it had been one of extensive repute and great success, every worldly inducement pointed in that direction. But all such solicitations he spurned, feeling bound to follow the great profession to which he had given himself. When urged to allow the use of his name, and told that his refusal might ruin the business, his answer was, "Though I throw away a fortune, I must obey the dying commands of my father."

But there was one care left to him, that of his widowed mother, from which he did not shrink, but supported with all the affection of his great manly heart, and thus he assumed the task :

"I do hope and pray that God will enable me so to conduct myself, that I may be a comfort and stay to my mother, and though my conscience tells me that I have often wounded you and roused your anxiety respecting me, and though I fear that the indiscretions and heedlessness of youth may often prove detriments to my designs, yet, it is my firmest and fondest resolution in a reliance on divine aid, to be indeed a son and a prop to my widowed mother."

Noble resolve, and most faithfully and lovingly was it kept. When the session of the Seminary began, he was at his post, his only regret being, that his mother was "seated by a lonely hearth, with none to comfort, none to console." Upon a visit, he became more impressed with her desolate condition, and proposed to sacrifice for her comfort his privileges at Princeton:

"The path of duty appears to me very dark, whether I should stay here, absent from her whom it is my natural duty and still more my fondest desire to protect and solace, or return to her to cheer, as far as possible, her loneliness, at the expense of a very few advantages. Next to my God's, I am my mother's. If by leaving P., I should necessarily interrupt my studies and thereby delay my fitness for the responsible work to which I am called, or if by leaving this I should necessarily deprive myself of many advantages, which nowhere else could be found, the path of duty would be clear, and God would order things as well with you and better than if I were to act in direct contradiction. But the case is not so. In New York, I should be able to prosecute my studies with almost equal advantages. My access to books would be equally free and unlimited, for the libraries of all the clergymen would be open to me."

After arguing the subject at considerable length, ingenuously advocating a course which love and duty prompted, with characteristic generosity, he concludes by making one condition, that his friend Williams might be permitted to remain. "I am not so selfish as to wish to deprive others of advantages which duty compels me to forego, or to wish others to choose the path which I think I am bound to tread." To this proposal his bereaved parent could by no means consent; but it affords a fine illustration of that filial affection which was so notable a trait of the man, which cheered her darkest hours, and which never fainted even in her days of childishness, nor ceased until he had closed her eyes in death.

Study was now vigorously pursued: and as evidence that the theological course did not distract him from former loves and elegant pursuits, he writes to a friend in England about an edition of "Valpy's Classics," which was expected to reach one hundred volumes. A fellow student speaks of his new parish as reminding him of auld lang syne:

"When I sat at the doors of the cottages of my poor friends, taking a smoke with the old women, I have thought of No. 22, in a large stone building far, far away. The house was different, the company different, the pipe, the tobacco, all different, still the associations were agreeable. I am sure if I reflected upon anything with pleasure it was the recollections of the theological smoking association of which I had the honor to be a member."

He alludes to the gift of the muse bestowed upon Bethune, which was confessed by all his young compeers, and might have reached a much higher standard had it not been restrained by a sense of the more serious and important duties set before him.

Sensible of his advantages, there was about the young man a certain uppish air, which called forth the following rebuke from his careful parent:

"Pardon a mother's anxiety, my beloved son. Beware of trusting in riches, and that vanity of heart which attends the possession of them. I did not like to hear you talk so much of *genteelity*. Remember the Scriptures, 'If any man would be great among you, let him be your minister.' Not many wise, not many noble are called, &c. Condescend to men of low estate. Who did the Great Redeemer choose for his associates? Fishermen, tanners. Nay, was he not to appearance the son of a carpenter? If any one in New York could boast of *genteelity*, it was your father; even the great of this world were his relations; yet even I, his bosom friend, never heard him once attach any value to it.

and his first religious associates were in the humblest walks in life. The first prayer-meeting he joined, he was the only merchant among them. A cartman, a stonecutter, a tailor, a carpenter, were the members; yet I have often heard him say, that by the mouth of one of these men, his path of duty was made plain to him. You know how much he was respected by all ranks. Nobody ever said he kept low company. Would you wish to become truly respectable in the eyes of the world? Follow your father's example."

He had a wise monitor.

About this time we date an intimacy with Dr. John O. Choules, afterwards the distinguished and witty Baptist Minister, of Newport, R. I. In some way old Mr. Bethune had done kindness to this young man, lately arrived from England, and the debt of gratitude was repaid to the son, with whom was maintained a cordial friendship.

Now it pleased the Lord to send upon his widowed parent much complication in business matters, attended with considerable loss of property. She meets the trial like a Christian, and her son "rejoices that she is enabled to throw herself so confidently upon Him who is alone able to support. I trust that in all your distresses the Lord will hear you, in the day of trouble the name of the God of Jacob may defend you, send you help from the sanctuary, and strengthen thee out of Zion." With such good words did these children of the covenant comfort each others' hearts.

In February of this year there came another sorrow, in the death of a beloved pastor, the Rev. Dr. J. B. Romeyn. He died of a broken heart, from the slanders and repeated attacks of persons in his own congregation. In his delirium, he took a text and preached from it. "Let not your hearts be troubled," &c., dispensed the communion, calling

Mr. Bethune to "take the cup," and appealed to his people that he had been faithful to them, and was free from their blood. The pious family mourned over his loss, as if one of their own number had been stricken. Shortly after the young theologian desires books from the dear Doctor's library. "If there are any sets of Poole, Calvin, Jonathan Edwards, the Biblia Critica, Turretin, John Howe, Jeremy Taylor, Horsley, Whitby, Milner's Church History; the German critics, Koppe, Kuinœl, Rosenmüller, Schultens, it would be well to get them."

An event occurred in the summer vacation, which made him "the happiest mortal on the face of the earth." His dear Mary yielded, with the sanction of her kind father, a return for that attachment, which, from the days of his boyhood, had ever bound him to her. He informs his mother, with the delight of an enthusiastic lover:

"I shall leave you to draw the picture of my feelings as you please, satisfied that no coloring would be too rich. To find that all those gay dreams which brightened my boyhood, but which opening manhood viewed as too much like enchantment to be real, are now realities; to be blest with the love of one so pure, so gentle, so lovely, yet so far above me in prospects, and not the least to find my dear mother satisfied with all, is what no thankfulness can express, no gratitude repay, and of which none bnt God who knoweth the heart can estimate the value. Life wears to me a new aspect; new motives, new inducements, new hopes, new enjoyments present themselves on every hand."

The prospect of this alliance gave much satisfaction to his remaining parent, who welcomed the young lady as her daughter, and as her son's first and only love:

"Now that both of you have given your hearts to the Lover of your souls, and your attachment will be strengthened by religion, my full heart overflows with thankfulness to that God who has granted my every wish for my beloved George, 'the only son of his mother, and she a widow.' I shall now close my eyes in peace; my son and the chosen of his heart have each sought the kingdom of Christ and his righteousness, and the promise to them is, that all other blessings will be added."

The correspondence between these young Christians often assumed a tone higher than that of ordinary love-making:

"But why," he says, sympathizing in the continued illness of Miss Williams, "but why seek the sorrowful influences of memory, when hope points cheerily onward, and like a good prophet speaks of days of bliss, and hours of joy. Blessed be the man whose trust is in the Lord his God; and has not he, who spake as never man spake, promised to the believing spirit, 'Lo, I am with you alway, even unto the end of the world.' Be thy promise, Man of Sorrows, Lord of Glory, our comfort, and may not our death, but our life, be the life of the righteous, and our end be like his. Blessed with the promises of God, and each other's love, we may challenge life to do its worst to mar our happiness. My desire to do something for the honor and glory of my Master, is, I believe and hope, true. I need not say, how much I desire the prayers of those who love me. Pray for my humility, yet confidence in the discharge of duty; zeal, yet prudence; tenderness, yet faithfulness in all my preaching and pastoral duties; for, next to God and his cause, my desire is that I may not in any degree fail the hopes of one whose hopes will be linked with mine, and who must share all my misfortunes, and all my successes."

This engagement soon brought with it responsibility, and led to an important change in his life. In the autumn, the health of Miss Williams began to decline, and Dr. Post advised that her life could only be saved by going to a warm climate. Who should be her escort? The youthful lover could not resign the charge to another, so the consent of his professors was obtained, the theological course suspended in mid career; he had been studying about two years; and a sum of money which had been carefully laid aside by his father for a trip to Europe, was devoted to a wedding tour to the West Indies. The first plan was to go to the South of France, but the very bad symptoms of the invalid compelled a more speedy change. On Nov. 4, 1825, the marriage was consummated, and soon the happy couple sailed for Havana, in the ship Berlin.

Their groomsman, Mr. Bleecker, had been saved from drowning at Rockaway, by young Bethune, at the risk of his own life. He had been carried beyond his depth, and as he could not swim, was helpless. The intrepid friend caught him as he came up the third time, and brought him near the bank, when the waves dashed them on the beach. Bethune soon regained his powers, but it was with great difficulty that Bleecker was restored.

The loss at Princeton was grievously lamented. It was apprehended that the Round Table would go down, and the Scandal Club become extinct, Mr. Green dcelaring himself unable to support it without Bethune's aid :

"The Professors were satisfied with the propriety of your conduct. Mr. Hodge said but little, though by his smiles he expressed full approbation. Dr. Alexander observed (in his own way), that the circumstances were very peculiar, and spoke in very flattering terms of recommendation, of your originality of mind, your readiness of thought, your talents as a speaker and preacher. Dr. Miller very gravely observed, 'that by such short-sighted creatures as we are, it would be termed an unfortunate occurrence, but he thought that if placed in the same situation, he should not have acted otherwise, adding that, even in Cuba, one possessing Mr. Bethune's active and inquisitive mind, might avail himself of many means of improvement from the opportunities of conversation with learned Catholic Priests, and from the facilities of access to many rare and valuable books."

Princeton could then boast of many students who have since become eminent. Dr. Edward N. Kirk was a resident graduate, and Drs. Hutton, Dickinson, Jas. Alexander, Erskine Mason, of New York ; Bishop McIlvaine of Ohio ; Dr. Plummer of Va. ; Drs. T. L. Janeway, John W. Nevin of Pa. Havana was reached, and the place described :

"The first object which strikes the eye is a miserable looking pile, called the Moro Castle. It stands upon a projecting rock on the north-east side of the harbour. The long line of its fortifications continued by the immense fortifications of the Cabanas, with its watch-tower, its loop-holes and portals, give you a very tolerable idea of the castles of the olden time. Passing thence up the small river which forms the entrance of the harbour, some two or three thousand yards, you anchor in the harbour of St. Christopher or Havana. On every side there are moles of immense strength, rendering the town completely inaccessible from the sea, by any hostile force however great. On the right is the Castel de la Habana, from which the place derives its name. The circumstances are as follows : In the year 1512, Christopher Columbus discovered the Island of Cuba as he was endeavoring to trace the course of the Gulf Stream. Landing some miles to windward, he followed the shore until his notice was attracted by the harbor of this now flourishing town. In prosecuting his journey, he was opposed by some of the Indians, who after a little resistance fled until they came to a clump of wide spreading trees, peculiar to this island. They there met a gigantic and majestic female, whom they considered a supernatural being whom they reverenced under the name of the Habana, and then partly by force and partly by stratagem, were led to form a rude treaty with Columbus, who in gratitude to God, celebrated mass under two of the largest trees, which are still standing and luxuriant, and took possession of the place in the name of Spain. They built a rude fort, calling it, to please the natives, Habana. The Spanish soldiers took possession of the country two years after. As you pass along the quay under the battlements of the Habana, you are struck by the singular appearance of all around you.

First, of the houses ; they are chiefly constructed of a crumbling stone, covered with a thick layer of plaster, built in the form of a quadrangle, the centre of which is open, communicating by an arched gateway with the street.

Ascending a flight of stairs, you find yourself in a gallery extending on every side of the quadrangle, from which doors open to the several apartments. The windows are closed and barred, which with the massive pillars and arched doorways, seem more like prison-houses or castles, than peaceful domiciles. It is easy, however, to see that though gloomy in appearance, at first, they are in reality the most convenient that can be made. The thick walls from four to six feet through, the heavy tiled roof and the shaded galleries, sufficiently exclude the sun, while the open windows give free circulation to the air which is retained by the plaster floors. Then the singular vehicles called volantes call for notice. They are not unlike a large old-fashioned chaise depending from the axis of two very high wheels, supported at the other extremity by shafts, which are borne by a horse or mule, according to the purse or caprice of the owner. On the back is seated the Calasero, or driver. It is not uncommon to see three persons in the volante and a footman behind, drawn by one poor brute with his driver on his back. They are, however, very safe; and, with the exception of five coaches, are the only carriages used on the Island. Another thing which strikes the eye of the foreigner is the number of soldiers, which amounts to six or seven thousand in the city alone, which within the walls, contains only sixty or seventy thousand people, though the suburbs contain, possibly, as many more. The churches are large, but with the exception of the Cathedral, (containing the bones of Columbus, and really a fine building,) are huge and unshapely. The monks though numerous, are not so numerous as previous to the first adoption of the Constitution. To give you some idea of their licentious life and the general state of religion, I need only say, that I saw on Sunday, at the same time that high mass was performing in the Chapel, a party of friars at whist in one of the cells. There is also a gambling house immediately opposite the church, supported entirely by the monks."

But the destination of the party was Matanzas, where a house furnished was generously offered for their use. Here they set up a small establishment, taking a poor orphan, Miss Gerard, under their protection, and beginning that life of kindness which was a leading feature in their history.

It was the practice of Mrs. Joanna Bethune to write to her son regularly on the 18th of March, and she does so in this year, 1826, to the following purport :

"And what, my dear George, do you think this day recalls to my mind? More than I can tell, of him who, twenty one years ago, first opened his eyes on *time.* You might indeed have been called by your beloved father, what the people of France called their king, 'Le Désire;' so anxious was he to have a son, that he might devote him to the Lord. Oh the prayers, the tears, the anxious desires that have been poured out and expressed before a throne of grace for you, my dear son. See to it that you 'be not negligent.' If you have no opportunity of benefiting others, which I hope you may, be much in prayer and reading the Scriptures, that you may gain that spiritual knowledge without which all other knowledge will be a curse rather than a blessing, in the profession you have chosen. Your father always esteemed it a peculiar blessing, that before he entered into business or married, he had a season of leisure to study and pray over the word of God. The diligent use that he made of that season was useful to him all his after life; and made him, even a layman, eminently useful to others, which you know. 'Whatsoever thy hand findeth to do, do it with thy might,' ought to be the motto of every Christian. Time is passing, the prophecies fulfilling, let us press into the ranks of those that are on the Lord's side, that we also, however feeble in ourselves, may be instruments in God's hand of bringing in the great and glorious day when all shall know him from the least unto the greatest."

We shall see how, until late in life, Mr. Bethune was aided, encouraged, warned and stimulated, by a constant succession of such noble letters, and how well the son appreciated his privilege. In answer to the above he writes:

"MATANZAS, *April* 4.

"I received, some days since, a previous letter by way of Havana, which gave me pain, because I learned from it that one of mine had caused pain to you, though He that knoweth the heart, knew nothing was farther from my intentions. With sorrow and regret, I sincerely crave your pardon, and my kind and forgiving mother will, I am sure, remember that there are some chords in the heart which are more morbidly sensitive than others; and I must say that the thought of being a married man with nothing to support my wife, and no immediate prospect of making anything, is to me exquisitely painful. But on this subject I have done.

You ask me in your last, if I find any opportunities of usefulness about me. There is perhaps, no place where such opportunities may not be found, if sought for. But there is scarcely any place where fewer are to be found than here. I had hopes to do some good among the negroes of the plantation, but they do not understand any English whatever; and are most bigoted and ignorant Catholics. The most of the foreigners are hooters at religion, and so fearful is the Government of anything like Protestantism, that my being connected with the clerical profession, almost lost me my passport; and nothing but high bribes to the Custom House, saved my two trunks of books from forfeiture for heresy. Were it known that I attempted religious instruction, imprisonment or banishment would be more certainly the consequence, than if I murdered or robbed. Still I hope the great day may reveal some little good, of doing which I may have been the means in the Island of Cuba."

Some effort was made with the house-servants, which was his first labor among the blacks, in whom he afterwards became much interested. He taught them to read, sing hymns, and gave such moral instruction as he could. The family was increased by a young Bostonian, whom Mr. Bethune rescued from a band of soldiers, who threatened him with the bayonet because he would not kneel before the host which the priests were carrying through the streets of Matanzas; fleet horses, and the feint of having pistols in their breasts, saved them. Now that they were known as Protestants, they always carried pistols in their holsters, in fact, Mr. Bethune slept with them under his pillow from his first arrival. In April, 1826, they left this inhospitable island, and brought along a little Spanish maiden, who was taught to love Jesus, and in later life returned to do good among her friends; after spending a few pleasant days in Charleston, they proceeded to Philadelphia and New York.

From this period the correspondence becomes voluminous,

and would be of itself, when arranged in order, a full and almost sufficient memoir; five thousand letters of all kinds have been examined and noted; a due selection of these will be inserted in their proper places, and they will in many instances tell their own story without the help of remark.

Perhaps it will interest our readers to know that in the large share of this mass of manuscript which is in Dr. Bethune's handwriting we have discovered not one careless or ungrammatical expression, and only one orthographical error. This frightful crime amounts to an "l" too much in "thankful" and had he not, in other places, given in his adherence to the use of the single labial, might have considered himself borne out by partial usage and not altogether despicable authority. We suspect that his pen slipped.

Solomon has used a vigorous expression touching the effect of dead flies upon the ointment of the apothecary; and the only effect of that questionable "l" is to call attention to our writer's sensitive purity in matter of style and diction.

REV. J. McELROY D.D. TO G. W. B. "*June* 13, 1826.

"MY DEAR SIR: I received your communication three days ago, and should gladly have replied to it immediately, but have hitherto been prevented. I have now only time to write a few lines.

We will agree in opinion, that had it been practicable for you to spend another year at the Seminary, it would have been better for you, and better for the cause which I trust we both love; better for you, as you would thus have been more amply furnished for the arduous work you have in view, and better for the cause, inasmuch as you would thus have been able to exert a still greater efficiency in advancing the Redeemer's interests. But under all the circumstances of your situation, I am clearly of the opinion that you should be licensed, and you need apprehend no difficulty in the way of that event.

I take the liberty of assigning you, as the subject of a popular sermon, Galatians VI., v. 14, stopping at the word 'Christ.' 'But God forbid that I should glory save in the cross of our Lord Jesus Christ.'

Wishing you, my dear sir, the Master's presence and blessing,

I am very truly yours."

The license to preach came from the Second Presbytery of New York and is dated July 11, 1826. The family were accustomed during the summer to resort to Rockaway, and Mr. Bethune's first sermon before the public was preached in a school-house near by, from the same text that had been assigned by Dr. McElroy; in this place, Mrs. J. Bethune had already established a Sunday School.

G. W. B. TO MRS. JOANNA BETHUNE. "SALEM, *Aug.* 7, 1826.

"MY DEAR MOTHER: We arrived here in safety, but at a house of mourning, on Saturday. Dear little Alexander had a return of the complaints which have troubled him since his birth, ... and on Saturday afternoon the dear sufferer exchanged this world of sin and sorrow for the presence of Him who said: 'Except ye become as little children ye cannot see the kingdom of God.' Poor dear Mary's grief was excessive, but her sweet Christian spirit, upheld by the consolations of the Gospel, has recovered at least calmness and resignation. The Colonel feels it very much; his heart was wrapped up in him. It has affected me very much. I have never loved a child of his age so much since John Mason Duffield. . . . The funeral took place yesterday. Of course I was silent during the whole of the day, though very much urged to preach by the Doctor. I received yours, with the enclosure, a short time ago, for which I thankyou sincerely. . . . I must manage in some way to preach one day in Troy. Mr. —— has been very imprudent, and his congregation is much displeased with his mode of preaching. He points at individual members from the pulpit, and repeats what he has heard they have said during the week.

Your affectionate and grateful son."

The rest of the summer and autumn were occupied in a preaching tour through Western New York, when the young candidate appeared before different audiences; he also distributed Bibles and Tracts in destitute places.

G. W. B. TO MRS. J. B. "SARATOGA, *August* 15, 1826.

MY DEAR MOTHER; I arrived here this evening from Salem, expecting to find Mc Cartee, in which I am both disappointed and alarmed, fearful lest sickness either of himself or of the family may have detained him. He should certainly have written to me and not left me to go about the country in this way after him. I am without any credentials whatever (having trusted to having him with me) and am yet on a preaching tour. I preached for Dr. Proudfit twice last Sabbath, I believe to the satisfaction of my friends. O! that I might be able to say it was convincing to the hearts of sinners. Well might we exclaim What is man! and yet O the consolation and encouragement of that promise or rather declaration, 'It pleased God through the foolishness of preaching,' not the wisdom, 'to save them that believe.'"

G. W. B. TO MRS. J. B. "SALEM, *Sept.* 15, 1826.

I had hoped to have preached in Troy, as a fine church is about to be organized in that place, but was disappointed. It seems strange that I have never yet preached in a vacancy. I pass my time here in study chiefly, though under some disadvantages from want of books. There is very little society out of the immediate family.

Do you know when the Examination at Princeton is? I have entirely forgotten the day, but wish to be there to see my classmates once more before they separate forever. I suppose it would give you some pleasure to learn that my preaching in Albany gave very great satisfaction to one of the most sensible and judicious congregations there. If he whose cause I serve would but make it means of making some wise unto salvation, how much richer the pleasure!"

Savannah, Nov. 6. Mrs. Bethune and he have arrived safely at this city after a pleasant passage, having preached on board the vessel to a congregation of ninety souls.

G. W. B. TO MRS. J. B. "SAVANNAH, *Nov.* 12.

I have been working since I have been here. I preached to a large congregation of negroes and whites in the negro church on Thursday evening. For Mr. How all day yesterday in a very large church and congregation, made an address and opened the Sunday school and preached to a crammed, overflowing house in the negro church at night.

I love this place very much, there seems to be a vast deal of Christian spirit and zeal, and the people generally, especially the poor negroes, seem anxious to hear. They are in point of privilege many degrees above the blacks in Charleston."

"SAVANNAH, *Nov.* 26, 1826.

MY DEAR MOTHER; You should have heard of me sooner since my last, but that my time has been occupied in going to and returning from Augusta. I am sorry that I am unable to state my prospects for the winter because as yet I have none. Augusta is at present in a very unsettled state. They have had a Unitarian among them, and they have promised him a thousand dollars a year to come to them. The Presbyterian and Episcopalian ministers, have both been attacked as to their character for sobriety, and though the charges have been investigated and proved to be false, there are many who yet believe and endeavor to spread them. When I sent up my letter, it was taken no notice of. But when in Augusta last week I was told by one of the session that they anticipated much pleasure from my being in Augusta, because were there no other minister there, I could supply them. They thought that I would come at any rate, and would be a kind of *corps de reserve*, a kind of forlorn hope to do when no other could be found. They seemed to have no idea of inviting to a regular supply. The good people of Savannah seem very anxious to keep me here and indeed I am desirous of staying. I know no place where I may be more useful than this, while I remain at the South. I have not been idle. I have preached, or shall have preached to-morrow evening, should God give life and strength, twelve times in sixteen days, besides addresses, and travelling three hundred miles. I will preach under the Bethel flag on board a ship, to-morrow. I am fulfilling as far as possible the command to preach the gospel to the poor; for negroes and sailors are my favorite auditors. Can I have any more tracts, little books for children and sailors' tracts especially? I have abundant use for many more than I have, and I hate to be economical of the Bread of Life."

"SAVANNAH, *Dec.* 11, 1826.

You must have received before this my letter containing an account of my visit to Augusta, and I am confident that so far from regretting that I have not obtained that situation, you must rejoice, owing to the unpleasant state of feeling and things there existing. One thing is certain that I have been treated very cavalierly by those gentlemen, and with the exception of the expense I was at in going there, I regret nothing more than that I exposed myself to their neglect.

Immediately upon my arrival here, a path of usefulness seemed to be opened to me which I would have left with regret for the most splendidly endowed situation our church has within its bounds. Nor would I have left it but from the conviction that your wishes and my own necessities demanded my seeking some employment, which, while it promised usefulness in my Master's cause, promised also, some means for my support. The prospect even of such a situation, Providence seemed to deny me. Wilmington I had kept as a forlorn hope, because the exposed situation in which it stands to the sea, would, had I taken it, have demanded my separation from Mary. On Friday evening, however, Mr. How, who has been very attentive to me since I have been here, called upon me at the instance of the Board of directors of the City Missionary Society, to request me to remain as their Missionary at the salary of fifty dollars per month, which after a prayerful consideration of two days, from the prospect of usefulness afforded me, I have been induced to accept. My labors shall be devoted in a primary degree to the sailors and the poor. Among the sailors my engagements are peculiarly delightful. To the number of two hundred and fifty, they crowd around me, and listen with the most breathless attention, and receive their tracts with a grateful expression, which is, I hope, indicative of good feeling. The mildness of the climate enables me to preach on the deck of the ship. But it is not to the sailors alone that my addresses are directed. There is a large number of men, chiefly young men, who never attend regular service, who follow me wherever I go, and to whom I hope the Lord, through me, may communicate some lasting instruction. The poor blacks also assemble in great numbers, when they know I am to preach, because they say, "I talk so plain. I no use big words. I talk plain." My meetings during the week are held on Tuesday evening, when I hope to have a full house from the attendance of the inhabitants of a part of the town which corresponds to the "Hook" in the city of New York. I assist, occasionally, the ministers here, Baptist, Presbyterian, and Methodist, black and white, so that I seldom preach less than six or seven times during the seven days, if extemporaneous addresses can be called sermons. For except in the large churches, for which I always write, I preach without writing. Such are my prospects and my engagements. If I have done wrong in making them, I hope I shall be forgiven by my mother and my God. It was not without many an anxious prayer, and careful examination that I thus determined. It belongs to man to err, and although this is no excuse with God, it may be some palliation with an affectionate mother."

"SAVANNAH, *Dec.* 28.

I preach frequently for the blacks, and Mr. How, so that I seldom preach less than three times on the Sabbath, and twice or thrice during the week. I have enough labor, that is certain, whether I do any good or not, the Lord only knows. I preached, or rather delivered an address for the Sabbath school in this place, and obtained for it about seventy dollars, about three times as much as they were ever able to obtain before. They, however, go on a poor plan here, they teach none to read, considering the free schools as sufficient. They employ themselves solely about instruction from the Bible. This is very good, indeed, the principal thing, but the other should not be neglected."

The fact was, that his knowledge of the character of seamen, together with his perfect familiarity with nautical phrases, and sea life, rendered his services among sailors extremely popular and successful. One of his hearers expressed the idea: "I like to hear you because you know the ropes." While in Savannah and preaching in the Bethel Chapel, the Pastor of the Presbyterian Church proposed an exchange. To this proposal Mr. Bethune was slow to respond well knowing Jack's dislike to see "a new hand at the wheel." But after due warning of the peculiarity of his salt-water congregation, consent was given. During the ensuing week, he, meeting one of his charge, naturally inquired how the boys liked the minister whom he had sent. Jack bluntly condemned him and called him "an old land-lubber." "Ah," said the Pastor, "that is wrong, you must not call the minister of the gospel a land-lubber." "Yes, but he is a land-lubber;" replied the tar. "Why, he talked about the anchor of hope, and spun a long yarn, of a storm at sea and a ship coming near land and in the very breakers: Then he said, 'what would you do but heave out your anchor?' Now, in such a case, I'd like to know, what in creation we could do with an anchor? No, no, we would order all hands on deck and try to claw her off shore." So the sailor walked off triumphantly, feeling justified in his assertion. Dr. Bethune, in after life, often told this anecdote with great relish.

G. W. B. TO MRS. J. B. "SAVANNAH, *Jan.* 12, 1827.

Your tracts arrived very seasonably. I was just out, and knew not where to turn for more. On Sabbath last however, my captains came around me after I had preached from that passage in Proverbs; —'He that hath friends must shew himself friendly, and there is a friend that sticketh closer than a brother'—and said that they ought to shew themselves friendly, and proposed that on the next Sabbath I should take up a *collection for tracts*, after service. This will be to-morrow. My audiences rather increase than diminish, and their attention is unequalled by any congregation I have ever preached to, and I have more than once seen tears streaming down a hard weather-beaten cheek.

One interesting circumstance I must mention, that, on board of the Scotch ship where I preached this morning, there was a larger attendance than at any time previous, and you might notice the crew with each his Bible, turning to the text, as if they were in the kirk at home. The 'tract collection', amounted to fifteen dollars and fifty cents, whereas my brightest hopes did not extend beyond five dollars. One old fellow came up with two cents between his finger and thumb, remarking that he would give more to-morrow when he was paid off."

"SAVANNAH, *Feb.* 24, 1827.

I received some thirteen thousand tracts by the Louisa Matilda, with a very polite note from Mr. ——— the Depositary. I am much obliged to you for your trouble, and am very much pleased with the selection, except that some which were sent might have been substituted for 'The Swearer's Prayer.' I am very thankful for the fifty dollars. At the time I received it, we had not three dollars in the world, and a month to go before any would be due, much less paid. But the Lord will take care of me. I fear it not: Something more than fifty dollars a month is necessary to do it with, however, unless the ravens bring us our food."

Dr. How* gives the following account of his work at Savannah: —

"Besides the sailors, a very considerable number of the citizens of Savannah, and among them some of the most respectable and intelligent and influential men, habitually attended our young pastor's preaching, and there is reason to believe that his ministry was useful to all classes of his hearers. The fidelity with which he set forth the great and fundamental truths of the Gospel, the earnestness with which he pressed them on the attention of his hearers; and the eloquence and power with which he spoke, arrested their close attention, and produced abiding impressions on their minds. His ministry, I doubt not, was highly useful and instrumental in leading some of his hearers to unfeigned repentance and faith in Christ. He occasionally preached to the slaves, especially to those on a plantation in the neighborhood of the city, belonging to an eminently pious lady. While they greatly admired his preaching, they also became strongly attached to him, because of his kind, familiar and gentlemanly intercourse with them. The slaves on this plantation, as also on a very large number of the plantations in the South, belonged to the Baptist Denomination. One of them was a Baptist preacher, strongly attached to his particular Church and confident that they were preëminently distinguished for holding Christian truth and practice in greater purity than they are held by any other religious body of Christians. He became very much interested in Dr. Bethune, and strongly attached to him. I have heard the Doctor very pleasantly repeat the following incident concerning this preacher: he was expressing to Dr. Bethune his approval and admiration of his preaching, when he suddenly changed his tone with much earnestness, 'But, Massa, in the Millennium they 'll all be Baptists.' The Doctor received this information without dispute."

In later years Dr. Bethune spoke gratefully of the wise counsel given by this excellent minister. He was inexperi-

* Rev. Saml. B. How, D. D., now of New Brunswick, N. J.

enced, and yet already enjoyed some of the popularity which attaches to the man of eloquence. Crowds often sought his ministry. The young preacher was inclined to careless preparation. Richly gifted with power of language he found it easy to produce a popular harangue and thus was preaching extemporaneously and allowing his talents to run to waste. Here the older workman did good service, he took the beginner to his study, explained his danger and urged him to write his sermons as the best method of securing proper forethought, a course which was faithfully pursued by the scholar in the period of his greatest success.

His labors here were very arduous, but his success was great and popularity general, his reception by all classes was enthusiastic and might have injured other young ministers. He preached to the negroes in the evening, and it is deserving of note that the interest which his early occupation created in his mind followed him through his entire ministry; those causes to which he was especially devoted being "The Seamen's Friend," and "The Colonization Societies."

CHAPTER IV.

RHINEBECK MINISTRY.

G. W. B. TO MRS. J. B. "SALEM, *June* 25, 1827.

I embrace the first mail since my arrival here to inform you of our welfare. Stopped at Rhinebeck, on my way up, as I proposed, and learned from my kind friends that there would be a meeting for the choice of pastor last Saturday. What the result of the meeting was I do not know. Some were flattering enough to think they would pitch upon me, at least by a majority. It should be a large one to induce me to accept. I have received, by this day's mail, two very pleasing letters from Savannah,—one from my excellent friend, Mr. How, enclosing a very pressing and affectionate invitation from the Ladies' Missionary Society, to labor among them during the next winter, with a salary of one hundred dollars per month. The prospect of usefulness which this presents, with the almost adequate support, makes an admirable *corps de reserve*. Mr. How accompanies the invitation with his warmest entreaties that I should accept it; the other is from my excellent friend Mrs. McQueen, sending me the thanks of my poor negroes for the little sermon which I sent them, and assurances of their kind regards."

He worked to great profit amongst the negroes of her plantation, and was enabled to establish a well ordered Church. Mrs. McQueen gratefully rewarded his fidelity and became his most attached friend.

G. W. B. TO MRS. J. B. "SARATOGA SPRINGS, *July* 30, 1827.

I received, a day or two since, a letter from Mr. Jno. Radcliff, of Rhinebeck, in which he says that the committee of the session were then engaged in taking up subscriptions to authorize a call for me. Thus far they had succeeded beyond their most earnest expectations. Many had subscribed more than at any previous period, and the friends of Mr. Labagh had testified their acquiescence in subscribing liberally. Until their subscription is completed, they will send me no official communication. As far as we short-sighted mortals can judge, there seems no doubt of their calling me. I look to God for guidance and strength. This is an important crisis in my life. But my faith is under the direction of God. To him I commit myself."

With this call from the Dutch Church at Rhinebeck, involving a change of religious denomination, a very serious question was presented to the young pastor. This step could not have been taken without deep thought and anxious prayer, as it was to define his future position. Some years later he published a sermon entitled "Reasons for preferring a union with the Reformed Dutch Church of North America," which give us a synopsis of his deliberation.

"Many who love ecclesiastical order, pure truth, and above all, freedom from contention, have swelled her members, and now the name *Reformed Dutch* has ceased to be so much a national distinction as the title of a sect holding certain peculiar features of government, possessing a certain religious character, and subject to certain distinct ecclesiastical courts." He preferred her Order; equally removed from the democracy of Congregationalism, the monarchy of Episcopacy, and the oligarchy of Presbyterianism she presents in her representative government united to rotation in office, the purest republican constitution. He liked her Liturgy, the most important parts of which are required to be used. In these, whatever may be the unfaithfulness of the minister, the great doctrines of grace in their unadulterated purity, are brought before the minds, and impressed upon the hearts of the people. He delighted in her sound Doctrine, yet with kind forbearance to those who were considered in error. He admired her "Spirit, 1. Steady, slow to change; 2. Benevolent to other sects and in charities; and 3. one of brotherly love. Her ministers are a band of brethren. When we meet it is as children of the same beloved mother. This I am bold to say, is peculiarly her character. It is obvious to all that are familiar with us. The same spirit pervades her laity. If we differ in minor points, we differ in love. The object of our discussion is not the triumph of party, but the peace of the church, and the discovery of truth by mutual counsels. Those who have seen us in our assemblies, must bear witness to the fact. We never meet but with joy, and never part but with tears and mutual benedictions. I am aware this is a high wrought picture, but it is faithful. My heart flows over with thankfulness to the God of love, while I draw it." Lastly, opportunities of usefulness in the Reformed Dutch Church are great.

"Our church is at peace. We are not called upon to engage in the controversies of the day, which so much distract the minds, divide the hearts, and occupy the energies of some sister churches. We may then give ourselves wholly to the work of saving souls for our Master. If it be necessary that other denominations should go to the war, we, a little band, may stay at home and cultivate the field of the Lord, and gather the harvest. We are united, we are respected, and hold a position of great influence. Such," he concludes, admitting into his serious discourse a little drop of native humor, "such are some of the reasons why we continue to love our church; why many who have no national claim to her appellation, 'seek her good;' and why we believe that 'they shall prosper that love her.' If any deem these reasons insufficient, we will yet remain where we are, until we can find a better spiritual home."

Of these reasons doubtless the two most potent in the mind of the young divine were the distracted state of the Presbyterian, church (then engaged in the struggles which resulted in its division), and the liturgical attraction. He had a taste for forms and inclined to give divine service a richer dress. Certain it is that his choice was the result of earnest conviction, for he gave his great heart with unflinching loyalty to the church of his adoption.

G. W. B. TO MRS. J. B. "LEBANON SPRINGS, *Aug.* 13, 1827.

I am in a little doubt upon a subject in which I wish your advice. In the event of my accepting Rhinebeck, is it better for me to be ordained in New York, or R——? I had rather receive ordination from my own

Presbytery, and Mc Cartee thinks it would be pleasanter for me; while on the other hand Dr. Mc Elroy, whom I met at Saratoga, thinks I would do better to consult Dutch feeling, and receive ordination from the Classis. Do send me your advice, as it will determine me. . . . . I think of you continually, and from very many people have the kindest inquiries addressed to me. . . . . I preached twice at Saratoga, and I received invitations from people of all quarters to visit vacancies in their neighborhood. Two of the Consistory of the Dutch Church in Schenectady were sent to me to request me to preach for them, one, and, if possible, a number of Sabbaths. . . . . Two persons whom I never saw before, introduced themselves to me, to request me, but not officially, to go to Portland, Maine, as Dr. Payson's health is so bad as to permit him to preach but seldom. I have of course given the negative to everything until this affair with Rhinebeck is settled."

MRS. J. B. TO HER SON. "NEW YORK, *Aug.* 15, 1827.

MY DEAR GEORGE: At last I can acknowledge a letter from you. If you think of me continually, you might find a few minutes to put your thoughts on paper. Had I not heard from others, I should not have known of your getting the call to Rhinebeck. Choules gave the first information of it, and last Sabbath evening Mr. Camp, of Rhinebeck, called to inquire for you, and spent an hour with me; he seems a good, pious man.

I agree with Mr. Mc Elroy as to your ordination. It would have been, perhaps, more pleasant for you to have been ordained by your own presbytery, but as it has not been done previous to your accepting the call, I think it would please your people better to have all done by the Classis. They would then acknowledge you more a Dutchman, as I presume you would need no dismission from any other body. But I speak without knowing much of forms. I trust the Lord himself will be your counsellor in that, and everything else. I should like to be present at your ordination and installation; both, I presume, at the same time, which is another reason for being ordained by the Classis."

He was ordained by the Second Presbytery of New York in view of his call to the Rhinebeck Church, and when he assumed the solemn vows, he stood upon the spot where his parents had offered him to the Lord in baptism, and where reposed the sacred remains of his father and grandmother.

Directly after, he was installed at Rhinebeck and had a most cordial reception. The original correspondence speaks for itself.

G. W. B. TO MRS. J. B. "RHINEBECK, *Dec.* 10, 1827.

We arrived here in safety, and are now enjoying as much comfort as our anxiety with regard to you will permit. . . . .

It is a delightful reflection, the omnipresence and universal providence of God, that in all places, and under all circumstances, he is ever at hand to bless, to uphold, and to comfort his people, that the prayer for his mercy, though ascending for a distant mother, is as effectual as if offered by her bedside. You are with him my beloved mother, with him in whom you have believed, upon whom you have trusted, to whom you have committed every temporal and eternal interest. He has promised and he is faithful; he will comfort you and stay you by the right arm of his righteousness, and this is my only comfort in being absent from you."

"RHINEBECK, *Jan.* 2, 1828.

Things go on here tolerably well, and I have my hands as full of business as they can well be, but I have reason to be thankful. I am succeeding better than I had any reason to anticipate. My operations in the quarter where the Methodists had broken in upon me, have been attended with signal success, my Bible class there already consisting of five and twenty.

I have also strong reasons for believing my project of a Classical School, will be successful. I have made Mr. Van Horn an offer of about seventy-four dollars per quarter, to begin with, with every prospect of rapid increase. Should he come, I shall enjoy some assistance of my Sunday schools.

Few changes take place in our little village of interest to you. The whole routine of my duties to a superficial eye, is very monotonous, but to my anxious mind full of interest. Preaching here, preaching there; catechising in this quarter or that; visiting this sick or that afflicted family, but it is my work, assigned me by the Master. May I fulfil the end for which he has called me."

"RHINEBECK, *Jan.* 3, 1828.

Every thing about us progresses (to use a Yankee phrase) very well. We live very retired and very happily. We have great reason to be thankful. My official labours are so numerous as to prevent my taking much enjoyment in my greatest pleasure, reading, and my separation from my beloved and affectionate mother hangs like a cloud over me. If I had time to relieve myself by frequent writing, it would be different, but my moments allotted to general writing must be had, when others would be asleep, and the duties which more than filled up the day are closed. But if all were sunshine and happiness here, we would not seek for heaven; if we had all the comforts of home in this poor world, we would not care for our Father's house. But I trust I am not entirely ungrateful for the mercies I receive. I feel a happiness and enjoyment of my labour, which I never knew in my leisure hours, and I know by experience, that the sleep and the food of the labouring man is sweet.

"RHINEBECK, *January* 10, 1828.

MY BELOVED MOTHER; Your kind letter I received and read with that attention which every suggestion from one so affectionate and tender towards me deserves. I thank you, my dear mother, for the gentleness and forbearance with which you warn me of my follies and my sins. Dear mother, I thought all the while with David, 'let the righteous smite thee, it shall be a kindness and let him reprove me, it shall be an excellent oil, which shall not break thy head.' I dare hardly make promises, I have so often promised yet failed; but my dear mother, your letter has reached my heart. I do feel and deeply too, that I have been foolish, sinfully, ungratefully foolish, and I pray God I may never give you cause to repeat the gentle reproofs conveyed in your last. It is not with any intention to extravagance but through carelessness — sinful, blameable carelessness — I acknowledge. Not to excuse, but perhaps to palliate, my folly, I may say, that, we are young housekeepers and may, perhaps, and I hope we will, improve."

"I have been lately thinking more and more about the instruction of the lambs of the flock, and it appears to me that the church as such by its government should take a more decided part in the instruction of the young. The old churches (spite of our boasted novelties) managed these things better, especially our church (Hollandsche), — she had all the schools under her care. Their masters were her choice, subject to her government. Now, suppose an infant school attached to each church. Then the Sabbath schools for more decidedly religious and doctrinal instruction. Then schools for higher branches until the classical branches should finish all. How perfectly could the church control the growing years and expanding affections of her young. Immoral teachers, dangerous books, all would be banished from the schools.

"I begin to be more and more of Dr. Green's sentiments, viz: That however beneficial Bible and Sabbath Societies may be, the church in her corporate capacity should be up and doing. The command is to the church, Go ye and preach. I wish we had your book, I feel quite impatient to see it. I have half a notion to turn author myself. I find that there is nothing more difficult in the country, than to find good well-informed teachers or even those who have an opportunity of informing themselves. Judson's Questions, or anybody's questions, will be of little service where there is no commentary to assist the teacher to explain. Bible classes and lectures do something towards this, but not enough — neither does the instruction of a bible class keep pace with the Sabbath school. .

"My plan is this — to begin with the creation — thence the fall — the promise of Messiah — the call of Abraham — Israel — the Passover &c., to Christ's birth — thence through the gospel — to write a short running commentary adapted to the higher classes of Sabbath schools — divided into proper lessons with short practical remarks and place at the end the questions which show the attention of the scholar to the commentary. This commentary to embrace geographical, archæological, doctrinal, explanatory and practical remarks, suited especially to children. The only thing which I fear is, the expense."

"RHINEBECK, *February* 18, 1828.

You have probably seen the result of our Bible meeting. It was very cheering. The resolution was entered upon our minutes, that within six months every family in the county of Dutchess should have a bible. The motion was made by a Methodist, seconded by a Baptist, and enforced by a Lutheran. When I saw they were about to disperse I rose and moved, with a few remarks, that a subscription be opened immediately; it was carried almost by acclamation and my mother will excuse my putting down $ 10, when it was followed immediately by $ 250 — and since, I learn, by more than $ 100 more — our county funds exclusive of the auxiliary societies, must now amount to nearly 400 dollars. I think that the Bible Funds throughout the county of Dutchess within the present year must amount to $ 1,200.

So much for prompt exertion."

The young pastor was made Honorary Member of the Delphian Society of Union College on the 1st of April of this year, and the diploma, being the first of many the like which he received, is carefully preserved in the family archives. On the 18th of September comes the first letter to beg for patronage and recommendation. Some years later such letters came by dozens and twenties. The last we see of him in 1828 is his leaving a letter to his mother to "do the courteous to his congregation, which has turned out almost *en masse* to build his fence for him."

His labors and meditations at this time are continually turned towards the schools of his charge, and he constantly has to thank his mother for aiding him with advice and money to keep them up.

In September 1829, his congregation made what he calls a "straggling attempt" to raise his salary. "The utmost point they try to reach is eight hundred dollars, and I doubt whether they will make that out. It is to be sure a rather unfavorable time." But better days were coming.

G. W. B. to Mrs. J. B. "Rhinebeck, *October* 26, 1829.

The Rev. Mr. Schemerhorn of Utica, came to make a proposal of very grave interest. You know, perhaps, that for a year or two back, they have been endeavoring to raise a Dutch Church in Utica, to recall the descendants of our church to the institutions of their forefathers and specially to stem the tide of error and disorder which is flowing at the West. The Church is now completed or nearly so, and Mr. S. has come to ask me to become the pastor, and says that he does so because I have been mentioned by a number of persons high in the Dutch Church, as the person adapted for the enterprise, and that he can find no other. Mr. Varick of Utica, who is one of the main pillars in the Church, having heard me at Oswego, and Mr. Broadhead also wish me. They secure to me a salary of one thousand dollars increasing with the income of the church, to fifteen hundred dollars. The price of living is far lower in Utica than here, and the station, one of the most prominent in the Dutch Church.

The prospect of raising a good church speedily, is great. They wish to have a minister the latter part of December, at least. Now, what shall I do? They press me for a speedy answer, but how can I give one. It does appear as if the Lord were calling me to another sphere of usefulness in some things, and others appear to bid me stay here. I write to you for your advice, I refer it to God by prayer and desire to be in his hands to do with me as he will, I feel my inability to discharge the duties of so important a station and think I am better here. But, if the Lord call me, then he will give me strength."

The answer comes, —promptly, and to the point:

" *October* 29.

You, and I with you, undertook your present situation fully convinced that the salary of six hundred dollars would not support you, but hoping that the Lord would honor you as his instrument in reviving an apparently neither cold nor hot congregation, that it would be a good place for study, and to form a character, and experience for future usefulness when the Lord should call you to a more enlarged sphere and you should see your way clear to accept such a call.

How have these expectations been realized? Of the first we need say nothing, but surely the second has been more than realized. The pleasure of the Lord has indeed prospered in your hand, the dry bones have been clothed with sinews and flesh. The word of the Lord has not returned to him void; but as the snow and the rain has watered the earth and resulted in seed to the sower. The blessed purpose of the Lord has been fulfilled in the salvation of many souls, and you, my beloved son, the honored instrument in His hand. You have also been instrumental in rousing the people to active exertion in the Lord's cause and to honor him with their substance, and through you much treasure has been cast into the Lord's treasury. You have seen an apparently careless people become a praying people, an apparently stingy people became a liberal people, and you have all along been treated with much affection and much greater respect than usually falls to the lot of young men. To balance this, you have not been supported, and your salary has not gone as far even as you expected, neither have the people done as much for you, in a pecuniary way, as they have done for others, but the worst part of your settlement is over, many expenses you have been exposed to, you will not have again. You will gradually learn experience and economy, and, even at Mary's calculation, you may live.

Taking the call into view I see nothing to tempt you to change, and much to frighten you. You would be in the very hot-bed of Hopkinsianism, you would be looked at with a jealous eye by all settled ministers, and you would have to labor in season and out of season, not exclusively with the sweet feeling of bringing souls to Christ and honor to your Master, but to build up a Dutch Church; both may be proper, but I must say, my heart shrinks from your engaging in any party work and of course being exposed to party feeling. A change may be necessary, but I do not advise it so soon. Your character is scarcely established, and were you to change for Utica, and probably from that to some other place, it might give an unfavourable impression of your stability. Besides, I see nothing to tempt you, even in a pecuniary way; one thousand dollars, without parsonage or wood, would be little better than what you have; your house-rent would be two hundred dollars at least, and you have loaded yourselves with so much "*thick day*" that the expense of moving would swallow up any overplus, and, though mentioned last, you will consider with me, the exposure of your dear Mary, at so inclement a season, as almost a sufficient reason itself for not attempting to move this season."

Meanwhile, however, there were other causes at work and while the zealous young minister was "proposing," the ill health of his wife forced him to leave Rhinebeck for the South. He went away on leave of absence, but never came back again.

His labors had been abundant. The congregation was spread over fifteen miles of country, and he was obliged to conduct four Bible classes. His audience was not composed entirely of plain country people, but embraced some who were distinguished in the land, such as Hon. Peter R. Livingston, and the widow of General Montgomery. Mrs. L. he loved to call his "Rhinebeck mother," and when she was dying he sang over her couch, "Angels are hovering round thy bed, to waft thy spirit home." He was most conscientious in work, never saving himself when the sick or sorrowful called. One evening he said to Mrs. B. we are both so fond of music, I am enticed to play the flute when I ought to be writing sermons. My flute is a temptation from duty. I will give it up. It was dispatched to a nephew with tears, and accompanied by a note, "I send you my flute, it tempts me from my studies. I love it, for it was the gift of your grandfather, use it tenderly for his sake." Frequently he was in his study till two or three o'clock in the morning, and when asked at a late hour, "Are you not weary?" replied "Yes, but I cannot sleep till I have made each individual visited a subject of special prayer."

Rev. Mr. Drury has supplied interesting particulars regarding this ministry.

"When Dr. Bethune came to Rhinebeck, the church, like many of its sisters in the country, was in a cold and lifeless state; though there was doubtless in it a little leaven of piety it was almost hidden in the great mass of dead orthodoxy and indifference by which it was surrounded. There was not a single unmarried person in the communion under the age of fifty, and of the members there were none who could lead in public prayer. Of course such a thing as a social prayer-meeting was unknown, and under existing circumstances, seemed well-nigh impossible. When after Dr. B. came he spoke of starting one, a young man, now a leading member of the Poughkeepsie bar, doubtingly asked, "But Dominie, who will make the prayers?" to which the Dr. had to answer, "If no one else, I."

He very soon filled the church with interested listeners to his preaching. With his natural gifts and abilities, he could not but be an attractive and eloquent speaker. His sermons while at Rhinebeck were characterized by the same practical and fervent spirit that is observed in his published discourses. At this period his pulpit preparations were less studied than they afterwards became, and many of his former people, on hearing him in after years would remark the difference, but yet insist, that although the Dominie had gained perhaps in grace and polish, he was more eloquent and effective to their minds, when his inspiration was gained more from daily intercourse with his people, than from the retirement of his study. At the second service he always extemporized, and these sermons are, I find, best, and most favorably remembered. But while the Dr. was effective in the pulpit, and by his preaching wrought a great work, his distinguished usefulness was due, in almost as great measure, to his diligent use of the *accessaries* of preaching.

As a *pastor* the Doctor was especially active. He seems to have recognized that in order to benefit his people he must get them acquainted with, and interested in, him, and to this end he spent much of his time with them at their homes. He took especial pains to interest the young, whom he regarded as the hope of the church. He was in the habit of remarking that the old people had become too set in their ways for him to do much with them, so he must, if he was going to do anything, attend to the young, as only in that way could he get such Christians as he wanted. He neglected no means by which he might hope to win any. If his horses needed shoeing, or he required in any way the services of a mechanic, he went himself to see to it, and in this apparently chance encounter was not unmindful of his higher work, and by his ready wit and conversational powers wiled many to hear him preach who were never before in the habit of attending church.

Much that he did as a pastor was not discovered until after he had left. About eight miles from the village is a slate quarry, at that time extensively worked, affording employment to quite a number of workmen. They and their families were in a great degree destitute of the preaching of the gospel and the means of grace. After he had left, for many years the Doctor's name was spoken of in these humble families with affection and respect. In each of them he had been a visitor, and quietly, and as it were, unknown, sowed the seeds of the word. He was famous for the speed of his driving. Such facts as these show in what service it was done.

Dr. B. was, moreover, the inaugurator of the Temperance movement in Rhinebeck, and accomplished in this direction a much needed reform. His sermon on the subject is remembered by those who heard it as an eloquent and stirring effort. It was published. This is the first record of his appearance in print although he had contributed to magazines under assumed names. The Doctor not only preached but practiced the new doctrine. In the early spring, soon after preaching the sermon, he attempted to drive to Poughkeepsie on the ice, and just before reaching Hyde Park he broke in and with his companion, got a decided wetting. When they reached Hyde Park his companion suggested "taking a little something to keep the cold out," but the Doctor refused, saying he had lately ridiculed the idea of taking liquor in winter to keep out the cold and in summer to keep out the heat, and he was going to try the virtue of doing without it, and afterwards testified that he was none the worse for his abstinence.

Bethune was fond of horses and was accomplished in their management. He owned one or two during his stay which he alone was able to manage. So noted was his horsemanship that some were even brought to hear him preach to ascertain if he could preach as well as he could drive. He had as a near neighbor, an old gentleman, who spent a great deal of his time in his garden. As he was something of a character in his way, the Doctor would frequently stop and converse with him over the fence. One day he said to him, "Well Mr. L——, now you are suited to a great many employments, if you fail at one you can take to another; but if I were prevented from preaching what do you think I would be good for?" The old gentleman stopped digging, and then with a twinkle in his eye, answered, "Well, Dominie, if you have to stop preaching you would make a first rate stage-driver." The Doctor accepted the compliment on his horsemanship and failed not to repeat the joke to his friends. Mr. L—— did not tell his Dominie, as he might have done, that other trades failing he could take to gardening. Helping hands were never wanting. A fine taste directed and a living energy urged on the work. A little gem of horticulture was the result. The tired eyes of the hard-writing pastor had a sweet object to dwell upon, flowers adorned the vases on the tables; and the great, much neglected truth that "beauty is cheap" received its fullest illustration. The parsonage was surrounded with beautiful scenery. A silver brook made sweet music at the bottom of the sloping ground on which the house stood, and the ruins of the old parsonage peeping through the trees reminded of good Dr. Romeyn, who was its first occupant. The first winter was employed in bringing forest trees on sledges and placing them in trenches prepared, and in the spring the grounds were laid out and planted with the choicest fruits and flowers. The neighbors gladly aided in the work. One day they were in despair at fruitless efforts to mark a circle for the flower bed. The Dominie came up in his light wagon and perceiving at a glance their difficulty, desired them to stand back, drove in, and, with a sweep of his wheels, marked the true curve amid the uplifted hands and loudly expressed admiration of the bystanders.

Rev. Mr. Hendricks relates that at a general training Mr. Bethune was chaplain of the day. Some of the people having fallen into intoxication, the minister reproved the fault severely, asserting that it was beastly, but soon corrected himself, saying no, that was a satire on the beasts, for they never debased themselves in such wise.

CHAPTER V.

MINISTRY IN UTICA.

On his arrival in Savannah, whites and blacks, sailors and civilians received their favorite Pastor with acclamation. He found a sphere of usefulness at once, by taking the place of Mr. Baker who was travelling for the Savannah Bible Society: "so that the Lord can find a place for me," he says, "and one too, in which I am, perhaps, aiding my favorite cause more than if I were personally and immediately engaged."

His somewhat exulting accounts to his mother did not elicit precisely the response that he may have expected. "What I most dread in your remaining at Savannah," she says, "is your popularity there; remember Bacon's prayer: 'When I ascend before men, O Lord, may I descend in deep humility before thee.'"

His satisfaction in his Savannah work too, was seriously lessened by the affairs of the Rhinebeck parish which weighed upon his mind, and of which he received no cheering accounts. The eye of the Master was wanting and it is evident that in spiritual matters his church was retrograding, in money matters not getting on. The call to Utica, though declined in theory, was yet an open question and the failure of the Rhinebeck Consistory to reduce the debt of the church and raise their minister's stipend, left him free to stand by them or go elsewhere as should seem best. Meanwhile, calls to other churches were not wanting. In the latter part of March a very complimentary letter from Charleston, invited him to fill the pulpit in the Second Presbyterian Church of that city. The wish of the congregation was unanimous, with the exception of a single individual, who desired it placed upon the minutes, that "he could vote for no one who had charge of another congregation without first consulting that congregation to know if they were willing to dissolve the connection."

He thus wrote:

"I preached three times yesterday to very full congregations and at night to an enormous audience. My charity sermon brought a very large collection. It may please you to know I have met with great applause, I pray God, with spiritual success. I have soothed my lonely feelings by writing the following lines:

TO MY WIFE.

Afar from thee, the morning breaks,
  But morning brings no joy to me;
Alas! my spirit only wakes
  To know I am afar from thee—
In dreams I saw thy blessed face,
  And thou wast nestled on my breast;
In dreams I felt thy loved embrace,
  And to mine own thy heart was pressed.

Afar from thee! 'tis solitude,
  Though smiling crowds around me be,
The kind, the beautiful, the good,
  But I can only think of thee;
Of thee, the kindest, loveliest, best,
  My earliest and my only one;
Without thee, I am all unblest,
  And wholly blest with thee alone.

Afar from thee! The words of praise
  My listless ears unheeded greet;
What sweetest seemed in better days,

Without thee seems no longer sweet;
The dearest joy fame can bestow,
Is in thy moistened eye to see,
And in thy cheeks' unusual glow,
Thou deemest me not unworthy thee.

Afar from thee! The night is come,
But slumbers from my pillows flee;
I cannot rest so far from home,
And my heart's home is, love, with thee.
I kneel before the throne of prayer,
And then I know that thou art nigh,
For God, who seeth everywhere,
Bends on us both his watchful eye.

Together in his loved embrace,
No distance can our hearts divide;
Forgotten quite the mediate space,
I kneel thy kneeling form beside;
My tranquil frame then sinks to sleep,
But soars the spirit far and free;
Oh welcome be night's slumbers deep,
For then, dear love, I am with thee."

During this winter Mr. B. stood as godfather for the son of Mrs. McCullister. He made him a special subject of prayer on Sabbath evenings, asking that he might become a Minister of the Gospel. The prayer is answered and he is the beloved pastor of a large congregation in San Francisco.

The Charleston congregation was treated with great courtesy and candor. Their offer was taken into respectful consideration; the facts not concealed, which rendered a decision difficult. When the call to Utica was renewed soon after, and the northern clergyman thought it a more advantageous offer for him, his southern friends had nothing to complain of in his course.

A clergyman's profession makes him fit to stand before kings and mean men alike, and in this fact, and in the fulfilment of his duty, he finds his reward for toil and exposure. But this world's goods are none the less acceptable for that. A present of three hundred dollars was made to the young pastor by his Savannah congregation, as a token of their regard for his person, and their estimation of his talents, and probably imparted equal pleasure to the giver and the receiver. Indeed a firm attachment appears to have subsisted between the minister and his people, and so much kindness was shewn to Mr. Bethune by the men of the south generally, as fully to account for a certain tenderness of feeling which he entertained for them when the war first broke out.

The Utica congregation have made up their minds finally as to the man they desire for pastor, and from that man they will not take no for an answer. Their church is not yet formed, and they will have but one man to form it. Their church is not yet dedicated, and they will have the same man to dedicate it. "We have appointed the *third Thursday* of this month (June, 1830), for the dedication of the church of Utica," writes John F. Schermerhorn, "and we expect you there on the occasion, and wish that you supply the pulpit on the Sabbath following." The church is duly dedicated on the day fixed. The "edifice is the neatest and most tasty building of its kind that can be seen, the congregation quadruple what our most sanguine friends could have anticipated, and we have succeeded in procuring a chorister of the best abilities for his office, so that everything looks fair."

G. W. B. to Mrs. J. B. "Utica, *July* 8, 1830.

My Dear Mother: I should have written before this, but time after time have been prevented by my multitudinous concerns. Not that my parish is so large as to occupy much of my time in visiting, as I can see my whole flock in one day. But the commencement of my Sabbath School Bible Class etc., has swallowed me up. By the way, my school does well. Seven of my men gave me ten dollars each to establish it. I have now sixty scholars, and we have only met once.

My church promises fairly as yet; although, of course, the experiment is only begun, but my congregation increases every day very evidently. We have no quarrel with any one, and will try to permit no one to have any quarrel with us.

Honesty is our policy—plain, open-handed honesty; a policy the God of truth will own and bless.

You will be gratified by hearing that the Scotch people gather about me. They say: 'There's something about these ither churches we dunna like; but ye are mair like our ain fouk at hame.' They do not understand Hopkinsianism, can't make out what they would be at. One of them was particularly pleased with one sermon of mine. He could not tell how it was, but it ran more like the sermons he used to love. I knew the reason. I had carried the doctrine of substitution and suretyship in a strong vein throughout."

"UTICA, *July* 28, 1830.

You will be pleased to hear that thus far we are doing very well. The pews are not sold, and will not be if we can avoid it, our wishes being to rent or lease them. I cannot therefore say who my congregation will be. It is however ascertained that a very good number, and among them the choice people of the town, certainly intend to join us. We have our opponents as we expected. Their attacks, however, they have not dared to make openly; but insidious attempts, to impede if not frustrate our designs, have not been wanting. As yet, thanks to our good God, we have been enabled to walk so circumspectly as to give no occasion for open censure; and the worse charges against me you will not be displeased to learn are, 'Triangularism,'* and others similar.

It is my firm conviction that this church may be instrumental in doing much good, not only as a centre for extensive missionary operations of

* A theological term of the day, derived from a book called "The Triangle," and signifying high-toned Calvinism.

our own church, but to the people of this village. It has already had the effect of allaying the bitterness of party rancor among other churches, and I hope may be an ark to preserve the law of the Lord entire, amid the flood of false zeal and falser doctrine by which we are surrounded. Already have they endeavoured to leave us out from the charitable enterprises of the day, by cautiously excluding my men and myself from all offices and even committees; but the effect of their schemes has been neutralised by our willingness to work among the lowest, and to give with the highest, and already my little church has taken a stand among the most energetic and liberal in this section of country."

The climate of Utica was too severe for Mrs. Bethune's health, and another southern trip became necessary.

"UTICA, *October* 5, 1830.

The communication to go south this winter and to leave Utica, has driven my friends here to apparent and I believe real despair. They think that it will be the death blow to the church and to all the efforts in the cause of truth here.

They appear to acknowledge the necessity of Mary's having a southern winter, but had not anticipated my leaving them altogether, and yet, if I go to the south, I see not how it can be otherwise. The mariners' church is my support if I go, and I cannot take that except I remain from November till the end of May; and then, again, the uncertainty of the subsequent winter. This is an important station. I am persuaded a congregation can be gathered with the ordinary blessing of Providence, if I remain; and, I believe, I would be paid the sum stipulated. I also think that I have opportunities of improvement here, and a fair opening for establishing my reputation in the Christian community. At the same time there are many difficulties in the way.

I do not wish this enterprise to fail. I believe it to be intimately connected with the cause of sound truth. I know not what to do. Darkness and doubt rest upon the future. I have thought and prayed, and yet I am in darkness. These people afflict me. The cause which has somehow become entangled with me, afflicts me. Do write to me speedily, decidedly and at large, and excuse my indecision."

Answer to the above from New York:—

"MY DEAR GEORGE: You imposed a hard task upon me, and as it is always better to take time to consider and pray for direction, I have not answered as speedily as perhaps you wished. Yesterday was our communion Sabbath, and you and your concerns were upon my mind. This forenoon I received a letter from Mr. Schermerhorn, laying not only the Dutch church, but the prosperity or ruin of his family upon the advice I shall give you, with a variety of appeals to my conscience. The words which came to my mind while reading his letter were those which the parents of the blind man said, "He is of age ask him." He proposes that if it is necessary Mary should go south, that you should remain and she go with a companion; or that you should go and return early in the spring. I presume you have heard all his arguments. . . . You may make a virtue of necessity, and consent to be installed in Utica, even though Mary's health render your going south necessary. But there is another circumstance which makes Utica less desirable to me. Many say that you are killing yourself. I called at Jersey City to see the Colonel and Mrs. Varick. He told me it would never do for you to labor so hard, that although you were doing a great deal of good, it was more than flesh and blood could stand. I must therefore beg, and if I dare, insist, that you do not preach more than twice on the Sabbath. . . . I can give no further advice on the subject. I cannot consent to take the blame of all the exertions made to establish a Dutch church, and to advance the cause of truth being ruined, as well as the temporal prosperity of Mr. Schermerhorn's family. It was no fault of either you or me that he put his money into such stock; and you and he both know that I never was quite satisfied that you should go to Utica. It has been accompanied by some sacrifices on my part as well as on yours."

In the latter part of October, the church at Utica was formed. The fears of the anxious mother regarding the want of a church, and especially of a consistory, proved unfounded; but in a worldly, temporal point of view, the wise lady's provisions were justified.

The zealous minister writes :—

"There is an unusual number of young men among us. . . . The other folks, the *extreme Hops*, emphatically *let us alone*; hold no communion with us and pass by on the other side. If there is determined opposition against us, (and I fear there is,) it is secret. No charges are brought and I am happy to believe none can be; for whatever unchristian feeling may have obtained in our hearts none has appeared in our acts. The motto I have endeavored to recommend and to practise upon is, when persecuted let us bless, when reviled let us revile not again. I am confident that I am in a good school; caution, prudence, upright walking, the government of the tongue, appear vital in their importance."

The installation at Utica took place on November 7th, and on the following Lord's Day he preached his Inaugural Discourse from 1 Cor. ii., 2, entitled "The cross of Christ the only theme of the Preacher of Truth." This sermon gives us the key-note of all his preaching.

"Your attention will not be diverted from the more important topics of eternal interest by the wire-drawn speculations of mere human philosophy, nor will the plain and simple rules of the Christian faith be obscured and entangled by the metaphysical jargon of modern theology, falsely so called. The description of any subject inferior to those of eternal interest will be considered profane and insulting in the house of God. All amusements or interest here, must be sought and found, not in the adornments of style or the playfulness of fancy, but in the grave examination of solemn truths and simple illustration of heavenly precepts. You will not be assembled on the Sabbath to listen to one who hath a pleasant song, or who 'can play well upon an instrument,' even were it within the compass of your pastor's talents; but to hear the words of truth and soberness. It will be his endeavor not to please the itching ear, but to instruct the inquiring soul and warm the pious heart. Like the Master, he will seek to draw with the cords of love, rather than drive with the scourge of terror. . . . Indeed, my beloved friends, the cross of Christ shall be my welcome and continual theme; and whether the rigorous demands of the violated law be thundered, or the sweet accents of forgiving love be whispered in your ears, the object will be to bring you weeping yet thankful, humble yet confident, to the feet of the crucified Hope of Israel. As the herald of His cross, the preacher of His gospel, the messenger of His love, never will your pastor descend from the sacred elevation until he hath pointed it out as the rest of the weary, the refuge of the condemned and the shelter of the lost."

In the evening there was an "Exhortation to prayer for the peace of Jerusalem." Both these discourses were published at the request of the people.

Nothing can be clearer than that our pastor had a most arduous and difficult task in building up the church in Utica.

Hovey K. Clarke, Esq., who was one of the earliest converts under Mr. B.'s ministry at Utica, and had been engaged in the founding of the church, kept up a continual correspondence with the man whose life we endeavor faithfully to set forth. He has furnished much interesting matter from memory and his own papers. We quote his statements:

"This Church had then been recently organized and was, in some degree, the result of a condition of religious opinion existing there; especially among those who accepted the Calvinistic standards of faith, with, nevertheless, such differences in their belief as would scarcely fail to be considered as of vital importance.

About three years before, the Rev. Mr. Finney had, during an entire winter, preached almost every evening in the First Presbyterian Church. That his preaching was attended by the power of the Spirit of God there can be no question, as numerous conversions abundantly testified; conversions which after the lapse of nearly forty years still attest their divine origin. But the sentiment prevailing in that locality gave such prominence to the doctrines preached by Mr. Finney and the practices employed by him as efficient instrumentalities in the work of conversion, that to oppose the "new measures" or to doubt their wisdom, was regarded as assuming a position of opposition to a manifest work of grace. Those to whom this position was assigned could not but regard Mr. Finney's preaching as a departure from the standards of the Church in which he was ordained; and his measures as unscriptural and therefore dangerous in their tendencies. But it was a fearful responsibility to seem to oppose a revival. It was easy to sail with the stream which seemed to bear on its bosom the glad fruits of numerous conversions to God. New measures were popular, and those who could not adopt them nor approve the doctrines, of which they were in some respects the outgrowth, were compelled to silence or to seek other religious associations. Such influences as these, combining with others which are seldom wanting on such occasions, resulted in the organization of the church to which Mr. Bethune was now called to be the Pastor.

It is not surprising that he found himself, to some extent, in a field of controversy. He had a new church to organize and build up; a church harmonious in all the substantials of its faith, and yet, if not discordant in the materials of which it was composed, as it certainly was not, it was nevertheless *not* perfectly harmonious.

He was not long moreover in making the sad discovery that there were those to whose recognition as a welcome fellow-laborer in the same service he might have supposed himself entitled, who regarded him as the representative of a dead orthodoxy — one whose qualifications for usefulness might be derided and whose influence might be crippled without offence to the cause of evangelical religion. Under such circumstances and environed by an atmosphere of prejudice did this young minister carry on his labors at Utica. His two sermons on the day of his inauguration have already been referred to. The inaugural itself most significantly indicated the defensive attitude which the preacher felt himself obliged to maintain by its frequent references to the Heidelberg and the Westminster Confessions. A note printed on the cover of the pamphlet which contained these discourses further indicates the personal hostility to which he was in some measure subjected.

As an appeal to the Christian public to be treated with Christian courtesy it is well remembered by those who sympathized with the author on the occasion of it. It was as follows:

"The author of these sheets is not without information that his theological opinions have been grossly misrepresented, and that he has been designated by opprobrious names, 'Triangular,' 'Antinomian,' 'A preacher of smooth things,' &c. His every discourse is a refutation of such charges, but such refutation is of no avail against their censure who condemn without hearing. He hopes these misrepresentations have been unintentional, and he assures all who have made them, of his earnest endeavor, by God's grace, to forgive the deepest injury he can suffer from man, the diminution of his usefulness in his Master's cause. He would fain forget what he has heard, as unfavorable to the cultivation of that high esteem in which he would hold the followers of the same kind and heavenly Master. To be altogether silent, however, would be to permit the circumscription of his ministerial influence. For the sake, therefore, of the truth he advocates, he has been induced to publish the foregoing discourses as an exhibition of his creed; though his youth, in other circumstances, would have exhorted him to retirement. He again declares that his creed is to be found in the books of his Church and those of the Presbyterian Church, in whose schools he was educated, and to whose ministry he was ordained, though subsequently, from deliberate preference, he entered the communion of the Reformed Dutch Church. If, therefore, he differs from any one, it is because that person differs from the standards of faith above referred to.

He is not ashamed of association with the many mighty men, since the Reformation, who have held the doctrines he holds by whatever name calumny may stigmatize them. He frankly acknowledges a dislike to the disposition of those who 'spend their time in nothing else but either to tell or to hear some new thing,' but loves sound, consistant, stable doctrine. His desire is 'to live in charity with all men,' especially 'with the household of faith;' and he asks for that charity in return 'which thinketh no evil,' without palpable evidence, and his reliance is upon Him, 'who endured the contradiction of sinners against himself,' and who 'when reviled, reviled not again.'"

To illustrate the nature of the controversies then disturbing the church, and Mr. Bethune's position, we quote a letter of Mr. Clarke:

"CANANDAIGUA, *Sept.* 24, 1831.

MY DEAR PASTOR:—Notwithstanding our separation, I shall persist in preserving the relation of Pastor and Parishioner between us, and although our intercourse will be seriously interupted, still, I trust that the pastoral visits of your pen will be neither 'few nor far between.'

As you anticipated I find in Mr. —— some things different from what I found in you; but what they are I am not able, clearly, to define. He will occasionally flash off from the pulpit a sentence, which from his tone, manner and emphasis, evidently is intended for the *Dutchman* of his congregation, or rather, as Mrs. —— styles me, the 'Consistory of the Dutch Church about to be established here.' On the first Sabbath that Mr. —— resumed the duties of his pulpit (three weeks since), he made a remark of this kind, viz: that he believed the Atonement to be sufficient for the salvation of millions of worlds and not merely efficient for the salvation of those that believe; this being so palpably an imitation of your language when expressing the contrary to the sentiment contained in the latter clause, that it needs no seer to explain to whom he pointed, especially when taken in connection with a remark he made to a gentleman (who resides near here) in my presence, and probably intended for my ear. On Mr. S. enquiring of Mr. —— if 'Mr. Bethune could induce all his people to believe with him in a limited Atonement:' 'Oh,' said he, 'Brother Bethune satisfies them by saying it is sufficient for all, and efficient for the elect.' Again Mrs. —— says, for I have conversed more with her upon these subjects, that you are a Triangular. Now, I am so innocently ignorant of the virtues and the vices of a Triangular, that I am ready to say with the Irish horse-jockey, who was asked if his horse were spavined, 'Och, sure he is, if that's any advantage to him.'"

On the 9th of January, 1832, Mr. Clarke thanks his correspondent for his views upon the nature and extent of the Atonement, and says that they appear more reasonable and consistent than any thing heretofore heard upon it. These views are contained in a letter which, to our great chagrin, is not forthcoming. It would be cheaply purchased with ten or fifteen pounds of the paper stock which has come safely to hand. Mr. Clarke writes again May 7.

"By the way, of this same limited Atonement I am excessively desirous of knowing whether the doctrine we profess, namely, the sufficiency of the merits of the death of Christ for the salvation of all, and its efficiency to the salvation of the elect, is the doctrine of the 'limited Atonement.' The idea that I have received here of it is that Christ weighed out, as it were, with scrupulous exactness, the amount of sin committed, or that would be committed by the elect, and by his sufferings atoned for that and no more. And that could we know who the elect were, we should have no right to offer salvation to any but to them. Can it be that this is the doctrine which so many eminent men have not been ashamed to avow? For fear that it should be, I will not in my ignorance of the doctrines of the Bible with all their collateral bearings, presume to impeach their wisdom. But really, if it is so, the innumerable invitations that are given in the Bible, *to all*, to 'come and partake of the waters of life freely,' appear to me very like a farce. God offering salvation to lost men, through Christ, *to all*, when he has made provision for only a part! It appears to me perfectly consistent with the character of God to offer salvation to all through an atonement, the merits of which, so far as it relates to their sufficiency, are infinite; although he knows that a majority will absolutely refuse to have that atonement made efficient in their salvation. But then means were provided and salvation offered; and man, in the free exercise of his moral agency, refused. I am well aware that my notions upon this subject are crude, and perhaps contradictory. It is for this reason that I am now consulting my proper spiritual adviser. I am also well aware that the weapon which many think proper to wield, and which they do at times with singular force, is ridicule. A doctrine of which, though they disbelieve it, a correct portrait might present some points favourable to belief; they choose rather to render odious, by making an infamous caricature. However I am thankful that I can adopt Gov. Granger's motto, 'Lux, Lex et Libertas.' Light to show me what the Law or doctrine is, and the Liberty of conscience to exercise my own belief, notwithstanding I am in a hot-bed of opposition."

The answer to the above is to be found *passim* in the writings of Dr. Bethune. In lecture xvii. on the Heidelberg Catechism, we read — pp. 358 et seq:

"But our Lord stood not in the room of a single sinner; he bore the sins of many, and heaven opened to us by the vision of John, shows a mighty host redeemed unto God by his blood. Hence his sufferings were incalculably more than the sufferings of any one mere man could have been. For though we unhesitatingly, and not without horror, reject the idea that his sufferings were weighed out to him in exact proportion to the sufferings which every individual of all he redeemed, would otherwise have actually suffered; we must see that they needed to be so great as to justify God in taking away his wrath from all the Saviour's people. It was, among other reasons, for the purpose of strengthening our Lord's humanity to endure this accumulated aggregation of suffering, that it was constituted in union with the Divine Nature, which also gave to his sufferings their infinite value. So the Catechism says that he sustained the wrath of God against the sins of all mankind.

This last sentence requires some little explanation, lest its meaning should be misunderstood, and we shall give it conformably to the comments of the learned and pious Ursinus, the author of the Catechism, and therefore the best expositor of its sense. The idea of the sentence is that of several scriptures, as where our Lord declares that 'God so loved the world' as to give his only begotten son; and the writer to the Hebrews, that Christ tasted death for every man; and Paul that he gave himself a ransom for all; and John 'that he is a propitiation for our sins, and not for ours only, but also for the sins of the whole world.' Yet Scripture must be read in harmony with itself, and as we know that all men are not actually saved, but only those who through grace being ordained to eternal life do believe and repent, it cannot be that our Lord bore the wrath of God against the sins of the whole world in the same sense or degree that he bore it in the room of his people. They were actually redeemed by his blood, he having taken the penalty they deserved on himself so that their satisfaction was certainly secured by his vicarious satisfaction; but the rest of mankind, though they have so far as the gospel is preached to them opportunities of salvation, are condemned to death eternal without violence being done to the covenant of the Son with the Father in the plan of salvation.

Thus Christ died for all mankind, because in him the blessings of salvation are not confined, as were those of the Abrahamic dispensation, to one particular people. The gospel is sent throughout all the world, to be preached to every creature, and whosoever will, be he a Jew or Gentile, may take of the water of life freely. As several of the later fathers following Tertullian phrase it, His merits are sufficient for all, but efficient for the elect. And Aquinas, whom the Papists call the Angelical Doctor, teaches, 'The merit of Christ, as concerns its sufficiency, equally belongs to all men; but as to its efficacy, the effects and fruits of it are mercifully bestowed on some, and, by the just judgment of God, withheld from others.' Nor can this be otherwise, since it were preposterous to make Christ the substitute of those that refuse his representation. But it is, on the other hand, positively true, that the benefits of Christ's merit do actually, though not in a saving degree, extend to all men; because for the sake of Christ all temporal mercies come to all, and the world is kept by his intercession from becoming a hell of extreme torture and despair; and very precious blessings, though not the most precious, are bestowed on mankind through the restraining influence of Christianity and the light which it sheds on every mind wherever the healing beams of the Sun of Righteousness shine. It is enough for us to know that, if we believe in Christ with our whole heart, his merit will certainly save us; but if we refuse the grace he offers, not all the mercy of God in Christ warrants the slightest hope of escape from everlasting death."

We add a passage from another sermon on quite a different subject, "The Strength of Christian Charity."

"The grace of God is infinite in the merits of Christ, the Saviour, for they are the merits of God incarnate. It was the Son of God who walked in all the duties of man. Who dare limit the reward of his obedience?

It was the Son of God who dwelt in the sufferer when he drank the cup of trembling, when it pleased the Father to bruise him and to put him to grief, and when, pouring out his soul unto death, he cried, 'It is finished.' Who dare limit the power of his atonement? It was the Son of God who burst the bars of death and cleft the heavens for the upward way of the man Christ Jesus, 'to make continual intercession for us,' not as a suppliant kneeling at his Father's feet, but as a Son and a Prince, the true Israel sitting at the right hand of the Majesty on high. Who dare limit the efficiency of his prayers?"

"Other calls will not be wanting," said Mrs. J. Bethune in the letter to her son touching the removal to Utica. To show how true this was, let us state that in the five years which elapsed from his entering the ministry to February, 1831, there came to him of official calls, or what might have been such, eight. To Savannah, to St. Augustine, to St. Mary's, to Rhinebeck, to Utica, to the Market St. Church, N. Y.—This last was most earnestly backed by the letter of his friend John Redfield.

But his heart was given to Utica, and every art of ingenuity was employed that could increase his usefulness and strengthen the Church. During the early part of 1831, great attention was paid to the young; and the professors and great lights of the Dutch denomination were introduced into his pulpit to advance the cause of sound doctrine.

Mrs. J. B. to her son, October 29, 1831. In this letter we have notice of an early and well-known poetical effort.

"I have been writing and getting printed a lesson on the Mariner's Compass. I read it to Mr. Seaton, and next day he wrote me a note, saying there was a beautiful Hymn in the 'Lyra,' which he thought would suit to close it. I sent for it and lo and behold, it was yours:

'Tossed on life's tempestuous billow.'

I bought the Seaman's Hymn Book to get it. I had, however, prepared one myself which, although not so poetical, is more suitable."

SAILOR'S HYMN.

"Tossed upon life's raging billow,
  Sweet it is, O, Lord, to know
Thou hast pressed a sailor's pillow,
  And canst feel a sailor's woe.
Never slumbering, never sleeping,
  Though the night be dark and drear,
Thou, the faithful watch art keeping,
  'All, all's well!' thy constant cheer.

And though loud the wind is howling,
  Fierce, though flash the lightnings red,
Darkly, though the storm cloud's scowling,
  O'er the sailor's anxious head;
Thou canst calm the raging ocean,
  All its noise and tumult still,
Hush the billow's wild commotion,
  At the bidding of thy will.

Thus my heart the hope will cherish,
  While to heaven I lift mine eye,
Thou wilt save me ere I perish,
  Thou wilt hear me when I cry;
And, though mast and sail be riven,
  Life's short voyage soon be o'er,
Safely moored in Heaven's wide haven,
  Storms and tempests vex no more."

We are at a loss to imagine how the Editor of the very popular "Songs of the Sanctuary" came to insert this hymn under the number 1322 as "anonymous." His taste in this direction is faultless and we cannot believe that he had seen the original, or the amendments upon Dr. Bethune would scarcely have been permitted. The alteration, we admit, is for the better, and yet question the propriety of even such a change. We want the master's work as he left it. Men may copy a picture, but it is a shame to retouch it.

G. W. B. TO MRS. J. B. "UTICA, *November* 25, 1831.

My congregation is in a very quiet state, too much so I fear. My heart, rather desponding, probably owing to bodily indisposition. I find my duties exceedingly arduous. The Lord, however, is, I trust, my everlasting strength. I am charmed with the Infant School lessons which appear from week to week in the Messenger. I read them all, and believe that I receive benefit from them."

Answer to the above, 28th Nov.

"NEW YORK, *November* 28, 1831.

MY BELOVED SON:—I have this day yours of 25th instant, and grieve to hear that you are not well, either in body or mind. How could you fly about when you had so heavy a cold? Mr. Nasmith told me you were out at the meeting when you were very unwell. I pray God to restore you and spare your precious life. I often tremble when I think how many of your companions have already finished their course and I cry out, O, that my son might be spared and live before God. O, George, for your poor, solitary, widowed mother's sake, for your dear Mary's sake, *two* at least, whose comfort in this world is wrapt up in you, take care of yourself. My darling son, my heart is pained and my eyes overflow when I write; would that I could fly to you and hold your aching head and cheer your desponding heart. I hope you are not so bad as my fears represent. O, my son, look to Jesus for strength, where alone it can be found. Remember him who endured. In him is abundant fulness for all you want. I wish you would give up one service on the Sabbath. It is too much."

"Iron sharpeneth iron, so a man sharpeneth the countenance of his friend."

"A man" (aye every inch) writes from Canajoharie, 16th April, to "his friend" in Utica.

"MY DEAR BROTHER:—I received your note of invitation yesterday—and at first I almost imagined myself reading the 'Lamentations of Jeremiah.' What is the matter? Is your church in a state of dilapidation, or had you got a little touch of the hyp? Your station is undoubtedly one of great importance and the prosperity of your church will exert an extensive influence upon the surrounding churches. It must, in time, become the Metropolis of the West. But, '*Nil desperandum,*' Rome was not built in a day. Neither your Master in heaven nor the church on earth expect that you will do more than your thought and abilities enable you to do. Preach Christ and Him crucified, and if in the end the ship is wrecked and the cargo lost you may cling to some floating plank and escape — or if you all founder together — your 'hands will be clean from the blood of all men.' But report says that your church is flourishing — increasing in numbers — in popularity — in influence, and that your labors are highly acceptable to the people and signally blessed of God. I cannot subscribe to one sentence of your letter — 'that the Ministry of the church should appear to ADVANTAGE in Utica.' They should be the faithful heralds of Salvation — the world over — wherever they go they should be about their 'Father's business' and, in Utica and every other place, leave the impression upon the minds of all — that they watch for souls as they who must give an account. If, as a church, we had far less of the spirit of unhallowed rivalry and vastly more of the self-denying and self-sacrificing spirit of Paul, the smiles of Heaven would shine upon us more brightly. But Utica has seen the very flower of the flock, the very quintessence of Dutch Reformed celebrity, the choice spirits of the day. Did not our men of renown come all the way up the Hudson and the Mohawk to edify, astonish and delight the inhabitants of these western wilds by their wisdom and their eloquence? Now, if the citizens of Utica are not deeply impressed with the conviction, that the Dutch Church abounds in talent of the first water, Pauls and Apolloses, then they must be stupid as oxen and ignorant as asses; or if these Anakims have failed to leave such an impression, what can such little men as compose the Classis of Montgomery do? RANSFORD WELLS."

This little correspondence speaks for itself.

It may be well to quote entire a specimen of our minister's style of pastoral letter-writing in 1831, in order to a comparison with his later efforts of the same kind.

TO MISS S. B. M. AND M. A. V. "UTICA, 1831.

MY DEAR YOUNG LADIES: — It is long since I promised myself the pleasure of addressing you — and more than once have I commenced a letter, but have been called away from the pleasing engagement by the many and various duties of my arduous office.

To say that I miss you is but poorly to express the reality. My heart goes after my absent lambs whenever I am reminded of your absence — I miss you from the church, the lecture room and the prayer-meeting, where you were ever glad to be — I miss you from the choir which you joined at my request — I miss you from the Sabbath school, to whose establishment and success you contributed so largely — I miss you from the Bible class, where you were ever attentive and well-informed — I miss you from your homes where you ever welcomed me with pleasure — I miss you in my walks where I so often met your smiling faces — I do not forget you, my sweet young friends — but many a prayer is sent up to God on your behalf, as well from the meetings of God's saints as from my lonely study.

I thank God, that though absent from me, I can bring you in my faith to Him who is everywhere present, and rejoice in hopes that the Shepherd of Israel will watch my precious lambs.

I am very anxious for your welfare — your advantages are, indeed, many — but many also are your temptations. Remember the first, the highest object of your desire should be 'the Kingdom of God and His righteousness.' All things else will be vain without this blessing. And all things else that are truly profitable will be added to it. You cannot have forgotten how earnestly and repeatedly, I endeavored to impress this upon your minds, neither can you have forgotten how seriously for a considerable time at least, it occupied your thoughts. May I hope that it is still the object of your care?

Have not your new pursuits changed the current of your thoughts to other channels? Have not new companions, new amusements, and new cares distracted your thoughts of God? Let me entreat you to guard against these dangers. The soul, the soul, my young friends, the undying soul, what can compensate for its loss! Make that your first care, and all other cares subservient. Let me earnestly request you to commence and close each day with private and personal devotion. I know you will have difficulties in the way: the want of sufficient privacy and punctual regard to necessary regulations of your school. But where there is a will, God generally grants a way. When I speak of devotion,

I do not mean merely *prayer*. Other duties are necessary to give prayer its proper character and efficacy. Self-examination for the past, and arrangement for the future will be found necessary to teach you gratitude and repentance, and the need of counsel and strength from on high.

'Sum up at night what you have done by day,
And in the morning what thou hast to do.'

Then read a portion of Scripture; it need not be long, indeed had better be short. Consider well its meaning; meditate upon its practical lessons; apply them to yourselves. Then, with a heart thus prepared, you may pray with profit, for you will pray with the understanding. Especially ask God's blessing upon your studies and pursuits. If unsanctified by Divine grace, they will prove curses and not blessings. If possible, have one text upon which to meditate during the day. Above all, cultivate repentance toward God and faith in our Lord Jesus Christ. Thus living, you will live with God, to God, in God, and God will live in you.

I will write you, I hope, soon again, but shall expect an answer to prove my letters are welcome. Mrs. B. is enjoying very good health, for her, and sends her warm love to you. All our other friends are well.

Yours affectionately,

GEO. W. BETHUNE."

In the summer of 1832 the city of Utica had a terrible visitation of the Cholera. The wealthy citizens deserted the place and nearly all the ministers of religion fled, Mr. Bethune being one of two faithful exceptions. Projects of aid to the sick and dying were formed but there were none to execute them, and much of the work devolved on the ministers themselves. Our pastor was indefatigable. One day going his rounds he found a person sitting on a bridge with strong symptoms of the cholera, and asked, "Can I help you home?" The poor man gasped, "I have been turned out to die." Kind arms were put around him and he was borne to the parsonage. The physician said, "We will have hard work to save him;" but the case yielded to active treatment, and the pains ceased. He proved to be a clergyman, who had come to visit a brother, but not finding him had put up at the hotel. Feeling in the night that he was ill, and calling for help, he was ordered to leave the house; and he laid down to die with anxiety lest it should be thought that his death was caused by drink, as his breath was strong with brandy, taken for his disease. Many expressions of gratitude were given by this disciple of Christ for the merciful kindness shown to a stranger. For three months the plague lasted.

Several meetings were held in behalf of the Colonization cause, at which appeared a young man in a homespun white coat, who, by his sensible remarks and deep interest, attracted general attention, but none knew him. After a while White-coat presented to Mr. Bethune a letter of introduction, recommending him as a pious young man, desiring to enter the ministry, but without means of support. The liberal pastor at once became his patron, offered him a home and the use of his library, and he became a pleasant member of the family. White-coat proved to be Thomas Buchanan. He followed Mr. Bethune to Philadelphia, but there abandoned the purpose of the ministry, and became the zealous and wise Governor of Liberia, and laid broad and deep the foundations of the African Republic. Such flowers of charity made beautiful all the path of our minister.

Mr. Buchanan died at Bassa Cove, in Sept., 1841. His pastor grieved for him as a brother, and exclaimed, "I regard my early and intimate acquaintance with Buchanan as one of the chief blessings for which I should give thanks to God." At the request of the Colonization Society, Dr. Bethune prepared a Memorial of his life and death, which has been preserved.

Returning now to his private life, we find him longing after and rejoicing at the prospect of a wider sphere of action. A plan is proposed by his friend Varick of building a large church for him in New York. He revels in the idea of a "metropolitan post away from the pettiness of a village life," and where his "time would not be cut all to pieces with trifling engagements." As this plan never went into realization, we need not discuss it; but it elicits a valuable letter to his mother, on the 13th December, 1832, in which remarks upon this matter and family affairs are so mixed up as to make the above brief abstract all that can with propriety be placed here. "But he was writing to his mother," as he fondly says.

The months pass on. He is written to for sermons to publish in a volume for the use of sailors at sea.

Dr. Spencer asks for advice on the question, whether he shall assume the Presidency of Hamilton College. His house is not comfortable, and he would fain buy a new one for $6000. He is urged by his mother to commence the memoir of his father, in order that she may aid him in it before she "decamps over Jordan."

He suffers from illness and consequent depression of spirits, thinks "his prospects of usefulness are very dark, and the fondness for nature, for which he was so well known, is his comfort in this every-day annoyance, and for which he gets so little sympathy.

About this date, too, occurred an event which brought great trial upon the minister's future life. A severe fall in the street occasioned injury to Mrs. Bethune, from which she never recovered, rendering her a confirmed invalid, and often a great sufferer.

On the 28th October, 1833, he writes:

"It is now more than autumn with us, it is almost winter, and would be quite so in any other climate. The air to-day has been filled with snow, which melted as it fell. I can only enjoy the scene from my window, but the leafless trees and the sombre sky, with all their melancholy accompaniments, though sad and soothing, seem to have a common sympathy; at least I am sure I love this season better than I could spring. I am becoming very fond of nature; it has a good influence on me. I am persuaded there is more of conscience than of romance in my awakened fondness for this first book of the Creator's hand. I think (I may be deceived, but I do think) my desire for doing good to my fellow-men increases, and my love to my race increases, but I have certainly much less fondness for society (as such) than I have had. I find it more than made up in nature, my books, and communion with my God. We are so liable to be misunderstood and hardly judged in our most affectionate attempts to serve others."

Again he writes:

"I am getting on in years, — twenty-eight! and what have I done? Alas! how much of life is made up of littlenesses and trifles, seemingly of importance at the moment, but as nothing in the retrospect. The ambitions, the jealousies, the strifes and the formalities of time, how do they keep the mind from eternity. And even we who are set apart for the altar, how much time is spent in mere professional arrangements, — making new theories and combating them, — contending and intriguing for power. Eternity! It seems as if that one word were enough to check all such vain imaginations. I have no wonder that more people become not Christians, when the Church busies herself with trifles; my only wonder is, that men do not stumble at our folly, and fall forever. What will Duffield's big book on Regeneration, and all the pamphlets for and against, weigh with one single soul? For my part I abandon controversy. I am determined to walk in the plain, obvious path of duty, studying the Scriptures as a child rather than a philosopher, and endeavouring to win souls for my Master."

In the early part of December of this year the information of a unanimous call to the church of Poughkeepsie gave a turn to his ideas. Perhaps there was a little wish that was father to the thought when he hints that his days of usefulness in Utica are over, but the unfailing counsellor in New York is ready with her advice.

"*Jan.* 6, 1834.

I have thought that a church that kept the good man who labored twenty-five years among them, with a growing family, on a pittance of $1000, while they can offer a young one $1400, cannot be a very liberal people. You would enter upon a people already formed, and habits fixed. They would expect all the attentions they were wont to receive, and your popular talents also. You might, indeed, not be under the necessity of studying so hard, and use your old sermons, but would that be conducive to your own growth in the divine life? Many other things occur to my mind connected with your query, 'How shall I leave my little people?' How indeed! A little flock gathered together by your instrumentality, for whom I trust you have travailed in birth for their souls, who love you for your Master's sake and their own sake, who prize your good qualities and make allowance for your faults, who have no former pastor to lead them to make comparisons.

Your next query, 'Who would take my place I know not;' neither do I; but this I know, they would be provided for, as long as these words stand in the Bible, 'I will never leave you nor forsake you.' Many of them, I know, think the church would go down if you leave them; they trembled at the idea of your leaving them even for the winter. I saw Mr. Varick on Friday. He fairly trembled when he asked me if you had received the call, adding, 'if he accept it the church will go down.' I begged him to write to you; he said he would be in Utica, D. V., this week.

The next thing you mention, that your days of usefulness are done. *It is not true.* You would not be so popular if they were. There may be a dry and dead time, to quicken you to greater diligence; to lead you more to look to Him who alone can direct the arrow of conviction, apply the word preached, to build up; and the balm of Gilead to heal the wounded conscience. What cannot prayer do? As to the other reason, 'that you would be nearer me,' I have 'not dared to trust my heart'; but neither that nor salary ought to weigh one moment with you. The former, your present people will probably increase. . . . .
Your dear father, grandmother, and your own mother 'lent you unto the Lord all the days of your life,' and solitary as your widowed mother now

sits, she would not take back the loan, nor interfere by any wish of hers to take you from or keep you in any place where the Lord's work is to be done by you."

In the year 1833 a discussion took place generally known as the "Wine Controversy," in which our minister bore a prominent part, and which involved him in much unpleasantness. At this distance of time we may strive in vain to awaken interest in the episode; but prejudice will have died away, and as the occasion served to display much of the man, and led him to take a position on the great moral question from which he never swerved, we shall, from the faithful papers before us, draw "a round unvarnished tale," and shall

"Nothing extenuate,
Nor set down aught in malice."

The Temperance movement was now taking a more radical position. Before it had aimed its blow simply at ardent spirits, now its advocates would forbid the use of all fermented liquors. In November, 1833, Mr. Bethune was, in his capacity as chairman of the Young Men's Temperance Society of Oneida County, a delegate to the Convention of the friends of Temperance, held in Utica. In the course of discussion, a resolution was offered that the drinking of wine and beer, as well as ardent spirits, was noxious, and denounced by the sacred writers. Mr. Bethune opposed this resolution on grounds of Scripture and expediency. The speech must have been eloquent and powerful, as it was feared that it would cause the loss of the resolution. It must have possessed much asperity, if we judge from the only quotation before us, "The drunkard who refuses to give up his liquor because you do not give up your wine, is not honest. If he tells you that is the reason, he lies." He was answered by Dr. Speed, another delegate, who remarked that it was the young clergyman's own fondness for wine, and his disinclination to give up its use, which prompted his opposition. Allusion was made to a certain occasion, when the delegate, who just sat down, had indulged in a glass of beer, and an impression was left on the mind of the assembly that this kind of indulgence was a matter of habit. A common report was also mentioned that the Dutch pastor's table was loaded with different kinds of wine. This attack was met, and the assertion passionately repudiated by Mr. B. The resolution was indefinitely postponed by an overwhelming vote, and another proposed, with special reference to the attack, regretting its personal allusions, and censuring its injurious imputations, and passed by acclamation. At the close of the meeting, the clergyman and physician met on friendly terms, and the former proposed, as a peace offering, to join in supplying the other's village with the Temperance Recorder. Thus the affair ended. But on Nov. 29th, Dr. Speed wrote to Mr. Bethune a copious letter, in which he apologizes for the attack, and hopes that the two are friends ; and still he reiterates his remarks, and supports them by the sayings of others, and in fact, opens anew the whole controversy.

Meanwhile Mr. Bethune addressed E. C. Delavan, Esq., protesting against the latter for having "called the time" to arrest him in his passionate disclaimer of the injurious imputation, and requests such statements in the Temperance Journal, as shall convince the friends of the writer, that he (Mr. D.) regretted the occurence.

Quickly Mr. Bethune replied to Dr. S., dated Dec. 6, 1833.

"Allow me to state in commencement that it was not the ridiculous charge of taking a glass of beer that drew from me the expression of indignant feelings; but the insinuation, nay, broad assertion that it was through unwillingness to abandon the use of wine myself, that I was led to oppose the resolution. I had expressly and solemnly stated that there existed no such unwillingness on my part. My language, as reported by the New York Evangelist, was as follows :

'Sir, I do not plead for the liberty of using wine; so impressed am I with the importance of the Temperance Reformation, that I am willing to go the whole if necessary. It would be no sacrifice to me. I confess that I do occasionally make use of it, but seldom, however.' Notwithstanding this positive and repeated declaration, you did not hesitate to lament 'that I could not make so small a sacrifice.' Sir, this representation of my motives was charging me with falsehood."

After denying any use of beer, he proceeds:

"Now, Sir, can no man differ from you upon a question of expediency without guilt or criminal motives? My difficulties are Scriptural and remain unanswered and unanswerable. If they are not, why did not you or some one else answer them? Mr. Dwight, of Geneva, said at tea, 'that all the argument was upon my side, the only question was present expediency.' I have abandoned wine, beer, and cider, myself, but do not see how I can condemn a proper occasional use of them in others. Here we differ. Is your opinion the sole test of sound truth and moral honesty? God promised to bless the vineyards of the Jews. Why? Two thirds of Palestine were devoted to the cultivation of the vine and olive. Our Saviour made wine; He instituted its use in the Eucharist, and in many Scriptures its use is expressly recommended and enjoined. Wine countries are proverbially temperate. I resided once for some time among a wine-drinking people, and never saw a drunkard. I do not believe that the common people can ever be persuaded to use water alone. By demanding it of them and placing every drink upon the same footing, you do, I conscientiously believe, retard if not ruin the cause.

I have not been an idler in the Temperance cause. Like Paul, when unjustly accused, I may boast. No man in the country, excepting Mr. Stewart, has laboured more in the cause of Temperance. In 1828 I preached upon the principle of Total Abstinence, when scarce a man in Dutchess County spoke out in favour of Temperance but myself. The sermon was printed. The Temperance Societies at Rome printed my address in February last. The Circular of the Young Men's County Temperance Society was written by myself. I am a member of that Society's Executive Committee. I am Chairman of a committee of eighteen who have gone a great way toward placing the pledge before every person in the county. I am Chairman of the Young Men's State Central Committee. In the communion of the church over which I preside, not a single person is engaged in the traffic in ardent spirits. Months have passed since I drank wine, except in one instance. . . . My experience has been that of my Master, to be called, unjustly, 'a winebibber and a gluttonous man, a friend of publicans and sinners."

Now, singularly enough, the two disputants referred their difficulty to Mr. Gerrit Smith, who decided that our minister had laid himself open to suspicion by his course in Convention, combined with the fact that he had not given up wine, but must always think that Dr. Speed's remarks had better have been made in the private ear of Mr. Bethune.

The next letter from Dr. Speed takes advantage of the impetuosity of his correspondent, complains of the reopening of the controversy, and declares that Mr. B. had mistaken the spirit of his epistle. Whereupon Bethune rejoins with spirit:—

"*January* 3d, 1844.

You seem to complain that I had ripped open an account settled. I had considered that account settled. You, sir, would never have heard a word from me on the matter. But in *your letter* the account was laid open. I had supposed yourself satisfied. I had supposed the Convention satisfied in my favor. You, then, in your letter took pains not to apologise for, but to justify your act, not to show sorrow for my outraged feelings, but to bring the testimony of other anonymous persons that I deserved it all. You thus proved to me that so far from having expiated the offence by the apology you offered, many still remained convinced from your testimony that I was a common swiller of such stuff, and that my objection to the wine question was not conscientious but personal. All this may have been done with good intentions, nay, I believed it was done with such, but one may have good intentions towards a criminal; and as a criminal was I treated, nay as the basest of criminals, a hypocritical falsifier of pretences. For I repeat, to believe I opposed the question from any other than conscientious motives, is to make me such. Had I then no cause for indignation at knowing that my good name had been injured in the estimation of individuals whom I never may see again and of whose names I am studiously kept in ignorance? But for those statements of your own of the injurious effects of your charge upon my character, I would never have dreamed of asking any further apology, for I had deemed yours before the Convention was sufficient and also that yourself would have been my vindicator after what you had said.

Even at this late day I cannot conceive the reason of your statement in Convention. I cannot imagine what it was intended to effect. Certainly to attack the character of a prominent friend of temperance (as you are pleased to term me), is not the way to sustain the cause. But you assert that your motives were good and I *believe you*. It is, however, faith entirely. Sight hath nothing to do with it. . . . .

My views with regard to the wine question, though a water drinker myself, remain unchanged. If you push that question I believe you will ruin the cause. . . . So thought the majority of our Convention. So thought the Connecticut Convention. If I err, I err in good company, or, do we all love our wine too well to be honest?

I shall be extremely happy in any way to testify my esteem for you, and again assert that the doubt of my candor by so respectable an individual as Dr. Speed gave me more pain than anything else.

With sentiments of unfeigned regard and respect,

I am yours,

GEORGE W. BETHUNE."

But he now has to deal with Mr. Delavan. This gentleman's course in the conduct of the Temperance Recorder, was calculated to misrepresent the action of the Convention. Mr. Bethune addresses him, declaring the resolution to be "unwise, proscriptive and unscriptural, slanderous to the character of our blessed Master, and damnatory of the very regulations of God."

Mr. Bethune disclaims any judgment of Mr. Delavan's motives, but says that his course was unfair and unwise.

"You will gain the victory," the pastor says. "There is fanaticism enough to carry it. But you will ruin your cause. We have done well here for two years past, or rather for the past year. But I tremble for the future. Look at your own city! behind us all, and in consequence of ultraism. A verdict over the dead body of the Temperance cause will soon be taken and it will be *felo de se.* Its epitaph is written. 'Died of the evil it opposed,—intemperance.' I do not know that I shall write against the question. I am unwilling to court more abuse, but I do trust that God will yet deliver us from ourselves."

To leave no stone unturned, a letter is written on the same day, 27th Jan., by our eager debater to his friend, Mr. Hopkins, urging him to suggest some means of stopping the wine question. "We are almost unanimous here in Utica," he says, "but the country members, in their honest but ignorant heat will all be led astray. We have seen an end of all perfection; I had begun to make the temperance cause an idol."

Such was the reward of his fidelity to a good cause. Because he could not utter the Shibboleth of the party, because he could not take the most extreme views, because he could not do that which reason and conscience alike forbade, he was subject to denunciation. It cannot be doubted that the accusation which was withdrawn by those who preferred it, still existed in the public mind; and a man, who, above most others, lived soberly, righteously and godly, acquired the reputation of a free-liver. Yet, we who love his memory rejoice that this controversy took place. His vehemence, his asperity, nay, even his mistakes, were the results of strong conviction and deep earnestness. He uttered the words that rose to his lips, not because they were expedient, but because they were right. His judgment was rarely wrong in any matter brought fully before it; his eye was single, and his whole body was full of light. It is fortunate that Time was to try the issue. This unfallible judge has vindicated his wisdom and justified his precision. Experience has shown that the cause of Temperance would be better off to-day had his conservative counsel been followed.

As there had been a division among the friends of Temperance, so about this period there was a separation of those who were devoted to the welfare of the negro, the parties forming the Anti-Slavery and Colonization Societies. Mr. Bethune, according to the turn of his mind, went with the Conservative section, and in May, 1834, he repaired to New York to speak on the Colonization Anniversary. The Anti-Slavery meeting had been held on the preceding day, and as it had been quite successful, some friend who met Bethune at the wharf, informed him that his speech could do no good, as his favorite society was dead. But his fame had preceded him, and the announcement of his coming drew together an audience unusual in size and splendor. It was an assembly of the beauty and fashion of New York. He took advantage of the occasion in the following witty style:—

"After my arrival in town, where I expected to meet a friend whom I had known for several years, and whom I was anxious to meet again, I was informed, to my grief and consternation, that he was dead and buried; for that the funeral obsequies of the American Colonization Society were attended yesterday. But when I behold this numerous audience, it seems as if there had been a resurrection, — for it is a collection of the most beautiful corpses I ever saw. They remind me of two lines of the poet: —

'On the cold cheek of death smiles and roses are blending,
And beauty immortal awakes from the tomb.'

Nor can I forget an anecdote that I heard in my boyhood, that may well apply to the premature interment by the reverend pastor of the Spring street Church yesterday. An old lady took it into her head that her husband was about to die, and proceeded to the undertaker's to procure the necessary apparatus for the burial, — accordingly, says the couplet: —

> 'Forth went the good lady to buy him a coffin,
> But when she came back, she found him a-laughing.'"

He spoke of the course taken by the Abolitionists to the Colonization Society.

The speech is represented as one of great power; but the reports are so imperfect as to render them unworthy of reproduction.

The month of August, 1834, saw the last of Mr. Bethune's labors in Utica, and the church which he had built up and made so strong was to be occupied by another. From the previous date no event of special interest is noted in his papers. We willingly take it for granted, that the latter part of his ministry was like the beginning; zealous, able, and useful to an unusual degree.

Again we resort to the valuable memorial of H. K. Clarke, Esq.

"Mr. Bethune's attention, most diligently and skillfully bestowed upon all the details of pastoral labor, by which his people might be benefitted or the welfare of his congregation promoted, did not fail to produce the most gratifying results. In the organization of the Sunday school, he was made its Superintendent, and though the practical details required of this office were performed by his assistants, yet his superintendency was real and constant, and those who remember it will add, delightful. By making the lessons of the Sabbath school and of the Bible class, which he conducted upon an evening during the week, identical, he became the teacher of the teachers, and thus left the impression of his teaching upon the whole school each week.

"During the first year of his ministry in Utica, and while the health of Mrs. Bethune permitted, she was also actively engaged in teaching the 'Infant' department of the Sabbath school. The method of instruction employed by her was then a novelty; but it was the most attractive feature of the exhibition or examination of the school which took place annually on Christmas. These occasions afforded an opportunity for the exercise of the fine talent which Mr. Bethune possessed for lyrical composition. For such occasions he was never unprepared. Many of his contributions to the interest of such and similar services are still known and cherished by thousands who have no knowledge of their authorship. Floating through the various hymn and tune-books employed by Christian people, some of them like the hymn so popular among sailors,

'Tossed upon life's raging billow,'

attributed in the collection to 'Anonymous,' these sacred lyrics have not only done delightful service in swelling the flow of pious emotion in Christian hearts, but they reflect also the sweet spirit of their author. They prove that he, — to express the thought in his own words, was

'Like him God loved, the sweet-tongued psalmist,
Who found in harp and holy lay,
The charm that keeps the spirit calmest.'

While thus the pastor and his wife were actively employed in the Sabbath school, neither were wanting in the manifestation of a kindly zeal in all the plans of minor moments, by which the school might be rendered more useful, or the scholars be gratified. Anything that would appropriately accomplish these objects was neither too trifling nor undignified to enlist the quick sympathy of Mr. Bethune. On a Friday evening previous to the Fourth of July, which was to occur on the following Monday, the teachers of the Sabbath school were assembled to make arrangements for the participation of the school in a general celebration of this anniversary by the schools of the city. Mr. Bethune overheard an expression of regret that the school would be obliged to appear without a banner, while it was known that several other schools had handsomely-painted banners that had been prepared for former occasions. He interrupted these regrets with 'Why can't we have a banner?' 'Because there is not time to get one painted; this is Friday evening and the celebration will be on Monday.' 'There is time enough,' he replied 'all we want is a simple field of white silk, — white, to indicate the purity of the gospel you are called to teach, inscribed *Hosanna!* the shout of the children as they greeted the Saviour in the Temple, surrounded by a fringe of orange, the Dutch color, and we shall have a banner, at once appropriate and descriptive.' And appointing two of the young ladies to procure the thread and do the needle-work, and one of the young men to procure the staff and the lettering, that arrangement for the coming celebration was made. The banner was completed on Saturday afternoon, and, in its place on Monday, it fully vindicated the ready wit and pure taste of its designer.

During the first year of Mr. Bethune's service in the church at Utica, that remarkable exhibition of the power of the Spirit, which will be recognized as the great revival of 1831, was felt in his as in other churches in that region. The absence of the 'new measures' in the services of the Dutch church did not hinder the work of the Spirit there. Nor did the employment of these measures in other churches interrupt the genial flow of Christian feeling, nor mar the harmony with which all denominations joined to praise God for the manifest tokens of favor, which these scenes displayed. During this revival, the pastor of the Second Presbyterian church, Dr. Lansing, was called to mourn the decease of his wife. The session of his church desiring to relieve their pastor from his public duties on the Sabbath following that event, invited Mr. Bethune to conduct the morning service. He promptly complied. It was a memorable and most interesting service. This young 'preacher of smooth things,' this 'antinomian,' this 'individual from a certain city, a circumlocution applied to him with injurious comments in a religious paper printed in the city, was now to conduct the worship of a congregation where the prejudice against him was the strongest. The circumstances, however, were propitious. The hearts of the people were subdued by the bereavement which they felt in the liveliest sympathy with their pastor. The presence of the Spirit as displayed in the conversion of sinners had drawn all who loved the Spirit and his work into close communion. It was to such a congregation, surrounded by such influences, that Mr. Bethune performed that memorable half-day's service, and those who remember with what pathos and power his soul went forth in the utterances of the simple truths of the Gospel, and what a wealth of tenderness he had in store for all who needed the ministries of consolation, will not wonder why that service was a memorable one to all who participated in it or witnessed any of its effects. On the succeeding Sabbath, the members of the Second church crowded the lecture-room of the Dutch church at the morning prayer-meeting, to overflowing; and the kindly recognitions of brotherhood in Christ, which were there interchanged, removed forever the asperity of feeling which had before existed. Differing opinions were doubtless still held with the earnestness of conviction; but the injunction to 'love the brethren,' was now remembered and obeyed.

The communion seasons in the Dutch church, in the months of January and April 1831, were signalized by large accessions to the church of the fruits of the revival; and if souls converted are 'crowns of rejoicing and seals to the ministry,' of those who were instrumental in producing the gracious results, then great will be the rejoicings of pastor and people in the great Day, for the wisdom and tenderness and faithfulness by which the new communicants at these seasons, were led first to the cross and then to the table of the Lord.

'My heart clings,' he writes in September 1834, after his removal to Philadelphia, to one who had been brought into the church under his instrumentality during the revival of 1831. 'My heart clings to dear, dear Utica, the scene of so many trials and joys, the place of warm friendships and bitter opposition. When I forget her, my right hand will have forgotten its cunning, and my tongue will cleave to the roof of my mouth. Dear little church! Peace be within her walls and plenteousness within her dwellings, for my brethren's and my companions' sakes, I will now say 'peace be within thee.''

And again in July, 1842, he writes, 'what a pleasant thing it is to know that our (it is still *ours*) little church at Utica is quite filled up. God's blessing be upon it. I must visit them this summer if permitted.'"

It is difficult to follow up all the efforts of his stirring life. Letters show that he was diligent in extending his denomination through western New York, and the churches in that district made continual appeals to him for help, and before leaving the city, he had devised large educational plans, by which he thought to strengthen the Dutch interest.

Two or three Utica anecdotes and we will go with him to Philadelphia. In the course of his ministration at Utica, Dr. B. at one time caught a breath of dissatisfaction on the part of certain individuals in his congregation at something he had said or done. It was mere gossip, but his extreme sensibility was at once alarmed; and agitated he hastened to his friend Rathbone, one of the consistory, and besought him to say wherein he had sinned. The counsellor knew that it was all trifling gossip, not worth a second thought, and quieted his minister's fears by telling him so. In due time, Bethune applied again for advice on a like occasion, and exacted a promise from his adviser, that should any, even unconscious, steps from the paths of strict decorum be discoved by Mr. Rathbone, he would instantly and frankly tell his friend of them. Within a few weeks, the Dominie was again in great alarm at his friend's office. He must have done something wrong! He was ready to humble himself and ask forgiveness first of his God, and next of his people, if he could only know what it was. "Well," said Rathbone with amazing solemnity, "I am obliged to tell you that you have at last been guilty of a very bad action, a dereliction of duty, sacrilegious and increditable, committed on the Sabbath day, and on your way to the sacred desk!" "Do my dear friend, if you love me," said the other, "tell me what it is! I know I am a thoughtless, wicked creature, but I will ask and deserve my people's forgiveness, if I may only know my fault." "Well, I suppose I must tell you," said Rathbone, without moving a muscle. "When you were going up the steps of the church, last Sunday morning, I was within twenty feet of you, and saw the act myself, you dare not deny it, you took two steps at once!"

It is related of Dr. Bethune that he did not trouble his friend Rathbone with any more cases of conscience.

When stopping at a hotel in Utica, a gentleman found himself, in a moment of excitement, betrayed into the use of an oath. Turning round, he discovered that Mr. Bethune was present, who met him with such a look of sorrow, mingled with tenderness, as overwhelmed him. It had more effect than the most powerful sermon. Not a word was spoken, it was only a look, and yet, the person relates that never in his life had he felt so reproved and penitent.

To the facetious belongs the following note from Dr. Cummins, the celebrated Romish priest:

REV. MR. BETHUNE. "UTICA, *Nov.* 2, 1831.

REV. AND DEAR SIR, — As I was returning home, this evening, after our very agreeable party at Mr. Devereux's, and pleasantly indulging my fancy on the subject of the first meeting of his reverend guests, a very singular and amusing idea crossed my mind. As you love a joke I would have gone back immediately, and presented you this trifle with all its laughing levity still fresh about it; but on reflecting that it belonged to the class of riddles, I thought it better not to set your wits a-hunting for the answer, at a moment when you were, perhaps, enjoying the luxury of the segar, to which you so politely invited me, or preparing for a comfortable nap after dinner.

If you don't soon find out the answer to my riddle, you may consult our other two reverend friends, as you will perceive that the literary fame of each of us four is equally interested in the solution of this most important question:

Query. — Why must Mr. Devereux's reverend guests of this day be recognized by every scholar, at the very first sound of their names, as the four most eminent and leading characters in the modern Republic of letters?

Je vous le donne à deviner en quatre, as the French say. En attendant, veuillez agréer, mon cher Monsieur, mes respectueux sentiments. CUMMINS."

The fourth gentleman of the party was the Rev. Mr. Adams of the Presbyterian church.

CHAPTER VI.

SETTLING IN PHILADELPHIA — WANDERINGS IN EUROPE.

TOWARDS the middle of March, 1834, Mr. Bethune received a letter, which was meant to sound him as to whether he was inclined to be a candidate for the pulpit lately vacated in Philadelphia, by the death of the Rev. G. R. Livingston. This prospect of change was the more welcome, as the cold climate of Utica was telling upon the health of his wife, and the medical advice which was thus rendered necessary, was to be obtained in Philadelphia. Added to this, good ministerial society, books, scientific lectures and ease of communication with New York, all combined to tempt him to change. The proposal was taken into serious consideration, and Mrs. Joanna Bethune's sage opinions were, as usual, elicited. But when in the next month, an invitation came to repair to Philadelphia and preach on trial, the proposal was repudiated on the spot. Our minister professed himself at all times open to a direct call, but his self-respect recoiled at the idea of an exhibition of his capabilities. "Other calls were not likely to be wanting," and he thought it well, even in a worldly point of view, to stand upon his dignity. Accordingly, in the latter part of May, he received a formal call from the First Reformed Dutch Church of Philadelphia, Crown street, and the sum of two thousand dollars a year was to free him from worldly cares and avocations, while engaged in the spiritual duties of that post. Great was the sorrow of the Utica flock, when, on the 29th June, their good pastor preached his farewell sermon. It was heard by a large congregation. "Shall I tell you how many tears have been shed, how many sighs heaved, and how many prayers offered for you? But no, I would rather say that the blessing of the poor and needy will follow you whithersoever you go," wrote a humble Christian.

The installation took place in September, and the sermon was preached by Rev. Dr. Mathews. The two inaugural discourses were heard by very crowded houses, and afterwards published, and it is related that at Mr. Bethune's first appearance in the pulpit, a most thrilling effect was produced by the simple recital of the Apostles' Creed. After standing some moments with his right hand raised, he began in the most solemn manner to repeat the words, his loud, clear voice ringing through the great building; the vast audience were spell-bound, and a most impressive silence ensued until broken by the sound of the organ. The new, popular and well-known minister found himself immersed in work, within reach of every necessary of literary life, and spurred to vigorous exertion by the rivalry of his peers. He writes, "There is a strange contrast between this dull population and lively New York. Indeed I have some fears whether I can ever make that impression upon the city I could wish. My temperament and mode of doing things is so different. However, there is nothing so good as effort, except reliance upon God. The more I see of my new people, the more I feel that I will be useful among them. Much labor and pains and patience will be required."

He writes to Mrs. Joanna Bethune, Nov. 19th:

"Every day for a week past I have determined to write, but have been interrupted until too late for the mail. I have been paying the penalty of a new-comer; I have spoken at some public meeting every week since I have been here, besides a thousand applications, &c., which I know not how to dispose of. I spoke last evening for the Methodist Ladies' Missionary Society, so that I am quite 'promiskus,' as the folks say. My own congregation is doing very well. In a few days there will not be a vacant seat below stairs. The value of the pews on sale has risen at least fifty per cent. My Bible class, also, has crossed the Rubicon, and is successful, at least in appearance.

I have now my excellent friend Dr. Ludlow * with us in town, whose sound sense will be a great personal aid to me, and whose official station will give influence to our congregation. He is to be my hearer. I think even that (if I do not carry the fear of man too far) will be of service to me; I will not dare to talk carelessly or crudely before him. I thought I would enjoy clerical society when I came here, but I find very little cordiality on the part of the clergy generally, and I have very little time to enjoy the intercourse of the few I know. Drs. Cuyler and Ludlow are my especial friends. I have been and am still labouring intensely hard; I never strained mind and body so much before."

When we learn now from a letter of 23d Dec., that, having formed the determination never to preach an old sermon if he could possibly get time to write a new one, he had just placed the No. 23 upon the last written since he came to Philadelphia, we gain a sufficient idea both of the fluency of his pen, and of his power to construe *hoc age.*

He was equally diligent in pastoral works, and, by the month of October, had visited half the congregation, having made 160 calls. His career of platform speaking was now fairly begun. He addresses the City Tract Society, promises a Charity Sermon, engages for a Colonization meeting. His opinions in politics, as on most subjects, were positive and well considered.

* Dr. Ludlow was Provost of the University of Pennsylvania.

H. I. KIP TO G. W. B. "RHINEBECK, *Jan.* 14, 1835.

I have been told that you too have veered round from your old position; but I did not design to enter into a political discussion, so I will merely say that if, upon mature deliberation, you have become convinced that the present administration is a dangerous one, you are justifiable in the course you have taken; else we might as well live under a king, if we are not permitted to change, right or wrong; but, as for myself, I think we are as safe and as prosperous as we should be by a change, for, to tell the truth, there is too little honesty in politics at the present day."

G. W. B. TO MRS. J. B. "*March* 19.

Yes, my dear mother, I am now thirty years of age. In all probability the larger half of my life is past; and while I feel grateful that so many opportunities of usefulness have been granted to such a young man, I have much cause for sorrow that I have improved them no better, and deserve so little the success with which God has sometimes been pleased to honor his own word by my lips. May the time past suffice me to have wrought so much for myself and the world, and the future find me more fervent in spirit, diligent in business, 'serving the Lord.' I think I was never more tried in my ministerial life than now, by the little apparent success attending my labours. There are, however, many moral causes in the past affecting the present and beyond my power to control. The people must be weaned from a dependence upon measures of their own contriving, ere we can expect God to remember them in mercy."

In May, 1835 he appeared at the Anniversary of the New York Colonization Society, and is thus noticed by the N. Y. Commercial Advertiser.

"Rev. Mr. Bethune addressed the meeting in his peculiarly happy vein, and delighted the audience for three-quarters of an hour with great effect. We have listened to few specimens of racy humor and sarcasm more felicitous than portions of this speech; particularly the form of the report which it will become Mr. Geo. Thompson to present to the venerable single ladies of Glasgow, who have sent him over to emancipate the slaves of the South, by abusing their owners at the North.

"He spoke as follows: The question then returned — how shall we do good to these people? Admitting that the power to liberate or not to liberate them, was *de facto* in the hands of the white masters at the South, two things were needful: first, to obtain the consent of their masters; and secondly, to show how the benefit may be conferred with safety to those who receive it, the poor slaves themselves. One thing was certain; you could never convince any such man unless you approached him in a spirit of kindness and moderation, a spirit which admitted and sympathized with the difficulties of the slave-holder. The gospel, while it testified of sin, came with the offer of grace in its hand, with sympathy and compassion in every look and every tone. So while it was a Christian duty to rebuke the sin of slave-holding, and to search it out, yet this was to be done only in a spirit of love and pity, and not in a spirit of denunciation, and rash and merciless judgment. What right had we to denounce? Were we ourselves so clear of guilt in this matter? And if we were, did not the Son of God, himself without spot, come down with Heaven's mercy, not to condemn the world, but that the world through him might be saved? Let us imitate his example: let us act in his spirit. . . . As to the second point, viz., the safety of the slave, the mode of relief must be distinctly shown. Every great object of a national kind must be accomplished gradually. History did not show a single instance where it had been effected of a sudden. The Southern people, in this matter of emancipation, held the power in their own hands; and it was nonsense for us on this side of the Potomac to talk authoritatively in the case. We could not emancipate the slaves of Southern planters, if we would: the duty was not ours, but theirs. Now it was obvious that when an address was directed to conscience, it was, and must always be, virtually an address to individuals. It must be so in the nature of things; and the appeal in behalf of liberating the slave must be an individual appeal. The Northern people came to a Southern slave-holder, and said to him: 'It is a duty binding on you to abolish slavery as soon as you can. If you will emancipate your slave we will provide him a home upon the soil of Africa. We are aware that the laws of your State forbid you to set him free where he is; but if you confide him to our care, we will place him where these laws cannot reach him, and where he may walk abroad in the erect majesty of a freeman.' To such a proposition there were many slave-holders ready to listen; many had acted upon it; and could any man doubt that one such example would have more influence toward the abolition of slavery than all the invectives and vituperations that could be poured out upon slave-holding? Beyond all question it would. It was upon the effect of such appeals that Mr. B. founded his hopes of ultimate success; and he believed that the great object might thus be obtained without sending out all the colored population from the country.

But it was said that to send them to Africa was impossible; it could not be done. Yet was it not a fact that millions upon millions of slaves had been brought from Africa, by the mere cupidity of bad men? Were there not in a single year forty thousand carried into the Brazils alone? And should it be said that the Christian philanthropy of America, backed by all our abundant and increasing national wealth, could not effect what the bare avarice of the slave-trader had done and was every day doing? Surely, if the Society had the pecuniary means this might be effected, and they should have had more of those means but for the interference of those who insisted upon the visionary scheme of immediate and universal emancipation. Yet no; he was wrong. The Society had not received less, but more, in consequence of the abuse of its opponents; a fact in which he recognized with joy, the fulfilment of God's ancient promise, that the wrath of man should praise him.

He was sorry not to see some more of our English friends present, and while speaking of them he could not help thinking what sort of a reception the agent of the Edinburg ladies (Mr. Thompson) would meet on his return to his constituents, and what sort of a report he would probably make on the subject of his mission. He could not but picture to himself the fair lady President enquiring,

'And pray, Mr. Thompson, what did you do in America?'

To this he thought he heard the agent responding,

'Why, ladies, I made speeches there; for which one part of my audience loudly applauded me, and another part as loudly hissed me.'

'And pray where did you make your speeches, Mr. Thompson? Did you go to that part of the country where slavery prevailed, and tell them how wrong it was?'

'Oh no! if I had they would have hanged me! But I went to the *Northern* States, ladies, and I told them what wicked people they were at the South.'

'But, Mr. Thompson, had the people of the North any power to emancipate the slaves of the Southern holders?'

'Oh no, no more, ladies, than you have yourselves.'

'Indeed! and then, Mr. Thompson, why did you not stay at home, and make your speeches to us?'

'But pray, Mr. Thompson, while you were in the United States were there no slaves *actually liberated* and placed in circumstances of comfort and happiness?'

'Oh, yes, ladies, there were one hundred and twenty emancipated and sent to Liberia soon after my arrival; and preparations were making to send one hundred more from Savannah, so that, in a few months, there were two hundred and twenty delivered entirely and forever from slavery.'

'And by whose agency was the emancipation of these slaves effected, Mr. Thompson?'

'Why, ladies, by the very people against whom I was all the while directing my vituperative speeches.'"

This speech was delivered at a time when feelings ran very high, and the excitement was much increased by the foreign agents.

"By the way," he writes, June 15th, "Mr. Garrison, the Abolitionist, after two or three columns of the foulest abuse, says my zeal for colonization may arise from the fact, that I am a large slave-holder in right of my wife. They are a beautiful set when they are all at home. The Patroon (bless his honest Dutch heart!) has given a thousand dollars to my new church, which goes on very well."

The Synod of his church met this year in Albany, where he assumed a commanding position, being elected Vice President of the body, and made Chairman of the Committee on Education. He was hospitably entertained by General Van Rensselaer (the old Patroon), and "had never seen a family so lovely as theirs. There is an unaffected piety and gentle quiet spread among them, truly remarkable, considering their circumstances."

Aug. 5 he writes to Mrs. J. B.

"You will be pleased to hear that I am to have my friend Gosman with me in Philadelphia. He has just given encouragement to the Spring Garden people that he will accept."

It was at the installation of Rev. Dr. Gosman that Mr. Bethune preached his sermon already alluded to, "Reasons for preferring a Union with the Reformed Dutch Church of North America"; an effort in which a structure of graceful eloquence is raised upon a base of accurate history.

Now came a new excitement to awaken the interest of our minister. The old church in Crown street was very crowded, the congregation too large and unwieldy for the care of a single minister; and as early as February 1835, the suggestion was made by Rev. Peter Labagh, "whether it is not almost time for your church to swarm that a new hive may be collected." This idea must have been greatly encouraged by the promise from Gen. Van Rensselaer of $1000 towards the enterprise. This promise was given in June, and directly a meeting was called, and subscriptions opened for the object; but no active steps were taken until Dec. 17, 1835, when, at a meeting held at the house of Mr. Bethune, it was solemnly and with prayer for God's help, resolved to commence building a house of God, on the lot at the corner of Tenth and Filbert streets. The corner-stone was laid by Gen. Van Rensselaer, May 3, 1836; Rev. Dr: Ludlow made an address, while Mr. Bethune stated the reasons which moved their action. It was in "no spirit of rivalry, they came away in peace, and left their friends and co-worshippers in the communion of the kindest feeling. But we return to the personal.

After some account of domestic trials, and personal

afflictions, he goes on : —

G. W. B. to Mrs. J. B. "*Jan.* 7, 1836.

I am, at the same time, in the midst of a very difficult set of sermons, the *doctrines* of the person and life of Christ.

I used to think I could feel the truth of Addison's lines, —

'Not the least gift a cheerful heart,
To taste thy gifts with joy.'

I can hardly get up to the cheerfulness *now*, but I can thank God for patience. I am the more submissive to his hand, because I think I have seen that I deserve much more than I have received of chastening. I am a very proud man, and need humbling; a reckless man, and need sobriety. I am learning, I trust.

But I am wrong in distressing you, who have so much trouble of your own. I ought to be comforting you; but I believe I shall be always a child, in running to my mother when I feel distressed. I have the sick with me, but you are alone; yet 'not alone,' I trust, for God is with you.

I have no other news, except that my friends have bought the lot for the new church at $18,500, and are about contracting for the building (Gothic), at $25,000. Total expense, $50,000. Their subscription is already above $21,000.

I have heard nothing more from Market street. It would not have done for me; I need a different sort of people to get along with than the mass of them. Besides, I would be almost as far from you as I am now."

G. W. B. to Mrs. J. B. "*February* 15.

You seem anxious, from some observation of M.'s, lest D. and I should quarrel about doctrine : give yourself no uneasiness on that score, I am determined we shall not. He is not, however, so scrupulous with me as with you; and I have not the slightest doubt meant to try and convert me when he came here. Only upon one occasion had we any warmth. He had denied that the expression, 'Ye are the temples of the Holy Ghost,' taught the doctrine of the Spirit's dwelling in Christ's people. He said it meant nothing more than that they had faith, etc., which are the influences of the Spirit. I told him I believed that the Spirit of

God did dwell in God's children. He laughed long and loud, and said it was nonsense. I then told him that he would oblige me either by speaking reverently of what he knew I held God's truth, or not at all, — that I could not bear to hear my own faith and the faith of my fathers ridiculed as nonsense. Since then we have got along very well together, as he finds me firm, and has given over the idea of converting me to his side."

A trip to Washington in behalf of his favorite Colonization Society brought him in contact with some of our great men, and his impressions are interesting.

"I spent yesterday in the Senate Chamber. I heard Mr. Poindexter, Mr. Benton, and Mr. Calhoun speak with great power in thought, but I was surprised not to hear better English. Mr. Clay made short but energetic speeches, and I admired him very much. I went to the President's levee. Last evening I spent at Mr. Forsyth's, among a brilliant crowd. Poor Mrs. Forsyth seemed sick of the whole parade, and asked me if I did not think it possible to keep religion alive, and yet be found where seeming propriety required her station to be. I met Col. Inly and some very distinguished foreigners. Mr. Webster talked delightfully with me; so did Mr. Calhoun. I addressed a little compliment, which he swallowed like any mortal."

Now the state of his affairs opened a brilliant prospect. Released from the care of Crown street church, and the fact that his new church was still in embryo, without a place of worship, afforded him a season of relief, and an opportunity to realize a golden dream of youth in a visit to the old world. Imagination may conceive the pleasure with which a mind, stored with classic memories, and rich with poetic beauties as was his, would revel in such an anticipation. Let us hear his own account.

After devoting a page to the account of a great missionary meeting, of which the whole burden and anxiety devolved upon him, he writes :

G. W. B. TO MRS. J. B. "*April* 2d.

We are getting on in our household the old way. Frances is, generally, better than she was, but Mary improves very slowly, and is frequently very ill. Dr. Hodge is very anxious that she should take a voyage; and, by the way, there seems a prospect of my having a better opportunity of going to Europe than would be likely to occur again if I could avail myself of it.

My new church, the corner-stone of which will be laid on or about the first of May, we had hoped would have been finished in November. This is now, to say the least, doubtful; and twelve months may elapse before its completion. If, therefore, I could employ the interval in a voyage and tour abroad, it might be serviceable. A fond day-dream I have had for some time has been, going to the Mediterranean in the summer and establishing Mary, with some attendant friend, in some place in Italy (Pisa, for instance, where living is cheap and the climate good, and consequently many English residents), and myself looking through Italy and Greece, and especially Egypt and the Holy Land. All this could be done before spring, when we could go to England in time for the May meetings, and have some months of the twelve there and in my fatherland. Such a tour I would much rather make than to spend a longer time in Great Britain, which is pretty much like our own country; and as a preacher, a visit to Palestine would be of great service to me. A very pretty *dream*, you say, — but when we cannot have the reality dreams are pleasant sometimes. Yet so many cross the water who have not the inducements to go I have, that I sometimes feel a little impatient. My new church once built, fetters will be around me, and the thing must be given up for life."

His address on Christian missions was printed in the Evangelical Magazine, July, 1836. Excepting this, no event of special interest for our memoir occurs, until in the same month we find the good Dominie and Yeffrow on ship board, setting sail from the land, and breasting the waves of the Atlantic. The sea afforded that repose which his overtasked faculties so much needed (there had been a fear of blindness), and we can imagine for ourselves the charm with which his genial converse and merry humor would enliven the tedium of the voyage; quite a successful one for those days, but tedious enough according to our notions. It was thirty days before they saw land, reaching Liverpool August 20, and Mr. Bethune was but little benefitted. Directly he hies to Scotland, and finds it "all that he had expected."

"When we came to 'merry Carlisle,' new associations were presented constantly to my mind. You know how fond I have been of ballads, particularly Scotch, and of Scott's novels, and everything relative to the border wars. Here every name was familiar; there was the castle of Carlisle, where Fergus MacIvor in 'Waverley' was confined, and from which he was carried to the scaffold; here, also, the three outlaws were brought to be hanged, as an old ballad tells us, which, perhaps, you do not remember. There we crossed the very river on the bridge of which MacIvor saw the ghost which foretold his death. Then on the right we passed Wetherby Hall, from which Lochinvar stole his bride; and then 'Cannabie Sea,' over which they chased; and the Esk, which he 'swam when ford there was none'; after that we passed the Teviot, the Clyde, the Yarrow, 'braw, braw lads on Yarrow braes,' the Ettrick, the Galla Water, leaving Melrose and Dryburgh on the right hand, passing in full view of Abbotsford, Walter Scott's place. Edinburgh is most beautifully situated, and excelling in beauty any idea I had ever formed of it."

At Edinburgh "on Sunday morning, I went to hear my cousin Mr. Marshall, in what is termed the Tolbooth, or Jail Church; it is the same building in which the famous escape of Robertson, the prisoner, occurred, as it is described in the 'Heart of Mid Lothian,' but the woodwork is very much modernised; under the same roof there are three churches, for it was originally an immense Gothic Cathredral. On Monday I went exploring universities in what is termed the old town, a great portion of which is built in ravines, over which are bridges also covered with houses, so that there is a city as it were over a city. First I sought out the house in which my grandmother used to live, which I found very readily; then I went through the libraries which are very large, in which I saw some fine old volumes and a few manuscripts; among the rest a collection of the genuine letters of my favorite Mary Queen of Scots in her own hand-writing, they were principally to her mother, and breathed much of the affection of a kind heart. I then went to the towers, saw the Highland regiment there stationed, and the ancient regalia of Scotland. I saw Allen Ramsay's house and his grave; and then the Grass Market where the martyrs suffered, passed a window from which John Knox used to preach to the people, and then to Holyrood Palace where I saw the State rooms of poor Mary, and the place of her many sorrows. Every spot has an historical association."

He visited the birth-place of his father, and had a warm reception from his Scottish cousins. He preached a Charity Sermon with good results.

"The beauty of Stirling exceeds almost any scenery of the quiet kind that I have yet viewed; the castle is a fine old pile, and of course the more attractive to me from its having been the residence of my uncle for so long a time. The river Forth winds in a most extraordinary manner near it, so that it makes twenty miles of circuit in going seven. Its banks are full of interest from the number of gentlemen's seats and ruined buildings. I entered Edinburgh to-day from a new quarter, and was again struck with its superiority to any place I have ever seen. I was, however, much amused this afternoon in visiting a panorama which is exhibiting here of New York — no one I am sure would have known the poor city, so metamorphosed is it from the reality. The people, however, that were visiting it, seemed highly delighted and pronounced it a most splendid city. The view is supposed to be taken from the house immediately opposite St. Paul's Church. Broadway seemed nearly three hundred feet wide, and Columbia College close to the river. I am perfectly delighted with my trip to the Highlands. The variety of scenery is beyond description, and entirely different from anything I have ever seen at home. I found Dalrymple House in fine preservation, only it is, I suppose, the residence of a dozen families; and there is a grog shop in the basement kept by a man of the name of Graham, who never heard of Dalrymple House in his life.

Returning to England, "I stopped at Glastonbury, where I saw the oldest Ecclesiastical buildings, or rather ruins (though one church is yet standing entire) in England; here tradition asserts that Joseph of Arimathea landed with eleven companions some forty years after Christ, and preached the gospel. Here, too, King Arthur was buried with his queen. I slept in the very place which was formerly the Pilgrim's House."

At Bristol a series of Missionary meetings demanded his attention and efforts.

"London turns one's head upside down more than any place I have ever been in; and not only one's head, but one's time, night is day and day is night; if you chance to be downstairs before ten, it excites quite serious astonishment; the morning closes not until six in the evening, and then dinner occupies you until ten, so that, with the best intentions in the world, I have been cheated out of my design of writing to you.

I had the pleasure of hearing Dr. Croly (the author of Salathiel) in the morning, and Mr. Melville in the evening. Croly was not at all profound, and of course shewed no great things, though I was gratified in seeing him and speaking to him afterwards. He is a very different man from what I expected — being tall, stout, and ungainly, with a strong Jewish accent. Melville, I feel inclined to pronounce the best preacher I have heard in England. His sermon was fervid though cautious and earnest without cant. The text he chose was from 2nd Thessalonians iii., 16: "The Lord of peace grant you peace *always* by all means." The tenor of the discourse was to show that from the name of God in Christ, the God of peace, we might, and ought, at all times and in every variety of circumstances to enjoy serenity and quiet of soul. It was sweet as well as strong.

I preached last night at Craven Chapel, to an enormous audience, and I believe with acceptance to the people; Oh! that it may be with God's blessing.

'There is quite a revival in Mr. Leifchilds's church; and you will rejoice with me when I tell you that my sermon on Sunday evening has been, with the blessing of Divine grace, the means of leading three or four that we know of to decide for the Lord. I spoke this evening for him also, and to do away some of the bitter prejudice which exists, I told them some of my Oatland stories, which affected many to tears. I have been requested to give a sermon for publication in the same series, if not in the same volume, with one of John Foster, and one of Mr. McCall of Manchester, and I have promised to write."

Oatlands mentioned above was the plantation in Georgia, where he labored amongst the slaves. In the course of this tour, the righteous soul of our minister was much vexed with the injustice done to his country; and he concluded "that they (English people) were too much beside themselves and too ignorant on that subject to be talked with."

While he was thus enjoying and wandering, disputing and preaching, perhaps he was not ill pleased to learn that the work upon his new church was progressing slowly, and that he would be at liberty to spend the winter in Europe, if so disposed. We soon find him at Dover on his way to France and Italy; he writes from Paris:

"Brighton is the place where, as I suppose you know, the king has a palace or, as it is called, a Pavilion. Here, in what seems to me a very odd taste, the English come as to a watering-place at this time of year (Dec. 4). You may imagine how great the resort is, when I say that the place contains some forty thousand inhabitants, which was only a fishing village before. The palace is a very singular building in the Eastern style, with singular bell-shaped turrets. There had been a violent storm a few days before we reached it, and the place, being entirely exposed to the sea, bore numerous traces of its devastating influence; yet in spite of the gale, the people, ladies and all, were walking upon the pier, with their garments blowing about in very odd style, yet as it is the fashion they bore it with no small philosophy. Hastings too, is quite a striking place, the buildings are really beautiful. That is the place where William the Conqueror fought his famous battle on invading England. Dover is the place where the white cliffs of chalk are, which have given to England the name of white-cliffed England. You remember Shakespeare's description of Dover in Lear; but certainly Shakespeare had never seen an American cliff, or he would never have made such a fuss about these.

I have seen nothing very remarkable in France, until we reached this city except the great number of wind-mills, which are so frequent that they are enough to turn one's head. A French *diligence* is, however, a most extraordinary affair. It is, properly speaking, composed of three parts; the coupé which is exactly like an English chariot; the rotonde which is like a post-coach, and the interieur which is the same only opening behind; besides these there is a place upon the top where all the baggage is stowed, the name of which I forget but which is capable of holding a number of persons, so that altogether there may be some twenty passengers with the driver and conducteur. This huge machine is upon four wheels, and drawn sometimes by four, sometimes by five and even six horses. If there are five, the three horses are put on the lead. The harness is made up of ropes and chains and wood and leather, in the most grotesque manner, and thus you are dragged over the paved roads at about four or five miles an hour. It is really quite astonishing that they do not upset the concern a dozen times a day, for the French drivers manage their horses apparently with the worst possible skill, yet they get along with very few accidents."

The following letter to an old friend gives a valuable resumé of our traveller's impressions up to this period.

G. W. B. TO MISS EUPHEMIA VAN RENSSELAER.

"PARIS, *December* 26, 1836.

I am sure your goodness will pardon my finding a solace for my feelings in expressing them to you, however unmindful I may seem to have been of the privilege you gave me of sending you an account of my wanderings. My excuses on that score have been already made.

It is too late now to begin a detailed description of the many places of interest I have visited. My extreme hurry prevents it at the proper time, and I must wait for that pleasure until I return; but you will not consider me too bold in saying that in every scene of natural beauty, or historical association, I found additional delight from the hope of being permitted to describe it to you at some future day. To say I have been gratified by my visit to the Old World, would not be half the truth. I have been instructed and rebuked; instructed by the perception of new claims upon my charity, and rebuked for a thousand prejudices I had insensibly allowed to grow up in my mind. Everywhere I have been met with kindness, unexpected as it was unmerited; and I hope never again to confine my idea of neighborhood to narrower limits than the family of man. O for a heart like His, who so loved the world as to give himself for it. How ungrateful I have been to waste so many thoughts and hours upon myself, when there are so many immortal beings whom he has commanded me to serve. I was much pleased with England. The English are truly a wonderful people. It is impossible to travel however rapidly through their country without being impressed by the mightiness of their strength. The majestic dignity of age is combined with the vigor of youth. Time, which wears away all else, has delighted to confirm and extend the foundations of their prosperity. It is little less than sublime to see their aristocratic families flourishing and happy, beneath the same gray roofs which have sheltered their fathers for a thousand years; or to join the rustic worshippers in the ivy-covered church, whose aisles are worn by the footsteps of many generations who have there breathed the same prayers and sung the same hymns of holy praise. There is poverty, bitter, hopeless poverty in England, poverty such as is unknown in our happier land, and it is painful to compare the price of humble labor with the price of food; but excepting in the larger towns poverty is rarely seen. The same taste which leads the rich man to study the effect of every tree in his wide domain, teaches him to hide from the eye the displeasing contrast of squalid want. The cottage of the village pauper is covered with the woodbine and creeping multiflora; while the starving wretch is forbidden to beg with the same sternness that he is forbidden to steal. I do not mean to say that there is no pity for the poor in England, on the contrary, their charity is unequalled, but from the density of the population it is impossible to relieve all the distressed, and many an outcast perishes from want before the parish almoners can determine who are the proper guardians of his welfare. There is, however, not a little ostentation in the manner of their charity. It is not an unusual thing for the visitor to be shown the almshouses of an estate as part of its architectural adornments. I could not help smiling at a pompous inscription over a row of three or four which declares them to have been 'founded and endowed by the bounty' of that Duchess of Marlborough, who, you remember, was notorious for her avarice. They shelter some half-a-dozen poor widows, and stand close to the princely portal through which you pass to find Blenheim House. It is very difficult to say how the many evils which undoubtedly exist in England may be remedied. After as careful a study as my opportunities allowed me to give the subject, I am rather inclined to be a tory in English politics. At least I would hold hard upon the wheels of reform to check if possible its too rapid descent. Even the abuses of their institutions like the excrescent humors that sometimes appear in the human frame, have been suffered to remain so long and to become so deeply imbedded that to sever them too rudely at once would be fatal to the life of the body politic. There are many arteries first to be bound up, and even then the knife should be in a skilful hand. The population in their little island is too numerous for such institutions as ours. There must be a strong hand somewhere to keep down such immense brute force, at least in the present state of public morals. It is true, that much provision is made for the education of the people, and the national schools which one sees in every few miles of travel, are among England's proudest glories. But I am not one of those who believe in the omnipotence of education, unless it be accompanied by the influences of the Spirit of God. Man can never know his true interest unless he sees it in the light of another world. When the people of England become generally and heartily religious, then, and not till then, will they be prepared for a popular government; and nothing but the same blessed leaven can keep our beloved country from the loss of her liberties, when our wide territories shall become crowded like theirs. There is indeed, much religion now in England. I very much question whether pure and undefiled religion does not flourish much more there than in the United

States. Certainly our worshipping assemblies might take many a lesson in decorum and solemnity from those which assemble in the churches of the establishment and the chapels of the dissenter. More holy, zealous and self-denied men I have never seen than many in both bodies of Christians, and, although too many of the clergy (which name is there confined to the ministry of the church of England) may have no true sense of the gospel they profess to teach, yet, the frequent reading of their admirable and instructive liturgy, with the many scriptural lessons appointed in the service, cannot fail to have a very salutary influence upon the popular mind. Certainly the evangelical clergy and the dissenting ministry are far more sound in the faith, and preach the gospel with greater simplicity, than the large majority of preachers with us. In only one or two instances have I heard doctrinal views given which would have been considered unsound in our own upright church. My sympathies were of course more naturally with the dissenters in most respects, but I cannot avoid trembling at the dangers which menace the establishment. An established religion with us, would indeed be a great evil, but the refusal to establish a church by the state is very different from putting one down. If the reform of the church, as it is called, could be placed in the hands of good men, the case would be different, but the party opposed to the establishment is composed of atheistical Jacobins, led on by such spirits as Hunt and Roebuck, the vulgar Catholics headed by the strong-minded but infamous O'Connell, many who care for none of these things, and a few candid, conscientious men. Must we not dread the result, when such unhallowed hands are put forth to touch the ark of the living God? It is sad, however, to see the effect which the intermingling of religious with political questions has had upon many good men on both sides. Once the pious dissenter considered his political inferiority as a cross which it became him meekly to bear, and he worked the better for his poverty of spirit; while the truly good churchman forgot his refusal to conform in admiration of his Catholic spirit; but now the dissenter buckles on his armor and contends with carnal weapons for his right, and the churchman like a strong man bars and bolts his house to keep it safe.

The Episcopalian, heaven knows, has temptations to bigotry enough at all times, but in England just now, he is fusing, and the dissenter not much better. Alas! that brother should thus contend with brother. If I were a dissenting minister in England, I would simply preach the gospel, and pray over it, leaving all the rest in the hands of God; but perhaps I would do just as they do, for we never know how we will act until we are tried. A good illustration of my last remark, by the way, is found in the present state of public opinion in England with reference to the United States. The religious people especially are actually mad upon the subject of American slavery, so much so that an American Christian can scarcely appear in a public meeting without being insulted. They will listen to no explanations, allow no difficulties, and, almost universally ignorant of the nature of our government, compound in one common condemnation, the North and the South, the slave-holder, and the non slave-holder. It was rather hard for me to keep my temper at times, though I carefully avoided placing myself in positions which exposed me to attacks. The testimony of Thompson is taken for truth against all that the well-informed and the candid among themselves can say, much more against our asseverations. On one occasion I did so far forget myself as to give one gentleman a rather sharp retort. I had been baited by a number of them at a dinner-table one day, when this person, more rude than the rest, bade me 'mark what England had done, how she had freed all her slaves; and let America go and do likewise, or be content to bear the scorn of the world.' I replied, 'Sir, when I read the news of the bill for the Emancipation of the West Indies, being passed, I said to myself, England is a glorious nation, she well deserves her rank among the nations of the earth. She has done one of the most glorious acts the world has ever witnessed; but sir,' I added, 'if the same spirit existed then which seems to excite you, I should doubt the genuineness of the charity after all.' 'How so sir?' rejoined my hero. 'Because sir, St. Paul tells us Charity vaunteth not herself, is not puffed up, and, you must allow me to add, doth not behave herself unseemly.' I was then let alone. I must however do justice in saying that the church people are far more considerate and less prejudiced in this respect than the ministry, and that there are not a few among the latter class who are willing to allow the difficulties of our situation. Indeed, the *liberal* party in England is sadly misnomered. Its chief strength is derived from the wealthy manufacturers who are jealous of the landed aristocracy, and a few of the very high and wealthy nobility, who are jealous of the crown, and willing to provide habitations for themselves in the event of an overthrow. The truly liberal men are very, very rare. Do not think I have been biased by my associations in England. I have been far more among the Whigs than Tories. The morals of England generally, will not bear comparison with those of our own country. The multitude of drunkards is far greater, and the unblushing audacity with which the innumerable tippling shops, or rather palaces, invite their customers, has no parallel with us. I have had the curiosity to count the murders which are described in their papers, and am persuaded that they exceed in frequency those of the whole United States together. I was sorry also to learn that profligacy prevailed, not only in the manufacturing towns, and larger cities, but also among the agricultural classes, who are generally so pure. This is to be attributed to the extreme closeness of the population, which induces poverty, and consequent recklessness of character.

But this is an unpleasant topic to dwell on, let me turn to one of a more gratifying character. We are told that John Bull is a rough, repulsive nature, cold and distant to strangers. I saw nothing of this. On the contrary, I mingled with all classes from the peer to the peasant, and everywhere met with the utmost politeness, and no rudeness or even carelessness of civility. There is, indeed, a certain reserve maintained in public places which I wish were oftener found at home, but it soon wears off when there is no necessity for it. The ready and willing attention of the servants is most agreeable to one accustomed to the republican indifference, which sits upon the brow of those we pay to do our bidding; while an English gentleman and lady are, just what gentlemen and ladies are all over the world. Everywhere you meet with intelligent people, who seem to think their kindness a matter of course without making such a fuss about it as we often see at home. The scenery in England is very sweet and quiet, but not various. With the exception of some fine mountain views in Wales, and among the lakes in Cumberland, I was rather tired of the monotony until I reached wild, rugged, yet ever fascinating, Scotland. The parks of many gentlemen are exceedingly fine. The oaks and cedars, centuries old, lift their arching branches or cast their profound shade over a turf shorn and levelled to a velvet softness, while the dappled deer are seen in the intervals gazing upon their beautiful shadows in the placid waters.

But there was too much of the hand of man visible for my taste. It is true, nature has been imitated, but man's nature is not God's nature, and it is not impossible to forget that every shadow had been calculated and that the stream had been dammed up to form the lake, while the melancholy eye of the fawn looked upon you with a familiar confidence which told he was not a free denizen of the forest. Were nothing else wanting there is no sunshine in England .to reveal the full beauty of the earth. Their clearest sky is a sort of *café au lait* color, and one can never go in search of the picturesque without an umbrella and over-shoes ; and as for a sunrise or a sunset they are matters of faith not sight. I would not give one glance of our deep blue heavens when the fleecy clouds are chasing over them, one glorious summer evening's western gorgeousness, or the streamy radiance of our Indian summer's morn, for the Duke of Northumberland's park, with all its ha-has and educated groves. I say educated, for every branch has been taught like a 'young idea how to shoot.'

But Scotland,

> 'Land of the mountain and the flood,
> Land of green heath and shaggy wood.'

My pen will certainly run away with me if I do not stop at once, and this awful elongation of an epistle be like poor Paddy's rope, the other end of which was cut off. I will not say Scotland is more beautiful than America, but certainly we have nothing like her scenery. But dear Scotland, thou shalt have another day to do thee honor. *Au revoir.* But I must stop again to say, I wish I could send your sister and yourself some sprigs of her heather to twine in your hair. It is worthy of the honor. As for the beauty of England's daughters, my fair countrywomen have no cause for jealousy.

I saw more loveliness at Gen. Cass's soirée last night, than I have seen since I left home, and there were none but Americans in the room. The English women are too — too — (I want a word) too *strong*, too *healthy*, if there be such a thing. Their cheeks are so red that they are almost blue. And such feet, they certainly gave the name to a foot measure. My conscience gives me, however, a twinge here, and bids me remember some delightful friends we had the pleasure of seeing, but there are exceptions, you know, to every general rule. I am told that among the nobility there are ladies of that high-bred beauty, which makes one almost hold his breath, it is so pure, so unearthly in its delicacy; and I suppose it is so, but I could match all the noble beauty I saw, from among the cotton-spinners of Lowell, and the onion-growers of Weathersfield, to say nothing of the Katrinas and Ariantzes, along our noble Hudson. I have heard, too, occasional laughter at the extreme delicacy (squeamishness they call it) and shrinking sensitiveness of observation, which characterize our American women. They say it argues *mauvaise honte*, but God grant that they may ever keep it. It is their highest merit, their most attractive charm. It is more precious than the richest veil that ever Mechlin weaver wove. You remember the tempter in Milton's Comus (how exquisitely delightful that poem is) says:

'Beauty was made for sports, as these,
For feasts and courts and high festivities.'

But when woman's feminineness is gone, she is not what God made her, and not what God would have her to be. Her throne is in the heart, her world her home. A proof of this is seen in the fact that, as no where else are women so retiring as with us, so, no where else have they so much real deference shown them.

It excited wonder in England, when I once gave up my seat in a stage-coach to a lady, a thing an American ploughboy would have done. Everywhere in England and in France, you see females at work in the fields doing the work of men. Here they make part of the pageant of an hour, but at home we honor them as our mothers, our wives, our sisters and our friends. In England they hold a higher rank than among these trifling Frenchmen; but in America they give to life its best and purest charms. I beg pardon for this unmerciful visitation. Your criticism I do not fear, for harsh you cannot be, and if I need forgiveness, I submit readily my case to so gentle a judge. You have, no doubt, met travelled Americans who affect a disrelish for their own country. Never did I feel so grateful to God for casting my lot in that dear land, as now. I must quote a verse from one of my own songs to express my heart.

'My country, oh, my country!
My heart still sighs for thee;
And many are the longing thoughts
I send across the sea.
My weary feet have wandered far,
And far they yet may roam;

But oh! whatever land I tread,
My heart is with my home.'

Please present my most respectful compliments to all your estimable circle, and allow me to be

Very truly your friend,

GEO. W. BETHUNE."

G. W. B. TO MRS. B. "PARIS, *Dec.* 13, 1836.

To describe Paris is impossible. It is a magnificent city, full of beautiful buildings and scenes of gaiety; yet there are far fewer external evidences of depravity than in London, or any English city I have seen. Luxurious and abandoned as a vast majority of the Parisians are, they have the good sense to hide their dissipation, or, at least, to veil it with graceful drapery. The pleasantest circle I have found was at Mr. Baird's on Saturday evening last, when I met some thirty or forty Americans, and a few English, in an old-fashioned religious meeting. It was very sweet and pleasant to sing the Lord's song in a strange land.

The gallery of the Louvre contains paintings enough to occupy me for a year. They are, besides, altogether of a higher character than any of those I have seen except a very few in England. I would soon become very fond of such matters. There is much fine music to be heard, and it is quite delightful to hear as one passes along the streets at night, the sudden burst of harmony from a band playing some familiar tune.

They tell a good story here, by the way, of Dr. —— He meant to ask his landlady for a chest of drawers to put in his room, and he asked for a *poitrine de caleçon*. It is said too, that he insisted upon making a speech before the French Bible Society, in French. The Parisians listened to him very gravely, but, &c."

G. W. B. TO MRS. J. B. "*Dec.* 28.

I have been endeavoring to improve my time as well as I could, and certainly think that upon many subjects I have acquired much information. My French teacher compliments me upon the readiness with which I improve in my knowledge of the language, and I can understand sufficiently well, to profit by the lectures in the different halls. I certainly have learned more in Paris than in London, and the society of well-informed persons is more easily reached. I was almost ashamed of the manner in which my time slipt from me in London; it seemed as if

I were continually employed in going from one street to another, the people are so wide apart.

Here, one can meet all they know in a very short time. There is much religious society here, at least much to what you would expect, and I enjoy myself as well as I can away from all I love. Mary writes me she is better, and begs me not to return to her until I have gone further, and, but for this, I believe I would have been on my way back to her before. I am haunted too with the dread lest you will blame me for staying in Europe, and spending so much money, though it is what I have not known how to avoid. I shall be miserable until I hear from you. I do hope the colonel will act a liberal part. He ought. But I must not write on this subject. I can not bear it. Dearest mother, forgive your son if he has done wrong.

We have been near seeing another revolution in Paris. Day before yesterday, Louis Philippe was going in his carriage to open the Chamber, when he was fired at in his carriage by an assassin. The ball passed close to his head and between the Duke of Nemours and his other son. I went to see the parade, and heard the shot, though I did not see the affair. I have been told since that it was well for us that the King was not killed, as the National Guards would have been so exasperated as to have charged at once upon the populace. Poor Louis Philippe! His crown is one of thorns. Yet God seems to watch over him in a remarkable manner. I believe he most conscientiously intends the good of his subjects, and certainly in private life is scrupulously moral. They say that the attachment of the Royal family to each other, is very great, and would be unusual any where, and in any rank in life, but especially in France and a reigning house. The poor Queen looked very, very pale and anxious, as she passed where we stood a few moments before the shot was fired. How near her fears were to being realized!

I can not say I like the French people. They are too flippant, too *external*, if I may use the expression, while the English are too heavy and reserved. I have found none like the warm-hearted, ready-handed Scotch. They are more like the Americans in character, and we, I think, contain many of the excellences of the French and English, with faults peculiarly our own.

I had hoped for a run into Italy, but the weather is so bad, the roads so bad, the cholera so bad, and the quarantines worse than all, that I believe I must give it up, but it is hard to do so.

Mr. Bethune was now made one of a deputation of Americans, who were to congratulate King Louis Philippe on his fortunate escape from the attempts upon his life. So he went to Court. "I had the honor," writes the traveller, "of a particular bow from his Majesty, which I attempted to return in my best style." On the same occasion, the English people had a deputation, and it was announced that while those of our country held the paper, containing resolutions of sympathy, the other party should express in words the sentiments of the house. Mr. Bethune related the marked difference in the conduct of the two delegations. The English appeared abashed in the presence of royalty, and spoke to each other in suppressed whispers, while the Americans stood up erect and self-possessed, talking together as if quite at their ease. "I have been to Court and exercised the cat's privilege of looking at a king; he behaved very well, and so did we."

"Paris now looks like home, the streets are covered with snow, and the people are enjoying themselves in the holidays. I have seen some sleighs in the streets, but they are the oddest looking things you can imagine. One of them is a reindeer stuffed upon runners, with a hole through the back, near the tail, in which a lady thrusts herself, and the gentleman, a Russian, sits behind and drives, and there is a gilded shell with a gilt cock perched upon the front. The horses have plumes of ostrich feathers upon their heads, and are covered with little bells. Did I tell you I was at General Cass's soirée last Monday evening? It was quite an American party, and I have not seen so much beauty since I left home."

The cholera having abated, and quarantine barriers being removed, our minister proceeded on his southern journey. We hear from him next at

"GENOA, *Jan.* 18, 1837.

What Hannibal and Buonaparte did I have done, 'crossed the Alps.' Whatever difficulties those gentlemen found in their way, I found none. It was, however, extremely cold. Indeed I have not been really comfortable since I have been in Italy. The scenery of the part of the Alps (those of Savoy) through which we came, is very wild, and sometimes extremely beautiful, but not so very different from mountain scenery at home, as I had imagined. Undoubtedly the season deprived it of many of its charms, but yet it must have given others; the fantastic forms into which the droppings of the snow from the cliffs were frozen, and the congealed waterfalls glittering like diamonds in the sun, were exquisitely beautiful. No art could carve, and no fancy devise tracery so inimitably beautiful. Winter scenery in a rugged country has always had great charms for me. I crossed by Mount Cenis, and it is wonderful how art has triumphed over nature in constructing a road over a heap (for no word seems to describe it so well) of mountains, nearly six thousand feet high, and so good that in summer the most timid woman might cross it without fear. I had for my companion a very pleasant man, a descendant of the Albigenses of whom you have read. He was quite intelligent, speaking every language of Europe, and delighted to give all the information, and shew me all the kindness in his power. To him I was indebted, not only for much pleasure, but instruction in the history of those mountains where St. Paul once preached, and the religion of Christ was kept pure and undefiled during all the reign of superstition in the dark ages. Descending on this side of the mountain, we were soon aware we had entered Italy.

The chestnut and elm began to abound, the sides of the precipitous hills were covered to the top with vineyards, and the graceful palace took the place of the Savoyard's Cottage. Sunday morning, very early, we reached Turin, the capital of Piedmont, the most beautiful city excepting Edinburgh, I have seen. Nothing can be finer than its two principal squares. The streets, too, are as straight and rectangular as those of Philadelphia, and, what is still more remarkable, as clean. I did wish for spring, however, to set off the beauty of the scenery through which we passed. Imagine if you can, a wide, high road, lined on each side by fine old chestnuts, winding along the foot of hills covered to the top with palaces, in the midst of vineyards, the vines growing on elm trees planted for the purpose, while below the road is the river Po, wide, placid, and majestic, wandering through the richest valley, bounded in the distance by the snow-peaked Alps, and you have the road from Turin. Oh! it is beautiful as a poet's dream; then the costume of the peasant women, a white veil thrown back from the head and flowing to the feet, is so graceful; while the very oxen, white and dove-colored, are beautiful features in the landscape. Now I look out from my chamber window on the Mediterranean. Genoa is situated on the shore of a harbor exactly like a horse-shoe, and is very rich and beautiful, but being built on the side of a hill, the houses are very high.

There are only one hundred and forty steps to my room, and in the palace of the Palacini, where I was to-day, the dining-room is up two pair of stairs. Here the costume of the women is very fanciful; they wear long veils of chintz, the ground of which is white and flowered. They look very pretty in them.

Pisa is remarkable for the beauty of some of its edifices. The principal is the leaning tower or campanile. It is about two hundred feet high, and circular, consisting of a number (eight) of stories with more than two hundred columns, but the greatest curiosity about it is, that in consequence, as is supposed, of an earthquake, it has been thrown from the perpendicular, and now leans over more than thirteen feet, so that you would suppose it would fall every moment, yet it has stood in this way for centuries. Near the town is a fine Cathedral, adorned with magnificent brass gates, and columns, and pictures. Behind the cathedral again is the Baptistry, which is a beautiful octagon temple, entirely of white marble. They have there, too, what is termed the 'Campo Santo,' or holy field, which is a burial ground, the centre of which is filled in with earth brought from Jerusalem, and the sides enclosed by fine Gothic ranges of windows. It contains many beautiful monuments, much antique sculpture, and old inscriptions. We left Pisa, however, the next day, and came through the beautiful vale of the Arno to Florence. We were very much struck with the beauty of the peasantry; the roads were lined with villages, and crowds of the peasants in their picturesque dresses were seen along. We did not see a young woman with a bad face; all were handsome; the ladies say the men are so, too, but I did not remark them. Report says, the peasantry are as virtuous and industrious as they are beautiful. Oh! it was a sweet ride, the vineyards on each side, the winding Arno, rolling its deep waves, tinged by the hues of an Italian sunset, or silvered over by a full, clear moon, which rose upon us long before we entered Florence. Here there is much to interest the stranger, more than any part of Italy, except Rome and Venice. It is now the season of the Carnival, and the Florentines are very gay. The public promenade along the bank of the beautiful Arno is filled every afternoon with crowds in their holiday dresses, many with the most ludicrous and grotesque masks and costumes, amusing themselves and the rest. The gentry go and drive on the Corso, which resembles the Paséa at Havana, where they ride backwards and forwards, throwing sugar-plums at each other. Here is the celebrated

Florentine gallery which contains the Venus de Medici, and many rare sculptures and paintings. I spent four hours in the gallery to-day, and shall spend as many to-morrow."

G. W. B. TO MRS. B. "ROME, *Feb.* 2, 1837.

Modern Rome is a sad commentary on the evanescent nature of human glory. It contains, it is true, many splendid buildings, and one unmatched in the world, St. Peter's; but there is the appearance of wretched, vicious poverty in the common people, and the streets are narrow and filthy. This is properly the week of the Carnival, when Rome should, according to custom, be very gay. You know that Carnival means, literally, 'Farewell to meats!' and precedes Lent; it is, in truth, feasting as much as they can before they are obliged to fast. But I understand the Pope is fearful of a revolt, and has forbidden masks, which these childish Italians consider so necessary to their amusement, that they think they can have no fun without them. They have, however, some of their amusements, among which are ridiculous races. The principal street in the city is termed the Corso, or Race Course, and the middle of it is covered with tan. At the appointed time the horses are brought out behind a rope, which is stretched across the street, and are without riders, but with a sort of saddle with flaps, in which are iron spikes. At the sound of a cannon the rope before them is dropt, and away go the poor beasts, spurred on the more, the faster they make haste, until at the other end they run against a large cloth hung across the streets, and are stopped. Nothing can be more ridiculous, yet, to see this, the Romans go in crowds; the Corso itself is full, and it is with the utmost difficulty the troops can preserve a lane wide enough for the horses. The glory of modern Rome, however, is her St. Peter's. This immense church I cannot describe to you: to say that it is more than 600 feet long, 200 feet broad, and 150 feet high, or rather, 450 feet to the top of the cross, would be to convey but a poor notion of its grandeur. Every part of this immense structure is finished in the most costly manner; mosaic pictures of enormous size, colossal statues and graceful tombs and altars, are on every side, in the greatest profusion. Not less than fifty millions of dollars had been spent upon this church in A.D. 1700; to say nothing of what has been added since. Yet I cannot say after all, that I admire St. Peter's; it is impossible not to be astonished at its vast size, but it is not to my mind truly grand. The gilt ceiling, the tinsel, the profusion of ornament are not to my taste. I had much more pleasure in Westminster Abbey, and some other Gothic buildings in England, and the Madeleine of Paris, which is pure Grecian, than in St. Peter's. It was, too, a strong rebuke of the pride which created such a temple, to see, as one continually does, a poor wretched man or woman huddling in the corner near the altar, which was most attractive to them for reasons they only could know. Surely the religion which was given for the poor in spirit, and teaches humility of heart, needs no such gorgeous temple as St. Peter's. The rooms of the celebrated Vatican contain a profusion of fine sculpture, but a small portion of which I have yet seen. The Apollo Belvidere, next to the Venus de Medici, is probably the most beautiful statue in the world, such dignity! such grace! such manly beauty!"

G. W. B. to Mrs. J. B. "Rome, *Feb.* 8, 1837.

There is a gay scene from my windows. They look out upon the terraces and esplanade of the handsomest gardens of Rome, which are now filled with gaily-dressed and merry people. It is the last day of the carnival, Mardi Gras, and the Romans, expecting to be half starved for the next forty days, are determined to feast to-day. This Italy is indeed a beautiful land, like one vast pleasure-ground, with a continual summer. Every one may here find his taste gratified. Here are amusements for the butterflies, who think of nothing else; because the Italian lives for amusement. Here are classical associations for the scholar, every hill, and lake, and river, speaking to him of times gone by, and here the lover of the arts, painting, sculpture and music, finds them in a profusion not elsewhere known. Yet it is a melancholy land. I cannot enjoy myself over the grave of buried millions; or when I see the indolent Italians lounging over the ground the masters of the world once trod, and yielding to the rule of effeminate and slipshod priests. The superstition of the people is awful. The other day I saw a dozen of them climbing upon their knees the Scala Santa, or stairs, said to have been those of Pilate's house which the Saviour went up; this was to gain a thousand days' indulgence, that is, to buy off a thousand years of purgatory. At another place crowds of well-dressed people and beggars of the most revolting description were kissing, one after another, a cross which gained them a hundred days. The Pope is continually issuing orders about ceremonies and processions, and the whole aim seems to be, to make a puppet-show of religion.

One could spend a month, yes, a year, in Rome, if his heart were not elsewhere, as mine is. I was yesterday at the Vatican Museum, where the galleries, taken altogether, are said to be nearly two miles long, and almost entirely filled with antique sculpture. The Apollo Belvidere — the celebrated group of Laocoon and his sons — the Antinous and the Jupiter are all there. Then the Capitol, likewise, contains an immense number of statues and bas-reliefs; while more than a half-a-dozen palaces in Rome have picture galleries, filled with gems from the best masters. In the Doria palace, the other day, we went through seven immense rooms filled with valuable paintings, before we reached the gallery, which comprises three sides of a very large square. The beauty of some of these works is indescribable, and the effect of some of them remains on the mind long, long after you have ceased to look at them. I remember now, as distinctly as if I had the picture before me, Sassoferrato's picture of the Virgin in grief, and Raphael's Madonna, which I saw at Florence. I think I never can forget those pictures, or one head of Beatrice Cenci, by Guido. I saw a grand exhibition of the Pope and Cardinals at the Sistine Chapel the other day, which I cannot describe to you by letter, but will amuse you with when we meet. It was last Wednesday; and the occasion of their meeting was for the Cardinals to have ashes sprinkled upon them which the Pope had blessed. The Pope is a venerable-looking old man, and it was sad to see him engaged in such mummery. Yet we ought to judge lightly, for none of us know how strong the prejudices of education may be. The environs of Rome are covered with ruins which speak of buried centuries."

CHAPTER VII.

SUCCESS IN PHILADELPHIA.

The Philadelphia church was approaching completion; kind friends had been busy in preparing a pleasant place of residence; time and money were both flying; everything called for a speedy return home. During his absence, Mrs. Bethune had been transported by water from Liverpool to London in order to consult Sir Astley Cooper and Sir James Clarke. At this place her husband joined her, to make the discovery that even the most learned doctors may be found napping. The accomodations not being extensive, when the two physicians retired for consultation, Mr. Bethune was in a position to overhear their remarks. They had a pleasant interview; one relating how he on a certain occasion came very near to fighting a duel. The difficulties and danger of the position occupied some time to describe, and they were about to separate when one recalled the patient. "But what shall we do with Bethune's wife?" "Oh, give her the old pill," was the ready reply. It is superfluous to add that this most expensive medical attendance quickly terminated.

It was not until the 7th of May, that the party sailed from Liverpool to the United States, and, in due time, reached Philadelphia. The church edifice, a very neat building in the Grecian style, was completed soon after his arrival, and solemnly dedicated to God by Mr. Bethune, who preached a sermon from Psalms xxvii., 4. Gratefully he had written from Rome: "What an excellent soul is Morris and the rest of them. How I will work for them when I get back." There was plenty to do and he plunged into it with all his might. His popularity increased; and his being talked of for other pulpits made his position towards his own congregation more commanding and easy.

In the month of July, he pronounced his discourse on "Genius" before the literary societies of Union College, and its opening sentence, "*Forsan et haec olim meminisse juvabit*" was a bit of true prophecy. This effort of his at making a public address of a character not purely or even chiefly religious, was the first of a long train of brilliant lectures, which brought renown and even money to the popular minister, but whose chief use was, as he himself intended, to induce many to come and hear him preach the Gospel who would otherwise have stayed away altogether.

G. W. B. to Mrs. J. B. "*October* 20, 1837.

I fear you will scarcely believe me when I say that I have been so driven, as not to have five minutes' time to write, for a fortnight past, any thing but sermons. I have a pile of letters lying unanswered before me, that is distressing to look at. I fear I have undertaken too much, for, besides my Sunday sermons, I am carrying on in the week a course of lectures on the Ephesians, which I write out, and which give me more trouble than any other service. The new members of the congregation are to be found out and visited, and adjusted in their proper places; besides which, I have to be at the end of everything, or it is ill done if done at all. You blame me for studying at night, but if it were not for those few still, uninterrupted hours of the twenty-four, I could not maintain my position at all. I am now placed in a dangerous situation, for I enjoy a great degree of general popularity. Double the number are turned away from my church doors of those who get in at the evening service. I know I do not deserve this from any talents I have, and therefore I must strive to preserve such an opportunity of usefulness by severe study, that study being directed as far as I can do it, to making the gospel simple and plain. My health has not suffered from it, but, on the contrary, the trouble and anxiety from which I find a refuge in study wears, or would wear me down much more. I do not wish to murmur. The lot which God assigns me is best for me, and it is not often I show my trouble to any one, for I endeavor for the sake of others to keep a cheerful face; but I have my afflictions and sometimes I think they are far from being light."

To the Rev. Mr. M—. "*Jan.* 4, 1838.

I am rather in difficulties myself (though this is *entre nous*), my church to outside appearance goes on prosperously, and there are few preachers in town, who seem to have the popularity I have just now, yet as an unfortunate author said to me the other day, 'It is very strange, that which every body praises, nobody buys.' My books, I mean my pews, go off very slowly. The hard times solve the riddle however."

G. W. B. to Mrs. J. B. "*March* 10, 1838.

During the whole of last week, I intended each day to write, but was really too unwell. I had to deliver a lecture before the Athenian Institute on Tuesday evening, and caught cold coming home. The Athenian Institute lectures correspond somewhat with those of the Stuyvesant Institute of New York. They have been overwhelmingly popular. It was computed that, after tickets for seventeen hundred persons were issued, they could have sold seven hundred more. My subject was 'Socrates,' his life and opinions. I only used it, however, for an indirect argument in favor of the necessity of revelation, in which, if I may credit the opinions of my friends, Dr. Ludlow, and Mr. Biddle, I was quite successful. The lecture will probably be published in the Knickerbocker Magazine, when I may have your judgment upon it.

I have reason to believe that my standing in Philadelphia is becoming higher and higher every day. People who should have known me as my father's son, when I first came to town, now seek to know me, and I have a decided and acknowledged position among the scholars of the city. All this I only care for so far as it increases my influence as a minister, and may enable me to do good. Fame and mere popularity are, of all human pursuits, the most vaporous; but to promote, as an instrument in God's hands, the kingdom of his blessed Son, and point wandering souls back to their Father's house, is indeed an honour. — I am sorry to say my congregation increases slowly. The hard times are against us."

From this period our minister became Doctor of Divinity. He received this degree *causâ honoris* from the University of Pennsylvania in 1838, and for ten years, from 1839 to 1849, was an active Trustee of that Institution.

MRS. J. B. TO G. W. B. "*January* 5, 1839.

Since you left I have often read over the sweet lines you addressed to me, and never without tears. — I have been asked for them for the Intelligencer. I don't know whether it would be well to publish them ; I fear your growing popularity will excite envy. Your sermon of the evening has been much talked of."

G. W. B. TO MRS. J. B. "*January* 14, 1839.

I am happy that you were pleased with the verses I addressed to you. If they have any merit it must arise from their being

'The flow of feeling,
Not of art.'

As to their being published, so far from having any objection, I wish it, and but waited to hear how you regarded them. I should like to pay openly a tribute of regard and grateful affection to my mother. But the Christian Intelligencer is not the place for them. In the first place they print abominably, making the most absurd errors, and then the lines would be buried there. No, if George Duffield will take the trouble to copy them distinctly into a clear hand, and carry them, or send them with my compliments to the Knickerbocker, I should like it better. My first verses to Mary were published there, and were copied all over from it.

My hands are full. It is, however, my weekly *sermons* which press me so hard. It is a sad thing to have a little popularity as a preacher in a regular pulpit. The drain upon one is excessive, and there is no *let up* as the Yankees say."

Some of our readers may have seen a beautiful engraving which appeared about this time representing Washington in the attitude of prayer. He appears to have retired from the camp which is seen at a little distance, and to have knelt down under the covert of a thicket to ask counsel and guidance of God in his sore perplexity. Perchance it was at Valley Forge where his fortunes and his hopes touched the lowest point, perhaps it was before Yorktown where his toils and his faith were crowned with success. The engraving was made in keeping with the representations of a Quaker who was eye-witness of the scene. This was used to illustrate the Christian Keepsake, and Mr. Bethune yielded to the request of Mr. L. G. Clarke to accompany the engraving with a contribution. In these minor efforts his pen had a facility which of itself would have secured fame and competency.

In the latter days of January, 1839, occurred the death of the Patroon of Albany, the excellent and venerable Stephen Van Rensselaer. That this was a cause of heart-felt sorrow to Dr. Bethume we need not say for he has left a record of his feelings on the occasion.

He writes to Mrs. Van Rensselaer on the 3d of February.

"My Dear Madam:

If I have not been among the first with words of sympathy, it was because I dared not intrude at once upon the sacredness of your sorrow. But I can forbear no longer. The many kindnesses of him who has entered into his rest, the precious memory of many days spent within the home hallowed by his meek and gentle affection, and the frequent privilege of kneeling with you and yours to implore the grace of God's presence in his hour of affliction, have given my heart the right to bleed with yours.

Yet what shall I say? I need not speak of consolation. God has already given it. You have marked the perfect and beheld the upright, that the end of that man is peace. The patient sufferings over which you have watched so long are ended. His pains have ended. He is asleep in Jesus. The venerable head, hoary in righteousness, is now crowned with glory, the fight has been victorious, the race won, the faith kept. O what gain has death been to him. 'If ye loved me,' said Jesus, 'ye would rejoice because I said I go unto my Father.' And he whom we love and mourn is with Jesus and the Father now.

As I close this letter I am preparing to go to my pulpit that I may speak to my people of him whose hands laid the corner-stone of our little church. The text that I have chosen is Jeremiah ix., 23-24. But how will I dare to speak of all his worth to those who knew him not as I have known him. Yet to God must be given the praise of an example the most excellent in meekness, in quietness, nobleness, and kindness we have ever witnessed or read of in modern days."

The sermon took True Glory for its theme and appeared in pamphlet form. It is also in the volume of "Bethune's Orations;" but this is the summing up of the whole, it is not tiresome to read and will be its own apology:

"*Glorying in the Lord is not incompatible with the possession of wisdom, power, or riches.*

The highest glory of man, in this life, is to be the instrument of God's 'loving kindness,' judgment and righteousness; and none can be said 'to know him' aright, or 'understand' the beauty of his character, who strive not to imitate him in the exercise of those admirable attributes.

If, then, any degree of *wisdom* be ours, it is our high privilege to use it in the advancement of his glory, and the best good of our fellow men; and the more wisdom we possess, the greater is our faculty for that blessed end.

If we have any degree of *power*, or influence in society, (and none of us is without some) it is our high privilege to use that influence for the vindication of the Redeemer's name, and the guidance of our fellow men in the way to glory; and the greater our influence, the more efficient our example and zeal may be.

If we have any degree of *riches*, it is our privilege, by a heavenly alchemy, to turn the dross that perisheth, into eternal and incorruptible treasures, which shall fill the treasury of God with the priceless jewels of ransomed souls; and the greater our riches, the greater means we have for doing good in Christ's most holy name.

Certainly, earth hath no nobler spectacle (and it is one angels leave heaven to contemplate) than that of a good man, preserving, amidst the temptations of wisdom, and power, and riches, his humble trust in God his Saviour, as his highest glory, and his delight in serving his fellow men, as his next chiefest good. His is a wisdom the most ignorant must venerate; a power the most malicious must approve; and a wealth, which envy itself would hardly dare to steal.

This wisdom, and power, and riches, may be attained by us all. For, though our learning may be poor, our influence narrow, and our means small, he 'that glorieth in knowing and serving the Lord,' hath done his duty, when he hath done, through Divine grace, what he could.

It was a magnificent tribute of respect and honor to one of the best of men. "These things did Araunah as a king give unto the king." Dr. Bethune occasionally reposes himself from graver writings with a bit of facetiousness, and then his pen is apt to run away with him. "Tell sister Bell" he scribbles to his mother, "that I owe her many thanks for her kind present, my *understanding* as well as my heart is clothed with gratitude; and my memory must become *slippery* indeed if I am ever *worsted* in an endeavor to recall her deeds of love, which have my warmest approval though she thinks they were but so so, *sew sew* indeed they must have been. By the way the shoemaker who put them together, before he sent them home, put them in his window before which I saw quite a crowd of lovers of the fine arts flattening their noses in gaping admiration."

Two other well known literary performances came from his pen during this year,—the discourse on "Leisure, its Uses and Abuses," delivered 9th March before the New York Mercantile Library Association, and the "Age of Pericles," read before the Athenian Institute of Philadelphia in the same year. These performances established a fame which future efforts maintained.

A funny story is told of the grievous mistake of one of Dr. Bethune's old parishioners concerning the aim of the "Age of Pericles." When the lecture was to be repeated in Boston, he met his former pastor and said "Well, doctor, I have bought a ticket and am coming to hear you to-night. When I told my wife about it, she asked, 'But who is this Perikels?'" The good man pronounced the last syllable as in "barnacles." "The fact was that I never had heard of the man, but I said, 'if you are such a fool as not to know that, it is high time for you to begin to study.' But now doctor do tell me, what is the reason that you are going to give a whole lecture about how long the old fellow lived?"

"Whilst his reputation was thus culminating in Philadelphia," writes the accomplished Dr. Dunglison, in his Obituary Notice for the American Philosophical Society, "he was energetically affording his powerful aid to every scheme for the promotion and diffusion of general literature and science, and for the good of his fellow men. Early and prominent among these was the 'Athenian Institute;' the object of which was to establish a course of lectures, to be delivered gratuitously by literary gentlemen of Philadelphia, and which, for a time, was eminently successful. The first course was given in the winter of 1838, and the last in that of 1842. Large and intelligent audiences assembled together to listen to the diversified discourses, of which none were more popular than those of Dr. Bethune.

In the different reunions of the respectable members of the Board of Directors of the Institute, he was placed in intimate intercourse with the first literary and scientific gentlemen of the city, by whom his sterling qualities were at once appreciated, and his claims to be regarded as a true lover of wisdom cheerfully conceded."

In April, 1839, a distinction was granted him, which he estimated as one of the highest to be found in our country. —"Among the honors conferred upon me lately," he writes to Mrs. J. B., "is a unanimous (very unusual) election to be a Member of the American Philosophical Society. Think of my being a philosopher." Of this Institution Dr. Dunglison furnishes the following sketch. "This venerable society which is so well known at home and abroad, and which reckons amongst its members many of the scientists of all nations, has been considered to owe its origin to a secret debating society called 'the Junto' formed by Franklin in 1727, which was limited to a small number of members, restricted in its objects and local in its character. This appears to have been kept up actively for a time, but on the increase of the Country it seemed to be necessary to have a society whose aims should be greater, and be more markedly a scientific body; and accordingly Franklin in 1743, issued a circular entitled 'A proposal for promoting useful knowledge among the British Plantations in America'; and this was the real origin of 'The American Philosophical Society.' It appears, however, that in the year 1750, a new society was formed, also called 'the Junto' and essentially resembling in organization the ancient Junto founded in 1727 of which indeed it was probably the sanctioned successor and this new Junto became amalgamated with the society founded in 1743, but not until the close of the year 1768, the united society assuming the name, as at present, of 'The American Philosophical Society,' held at Philadelphia for promoting useful knowledge, and on the second of January, 1769, held its first meeting and its first election. The society has from time to time published valuable volumes of its 'Transactions,' which are issued regularly and distributed to its members and to the various scientific institutions of all countries; from which it receives in return, as well as from distinguished physicists everywhere, the published accounts of their important labors."

"It was," says Dr. Dunglison, "at one of the meetings of the Board of Directors of the Athenian Institute that I first saw Dr. Bethune, and I well remember the favorable impression he made on me, as he did on all. We generally walked home together with Dr. Patterson, Judge Kane and Professor Dallas Bache, and often with our friend Mr. Benjamin W. Richards, taking our wives by surprise; who, at times, were wholly unprepared to entertain us as they would have wished. And Dr. Bethune often mentioned the equanimity and hospitality of my own excellent wife when there was nothing but boiled eggs to offer us for supper, and referred with enthusiasm to its being one of the most agreeable reunions he had experienced. This was before the four gentlemen first mentioned had resolved themselves with me into the Club, if it may be so called, which Dr. Bethune suggested we should call "The Five."

In this club we had no fixed evenings for meeting. It depended so much upon our meeting together at the American Philosophical Society, or elsewhere. Occasionally a stranger was admitted; but usually we were alone. In my memoir I state how much the pleasures of the evening were owing to Dr. Bethune, who was ever cheerful; full of anecdote; and pointed, but judiciously and amiably directed, repartee. Never did I hear from him any allusion that could be the cause of discomfort to the most sensitive.

After this period we were in the habit of seeing each other often. His mind was of the most scrutinizing kind, and many subjects we had been equally engaged in investigating. Philological inquiries he was very partial to; and when we returned from listening to public or private lectures, there was always something we had heard which furnished matter for inquiry, and which we had to decide at times by a reference to some work in my library, with the richness of which on particular subjects, he often expressed his gratification.

During his visit to me after he left Philadelphia, occasion often occurred for such reference; and it was a source of real pleasure to my boys to aid us in our re searches. His advent on the occasion of such visits was always hailed with pleasure by my excellent wife, of whom, on the occasion of her death, he speaks in one of his letters (March 10, 1853) with so much of feeling and truth, as well as by my children."

Having requested from Dr. Dunglison some account of the individuals composing this remarkable club, he replies, that he might be justified, in saying with the great dramatist, of each of them:

> "'His life was gentle, and the elements
> So mixed in him that nature might stand up
> And say to all the world, 'This was a man.'"

"These are designated in my 'Obituary Notice' as congenial spirits; and it is difficult to imagine five that could be more so. Although by their avocations they had all been more or less restricted in their reading and studies, all might be regarded as conversant with those general accomplishments that appertain to the educated gentleman. It was difficult, therefore, to start any topic of inquiry and discussion in which they could not generally participate, and on which light could not be thrown by one or more of the party; and hence it is, that their meetings were happily designated by Judge Kane as 'quiet, joyous and instructive.'

The very nature of their avocations necessarily led to their arguments being diversified. Dr. Robert M. Patterson, at the time Director of the Mint of the United States, had been, for many years, Professor of Natural Philosophy, first in the University of Pennsylvania, and, afterwards, in the University of Virginia. Judge Kane was an accomplished member of the bar, and afterwards Judge of the District Court of the United States Professor Alexander Dallas Bache was Professor of Natural Philosophy in the University of Pennsylvania, and afterwards, and at the time of his death, the distinguished Superintendent of the Coast Survey of the United States. Dr. Dunglison was Professor of the Institute of Medicine in the Jefferson Medical College of Philadelphia; and every one of 'the five' had held offices in the American Philosophical Society, — Dr. Patterson, Judge Kane, and Professor Bache as President, Dr. Dunglison as Vice President, and Dr. Bethune as a Member of the Board of officers. All are, alas! gone except Dr. Dunglison."

Between these gentlemen there was not only a pleasant intimacy, but a league for mutual defence. When, after the death of Judge Kane, his reputation was assailed on political grounds, it brought forth a rebuke from Dr. Bethune, perhaps the most severe he ever penned; and when, at a later period, Professor Bache requested that the interests of Dr. Kane, the Arctic Explorer, should be promoted, appealing to the memory of "the Five," Dr. Bethune felt the obligation and responded handsomely.

He made good his right to these elevated distinctions,

by repeated and highly applauded lectures at the Smithsonian Institute, urgently called for by Professor Henry, who was at the head of that foundation. Connected with the American Philosophical Society, there was a very remarkable social entertainment which went by the name of "Wister parties." The name originated from Dr. Wister, who was President of the Society, and these meetings were designed to discuss scientific and philosophical subjects. They assembled the choice spirits of Philadelphia, and distinguished strangers, in the most charming reunions, and became quite renowned. Drs. Bethune and Ludlow were constant attendants, and it was evident that their dignified presence gave a higher tone to the gatherings.

In many ways this year, 1839, was an important era in Dr. Bethune's life. In the spring he printed his first volume entitled "The Fruit of the Spirit." He had already published addresses, contributed frequently to Magazines and Annuals, but now he came prominently before the public as author. The work was issued at the request of his congregation. Dr. W. J. R. Taylor says,

> "It had passed through three separate processes of delivery to his people; first, briefly in the prayer-meeting, at another time in more enlarged form, in the weekly lecture, subsequently, in a course of Sabbath sermons, and finally, he revised it for the press. It was his favorite work, has passed through several editions, and bids fair to remain a household treasure for generations to come."

In the autumn, the chapel of the New York Orphan Asylum, at Bloomingdale, was to be opened. This magnificent charity had grown up under the care of his mother, and now that it had become well established in a beautiful location, the son was requested to preach the sermon for the occasion. In the month of June he was elected President of the General Synod of his church, and in this capacity addressed a letter to the Court of Holland, in reference to the Mission work in the Dutch possessions, and held frequent correspondence with the missionaries in the East.

Dr. Hazlett relates his first introduction to Dr. Bethune:

"Capt. Magruder said, 'Come go with me to hear Dr. Bethune lecture to-night.' It was very stormy, and they found only the sexton and an old woman as the audience; but the Dr. rose, gave out a hymn, and sung it himself. After prayer, and eloquent reading of scripture, he delivered one of the most profound lectures I have ever heard. My friend said, 'Why did you not keep that lecture for a better night. It was too good to throw away upon us.' The Dr. replied, 'It is my duty to preach the gospel to the best of my ability under all circumstances, and it is wrong to punish those who come in stormy weather, for the delinquency of others.' I set him down then for a great man, and concluded that he preached the truth for the love of the truth, and not for the praise of men."

On the 10th of April, 1841, news of the death of President Harrison reached Philadelphia, and the next day found our ready preacher in his pulpit prepared to improve the solemn occasion. The sermon, which was a tender appeal to his countrymen, and thought worthy of publication, must have been prepared in the course of a few hours. The speaker did not belong to the same party as the President, and with the greater freedom pronounced this sharp rebuke upon political bigotry:

"Standing, in our imagination, this morning, beside the grave of our departed patriot, who, even of those that struggled most against his rise, can look down upon his sleeping dust, nor feel a pang of keen reproach, if ever he hath done his honor wrong, or breathed a hasty word that might have touched his honest heart, or cast an insult upon his time-honored name? And vile, yes, very vile is he, whose resentments the grave cannot still. Whence this sacredness which death throws over the memory of character and life? Is it because the dead are defenceless, and return not an answer again ? Is it because God hath come in between us and our fellow creature, and vindicated his right to be judge alone? Is it because in the humiliations of the sepulchre, we see the frailty of that nature we share with the departed, our own aptness to err, and how liable we are to be misjudged? O, my friends, why should we wait for death to teach us charity, when it is too late to practice it, and repentance hath become remorse? Why not remember that the *living* require our candor and forbearance? Why reserve all our gentleness of judgment for the dead, who are beyond the reach of our absolution? They were once as the living, and the living shall soon be as they. It is, indeed, enough to bring us back to a better opinion of human nature, to witness such a spectacle of union in sorrow and in honor for our departed chief among those, who, a little while since, were divided into earnest and opposing factions; but oh! would it not be far more ennobling, to see the living pledging themselves to the living over the fresh earth of his grave, that henceforth, though they may honestly differ in their doctrines and policy, they will yet believe in the uprightness of each other's motives, and the sincerity of each other's belief? How hateful does censorious bitterness, and sneering suspicion look, in the face of your opponent! Yet such is your deformity in his sight, when you revile his principles and rail against his friends. When, oh! when shall this rancor, this cruel persecution for opinion's sake, this damning inquisition after false motives, this fratricidal rending of heart from heart because our mental vision is not the same; this exiling of the honorable from the honorable, because they have not the same sibilation in their Shibboleth; this waste of wealth, of mental power and untiring zeal, which our country, and our whole country should enjoy; when shall it cease? Must it be perpetual? I know that the words of a poor preacher are weak against this strong and vast-spreading evil; but as I love my country, and God knows I love her from my inmost heart, and never more than in this hour of her sorrow, I must speak. I cannot believe that I have a right to hate and despise my brother, because he reads another book than my own, or that he should hate and despise me, because conviction forces me to cling to mine."

MRS. J. B. TO G. W. B. "*April* 30, 1841.

I was much pleased with your short discourse on our poor old President. I was afraid you would not acquit yourself so well, as you did not think as highly of him as some did. What a lesson we have had as a nation. I did not think I had as much American feeling in me as I felt on reading the account of his death; my blood all tingled through my veins and I found relief only in tears. I retired as soon as I could and fell on my knees and prayed to God to sanctify the dispensation to the nation, a sinful, Sabbath-breaking and otherwise guilty nation, though exalted to Heaven in point of privileges."

G. W. B. TO MRS. J. B. "*May* 1.

I am glad you liked my little sermon. Would a Harrison man have done so much had my friend Van Buren died? I felt as an American and as a Christian (I trust) and forgot party."

And now we have to carry our popular minister through many months of gloom and depression. His continued speaking and the failure of his health from overwork brought in the earlier months of 1841, an attack of "bronchitis, laryngitis, or both," as his letters express it. He was peremptorily forbidden by his physician to preach for two months; and could he have quietly submitted he might have bided over the trouble and saved himself much annoyance. His congregation paid him the compliment of declaring they could not do without him; and forced him to obtain a written opinion from his physicians, Bell, Chapman and Hodge, that a sea voyage was absolutely necessary to him, before they would consent to his absenting himself. This paper convinced them, and with a total change of tone the Consistory voted a leave of absence for such time as should be necessary, and the substantial accommodation of two quarters' salary in advance was superadded. He writes in acknowledgement:

"*May* 15, 1841.

I thank the gentlemen of that meeting for their kind sympathy, for the leave of absence granted me, and their recommendation to the Board of Trustees that two quarters of my salary (for which I have no just claim) be advanced to me in the present exigency. Every added proof of kindness from the people of my charge, deepens my affliction in being compelled to intermit for a season the labors in which I have found my great delight.

I shall pursue, with the leave of Providence, the advice of those medical gentlemen whose opinion is before you; because their opinion in a matter of health, would naturally be preferred by a sick man, to that of any unprofessional adviser; because past experience of the effect of the sea on my constitution, and my present symptoms confirm me in believing their advice to be good; and because I owe it to myself, to the church, and to God, to recover and preserve, so far as means may, that health without which I should lose my usefulness.

That some proofs, that I have not acted precipitately in this matter, may be preserved, permit me earnestly to request that the letter of Doctors Bell, Chapman and Hodge be copied on the minutes of the Consistory and the Board of Trustees. No one, who may read it, will have a right to blame, but will think that it was not unreasonable to grant me, after nearly four years' hard service of mind and body, a furlough for a few months when rest seemed essential to my recovery, and that rest, in the opinion of those who ought to know best, would be most profitably spent on shipboard."

Accordingly Dr. Bethune sailed with his wife on the twenty-sixth of May, and arrived at Gibraltar on the twenty-fourth of June. On the nineteenth of July the travellers reached Naples, and a letter is at once sent homeward.

G. W. B. to Mrs. J. B. "NAPLES, *July* 19, 1841.

Among our passengers on board the Oriental, was the second son of Walter Scott, rather a nice young man, going out as secretary to the Persian embassy. We made a little acquaintance together. Malta, you know, has been quite famous as the place where St. Paul was shipwrecked, and we went to see the place where he is said to have shaken the viper from his hand. But alas for our antiquarian enjoyment, very good arguments are given to show that the apostle never was at Malta,* but that Melita was, and is, an island in the Adriatic."

* Better arguments to show that he was. ED.

Naples was found delightful, Sorrento charming, every thing rose-color, and we may imagine that our classic minister enjoyed the time at Pompeii and Vesuvius. A letter received at Florence, from E. T. Throop, Esq., enclosed money and a sort of apology for the Rothschilds of Naples, who had hesitated to make a small advance; and thus helped on his way, he made a hasty trip down the Rhine and pausing but little in London, reached home before the beginning of September. His trip had done him some good, but not as much as was hoped. But still "*objecta minoris resistentiæ*" he chafed at the enforced quiet. "It is impossible," he says, "to prevent myself from anxiety, but I pray to be able to look to Him who can and will sustain his tried but trusting children. I try to keep my spirit willing, but my flesh is weak." He was forbidden the segar by the inexorable Bell, and the deprivation was great. It is related of him that a brother clergyman with whom he had frequent disputes on points of doctrine, came into his study one morning and found him enveloped in the blue and fragrant wreaths. "What, smoking?" gasped the visitor, uplifting his hands in astonishment. "Yes," said the doctor, very coolly, "I am trying to *preserve* my orthodoxy."

But he could better bear the loss of nicotine, than the secession of a part of his congregation, which came with the frightfully hard times.

He writes to Mrs. J. B., February 14, 1842.

"Every thing here is upside down, far worse than in New York. We have no money at all that we can rely upon. I went to tea one night last week thinking that I had twenty-five dollars in my pocket, and when I went out next morning, found that it was barely worth fifteen. There never was such difficulty known before.

'Eheu fugaces
labuntur anni.'"

He writes a little later to his friend Mr. May:

"*Feb.* 22, 1842.

My health, about which you so kindly express anxiety, is, I am happy to say, improving. My voice is still weak, and I suppose must remain so for a time at least. I continue to preach but once a day, and keep in the house at night. I am sometimes impatient I fear, but then again I remember the goodness of my gracious Master to me in times past. How much permission he has given me to work for him, how long my voice has been granted to me! O surely then I ought to rejoice that I am in his hands, yes, in those faithful hands, the hands of my elder brother, that was nailed for me upon the cross. That dear union of Divine strength and human weakness, (except sin) how precious is the thought of it to our hearts when we feel ourselves weak and unworthy! We have a good master to serve. The joy of serving him is wages enough.

The flare-up in my congregation has subsided; instead of doing me hurt, they have done me much good.

My heart has been very sad from the loss of many friends by death. Four or five gentlemen of high intellectual character, with whom I was in the habit of frequently associating, have been buried within a few weeks, and another now lies very low."

G. W. B. to Mrs. J. Bethune, March 14.

"Next Friday I shall be thirty-seven. I feel much older. I have grown ten years older in the last year. It is impossible for me to rise above the weakness of mind and heart. I know God is good, that I have ten thousand blessings, that I deserve none, yet I am depressed, not ungrateful, I hope, nor murmuring, but depressed."

The secession or flare-up in the congregation was occasioned by a visit to San Carlo in Naples, the largest opera-house in Europe. It was the Queen's birth-day, and there was to be a grand performance, and an assembly of all the nobility. Mrs. Bethune had a great curiosity to see the show and hear the music; and the faithful husband would not allow his invalid wife to go alone. The house was brilliantly lighted, and with their cultivated musical taste the entertainment must have been delicious. They did not go for the opera, but rather to see the great people, and soon retired. The *chaise á porteur* in which Mrs. Bethune went was likely to attract attention, and the news was straightway sent across the Atlantic. Upon Dr. Bethune's return home, and after his first sermon, he was assailed on this account by a prominent lady of his congregation. Endeavoring to explain the circumstances, she would listen to nothing, but said "That is enough, take my name off your church books." Others left with her, and the affair brought the persecuted minister to a sick bed.

The following anecdote has been carefully shaped and sent to us, giving another instance of unkind judgment of this most godly man.

"On a former visit to Europe," writes our friend "the Rev. Mr. Kirk, now (1845) Dr. Kirk of Albany, being in Paris at the same time, they used to gratify their love for music together. On a particular Sunday evening they had been singing some songs appropriate to the day, when a third party, a gentleman of many admirable qualities yet having no deep sympathy with religious men, but still professing to do justly, love mercy, and walk humbly with God (by the way the last clause is rather as the Hebrew of Micah has it, vi., 8, and in the margin *Humble thyself* to walk with God), was occupying apartments in the same house. Their exercises had ceased, and Mr. Bethune was passing to his own room. Our young friend, who now holds a prominent position in his profession, was then on his travels, and greatly was he scandalized, and at a very low figure did he estimate the genuineness of Bethune's earnestness when he overheard him on that Sunday evening in Paris, after those sacred harmonies, humming on his way the melody of an amusing secular song very common then or before in New York.

It was the mind relaxed from its attentions roaming free in its associations, the playful predominating, all unconscious to its possessor. Quite as unconscious doubtless was he of the tune he struck upon as of the listener, and of the impression he was making, or that the incident was to be remembered and told again. Ah! if people had known the man in his close walk with God how would he have been saved from this censorious spirit.

About this time he was frequently called to meet Dr. Stephen H. Tyng on great public occasions. They were the leading ministers of the city, both in the prime of life; sometimes they would indulge in sallies of wit directed against each other. It is related that one year at the conclusion of the Anniversaries, Dr. Tyng expressed the great pleasure that he had derived from the meetings; the union of Christians here giving him a sweet foretaste of that perfect communion which would be formed in heaven; when he was unfortunate enough to hint that all the good people would come to his stand-point and occupy themselves with prayer-books. Instantly Dr. Bethune was on his feet. "He felt exactly the same delight as his Reverend Brother, in the privilege of mingling with believers, the joy of union in the Lord; and it brought vividly before him the idea of that great heavenly concert which had been so beautifully described by the preceding speaker, but he concluded there was one thought that had never before occurred to his mind, that in heaven all the Christians would become "Dutch Reformed." It is needless to add that the audience were convulsed with laughter at this most ridiculous proposition.

In April, the hospitality of Dr. Bethune's house was offered to Mar Johanan, the Nestorian Bishop ; a truly pious man, who became so fond of his host, that he could not be persuaded to change his residence during his stay in Philadelphia.

In the summer of this year, he visited Boston and mingled freely with the celebrities there. Speaking of the Phi Beta Kappa, he says: "Mr. W. B. Reed did capitally with his oration," and he adds, "certainly I never heard more wit in the same time from the different speakers. It was a constant coruscation. I had to speak among the rest, and they say I did pretty well, but it was totally unexpected to me, and I was miserably frightened. I have received much attention from literary men and others, indeed my time has been constantly occupied. Bancroft, the historian, has been indefatigable in his attentions. Mr. Justice Story has also been very kind. I spent an evening with Allston, the great painter of this country, and have been all to-day and yesterday looking at his and other pictures; there are a great many good ones in Boston. Prescott sent me a kind message, but I have been unable to see him or Dana. I have been invited in the evening by a Mrs. S., sister-in-law of our Mrs. S. Mrs. L., (wife of the eminent lawyer) Mrs. H., who is the very sweet wife of a most accomplished young man, and Mr. Abbot Lawrence have paid me attention.

G. W. B. TO MISS C——M——. "PHILADELPHIA, *September* 28.

MY DEAR CHILD: I have really been trying to find time for an epistolary chat with you ever since I received your last and abounding letter, the more welcome because abounding, but I have not had a moment's leisure except when completely tired of holding the pen, and unfit to think. I am writing now with a sermon just brought to its divisions, looking up imploringly in my face; that must be finished, and another, with diverse other things, before Sunday. I am also busy upon my lectures, the four for the Athenian Institute, which require much time in searching out references and in making plain my style upon such abstract subjects. I have also to write within two weeks the first lecture of the season for the Sunday school teachers, who turn out in great numbers, and expect something elaborate. All this and much more could be done very well if I had my time without interruption, but you know how it is here. I want very much to get at my book on the angels, which I am determined (Providence permitting) to write this season. I have become so full on the subject that the distension is painful.

By the way, speaking of books puts me in mind of Tayler Lewis, whom you spoke of in a letter sometime since as being a neighbor of yours. You may well like his 'Believing Spirit,' (is not that the title?) for it is a glorious burst of high philosophical feeling. No doubt Plato was wrong in many things, he was not the sober, unromantic though earnest thinker that his master was, but his immortal longings were very noble. Transcendentalism is platonism run mad, and yet, transcendentalism, mad and mischievous as it is, has done much good in Boston, and bids fair to destroy old Unitarianism by spiritualizing the reasonings of people. Unitarianism is the offspring of materialism, and the day of materialism is wellnigh at an end.

The Synod made me one of their committee to select hymns for a Sunday school book. At first I thought I would have nothing to do with it, as we can not have a better book than the American Union's. But then I thought again, it will add so many to the hymns appointed to be sung in our churches. Now here 's a chance for *you*. Mark for me all the hymns you love, and your father loves, and your mother loves, and your sisters love, that the object can allow, and we will try to get in as many as we can and have nice times in singing them by and by. Give me some of your own also. Just put on a paper the numbers and then mark the book in which they are.

Your punning in your last about my Phi Beta Kappa toast was

*Kap*ital. Dr. Johnson himself could not say Phi! upon such wit, but would exultingly exclaim of you, Let the *Pun* dits try to Beta (beat her). But really this is terrible. My trying to equal you reminds me that the over-ambitious are liable to the fate of Esop's frog and steam boilers. You will not believe me the less, because I put it just at the close, that I shall be very happy, and I am sure my dear wife to whom you have been such a comfort will be, to have you with us this winter. Come as soon as you can, and thank your kind parents in our name for letting you come. Love to all.

Yours very sincerely, G. W. B."

The month of September, was marked by the delivery of the discourse on the "Eloquence of the Pulpit," before the Porter Rhetorical Society of the Theological Seminary at Andover. This oration has the distinction of being the longest, if not the greatest, of his printed addresses.

MRS. J. B. TO G. W. B. "*December* 30.

I write to state that Miss Murray called to ask if it would be agreeable to you to preach the sermon for the widows in the Dutch Church, Lafayette Place. Dr. Knox expressed a wish to have it there. Dr. Potts also said he would like to have you in his church; of course I said Lafayette would be the most suitable. I heard Dr. Potts preach two charity sermons last Sabbath; both admirable, one for Home Missionaries in his own church which brought out $500, the other in Hutton's church in the evening; text, 'He hath dispersed, he hath given to the poor.' . . . . In speaking of relieving the wants of the poor, he said we ought not merely to supply their immediate wants, but endeavor to elevate. Now a political economist would rather take another view; endeavor to sustain and prevent from falling into irremediable indigence. At least this must first be done."

This letter relates to Dr. Bethune's sermon before the Widows' Society; and his provident mother gives him full advice concerning the way in which to preach it.

G. W. B. TO MRS. J. B. "*April* 30, 1843.

We are surrounded by excitements with reference to the Episcopal Controversy, and certainly the tendency that way is checked, but the fashionable world is on their side. I am sick of the whole business, and have been busy preaching justification by faith."

The controversy thus alluded to, was the famous one between Drs. Potts and Wainwright, originating in the sentiment uttered by Hon. Rufus Choate, in his celebrated oration before the New England Society, delivered in the old Broadway Tabernacle, Dec. 20, 1842, 'A church without a Bishop, and a State without a King.' There were several points in it which must have made it a peculiar trial to Dr. Bethune. Dr. Potts was the pastor of his mother, and they were frequently brought into the closest relations, while Dr. Wainright was a most intimate friend. Perhaps there were few houses in New York where Dr. Bethune was so frequently and generously entertained, as at that of his Episcopal brother. The debate waxed hot and wrathy, and good Dr. Potts, with all his strength of argument and classic beauty of style, did not shew the same dexterity in management as distinguished his acute assailant; and the proud Presbyterian banner for a time passed under a shadow. A caricature appeared of a man hurling a big wheel at a large assembly of jars, which were thrown into great consternation.

Short sketches of the more distinguished public characters now appeared in the New York Sun. In this gallery our illustrious Doctor shone conspicuously. "I send you," he writes to his mother, October 28, 1843, "for your *amusement*, the sketch of your *son* in the *Sun*, the man in the moon is nothing to such a solar luminary. It is perfectly ridiculous." This paper, while it has little merit in itself, yet serves to show the high position he already occupied in the public view. During one of his summer excursions in Pennsylvania, he came in the vicinity of a preacher of the doctrine of "Perfection," and was led by curiosity to attend his lecture. These men are not settled preachers, but rove about the country addressing such audiences as they can collect, assuming an air of superior virtue, and unsettling the minds of good people, by extravagant views. On this occasion the preacher had his house full, and Dr. Bethune found it more agreeable to take his position at a window. The argument being ended, an invitation was given to any one present to reply ; this was done for effect, as it was quite certain that in a plain country audience, no one would be prepared to make a speech. But, to the dismay of the orator, a clear voice from the window rang through the church :

> "Paul said in his Epistle to the Galatians, that when Peter was come to Antioch, Paul withstood him to the face, because he was to be blamed. Now if Peter was right, then Paul was wrong, if Paul was right, then Peter was wrong. One of these great Apostles must have been imperfect."

The Perfectionist, not seeing the person who spoke, and confused with the well-made point, cried out, "Is that the voice of Satan, or one of his imps that I hear?" Our brave Doctor, thus challenged, quickly presented himself to the people. Announcing his well-known name, he said, that the simple Scripture he had quoted, refuted the long harangue, and advised them all to go home and not be disturbed by such folly. Wherever the man afterwards went, he had dinned into his ears, "If Paul was right, then Peter was wrong, and if Peter was right, then Paul was wrong."

For some years there had existed in Philadelphia a spirit of lawlessness, which was rather encouraged than subdued by the weak City Government. The Native American party was now putting on its strength, and as its efforts were directed against the foreign element in the population, its advance created a corresponding bitterness of feeling on their part. An important election was now in prospect, and animosity ran high, until in May, 1844, the forces came into actual conflict. For some days the streets of that city were turned into a theatre of civil war. As nearly as we remember, the Romish party took the lead in aggressive movement, and the discovery of a large number of fire-arms which had been concealed in the church of St. Philip de Neri, excited the most extravagant fears among the Americans. The riots now assumed more alarming proportions; the military were called out, and many of the mob were shot down before the disturbance was quelled. A reference to these disorders occurs in the following letter:

G. W. B. TO MRS. J. B. "*May* 21, 1844.

MY DEAREST MOTHER: You will be glad to hear that we are all well, after the exciting times through which we have passed. Persons at a distance, I find, estimate our danger to have been greater than we thought it ourselves. It was very dreadful to hear the roar, but the noise came not near us, and, perhaps, we never were safer, because guarded on every hand by vigilant patrols. The catholic population are prodigiously frightened, and they ought to be, as it was their outrageous and murderous violence, which led to all the mischief. The disgrace is great, but I cannot doubt that the effect in the long run will be good."

At this exciting period, perhaps a little earlier, Dr. Bethune delivered the annual sermon before "The Foreign Evangelical Society," which was organized to oppose the power of

Popery. The text was 2. Cor. ix., 8 – 14, the subject, "The strength of Christian Charity." It was a most elaborate production, and while teaching love to all, it was a strong blow aimed at the Romish system:

"But the advocate of this cause may take yet higher ground. It is, as we have proved, indispensable to the triumph of evangelical truth, that its friends be united in catholic love, and concert of action. We must make practical that article of our faith, which holds to one church, and one communion of saints. The hosts of anti-Christian Rome are many, but never divided. One heart, beating within the Vatican, circulates one zeal through all the monstrous body, which returns again to feed the fountain of its pernicious life. Popery knows no country, but mingles with all people; speaks all languages, but one creed; shouts for democracy in America, and excommunicates the liberals of Spain; demands repeal for Ireland, and arrests in France the movement of July; tolerates no other religion when it has the power, and whimpers of persecution if, in Protestant lands, the Bible is read in the schools. It speaks from the imperial city, and in all the world, cardinal and prelate, and monk and priest and penitent own, by mystic sign and ready genuflexion, devout submission. Its eyes are upon every man; its voice is heard in royal cabinets and republican legislatures; its hands tamper with the absolute sceptre and pollute the ballot box; its learning gives tutors to the children of the great, and opens free schools of error for the children of the many; its charities mingle the poison of idolatry with bread for the hungry and medicines for the sick. Everywhere it is one, though in a thousand shapes. Who can avoid admiration of the vastness, the energy, and the system of its combination! No wonder they are so strong, when they are so united.

Brethren, let the tactics of an enemy teach us the method of success which the Gospel has taught in vain. There are portions of the Christian world not papal, whose narrow bigotry refuses union with us; but what, except unworthy suspicions and weakness of faith, prevents a catholicism of evangelical servants under one Head and High Priest, Jesus? Why should we know country, or language, or race, when we are children of one Father and servants of a mission to the world?

Let us also consider the opportunities and means of usefulness which our European brethren enjoy. The fabrics of superstition which here are new and modified, there are crumbling to ruins, tottering in decayed ugliness to their fall. The people more than suspect the alliance of priesthood and tyranny to grind them in bondage. Every blow now aimed at the despot, strikes the bigot ministers of a desecrated cross. If the Bible be not recognized as the charter of freedom, the right to read it will be claimed as the privilege of freemen. The sympathies of every liberal heart are with a free religion, every advance of popular rights opens the way for the Gospel, and each hour is big with portents of far-spreading changes.

I would not speak in disparagement of learning with proper limits as an aid to religion. But the church has too much idolized learning and authority, ever since the Reformation. And what has been the consequence? In university after university, on the continent of Europe, professors of theology have substituted a proud rationalism for the child-like faith of Jesus; and still more recently the most venerable seat of learning in Britain has startled the Protestant world with the bad design of uniting learning, genius and taste, in a conspiracy to bring back the ages of darkness upon the world, when the few ruled the many and fattened the priesthood. Popery again uplifts her bruised and brazen face in hope, as she sees one so hoary with years entering her noviciate, aping her pretensions, copying her garments, and practising her mummeries; boasting her titles, bearing aloft her symbols, and attempting, with ridiculous failure, the thunder of her anathemas. Not a few Christians prognosticate a general mischief, and would invoke some Christian Hercules to slay the Hydra that comes forth from deeper shades than the Lernæan swamp to ravage the Church.

Our friends in France and Switzerland have taught us better means and better hopes, by sending an army of simple men, with no other weapon than the pure Gospel on the holy page; and God, who blessed the rod of Moses, and the hammer of Jael, and the labours of primitive Christianity, has blessed, and will bless, the colporteurs with their Bibles and their Tracts. Already they diffuse the holy leaven. Already have many souls been brought to God. Already does superstition gnash her teeth, as she feels the net drawn closer and closer around her by the multitudes of these faithful men. Let us but increase the army as we may, and Babylon herself shall fall before them. Strength is in their weakness, for the excellency of the power is of God.

Consider, also, our deep interest in their successes. Already do many Christians tremble at the incursions of popery upon our own soil. A little while since, some of us may have smiled at these fears as visionary. The light of the nineteenth century seemed too great in this land of free thought to allow the influence of such superstition over a single mind not educated under it from early life. But have we not seen within a few years past, thousands of converts flocking round the standard of a vulgar, ignorant, and vile leader, whose pretensions to prophecy would have been contemptible had they not been so mischievous. Have we not also been astonished at the defection of grave and educated men from the simple Gospel, as it is written in God's own word, to the authority of shadowy tradition; who, while they insist upon a church in a priesthood of doubtful genealogy, would revive the aristocracy of ancient Pharisaism, which accounted the common people as little better than profane. The growth of Mormonism among the vulgar, and of this perversion of Christian doctrine which has no name of sufficient dignity for utterance here among the more refined, shew us too plainly that the human mind in no circumstances can be preserved from superstition except by the Spirit of God.

We are not then safe from Romanism. Every eastern wind wafts hitherward its priests and adherents laden with gifts to corrupt our people. Already has the cry been heard arousing Christians to defence of truth and freedom. But whence do they come. Why stand we only on the defensive. Why may we not cross the sea and besiege Carthage? Why not plant our vanguards on the passes of the Alps, send our spies into the very camp of the enemy, and await the happy moment (which, if it please God, is not distant,) when, like Atilla, though with better weapons and higher aims, we may thunder at the gates of Rome itself ? When ancient Rome fell, the empire was broken into fragments. When papal Rome falls, popery will soon be no more. One blow on the head is worth a hundred at its extremities. One thrust to its heart, and all the convolutions of its myriad folds will relax in death. Are there no smooth stones in 'the brook that flows fast by the oracles of God'? Is there no shepherd boy nor herdsman's son among those mountain Christians to wield a sling?

Christian brethren, I have done."

This sermon was originally delivered in New York, but

either this discourse, or one similar in spirit must have been spoken in Philadelphia, and produced a happy effect. Dr. Bethune seems to have consented to its publication, but upon reflection changed his mind, when we find the matter urged upon him in the following courteous letter.

HECTOR ORR TO G. W. B. "*May* 27, 1844.

REV. SIR: I have received your note instead of your MS.; no personal inconvenience will be felt through your decision, for which you certainly have high authority, since *John Knox* himself turned back from Scotland, through the advice of friends. (I had written this when Mr. Clark came in to get the 'copy'; I made him acquainted with your latest views, and he in return informed me you were most probably out of the city. My first inclination was to lay down the pen until a better excuse for using it arrived, but having thought much about the sermon and caused you to send more than once, from more than a mile's distance, 'I wish to put on record' my reasons for urging the publication.)

It has been my high privilege from early years to have intimate intercourse with some of the most devoted Christians of this my native city, an intimacy such as few without the pale of the church have enjoyed — qualifying me to some extent, to enter into the feelings of this great and venerable class at this time. The peculiar point on which attention was first excited in this movement — the banishment of the Bible — touched a chord in these men's breasts such as is unknown in the moral anatomy of the demagogue; next, the murder of their friends and neighbors wrung this chord to torture, and their desertion by the secular press completed the outrage; and while suffering under this delirium, infidel eavesdroppers have been apt to catch their exclamations and report them as 'the sentiments of the party.'

To you, much honored friend, who, through elegant leisure or refined toil, have long been familiar with 'man's duty and the reasons of it,' *I* need not stop in my drudgery to say that this fever in the whole evangelical community is undesirable, or that it would be high Christian kindness to allay it; but this fact may have escaped you, that nothing well adapted to this end has yet appeared, except your sermon. In my short experience I have found it a first requisite to the pacification of chafed human nature, to evince a hearty appreciation of the *exciting wrong*. Thence springs that confidence so indispensable to successful persuasion, through which we become willing to be led in the way of peace, which in the present crisis is so eminently the path of duty. This real sympathy with the torn heart of Philadelphia you alone have exhibited, and I sought to extend the influence of this word fitly spoken, beyond the mere compass of your voice."

About the same date wrote the Hon. Charles Sumner, of Boston:

"How exalted in the scale of beneficence is he, whose labors contribute to extend the culture and capacity of the human soul — to open new vistas of knowledge, to awaken dormant impulses and susceptibilities, to enlarge the sphere of study and action, to strengthen faith. Your generous exertions in this field, have already found a reward in the applause of good men, and in the consciousness of doing good, to which my mite can add nothing."

"From grave to gay".

G. W. B. TO MISS CAROLINE MAY. "SARATOGA SPRINGS, *Aug.* 3.

My dear child: I write to you because you sent me such a nice letter, on the first, which I received this morning, and because I wish to talk music.

I have heard Ole Bull; my ear is now vibrating with the most attenuated, sweetest, softest note it ever heard; his last this evening. He is about six feet one or two inches high, and well made, his head good though rather low, but long, and particularly square or rectangular at the sides. He wears his hair very plain and no moustache. His face is not handsome but honest, and at times intense. His music disappointed me. Ever since he came here I have been accumulating expectation, and as that has been for months, it was very high. I am disappointed. He has exceeded my highest imagination. No trick, no playing on one string, no convulsive efforts, but clear, perfect tone, steady bowing, and a perfect mastery of *all* his instruments. His opening piece was in three parts; a sweet, subdued allegro, then a very pure adagio, and then a graceful pastoral; in the first, he played at one time a complete trio with the bow, each part distinctly marked, and the harmony admirable and somewhat complicated; in the second he had a pizzicato passage beyond any thing I could ever dream of; it was better, yes, better than any harp, and while this was going on with his finger, his bow was busy with delicious, steady accompaniment to the staccato movement. The last part was distinguished by a passage so like a piccolo, that no piccolo was ever so good. His next piece was his Carnival of Venice. His imitations were of Punch and Judy in their box; you could almost hear the words. Then a lady sang who was very frightened, you could hear her gasping for breath; then a bird sang; any canary would have broken its heart with envy to hear itself out-warbled, and all this on the theme of "O come to me when daylight sets." After this he played a mother's prayer; slow, sweet, solemn, and reverent, than tender, pleading, earnest — then anxious, deprecatory, and then by chromatic crescendo, shivering with importunate supplication, until the mother's heart was poured out, and peace filled it, and she hushed herself to repose. His last piece on the bill was a warlike Polacca, various in character, and bringing all his powers in play, the last twenty bars of rich, steady bowing the very best of the evening, and beyond conception good. An encore brought him out again, when he played Hail Columbia and Yankee Doodle, but not as astonishingly as Max Bohrer."

We give here another letter on the same subject, to the same young music-loving friend.

"PHILADELPHIA, *Nov.* 11.

MY DEAR CARO: (Is it the 11?) (Monday it is.) I should have written before, but have been sick in bed with a cold, not aple to preach any yesterday, and only once the Sunday previous and Mrs. B. has been and is still (for I am better,) worse than I, with the same influenza. So it is when *you* are not here.

"*There's nae luck about the house*" when Caro's in New York.

I thank you for your kinkness in writing, your letters are alweys welcome for your sake and their own. Let me see what I can tell you in return.

We can get no organist to suit us: M. L. has turned out an astonishing genius, and we think of trusting to him, at least till we can find one really excellent. Maggie S. and I went some time since to hear an Englishman (and I think a Jew), Henry Philips, sing Handel, and liked him very well. He told us, by the way, that Catalani and Malibran and Paganini were of Jewish blood. I knew Rossini, Meyerbeer, Mendelssohn, Braham &c., were, but never thought the three names above could be.

'Apropos des bottes', as our friend Dr. B. says, talking of Paganini puts me in mind of what happened last Monday to Mrs. B., at about one o'clock. In came Mr. Scherr and, and, and, — *Ole Bull* — and, and, and, his VIOLIN!! I had said to Mr. Scherr, a day or two before, that Mrs. B. would be so happy if she could hear Ole Bull, when he said he would ask him, and on Saturday he sent me word that he would come on Monday at noon; and (being told to ask nobody) Mrs. E. came over to be the dowager, and Maggie came to be the young lady, and good Mr. Nevius, the missionary, happened to be here, and Ole Bull after chatting awhile with Mrs. B., who sat in her wheeled chair to prove that she was an invalid, opened the violin case, and said that his 'effects' were calculated for a greater distance than he could have in Mrs. B's little parlor, and so, to Annie's utter consternation, he went into the back room, which, like Richard III., was but half made up. He stood before the wardrobe, the doors open between the rooms, and played — first the famous Melancolie, with the tremolo passage, and then an air or two varied in the most exquisite style; then we all thanked him, Mrs. B. with tears in her eyes (I told her to cry if she could). Then he began again and played 'Auld Robin Gray;' you could tell the very place where her father 'broke his arm,' and where 'we tore ourselves away'. From this he passed on to an air of Rossini, and then went into the best parts of the 'Carnival of Venice.' I have heard him play three times in public, but never better than here. Now think, my little lady, what you missed by not being here. Maggie sang 'Solitario,' and then he promised Mrs. B. to come in the evening and play 'The Mother's Prayer', which needs a piano accompaniment, so please to come and play it. Annie thought Bull was well enough, but that Miss S. was better than all the fiddles (fiddles was the word) in the world!!!

I told her that Bull was the *bow* ideal of music — but she did not take. 'Dear o me,' I have filled my sheet with Ole Bull, which I did not mean to have done.

I am very glad Dempster was grateful enough to you for the trouble you took, to go up and sing for you. I should like to have his airs to my songs.

Here is a letter all about music, as if I thought of nothing else; but somehow music and Caro always go together in my thoughts. *Caro* and *caro lling.*

My best regards (Mrs. B. is asleep) to all your kind family, and believe me as ever, my dear child,

Your affectionate friend,

GEORGE W. BETHUNE."

W. R. DEMPSTER TO G. W. B. "*October* 8, 1844.

Rev. and Dear Sir: I received your valuable and agreeable correspondence on my arrival home, and ought to have acknowledged the favor before this time, but I was desirous first to be able to give you some account of my progress. I am now extremely happy in being able to do so, so far satisfactorily. The four songs which you sent are all beautiful. I have set two of them. '*I hae a cup,*' I have sung before the public, and it has made quite a sensation, it is constantly encored. I think I have been more than usually successful in giving it an air. Mr. Lewis Gaylord Clark says it is a perfect gem, and wishes to publish it in the Knickerbocker. I told him I was not at liberty to use your name with it, but that I would furnish him with a copy. The other one I have set begins 'I know not if thou'rt beautiful,' which to my thinking is a beautiful song, but not so effective as the other, although I have not yet sung it in public.

Upon reflection I feel a little delicacy in resetting the first one, as the former composer may think it invidious in me to do so, but we shall see. I may try my hand on it if I do not publish it.

The other one about the '*gloaming*' which you have been kind enough to write expressly for me, is truly beautiful, and I wish to take my happiest moods and greatest pains to make it shine out.

I know it will be pleasing to you to hear that I have been so successful thus far. I am truly delighted with the 'cup o' gude red wine,' and hope to let you judge of its flavor as soon as I come to Philadelphia."

In November of this year (1844) another membership was added to his already long list. He was elected by the Historical Society of Pennsylvania, and having been invited soon afterward to a public dinner by the New York Historical Society, made an extempore speech at that banquet. He had contemplated one of a different character; but finding that the tone of the meeting was not what he had expected, he, with native versatility, changed his line and disappointed the Manhattan audience of the racy references to the original Dutch colony of New York, and the dear old Knickerbockers, which they had naturally looked for. The meeting took altogether too much of a Plymouth Rock, Mayflower, Pilgrim Father tone to suit New Yorkers, and Hendrick Hudson was cruelly ignored. The opinion gained head that this was a New England festival, and to correct this a copy of Dr. Bethune's intended speech was requested for publication.

G. W. B. to Mrs. J. B. "*Jan.* 1, 1845.

One of those many things which will occur just at the moment you would rather they would not, prevented this being on your table this morning, about the same time that I received your most affectionate and gratifying letter. Still, though you may not hear it until the 2nd, it is in the morning of the 1st day of the New Year, that I call upon God to bless my dear mother, and thank Him for having made me her son. May His angel, the covenant one, be near you to sustain, comfort, and direct the steps of your age as He has been your guardian and guide from your youth up.

As I grow older and see more of mankind, I can better appreciate the restraining and converting influence of religion, while I cherish more fondly the few whose affection and piety have rendered them dear and useful to me. You, my mother, have been to me more than a mother only, you have been my teacher, my counsellor, my considerate friend. I do not know whether I ever made an allusion to it before, though it is likely I have, the association being strong in my mind; but there is an expression of Cicero's, in reference to Tiberius Gracchus, that has always seemed to me as peculiarly applicable to myself, and true of me in a far higher sense than of him. 'He was the offspring,' says Cicero, 'not more of her womb than of her soul, and nourished by her instruction as much as by her bosom.' I give a free translation, but the thought. I am persuaded that I owe you for that which makes the life I derived from you, under God, most valuable, and there is not a thought that I give to you, but makes me more grateful, and you more dear.

This is the honest outpouring of my heart, dear mother, an expression, which you must allow me, once a year, of my true feelings. Would that I were near you, with the opportunity to show by acts, what now only words must show, how much I consider my life to belong to you, and how much my happiness is wrapped up in yours.

I am not yet well, having a very severe cold, which I cannot succeed in shaking off; but have been busy at this busy season. Our Christmas passed off very well, the children singing my hymn and *tune.* We had a small, but very gratifying addition to our communion on Sunday, four on confession, and the same by letter; few, but *good* people."

G. W. B. to Mrs. J. B. "Phila., *March* 22, 1845.

My Dear Mother: You might have supposed that my first wish on the morning of my birthday, was to have written to you, as in other circumstances it would have been my first duty; but it has rarely happened in all my pastoral life, that so much engrossing and exciting engagement, has been crowded into one day. I was, between 10 A.M., and 7 P.M., at *three* death-beds; two of the persons, it is true, still survive, but with no possibility of recovery. They are dying, and have been for a week. A visit to another in very deep and peculiar affliction, added to my trials, so that I had not a moment to write, or if I had, not the heart.

Yet I did not forget you, my mother; but remembered you where I loved best to remember those I loved best, and loved best to be remembered. My days are fast fleeting. I feel that I am no longer young; that my step is now down the hill. For several years past, death and eternity have been growing more familiar to me; before, they were rather matters of faith, now they have a real, almost sensible presence. It is well it is so, so that our estimate of life be honest, not sickly, and our thought of the future hopeful, not gloomy.

I am rejoiced that your anxiety about the Orphan Asylum is relieved.

God may have already sent his angels (for I believe that all Providence is in the hands of angels) to bring you comfort. I wish that I had more to comfort me. My communion is drawing nigh, and, as yet, I know of but one person who is coming forward on confession."

With all the success that had crowned his efforts, and the general applause awarded him by the great and the good, Dr. Bethune had the modesty that graces the true scholar. Of his famous sermon before the Foreign Evangelical Society, he writes, "that it does not suit him ; he took too much pains with it. But possibly it may read better than it sounded." His mother has no regret over this feature, but replies, "You always say your sermons are not good, I am not afraid of you now." But if he fails, it is not from any lack of due diligence on his part. "I am now in my study laying out work for many weeks to come. Work is a blessed thing for us mortals, I am sure that nothing, except grace, does me more good."

We have reached the year 1845 in our track of Dr. Bethune's life and sentiments ; but eighteen years still intervene between this point and the day of his lamented death. We must hasten on and shall find it convenient to dwell less particularly than before upon the periods of quiet residence in the same place, and pay more attention to his changes of life, their causes and their consequences. On the 6th July, 1845 was pronounced the "Discourse on the duty of a Patriot" with some allusions to the life and death of Andrew Jackson. This panegyric was a labor of enthusiasm ; Jackson being a hero, and a hero of the right sort. Bethune was just the man to appreciate and praise with a will him, who, "in the darkest hour of our country's history, when a narrow sectionalism counterfeited the color of patriotic zeal, and discord shook her Gorgon locks, and men shuddered as they saw, yawning wide in the midst of our confederacy, a gulf, which threatened to demand the devotion of many a life before it would close again, sublimely proclaimed over the land that doctrine sacred as the name of Washington, '*The Union must be preserved!*' and the storm died away with impotent mutterings." This effort was published, and well received; the same may be said in a still greater degree of the "Plea for Study," delivered August 19, before the literary societies of Yale College. This plea for study is also a plea for the regimen which shall best fit man for study, a plea for exercise and fresh air, and fishing and genial society, and moderation in eating and drinking. The lecturer states facts that every one knows, that he knows are known to all; but he states them that he may urge upon his hearers the practice in accordance with them. He instances himself, a man with a constitution better adapted to follow the plough, or to sling a sledge and yet a close student, an excessive student, and worst of all a night student, yet he feels no inconvenience from it, solely, he believes, because he follows a light, regular, but not whimsically abstemious diet.

"I am happy", writes Hon. Charles Sumner, "that the master key and talisman of knowledge and scholarship is commended so persuasively as it has been by you. No person, whose soul is not of the lowest potter's clay, can read what you have said without confessing new impulses to learning and to those good habits which promote it."

"I like you, Bethune," writes Dr. G. W. Blagden, Dec. 11. "I hope the Lord will bless you. It does me good to see a frank whole-hearted minister of the Gospel now-a-days. Sometimes I have thought that I would *dare* to say to you that, in your really generous-hearted honest use of the creatures of God, particularly the weed and the thing that forms a good alliteration with it, you might go a little too far, but then again, I really like your independence so much that I doubt whether it be best. And yet you see I have done it. All I want to say is remember our 'beloved brother Paul's' doctrine of expediency, and love me as one who at this moment prays God to bless you, and make you unceasingly useful every day and year you live. I have inflicted quite a letter on you, but retaliate as soon and as long as you can."

PROF. FELTON TO G. W. B. "CAMBRIDGE, *Oct.* 10, 1845.

MY DEAR SIR: I received a copy of your Yale Discourse yesterday, just as I was getting into the omnibus. I ran over it as well as I could then, but this morning I have read it carefully through, and I cannot help writing you immediately to say how well I have been pleased by the manner and the matter of it. In particular I say a hearty amen to your views of water exercise, and Political Economy. You might, in my opinion have substituted on page 36 '*no instances*' for 'very few.' I have known a great many cases of young men, and old men, who have pretended that they were injured in health by 'hard study,' and have been sympathised with accordingly, but I never knew a single person who might not have done, without harming his health, a great deal more literary work by the application of common sense and cold water. I once had a fancy of that sort myself, but a little reflection convinced me that it was all a humbug. My Greek studies taught me that bathing and gymnastics were nearly as essential as languages and mathematics, and I devised with forethought and deliberation, a system of shower-bathing and dumb-bells, which changed me in a few weeks from a 'vertiginous' weakling unfit for anything, to a sturdy fellow, fitted, if need were, 'to sling a sledge or follow a plough.' I reverence the dumb-bells and the shower-bath, and were I a Pagan some allegorical representation of these should soon find a place in my Pantheon. I do not quite agree with you about animal food. My own experience teaches me that I am better with a moderate allowance *in the morning* as well as at noon. I can work better through the day with such a distribution of the flesh pots.

The system I mention I have now continued nearly ten years, and perhaps you remember enough of my outward man to know that I have not, any more than you, those lanthorn jaws, cadaverous sides, stooping shoulders, that narrow chest and ghostly complexion which have been considered indispensable requisites to the American literary character.

Your discourse cannot fail to do good. They need such doctrine at Yale as much as anywhere. They are too stiff, solemn, and dyspeptic. A friend of mine returning thence a short time ago, asserted as of his positive knowledge, that it was a common custom there, to take every morning a strong mixture of ramrods. How can they be cheerful with such a habit as that ?

Excuse this nonsense. I may urge in extenuation the authority of one whom you will admit to be worthy of reliance.

'Quid vetat ridentem dicere verum ? '

Thanking you for your kind attention, I am Dear Sir,

With high regard your friend,

C. C. Felton.

Geo. S. Hillard to G. W. B. "Boston, *Oct.* 13, 1845.

My Dear Bethune : I have read with great pleasure your oration delivered at New Haven. It strikes me as one of the best things you have ever done ; it is vigorous, learned, original, and true. It contains the doctrines of the true church, upon the great subject of 'study' that 'vehemens et assidua animi applicatio' as Cicero so well defines it ; only I don't know about angling. The poor fish that you pull out of the water with a hook in his gullet, might well ask if the Lord had made him a mere medicine to restore a dyspeptic scholar, and had not given him a pleasant life of his own in the silver streams. If the fish were not alive, angling would be delectable, but after reading Wordsworth's 'Hart-leap Well' I pause over the rod as well as the gun, in spite of dear old Izaak. But your counsels and your admonitions will do the boys good. As your discourse was lying on my table, a friend came in whose hobby is political economy, and he casually opened it on page 21 and read your eulogium on his favorite science with sparkling eyes, and sat down and copied the sentence and made a memorandum of the discourse with warm expressions of admiration, and a purpose of sending for it."

There is a fact about this very successful address at New Haven which it may be well to record for the benefit of literary institutions. The Doctor felt his reception to be very chilly, almost ice-cold ; there was a strange lack of interest in the orator of the day. He had to find his own way about town and when he came to the College Assembly, it presented one of the blackest looking audiences to be imagined. There was no relief in the back-ground, nothing but an array of sombre black coats, and these not easily to be moved from their quiet decorum. The President received him with a dignified bow, but not a word of sympathy consoled the sensitive heart of the speaker. He returned to his hotel, discouraged, and inquired of the clerk at what hour the first train in the morning left the city. An early hour being mentioned, he said, "Iwish to leave at that time," and speedily departed from the land of steady habits without having received the most favorable impression of Yankee hospitality.

During one of those years he was suddenly called upon to proceed to Washington, in reference to his favorite cause of Colonization. A Sunday at the Capital was quite sure to make demands on the popular preacher, and he caught up a few manuscript sermons and put them in his carpet-bag. Invited to preach in two churches, he found that only one of these sermons pleased him, which he reserved for the evening. In the morning he gave a very simple and unpretending discourse, on the "little child that our Lord set before his disciples as a pattern". The minister of this church, meeting him the next day, complained, saying, "I hear that last night you thundered and lightened in the Methodist church round the corner, but you did not take much trouble for us." The Doctor, having a modest opinion of his efforts, could make no defence ; but some months later, received, in an incidental way, a most agreeable compliment from a high quarter. A friend of his, conversing with Justice McLean, of the Supreme Court of the United States, said to him, "Since all the leading ministers of the country come here, you must have great privileges in the preaching line at Washington." "Not so much as you imagine, they all come with their grand discourses and high-flown elocution, but we have little of the simple gospel that edifies. There was, however, a man named Bethune, from Philadelphia, who pleased and profited me very much; he is a preacher of some distinction, but he took for his text, 'a little child,' and then he sought to bring all of us statesmen, judges and counsellors, to the position of little children before the Saviour; now that was a sermon to do a man's heart good."

Let preachers going to Washington gather wisdom. Manifold engagements pressed upon him, and yet he found time for the labors of authorship.

He really did dispatch a large amount of work. Besides the constant preparations necessary for a city pulpit, and care for the sick, he was engaged in extensive correspondence with home and foreign parts. There is a record of as many as forty-five letters written on a single day. Then he was expected to speak on important public occasions; he was President of the Pennsylvania Seamen's Friend's Society; a leading officer in the Colonization Society; neither did he neglect his readings of the Greek and Latin Classics; he told a friend "that, in the course of the winter, he had read through the plays of Euripides," which this friend being a ripe scholar, thought by itself a sufficient task for the season. Racy lectures must occasionally be produced; he was a frequent contributor to Magazines and Annuals, yet, in addition to all, he was able to get several volumes through the press. The first was a book of "Sermons";

"he yields to the wishes of some friends" in this publication. "The selection has been made out of the discourses preached by the author from his own pulpit, with some regard to variety, but principally, to the practical characters of their subjects." He adds with modesty, "The prospect of their being widely read, when there are so many better books, is small; yet the attempt to serve the cause of our beloved Master is pleasant, and if he smiles upon it, it will be successful, not in proportion of our talent, but of his grace." Mr. Wm. H. Prescott writes, "One does not look into a volume of sermons for novelties, yet you put your readers on trains of thoughts that are not opened every day. I have not read any thing from the pulpit for a long time that has pleased me so much, or which I think more calculated to benefit the hearers." Perhaps a more substantial compliment was given by the public in its rapid sale. "You will be pleased," he writes to his mother, "to hear that my book of sermons does so well. There must be another edition by September at farthest. My 'Fruit of the Spirit' sells steadily and well. My publishers say that they are now sure of its being a stock book; which means a book for which there will always be a good demand." In quick succession appears, "Early Lost, Early Saved." "A childless man himself," says Dr. Taylor, "it is somewhat remarkable, that in this little volume he has left one of the sweetest books of consolation for bereaved parents, founded upon an argument for the salvation of infants, which is at the same time a powerful vindication of that grand old system of doctrinal truth, taught by the Reformed Churches, which, as he declared his conviction, has been so often foully accused of consigning departed infants to a miserable eternity; but which 'affords the only satisfactory hope of their salvation,' which is by free and sovereign grace in Christ." Then followed "The History of a Penitent; a Guide for the Inquiring, in a Commentary on the One Hundred and Thirtieth Psalm." This was also the result, first, of pulpit exposition, and then of careful preparation for the press, and I need only add that it is admirably adapted to its great design."

These substantial volumes, while they increased the reputation of the author, also yielded financial gain. He made more money from them than from anything he did in the way of book making. By way of variety, we may relate that he was appointed Commissioner of the U. S. Mint, one of three to attend the annual assay and examination of the affairs of that branch of the public service; he accepted, and says he is "prepared not to be surprised at the offer of a large salary as special ambassador to the University of Timbuctoo." This important Mint function he afterwards referred to on a great public occasion. "I once," he says, "held an office under the general government, and I was offered another. The other I did not like, the first I did. It kept me five hours, and I was allowed my expenses as emolument, but as there was no omnibus riding in that direction, I did not get sixpence." On a visit to Boston, he quite startled the audience by a criticism on their book of praise. In giving out the Hymn, beginning,

"There is a fountain filled with blood"

he found that the last verse had been altered and read thus:

"And when this feeble stammering tongue
Lies silent in the grave,
Then in a nobler sweeter song,
I'll sing thy power to save."

"I should like to know," he sternly said, "who has had the presumption to alter Cowper's Hymn; the choir will please sing the hymn as the poet wrote it."

About the close of 1846, he received from President Polk the appointment of Chaplain, to the Military Academy at West Point, and there is much proof of his popularity at the White House. The office, although possessing many advantages, could not seduce him from his pastoral work. A letter from Littell, of the "Living Age," embodies a very neat compliment to Dr. Bethune, calling his letters a "brook by the way. I wish you would write to me at any time when you see any thing which you would especially like to see in the Living Age: I wish to put myself into magnetic communication with as much intellect and heart as I can, for the *good of the public.* I hope this plea may get me a line from you now and then."

CHAPTER VIII.

ART OF ANGLING — FOREST LIFE.

In the year 1846, the new edition of Izaak Walton's Complete Angler, appeared with the Instructions of Cotton, and, as says the preface, " with copious notes, for the most part original; a bibliographical preface giving an account of fishing and fishing books, from the earliest antiquity to the time of Walton, and a notice of Cotton and his writings, to which he added an appendix, including illustrative ballads, music, papers on American fishing, and the most complete catalogue of books on angling ever printed."

"For such an undertaking," writes Dr. Dunglison, "no one could have been better qualified and prepared. Fond of the sport to enthusiasm, perfectly acquainted with his authors, and possessed of an admirable piscatorial library, diligently accumulated at considerable expense,* he brought to the subject an amount of familiar knowledge, and opportunities for research, possessed by few, if by any, in this country. The references, with rare exceptions, were verified by his own examination, whilst for the literary annotations he held himself responsible. Many of these, especially of a philological character, were the subjects of occasional playful, but delightful and profitable correspond-

* The number of works that he had collected on fishing and kindred topics, composed about seven hundred volumes, and was probably the most perfect collection of the kind in the world.

ence between the writer of this notice and himself, and the whole work affords abundant evidence of rare learning, and ample practical knowledge."

That much time and pains must have been given to the above work is evident, and when it was objected that this occupation interfered with the duties of his sacred office, the doctor replied that he had accomplished it at odd seasons, while other people would have been looking out of their windows. The following bit of erudition is a specimen of the labor expended on his references.

"NEW YORK, *March* 19, 1847.

REV. AND DEAR SIR: The passage of Aristotle to which you refer, does not occur in any part of his extant writings. Heyne alludes to it in his note on Iliad. xxiv, 81., but merely mentions Plutarch as his authority. If Heyne could not find it, we may be very sure that it has not come down to us. Heyne's words are as follows: 'Melior interpretatio de cornu bovino Aristoteli deberi *discimus ex Plutarcho*, de Sollert. Animal. p. 976, ubi ejus auctoritate refellit acceptionem de pilis bovinis e quibus hamum contextum esse putarint alii.'

The passage of Plutarch occurs in the 24th chapter of the treatise de Sollert. Animal., (vol. iv. part ii , p. 961, seq. of Wyttenbach's edition of the Moralia; and vol. x., p. 65, seq, of Reiske's edition of the entire works) and in it, after giving the opinion of some, that κέρας in the passage of Homer, means τρίχα, and that the reference is to hair line, he quotes the more correct explanation of Aristotle. According to the old Stagyrite, a small horn (κεράτιον) was put around the line just above the hook, to prevent the fish from biting it off. This solves the mystery. Plutarch's words are as follows: 'Αριστοτέλης δέ φησι μηδὲν ἐν τούτοις λέγεσθαι σοφὸν ἢ περιττόν, ἀλλὰ τῷ ὄντι κεράτιον περιτίθεσθαι πρὸ τοῦ ἀγκίστρου περὶ τὴν ὁρμιάν, ἔπειτα πρὸς ἄλλο ἐρχόμενοι διεσθίουσι.

It appears to me that Heyne has made a slip in his note, and that for '*hamum*' he ought to have written '*funiculum*,' for the Greek of Plutarch is, θριξὶν οἴονται πρὸς τὰς ὁρμιὰς χρῆσθαι τοὺς παλαιούς. This, however, does not affect the main point.

With many thanks for your kind opinion of your old friend, and for your allowing me to claim some little part of the early training of one as eminent as yourself,

I remain, very truly, &c.,

CHAS. ANTHON.

REV. DR. BETHUNE, PHILADELPHIA."

For the use that is made of this morsel of scholarship, see the Bibliographical preface to the Complete Angler, p. ix.

On the same subject Dr. Bethune wrote to Charles Lanman Esq., Librarian at Washington:

"The truth is, I am very modest as an angler, but have exerted myself to the utmost in the literary illustration of our father's delightful book. As I wrote Mr. Duyckinck, it is impossible to make a *fishing*-book, especially an American fishing-book, of Walton. Permit me to say, that, though I am far from being ashamed of the gentle art, I do not wish to have my name formally associated with the book, as it will not appear on the title page, and whatever comments are made on the American edition, (particularly as to my part of it) I should like them confined to the literary character. You will understand my reason for this. My library is very good, piscatorially the best in the country, and my notes have been accumulating for years."

This edition of Walton is conceded in England, as well as in this country, to be the best one issued.

The sport of angling was a great aid to him in getting through his year's work. He always had an amusement to turn to; the course of his thoughts was completely changed, the mind relaxed, and the body restrung. We can give the testimony of eye-witnesses to the intense bodily and spiritual enjoyment, which the return of the fishing season always provided for him. We say spiritual, for who does not know how a pleasant book is enhanced by green fields and summer floods; and our angler appears to have had a small library in his head. We quote the words of his companion, Rev. Joshua Cooke.

"Dr. Bethune was an ardent *lover* of *Nature.*

He was not a worshipper of Nature. He had none of that regard for it which some of our day seem disposed to nurse up into idolatry; at least, into a feeling that if Nature be not divine, they know nothing more so. Of that religion which, to the call of a sinning man for bread of the soul, would offer Nature, give him a stone, our honored friend had not an element.

But Nature, as the beautiful and glorious handiwork of One whom he loved better than Nature; and as created, preserved, multiplied into her manifold forms, expressly for the honor of His name, in the happiness of His creatures: Nature, as such, I have never seen more fervently loved, and more eagerly resorted to, than by Dr. Bethune. It was not as her processes are developed under human training that he sought her, but as she exists in the forms and sounds of the perfect wilderness. And he sought them there in yearly pilgrimages, far from the haunts of men; associating with his enjoyment of wood and stream that of his favorite recreation, angling. There, his tent pitched, his camp-fire kindled; his implements of recreation around him; and what was more than all to him, with genial companions, he would look forth on wood, and stream, and lake, with a happiness known only to the lover of Nature; and which, in him, none will ever forget who had the happiness of seeing him there. And, as he felt deeply, so he would speak eloquently of the delightful calm, the unbroken repose; the freshness of all, as if just from the divine hand; and of the wondrous change in all this, from the excitements and conventionalities of life among men. He did not dislike men; he did not dislike society. On the contrary, he had a peculiar interest in being among those to whom he could listen with pleasure, and by whom he could be himself heard. And it was the one desire of his life to preach the gospel. This, also, made the concourse of men welcome to him, for he could discharge his office, and hope to save some.

But, after months of duty, in its routine; and, especially, if there had been trial of feeling, or controversy, he repaired to the stream and forest as a refuge and rest from excitement; and as one who found in their quiet, gentle, changeless beauty, a balm. He has embodied this feeling in a few of his own beautiful lines, now lying by me.

'Oh, for the rush of our darling stream,
With its strips of virgin meadow;
For the morning beam, and the evening gleam,
Through the deep forest shadow!
For our dovelike tent, with white wings bent,
To shield us from the weather,
Where we make our bed, of hemlock spread,
And sleep in peace together.

Oh, for the pure and sinless wild,
Far from the city's pother,
Where the spirit mild of Nature's child,
On the breast of his holy mother,
In the silence sweet, may hear the beat
Of her loving heart and tender;
Nor wish to change the greenwood range
For worldly pomp and splendor!

Oh, for the laugh of the merry loon!
For the chant of the fearless thrushes!
Who pipe their tune to sun and moon,
In clear and liquid gushes!
For the roar of floods, and the echoing woods,
And the whisperings, above us,
Of the twilight breeze, thro' the trembling trees —
Like words of those that love us!'

To write such lines, one must not only have looked upon such scenes, but have looked with the most hearty appreciation, and the most entire enjoyment. His feelings were so much in unison with everything around him, that he counted himself but as a part of the scene, or as a child visiting his mother. How beautifully l as he expressed this in the second of the above stanzas! All, who have spent nights in the wilderness, 'making their bed of hemlock spread,' will remember how, in the stillness so weird and solemn, one's own pulsation becomes, not only to fancy, but almost to conviction, the throbbing of the earth he lies on. And so,

'The spirit mild of nature's child,
On the breast of his holy mother,
In the silence sweet, may hear the beat
Of her loving heart and tender.'

His unconsciously delicate sense and discrimination were very apparent in his relish for fine poetry. It led him not only to produce much himself that was fine, but still more to enjoy the productions of others, and to love the very man for the thing he had produced. When he met with a piece where true poetical conception was expressed in becoming form and harmony, it was, with him, as when a diver finds a pearl. With what enthusiasm and happy rendering, would he repeat such pieces as the following, from the Englishman Stoddart:

'Oh, waken winds, waken, the waters are still;
And the sunlight, in silence, reclines on the hill;
And the angler is waiting beside the green springs,
For the low, welcome sound of your wandering wings.

His rod lies beside him; his tackle's unfreed;
And his withe-woven pannier is flung on the mead;
And he looks on the lake, through its fane of green trees,
And sighs for the curl of the soft southern breeze.

Calm-bound is the form of the water-bird there;
And the spear of the rush stands erect in the air;
And the dragon-fly roams o'er the lily beds gay,
Where basks the bold pike in the sun-smitten bay.

Oh, waken, winds, waken, wherever asleep!
On the cloud, in the mountain, or down in the deep!
The angler is waiting beside the green springs
For the low, whispering sound of your wandering wings.'

I think I see him now, as seated under the shade of our pleasant woodland home, and looking out on the little lake, so in keeping with the above piece, he would dwell on its fine alliteration and musical flow; but still more, on its exquisite pencilling of natural features. 'Don't you see', he would say, 'the impatience of the man as he looks at the glare of the sun, and the mirror-like surface, and knows that it would be as useless to make a cast of his fly before the eagle-eyed trout, under these conditions, as to make it into the woods behind him. And then, the water bird, the loon, or the diver, far out on the water; *really* asleep, but *seemingly* unable to stir till wind or wave should move; *calm-bound.* And the rush'; and here his finger, graceful and flexible as the rush itself, would shoot upward; 'the rush, the most pliant and yielding of all things, now upright as the bole of the pine, so still is the air. And the *sun-smitten* bay; the heat pouring down as a molten substance, and holding the helpless waters waveless as under pressure of a burden!'

He was equally sensitive to the devotional and the sublime. We had spent a Sabbath evening, four of us, in one of the tents, from dusk till near midnight, in delightful conversation on religion, and religious experience, when one of the party, alluding to the day, asked the doctor, if he remembered the fine lines of Spenser;

> 'Then 'gan I think on that which Nature said
> Of that same time when no more change shall be;
> But stedfast rest of all things, firmly fixed
> Upon the pillours of Eternitie;
> For all that moveth doth in change delight;
> But thenceforth all shall rest eternally
> With Him, that is the God of Sabbaoth hight.
> Of that great Sabbaoth, God, grant me that
> Sabbath's sight.'

The Doctor was visibly affected. He arose, and said, 'Where did you find those lines?' 'In the opening of the unfinished Canto of the Faerie Queen.' 'Beautiful, beautiful,' said he; 'it is strange I never met with them!' And he retired to his own tent, evidently filled, ear and heart, with the majestic numbers and sublime prayer of the poet.

And so he would pass, to and fro, among those beautiful little lakes of Canada, and up and down the clear, pebbly, forest-shaded brooks of Maine, his recreation, his exercise, and his few chosen friends of like mind in these things, his companions. So deep was his regard for those remote and untainted homes in the wilderness, that one might almost feel that their regard was responsive; and that it would hardly be fancy to apply to him, in death, the lines he so thrillingly applied in public to our great painter of Nature, Cooper:

'Call it not vain: — they do not err,
Who say, that when the Poet dies,
Mute Nature mourns her worshipper,
And celebrates his obsequies!
Who say, tall cliff and cavern lone
For the departed bard make moan;
Through his loved groves that breezes sigh,
And oaks, in deeper groan reply;
And rivers teach their rushing wave
To murmur dirges round his grave.

Not that, in sooth, o'er mortal urn,
These things inanimate can mourn;
But that the stream, the wood, the gale,
Are vocal with the plaintive wail
Of those, who, else forgotten long,
Lived in the poet's faithful song,
And, with the poet's parting breath,
Whose memory feels a second death,
* * * * *
All mourn the minstrel's harp unstrung
Their name unknown, their praise unsung.'

Certainly I was startled, on revisiting one of those favored spots, after he had left for home, by the vividness of association which made his presence there, hardly fanciful; and which gave to each tree, and shrub, and even to the ashes of the forsaken camp-fire, the aspect of a sentient companion.

But all this, with Dr. Bethune, was without the least laying aside of the proprieties of his calling, whether as minister or as Christian. Rude boatmen of the St. Lawrence, speak to this day of his Christian interest and benevolent action on their behalf, when visiting their vicinity; and, on the extreme confines of the Canadian wilderness, men tell feelingly of the tenderness, the simplicity, the earnestness of his prayers. Frequently, he would arise quietly from our little circle about the fire, and take his way to the depths of the forest. We knew well that he had gone into solitude for that communion with his Saviour, without which no scenes were lovely, and no day was bright. The escape from social pressure and conventionality was, with him, no flight to lawlessness. In the change of earthly scene, he sought no change in his Redeemer's presence and fellowship. The God of Nature was the God of Redemption; and, a lover of Nature, he made his enjoyment of its scenes and pleasures, one with his service of that Lord of all, who had bought him with His own blood."

We have mentioned the "plea for study," and a page from that vigorous discourse will put on record our minister's feeling for angling, and his authorities for believing in its hygienic efficacy.

"A catalogue of men," he says, "illustrious in every department of knowledge, who have refreshed themselves for further useful toil by the 'gentle art,' as its admirers delight to call it, would be very long; and those who would charge them with trifling, perhaps worse, might, with some modesty reconsider a censure which must include Izaak Walton, the pious biographer of pious men; Dryden, Thompson, Wordsworth, and many more among the poets; Paley, Wollaston, and Nowell among theologians; Henry Mackenzie (the man of feeling), and professor Wilson the poet-scholar and essayist; Sir Humphrey Davy, author of Salmonia; Emmerson the geometrician, Rennie the zoölogist, Chantrey the sculptor, and a host of others, who prove that such a taste is not inconsistent with religion, genius, industry, or usefulness to mankind. It has been remarked that they who avail themselves of this exercise moderately, (for, as one says, Make not a profession of a recreation lest it should bring a cross wish on the same) and are temperate, attain generally an unusual age. Henry Jenkins lived to a hundred and sixty-nine years, and angled when a score past his century. Walton died upwards of ninety; Nowell at ninety-five; and Mackenzie at eighty-six. Such frequent instances of longevity among anglers, says a writer on the subject, cannot have been from accident or from their having originally stronger stamina than other mortals. Their pursuits by the side of running streams whose motion imparts increased vitality to the air, their exercise regular without being violent, and that composure of the mind so necessary to the health of the body to which this amusement so materially contributes, must all have had an influence upon their physical constitution, the effect of which is seen in the duration of their lives."

Mr. Macomber, in the following account, proves that the apostolic art has its sorrows as well as its joys.

"Dr. Bethune was not one of those who understand the art of economizing by the profession of a 'rough-and-tumble' suit of clothing, fitted to such excursions; and, as the judicious charities of his excellent wife always found use for the half-worn garments of the doctor, and as he generally purchased the best, the natural result was, that he was a well-dressed man, and fine broadcloth, *and plenty of it*, went a fishing on all occasions when the wearer did. But let not one infer that the doctor was careful of his dress on such occasions. On the contrary, his black broadcloth was totally unheeded, and mud and water were disregarded, where *trout* was plenty.

On one of these trips, while whipping a fine mountain stream in the wilds of Pennsylvania, he with a companion had stopped at noon to lunch, and, while doing so, the doctor discovered ahead, a deep pool overshadowed with lofty trees and almost shut out from the sun-light, clear quiet and unvisited, the very spot to make glad the heart of an angler. He, who was a light eater, (his portly person, and the general belief to the contrary notwithstanding,) was quickly satisfied, and leaving his friend to finish his lunch and 'pack up,' he began, tackle in hand, to approach the pool. With wary and cautious steps he made his way through the thick underbrush which bordered the stream, until to his joy he discovered a fallen tree, one end buried in the soft earth, and the other elevated quite high directly above the quiet pool. To 'take to the tree,' and quietly work his way along to the elevated extremity, was but the work of a few moments, for the portly, and now somewhat excited sportsman. To say truth, he had not had 'good luck' during the morning. His brass-bound joint rod, patent self-winding reel, silk-laid casting line, and superb 'English hackle,' had been sadly out of place in fishing this narrow, swift, and brush-fringed mountain stream, and he had been fairly beaten at trouting, by his less skilled friend with plain cut pole, short linen line, and stump-grub. But here was a chance, a glorious chance, to show his friend the beauties of the science of angling — the doctor had already commenced his revision of the works of Izaak Walton, — and he challenged the attention of his companion to a beautiful 'cast' over that broad, silent pool. The tree on which the doctor stood, although large, and covered with bark and moss, having long been prostrate in its cozy bed, was rotten to its very core, and, just as he straightened himself for his 'beautiful cast,' it broke square off behind him, and doctor, broadcloth, and fishing tackle, fell ten feet into the pool, up to his neck in the 'still water,' now foaming with twenty stone weight of clerical humanity. The crash of the log and the souse of the doctor, brought the startled friend to his assistance, with the exclamation, 'Are you hurt?' 'No,' replied the immersed doctor, coolly shaking the water from his dripping locks, 'but I've frightened every fish out of *this* creek!'"

On one occasion, while fishing in lake Champlain, the Doctor fell from a boat, and a change of apparel became necessary. Nothing could be found for the emergency but an English dragoon's scarlet jacket. When the steamer passed, those who could recognize his lineaments would have seen his dignified episcopacy ensconced in a glittering garment better fitted for the Pope of Rome than the staid habits of a Protestant minister. Here is another story not altogether destitute of point:

"In the month of August, 1849, the doctor had determined to give himself a little relaxation from his clerical duties, and in company with his friend L., an excellent young man, and member of his church, they set their faces towards the mountains of Pennsylvania, to have a bit of angling. Arriving at H. they found that Mr. M., a resident of H., who had agreed to accompany them, had not received the Doctor's note announcing their coming, and had left for New York.

Not willing to lose the fine weather, they procured a conveyance, and although strangers to the roads and streams, found themselves at night, after a fatiguing day's ride, at the quiet tavern of Elder S., situated in a romantic gorge of one of the coal mountains of Pennsylvania. The Elder, an old acquaintance of Mr. M.'s, but entirely unknown to the Doctor and his friend, was unremitting in his attentions to his guests, and their creature comforts; and as they had explained their disappointment in not meeting Mr. M., who was to have been their guide, he offered to furnish a vehicle and accompany them the next day to the trout stream, up the mountain. But the good Elder, once a fast man himself, had long ago abandoned not only 'poker' and 'brag,' but also the 'rifle' and the 'rod,' and his knowledge of the whereabouts of the best trout holes, was extremely limited. He dragged his guests up steep mountains and down deep vales; sometimes his grey would get fairly stuck in a mud hole; and to extricate the rickety 'carryall' from the mire, all hands must alight and, up to their knees in water, pull the old horse and wagon out on to dry land. But Dr. Bethune, whose good humor and patience never deserted him, was always ready with his broad shoulder to lift away, and the conveyance was soon under weigh again. But they caught more ducks than trout, and late at night brought home more mud than fish. It was one of Dr. Bethune's peculiarities to travel about on these excursions *incog* when he could do so, and as his friend L. had, from the time of their arrival, only designated him as the 'Doctor,' Elder S. had naturally come to the conclusion that he was some jolly medical man from Philadelphia, but had not the face fairly to ask his name. He was however delighted with him as a companion, quickly abbreviated the 'Doctor' into 'Doc.,' and, often slapping him on the back, would exclaim, 'That's it Doc., give us another lift.'

When the labours and disappointments of day had ended, and clean water and a good supper (for Mrs. S. was famous for her cookery) had set all to rights again, the old Elder felt bound to express to his guests his satisfaction on one point. 'Now,' said he, 'gentlemen, we've had a hard time to-day, but through all the upsetting, sticking in the mud-holes, losing our way, and catching no fish, I am much gratified to say, I haven't heard either of you swear a single word. We have a prayer-meeting to-night, can't one of you do the singing?' "

As we write, an excellent likeness of Dr. Bethune looks down upon us from the wall ; it is a photograph, taken a few years before his death, under the following circumstances. He was arranging to start for one of his vacations, and in expectation of its relief and pleasure, was in one of his happiest moods, when Dr. Francis Vinton, of New York, entered his study. The Doctor has been kind enough to relate the incident :

"TRINITY CHURCH, NEW YORK, *September* 20, 1867.

MY DEAR DR. VAN NEST : One pleasant morning in the autumn of 1853, I was ushered upstairs to Dr. Bethune's Library Study. In response to my knock at the door, I heard his voice, rather bluffly, bidding the intruder to 'Come in.'

On opening the door, the scene, pictured in the photograph, to which you allude in your letter, presented itself to my eyes.

I stood still, while the Doctor, with pen in hand, and surrounded with his folios, looked up, with an expression, first of annoyance, but melting into a sweet smile, wherewith he welcomed me.

'A boon, a boon, my lord,' said I, jocosely.

'Come in, come in, take a chair ; I am delighted to see you,' he replied.

'A boon,' I repeated. 'First grant my request.'

'Granted, granted. What is it?'

'Let us have your photograph for the club, just as I see you now.'

And then he broke out into his cheering laugh at the singular petition, a laugh that was so hearty, so contagious, that we both indulged in it.

After some coquetting with his reluctance to appear in his study costume, and the surroundings of books, and creel, and fishing rods, he fell back on his rash promise and consented ; *provided* that the artist should destroy the negative after printing enough of the photographs to distribute among the club, and a few other intimates.

The photograph of 'Dr. Bethune in his Study,' had this origin ; and if the story shall enrich your memoirs, it will gratify me to be associated in its pages, with that noble man. 'We shall ne'er look upon his like again.' Yours faithfully,

FRANCIS VINTON."

There he sits in his habit as he lived, the learned-looking cap, gold spectacles, and easy morning gown, the ponderous authority he is in the act of citing on the table before him, the others whose turn is to come, piled up on the floor; "his orthodox pipe," leans against the table, the implements of his well-beloved sport adorn the walls, and the man's very look, at once humorous and serene, greets us as we turn towards it. We owe many a fervid page, and many a burst of eloquence, which there was, alas, no short-hand writer to record, to that same creel and rod, for they kept his heart young and his body manageable.

The Piseco Trout Club was the name given to a confraternity of gentlemen, whose annual habit it was to repair to the north of New York, with the full intention of catching and killing as many trout as they could. Their meetings were genial and jovial; a "Report" was made of the devastation they had caused each year, and it is fair to conclude that much provision was consumed. Without allowing ourselves to be stupefied with amazement at the figures which represent their success, we may say that the Secretary of this Society was Mr. Alfred Brooks; the Chaplain, Dr. Bethune; the President, Mr. Henry Vail, of Troy; and the other individuals of which it was composed exercised functions either private or official, according to posts they occupied, or duties they had to perform.

The "Reports" are before us, very whimsical and nonsensical; just such stuff as these noble "boys at play" might be expected to have got off, at a time when anything serious would have been out of place. The President has a song improvised in his honor by the Chaplain, of which a verse may suffice as specimen.

"And when the clock beneath our belts proclaims the hour to dine,
And we to seek the 'Tree Tops shade,' our busy-rods resign,
We love above our smoking board to see his bright face shine,
And hear him smack his lips and say, 'how very, very fine,'
Just like the honored President of our Piseco Club."

It was sung to the tune of "The Fine Old English Gentleman."

These fishing excursions resulted in something besides pleasure. "Come ye after me," said our Saviour to certain who were casting their nets, "and I will make ye to become fishers of men." And accordingly the church of the Thousand Islands rose and flourished, and did much good, because a man whose eyes were always open for a chance of doing good, went into the neighborhood for his amusement.

We gratefully make use of the statement of the Rev. Anson Dubois, D. D., upon this matter, and acknowledge our inability to improve upon it:

"You are aware that Dr. Bethune originated a Mission at Alexandria Bay, in the St. Lawrence River. He used to call it his pet child of the Thousand Islands. He was one day trolling for black bass among these beautiful Islands, when he said to his oarsman, 'Tommy, where do you go to church?' 'No where,' said he, 'no church to go to.' 'But do none of these people go to church?' 'No, we used to have Methodist preaching sometimes at the Bay, but they seem to have given us up of late years.'

This excited the Doctor's sympathy. He had it published in the district school and among the neighbors, that he would preach at the school-house the next Sabbath, and form a Sabbath school. It was a new thing, and quite a wonder. The people turned out largely. After the sermon to the adults, the Doctor gathered the children to the front seats, and held a Sabbath school, greatly interesting them with his Scripture stories and remarks. 'Now,' said he, 'my friends, we must have a Sunday school here. Who will superintend it?'

No one volunteered. He then cast his eyes around the audience in that small but crowded house. It rested, after a moment, on the intelligent and energetic countenance of a middle-aged lady. 'Madam,' said the Doctor, 'will you take charge of this school?'

The woman tried to excuse herself, but finally consented, and for the whole season managed the school with great success, although she made no profession of religion, and was the wife of a tavern-keeper, an irreligious man.

The Doctor soon after sent a ten-dollar library, and music books to the school; and a friend, an enthusiastic old gentleman, in acknowledging their receipt and use, said, 'If Dr. Bethune could hear these little children singing out of their new books, he would think it was the angels in heaven.' The next season Dr. Bethune sent a missionary, Rev. J. A. Davenport, to this field, who maintained preaching and Sabbath schools, sometimes to the number of ten, upon the Islands and adjacent shores, and was supported for three years by funds, contributed by the Doctor and his personal friends. That mission, begun in 1846, is still maintained, and has been productive of very great good.

The Doctor's intercourse with the less cultivated people in the remote sections of the country where he so loved to resort during his summer vacations, was always easy and free, though never approaching vulgarity. He loved especially to devote his Sabbaths to their religious profit, making it a matter of conscience to preach at least once, and frequently oftener. He used to tell some good anecdotes of their appreciation of his services. I will give you one as a specimen. He was at one time among one of the roughest sections of the lumber regions skirting Lake Champlain. The little log hut in which he preached was crammed, and many hardy backwoodsmen sat about the door in the shade. He discoursed earnestly to attentive hearers. After meeting broke up, some little consultation was had among the men, and one of them came up with the Doctor on his way to his tent. Said he, very respectfully, 'Preacher, we have made up our minds that we want you to stay here and preach for us.' 'Well, but,' said the Doctor, 'can you support me here? How much can you raise?' His friend was not discouraged. They had thought of that too. 'Yes *Sir*,' said he, 'we have made up our minds to give you one hundred dollars a year, and we'll build you a new church.' 'What!' said a bystander who had not been in the council, 'will you build a church of logs ?' 'Build a church of logs! No *sir*, we'll build a church of *sawed stuff*'! The Doctor had to take the thing seriously, and show them why he could not come and live there. He sometimes laughed heartily over his call of a hundred dollars' salary, and a new church of sawed stuff, though he declared he never felt himself more highly complimented in his life."

Mr. Dubois was pastor of the Thousand Islands' Church for some time after Mr. Davenport quitted it, and perhaps there is no better place than the present to insert a letter written by Doctor Bethune to Mr. Dubois, embodying certain important opinions, although the date is several years later.

"*April* 12, 1852.

You ask my advice and shall have it in all friendship. As a general rule no man ought to change his settlement, I mean his first settlement, for several years. That settlement is his apprenticeship to the pastoral office, and he cannot fairly learn its lessons in less time.

A minister's character is made in his first charge. If he be faithful and successful there, he establishes a reputation which will follow him through life, because it will be reputation among his clerical brethren, who are, after all, the best judges. The school you are in is a hard, but a good school. You have time for thought. You meet with a variety of human nature. Your work does not overtask your brain, and every hour is a preparation for a more important sphere. Two or three years longer there will do you much good, and there is scarcely any position, except those of the first class, which will give you greater prominence. By declining preferment now you do not lose it but only postpone it, for Providence has other places in store than that which you refer to.

Another general rule which should be very rarely broken through, is not to preach as a candidate. Young licentiates, or unsettled ministers, perhaps must,—but very rarely should a minister who has a pulpit, put himself forward, or be brought forward, as a solicitor for another. It always lowers him in the sight of his own people, and in that of the people he seeks. The seeker is always underrated. Let yourself be sought, which you will be if you are faithful, and God blesses you in the place his Providence assigns you. Do not try to be your own Providence, but do your duty and trust the providence of God. Candidating has been the curse of our churches, and has belittled our ministry. This is not the popular doctrine, but it is the true one. I could point you to several of our best men who have destroyed their hopes of advancement by seeking it.

These are general rules—but of course there are exceptions, yours may be one — and deeply interested as I am for the Islands, I would not stand in the way of your usefulness or comfort. I am impartial in the counsel given above. In any case you may rely on me, as far as you may think it worth your while, as your constant and ready friend,

George W. Bethune."

In this Church of the Thousand Islands a beautiful mural tablet has been erected by the Messrs. Stewart of Brooklyn, to the memory of Dr. Bethune.

There is a touch of sentiment in the following refusal:

"I cannot meet you at Lake George. The friend* who was always my companion there, the man whom I loved best and as whom I can never love man again, is sleeping in sacred rest till the illustrious morning breaks. He is associated with every nook and island of Lake George, and I can fish there no more."

Several allusions have been made to friends; those who were his most frequent companions in these excursions, besides the Rev. Mr. Cooke of Lewiston, were Mr. George Trott and the Rev. Dr. J. Wheaton Smith of Philadelphia. Mr. Trott states that they were under canvas for two weeks in the spring and autumn, and estimates that the time he spent with Dr. Bethune in the woods, would cover the space of an entire year. He relates a meeting with an old clergyman in Canada who was greatly astonished to find the pastor in such trivial employ. "What!" he said "is this the

* Probably his brother-in-law, Mr. John Williams.

"CHURCH OF THE THOUSAND ISLANDS"

great Dr. Bethune, and can it be that he has come all this distance to amuse himself with fishing ?" Afterwards he heard him preach to the backwoodsmen, and at once declared that Dr. Bethune had acquired more influence over these people in that brief visit than he had gained in years. A lumber merchant said, he would be glad to pay all the expenses of Dr. B. and friend, simply for the benefit that resulted to his working people; and only last summer, Mr. Trott met with a blessed result of those preachings. A man in Maine told him that his first religious impressions had been produced by Dr. Bethune's sermon.

Preaching to these plain people, his pulpit either a stump of a tree, or a rock, was often attended with ludicrous scenes. One Sunday in Maine, just as he concluded a solemn service, before the people had risen, the quietness was disturbed by a shrill voice, "Has any of the congregation found a new jack-knife? If they have, I've lost one, and they'll please hand it over."

During these excursions, the diet was of the simplest character ; alcoholic drinks, and even wine, were excluded from the stores. It may be imagined that in these remote regions, the forests of Maine and the wilder British Provinces, the visit of such a distinguished stranger would be a great event ; and he had a servant, named Ernest, who was frequently sent forward to make arrangements for the party, and he would amuse himself by exciting public expectation to the highest point. The entrée of the Doctor and his "fidus Achates" the Major, was like that of lords of the realm, but they would find its consequence in the greatly increased bills that ensued.

Dr. Bethune himself has given a touching incident of his mission work in the woods, narrated in an annual for Mr. L. G. Clarke.

It occurred in Northern New York, when in company with the Piseco Club* on the romantic banks of those waters which had given them the poetic appellation, and where they had erected a simple lodge. The article is headed "Piseco."

"The Sabbath there had peculiar charms. No church-going bell rang through the woods, no decorated temple lifted its spire, but the hush of divine rest was upon all around. A sense of the Holy One rested on the spirit, the birds sung more sweetly, the dews of the morning shimmered more brightly, and the sounds of the forest were like the voice of Psalms. As the day went on toward noon, the inhabitants, — whose dwellings were scattered for miles around, some down the rocky paths, others in boats on the lake, — singly or in companies, men, women, and little ones, might be seen drawing near to the lodge, where, when all assembled, they formed a respectful and willing congregation of perhaps fifty worshippers, and listened to the words of the preacher, who sought to lead them by the Gospel of the Cross through nature up to the God of grace. Such opportunities were rare for them ; never, indeed, was a sermon heard there, except on these occasions. The devout (for God the Saviour had a 'few names' among them) received the word with 'gladness'; all were attentive, and their visitors found, when joining with them in the primitive service, a religious power seldom felt in more ceremonious homage.

On one of those sacred days, there came among the rest, two young, graceful women, whose air and dress marked them as of a superior cultivation. Their modest voices enriched the trembling psalmody, and their countenances showed strong sympathies with the preacher's utterances. At the close of the service, they made, through one of their neighbors, a request that the minister would pay a visit to their mother, who had been a long time ill, and was near death. A promise was readily given that he would do so the same day ; but their home lay four miles distant, and a sudden storm forbade the attempt. The Monday morning shone brightly, though a heavy cloud at the west suggested precautions against a thunder shower. The friends parted from the landing, each bent on his purpose ; but the chaplain's prow was turned on his mission of comfort to the sick. Had any prim amateurs of eccle-

*This club was a different institution from the *friends* mentioned just previously.

siastical conventionalities, seen him with his broad-brimmed hat, necessary for shelter from the sun, a green veil thrown around it as defence from the mosquitoes near the shores, his heavy water-boots, and his whole garb chosen for aquatic exigencies, (for like Peter, he had girt his fisher's coat about him) they would hardly have recognized his errand. But the associations of the scene with the man of Nazareth and the Apostles by the Sea of Galilee, were in his soul, carrying him back to the primitive Christianity, and lifting him above the forms with which men have overlaid its simplicity. The boat flew over the placid waters in which lay mirrored the whole amphitheatre of the mountain shores, green as an emerald. The wooded point hid the lodge on the one side, a swelling island the hamlets on the other. No trace of man was visible. The carol of birds came off from the land, now and then the exulting merriment of a loon rang out of the distance, and soon a soft, southern breeze redolent of the spicy hemlock and cedar, rippled the surface. The Sabbath had transcended its ordinary hours, and shed its sweet blessing on the following day. His rods lay idly over the stern as the chaplain thought of the duty before him and asked counsel of the Master, who, 'Himself bare our sicknesses and carried our sorrows.' He remembered the disciples, who said, 'Lord, he whom thou lovest is sick;' and the gracious answer, 'This sickness is not unto death, but for the glory of God, that the Son of Man might be glorified thereby.'

It is not the imagination merely that gives such power to the living oracles, when they come to us where the testimony of nature unites with the inspiration. It is the blessing of Jesus, who sought the wilderness, the shore and the mountain side to gain strength from communion with his Father. It was in such solitudes that our example and forerunner found courage for his trial and suffering. Religion is eminently social, but its seat is the heart of the individual believer, and whatever be the advantage of Christian fellowship, the flame must be fed in private, personal converse with the Father of our Spirits. He who has not been alone with God, can seldom find him in the crowded church.

A brief hour, briefer for these meditations, brought the keel of the boat to a gravelly nook where the mouth of the inlet found a little harbor. There, awaiting the chaplain's arrival, stood a tall, upright, man, past the prime of life, who, with a style of courtesy evidently foreign, bared his gray head, and greeted his visitor by name of a friend.

'You have kindly come, sir, to see my poor wife, I thank you for it. She is now expecting you, for we heard the sound of your oars as you turned the island.'

A rough stone house, built by a speculator of former days, stood on a knoll a little way from the stream, and the garden around it was trimmed with some taste. As they entered, the owner said, 'Welcome to the mountain dwelling of an old soldier. He (pointing to an engraved portrait of Blucher wreathed with laurel leaves) was my general, whose praise I once received as I lay wounded on the field of battle. I am a Prussian, sir, and came to this country, when my fatherland had no more use for my sword. I have not been successful in my peaceful life, and misfortune after misfortune drove me here, hoping to gather about us a few of my countrymen, and make a German home; but in that I was disappointed. The severe winters chilled their resolution, and now we are by ourselves. The few neighbors about us are not of our class, but they are kind and honest, and the world has nothing to tempt me back to it. I have one brave son at sea. My two daughters you saw yesterday. We had another, but she sleeps yonder.'

He turned abruptly from the room. The chaplain, left to himself observed about the apartment various articles of refinement and faded luxury, telling the story of more prosperous days. The subsequent acquaintance with the family confirmed his first impressions. Though not of high rank, they were educated, of gentle manners, and though for years remote from cultivated society, preserved the amenities which now distinguished them. Only the father seemed to have suffered from want of occupation and, not unlikely, from habits formed in camp, habits doubly dangerous in seclusion.

At a signal from another room, one of the daughters led the chaplain to the bedside of the sufferer. The father sat with his face averted, near an open window, through which came the laughing prattle of a child, and a half idiot serving-woman looked in wonderingly across the threshhold of an outer kitchen. The daughters, having raised their mother's head on a higher pillow, and affectionately smoothed her thin, gray hair under the snow-white cap, withdrew to the other side of the bed. The chaplain placed his broad hat, with its green veil, on the little table, and sat silent for a while, not knowing how to begin, since, as yet, nothing had given him a clue to the woman's state of mind. She lay still and stone-like; her eyes were dry, with little 'speculation' in them; her lips moved, but uttered no sound, and her hand feebly stretched out, was cold and stiff. Her whole frame was worn to extreme thinness, and the color of her skin told that the seat of her disease was the liver.

At length the chaplain, seeing that her soul was near its dread passage into the eternal future, said: 'I am sorry my friend, to find you so very ill. You are soon to die!'

'Yes.'

'It is a fearful thing; are you not afraid?'

'No.'

'But to go into the presence of God, our Judge, is a most solemn change.'

'Yes.'

'And are you not afraid?'

'No.'

The preacher was confounded; the short answers, almost cold, without emotion, the glazed eye, the rigid countenance, caused him to doubt whether he had to contend with ignorance or insensibility. Anxious to rouse some feeling, if possible to startle into some attention, as a physician applies the probe, he pushed severe declarations of certain judgment and the danger of impenitence, reminded her that Christ, the Saviour of the believing, will be the Avenger of Sin, and that 'there is no work nor device in the grave, and as the tree falls so it must lie.' The tearless eye unwinkingly gazed on him, and no shrinking followed his keen surgery.

'Madam, you are going before God, and do you not fear?'

A faint smile stole struggling through her thin features, and a light, like a star twinkling under a deep shadow, was seen far within her eye, and, pointing with her finger upward, she said, in a firm, low tone, 'Though he slay me, yet will I trust in Him.'

The chaplain bowed his head on the pillow and wept thanks. Here was no ignorant or callous soul, but a child of God, whose perfect love had cast out fear. 'Yes, Christian soul, you are not afraid of evil tidings; your heart is fixed, trusting in Him who went this way before you. Fear no evil; His rod and His staff, they will comfort you.'

'Amen! blessed be His name,' replied the dying woman. 'It is true. I know in whom I have believed, and that He is able to keep what I have committed to Him. Because He hath been my help, therefore under his wings do I rejoice!'

It seemed now as if the fountain of her speech was unsealed, and, though no moisture was in her eyes, and the few drops which started out on her forehead were cold and clammy, and the worn lineaments had lost the power to smile, and she lay still as marble, yet, with a voice clear and unfaltering, she went on to testify her faith in *Christ*, and of the peace that filled her soul. A strength denied to her body came from within.

'Oh, sir, I thank you for coming. I thank God for sending you to me, like the angel to Hagar in the wilderness; I prayed for it. It is four long years since I heard the voice of a Christian minister; and all that time I prayed for one to hold the water of life to my lips once more. Now I know that *He* has heard me, blessed be His name!'

The preacher interrupted her to say, that she had not been left alone by her God, who needed not man's lips to comfort his people.

'Alone! no, never alone! I have seen *Him* in his mighty works. I have heard Him in the storms of winter, and in the summer winds. I had my Bible, His own holy word. His spirit has been with me. But I thank Him for the voice of His commissioned servant, whose duty it is to comfort his people.'

The readers of this imperfect sketch can have little idea of the eloquence, almost supernatural, pervaded by Scriptural language and imagery, with which she spoke. It was the soul triumphing over the fainting flesh; truth in its own energy, unaided by human expressions; a voice of the dead, not sepulchral, but of one near the gate of heaven.

The chaplain knelt beside the bed, and all the rest knelt with him; but there were more thanks than petitions in his prayer. The clouds that hung about the borders of eternity, were so bright with the glory beyond, that sorrow and pain were forgotten, as he gave utterance to the dying woman's memories and hopes, the memories of grace, and the hopes of immortality that met together in her faithful heart. Nor need I add, that his own gratitude was strong to the *Good Shepherd* who had sent him to find this sheep among the mountains, not lost nor forgotten, but longing for a token of her Saviour's care.

When he rose from his knees, she thanked him again, but with more visible emotion than before, and said: 'Sir, I doubt not God directed you here, and there is one favor more I have asked of Him, and now ask through you. Three years ago my eldest daughter died in my arms, assured of rest, but leaving behind her a babe not two weeks old. Mother, she said, just as she was dying, I leave my child with you, to bring her to me in heaven. You will do it for Christ's sake, and mine, and hers, mother. And mother, He has told us to give little children to Him in baptism. Dear mother, promise that my child shall be baptised. I promised, and her spirit departed. Ever since, I have been praying and waiting for some minister to find his way to us, but in vain. More than once I heard of some who had come as far as Lake Pleasant, but none reached Piseco, and I almost feared that I should die and not be able to tell my child in Heaven that the blessed water had been on her baby's face. Yet, even in this, God has been good to me. You will baptize my little one? How gladly the chaplain assented, may be easily imagined. The child was called in from her play on the grass-plat, her rosy, wondering face was gently washed, and her light brown hair parted on her forehead, and she stood with her bare, white feet, on a low bench by her grandmother's pillow. The grandfather filled an antique silver bowl with water, freshly dipped from a spring near the river. An old brass-clasped folio of Luther's Bible was laid open at the family record, beside the water, the chaplain's broad hat on the other side; he thought not, and none thought, of his coarse grey coat, or his heavy boots: he was full of his sacred office, and the presence of the Invisible was upon him. The feeble woman, strengthened by love and faith, raised herself higher on the bed, and put her wasted arm over the plump shoulders of the fair, blue-eyed child. The old man and his daughters, and her dull-witted servant at the kitchen door, reverently standing, sobbed aloud; and amidst the tears of all, except her whose source of tears was dried up for ever, the chaplain recited the touching prayer of the Reformed Churches before the baptism of infants, and with the name of the departed mother breathed over her orphan, in the name of the Father, and of the Son, and of the Holy Ghost, she was dedicated to God by water, sprinkled three times on her sweet grave face. The grandfather handed a pen to the chaplain, but it was lightly pressed to trace the inscription, for the page was wet with the big drops that fell from the old man's eyes.

Many moments elapsed before the thanksgiving could be uttered, and then the happy saint joyfully exclaimed:

'Bless you, sir! I bless God that he has granted me this peace before I die. Now I am ready to go to my child in Heaven.'

'My dear madam,' answered the preacher, 'it is, indeed, a blessed ordinance; but the child of prayers for two generations would not have missed the promise because of an impossibility on your part.'

'No, no! The spirit is better than the form. She had the promise; I knew that she was in the covenant, but I wanted her in the fold.'

The chaplain entered his boat. Never did lake and mountain and green shore look so beautiful, for they seemed all bathed in holy light; and that noon, when, with his friends reclining on the sward, he told the story of the baptism in the wilderness, their moistened eyes expressed their sympathy with his joy.

Heaven opened for the grandmother a few days afterwards. The next year her Saviour took up her child's child in his arms, and the three were together among the angels. The grandfather lived but a short time. One of the daughters having married a farmer, moved with her sister, down into the open country, where she also died in her young beauty. Of the two other members of the family, I have heard nothing since.

The old stone house still stands near the rushing inlet, but the storms beat through its broken windows. Rank weeds have overrun the garden, and brambles hide the spring near the kitchen door. Yet the path from the landing-place can be followed; and should any of my readers ever visit Piseco, now more accessible, but charming as ever, they can easily recognize the scene of my story. It is ever fresh and hallowed in my memory; for there I learned, by precious experience, that the good God never forgets those who trust in Him; and still, go where we will, we may carry this blessing with us to some heart thirsting for His word."

What a commentary on his own words in the preface to Walton and Cotton's Angler:

'I trust that I have drunk enough of the old angler's spirit not to let such pastime break in upon better things; but, on the other hand, I have worked the harder from thankfulness to *Him* who taught the brook to wind with musical gurglings, as it rolls on to the great sea."

He practised on the advice given to the young men of Yale College should they go a fishing:

"Nor should the angler forget the best of books in his pocket, and a few well-chosen jewels of truth to give away as he enjoys the simple fare of some upland cottage, or chats with the secluded inmates during the soft twilight, before he asks a blessing upon the household for the night."

CHAPTER IX.

LITERARY AND PUBLIC LABORS.

THERE is little to note in Dr. Bethune's life at this time beyond the literary works which proceeded from his incessant pen. In 1848, the "British Female Poets, with Biographical and Critical Notices," was edited by him, "and the specimens which he gives are well chosen, the biographical sketches ably written, and the characteristics of each writer skilfully discriminated." It was also expected that he would follow this with the "Female Poets of America," but that task was transferred to a young friend,* in whose judgment and taste he had great confidence. A little earlier, Lindsay and Blakiston issued a volume of his poetry, entitled "Lays of Love and Faith, with other Fugitive Poems." Dr. Bethune did not give himself to making poetry, it was merely an incident to his more severe labors with which he occupied his leisure hours. "Many of these lays were tributes of affection to those most dear to their author, whilst others were devotional, epigrammatic, patriotic and miscellaneous; and all exhibit a rich and vivid imagination, much delicacy of sentiment and expression, and melody of versification." Mr. William H. Prescott writes, "I asked my wife as she read them to me (which is my way of reading) to mark those we liked the best; but I soon found they were nearly all to be marked, that is, the original pieces: They are warmed by a genuine feeling, and often have a vein of

* Miss Caroline May.

tender melancholy running through them, which looks for repose to a better world than this; you are certainly the poet of the heart as well as of the head. One would hardly have looked for this vein, in one of so cheerful, not to say comical, turn in conversation. Are the man and the author of different natures?"

It was the custom of Dr. Bethune to prepare hymns for his Sunday school children on their festal days, and we present the following, as a happy specimen:

CHRISTMAS HYMN.

"Joy and gladness! joy and gladness,
O happy day!
Every thought of sin and sadness,
Chase, chase away.
Heard ye not the angels telling,
Christ, the Lord of might, excelling,
On the earth with man is dwelling,
Clad in our clay!

With the shepherd throng around him
Haste we to bow;
By the angels' sign they found him,
We know him now!
New-born babe of houseless stranger,
Cradled low in Bethlehem's manger,
Saviour from our sin and danger,
Jesus, 'tis thou!

God of life, in mortal weakness,
Hail, Virgin born!
Infinite in lowly meekness,
Thou wilt not scorn,
Though all Heaven is singing o'er thee,
And gray wisdom bows before thee,
When our youthful hearts adore thee,
This holy morn.

Son of Mary, blessed mother!
Thy love we claim;
Son of God, our elder brother,
O! gentle name!
To thy Father's throne ascended,
With thine own His glory blended,
Thou art all thy trials ended,
Ever the same.

Thou wert born to tears and sorrows,
Pilgrim divine;
Watchful nights and weary morrows,
Brother, were thine;
By thy fight with strong temptation,
By thy cup of tribulation,
Oh, thou God of our salvation,
With mercy shine.

In thy holy footsteps treading,
Guide, lest we stray,
From thy word of promise, shedding
Light on our way;
Never leave us, nor forsake us,
Like thyself in mercy make us,
And at last to glory take us,
Jesus, we pray."

G. W. B. TO MRS. J. B. "*March* 18, 1848.

MY BELOVED MOTHER: Before you receive this, you will be praying to God for your son on the anniversary of his birth, and I shall have blessed him for giving my opening life to the care of such a mother. I desire to renew my filial obligations, and declare to you, out of my heart's truth, that I am still in all reverent obedience and affection, your grateful son, your *child*. Would that I could have better opportunities of proving how devotedly I am yours. Dear mother, I was a wayward youth, and am a very faulty man; forgive me all the past and give me your blessing in my future. God will hear us both, you for me, me for you."

DR. BETHUNE TO DR. VERMILYE. "*April* 17, 1848.

MY DEAR VERMILYE: I am at a loss, principally from lack of proper information, how to act in reference to some present circumstances. Rumors uncertain and indistinct have run through my congregation, of my name having been used in several ballotings of your consistory for an additional minister, and, as might be supposed some uneasy inquiry has been excited. I find also that some out of your congregation, and some in, have thought me a candidate for the vacant place. It has even been said, though by those who had no right to speak on the subject, that I ought to withdraw my name. This you know I cannot do, as I never directly or indirectly presented it; nor can I, without impertinence, presume to know any thing of proceedings in your consistory about which I have no legitimate information. At the same time, while I duly appreciate the honor of being named by any one or more individuals, as at all fitted for so high a station, I have a great repugnance to being thought a candidate for any pulpit whatever. Other brethren may, if they choose, as they have a right, take another course; but, for myself, since the beginning of my ministry, I have carefully avoided any step that might bring me under any suspicion of offering myself to any congregation, and I am anxious to maintain my character. From your own high sense of Christian honor, and the unrestrained confidence of our friendship, you will, I trust, appreciate my feelings when I confess myself annoyed by the supposition, in any quarter, of my having deviated from a rule of ministerial conduct which I early adopted, and have never varied from. I am not sure that any thing needs to be done, but as you have a better opportunity of knowing, I beg you to act for me as, in like circumstances, I would act for you. The delicacy of my position compels me to throw myself upon the kindness you have ever shown to your affectionate friend and brother, GEORGE W. BETHUNE.

P. S. This note is confidential, but only so far as not to prevent your using it to secure the end for which it has been written."

The above letter defines with perfect accuracy Dr. Bethune's position with reference to a question of interest, namely, a possible call to be associate pastor of the Collegiate Church of New York. The communication did not and was not intended to prevent further movement in the matter, but solely to bring any possible negotiation to a point. In due time, September 15th, he was distinctly informed by Dr. John Knox, that he had been elected by the consistory, but the question was set at rest by Dr. Bethune's reply.

"*September* 25, 1848.

'Grace be unto you and peace be multiplied.'

DEARLY BELOVED BRETHREN: It is with a deep sense of my unworthiness, that I gratefully acknowledge having received on the 23d inst., from the hands of your committee, the enclosed call to exercise my ministry within the sphere of your church.

You are aware, brethren, of the responsible station I now hold as the Pastor and Bishop of a church not undeserving of your fraternal regard, which is very dear to me because of its eminent fidelity in our Master's cause, and the affectionate kindness ever shown by them to their minister, for the Master's sake. This, with other circumstances, rendered this question submitted by you to my judgment, one of great gravity, from the influence my decision must have upon both the churches, and upon my future course as a Christian man, and a minister of the gospel.

The result of my conscientious deliberations, and I trust, not insincere supplications for Divine help, has been that I ought to decline respectfully but firmly, the call which I was unworthy to receive, yet am not free to entertain."

Dr. Bethune had a mulatto servant,* who rejoiced in the Scripture name of Aquila, or Aquilla, as he was usually misnomered. This faithful man always knew where his master's books were to be found; often too, when the owner himself had forgotten, or never given himself the trouble to find out; so the two were continually in the study together, and the servant was of all his master's council.

* There was something very pleasant in Dr. Bethune's relation with his servants. Aquila lived in his family for fourteen years, and died in the arms of the Doctor, who at his funeral followed the hearse as chief mourner.

"Aquila," said the Doctor, when he was pondering on the letter we have just given, "What do you think of this call to the Collegiate church in New York, should I accept it?" "How many gentlemen did you say signed it?" "Twenty-four." "Hard thing to serve twenty-four masters, sure to get into trouble with some of them," was the sententious and, we may fairly believe, decisive rejoinder.

Many contingent advantages were sacrificed by this rejection of the Collegiate call: a nearly doubled salary, easier work, greater leisure for literary pursuits, the near neighborhood of Mrs. Joanna Bethune, and a home in his native city; but, acting to the best of his not unassisted judgment, Dr. Bethune chose to forego all these, and it is useless to speculate whether a different course of action might not have prolonged his life.

This event gave occasion to a Report which was presented to the Third Dutch church of Philadelphia, and presents a valuable expression of sentiment as well as a sketch of ministerial success. It was accompanied with the substantial donation of one thousand dollars. We quote some sentences.

"How shall your committee characterize the ardent desire that met them every where, not only for the health and happiness of their pastor, but for the continuance of his usefulness in a sphere where he has hitherto shone with unsurpassed lustre?

That their efforts have through the blessings of God been crowned with success, no one can or does for a moment doubt; and such success, without endowments, without great wealth among our early pioneers, this pile arose at a cost of fifty-five thousand dollars. A little more than twelve years ago the seed was planted. The fruit has been, the reduction of the debt to about sixteen thousand dollars; voluntary contributions by the members of the society, exclusive of private benevolences, for various religious and charitable associations of between thirty and forty thousand dollars; a large number of communicants; almost every pew, and almost every seat in the pews, either owned or rented; an agreeable, attentive and enlightened audience; the most entire and perfect harmony on all our concerns. Surely the seed has fallen in good ground. But sever the tie that binds us, and who shall answer for the consequences to this society? Who is to sustain them, to guide their tottering feet through an unaccustomed path? To them the cloud may vanish by day, and the pillar of fire by night be forever extinguished. The picture must not be dwelt upon. We have done something, will do more. But the tie which binds us to our pastor, our friend, our Bethune, cannot, must not be broken."

On the 23d of October the call to New York was again forwarded to Dr. Bethune with urgent letters and verbal messages, but met with a similar answer.

G. W. B. TO MRS. J. B. "PHILADELPHIA, *October* 23, 1848.

MY BELOVED MOTHER: I have been reproaching myself ever since declining to preach for your Liberian school. For you I should be glad to do anything. That thing requires time. If it will do after a while, tell your boy what your wishes are and he will try to be a good child.

My old friend Mr. Labriskie came in again on Thursday, with the call in no way altered except that the additional five hundred is endorsed upon it. Indeed I think my people would give me any thing I ask now, but alas, they cannot give me my dear mother. My time is filled with duties, yet passes sadly and solitary enough. You are not out of mind for an hour except when I am asleep, and then I often dream of you.

I had a sweet subject for a sermon yesterday morning: The youth of Jesus, embracing his questioning with the doctors. It is full of delightful interest, and I got light upon it I never had before.

I send the call back to-day, but with a pang in thus consenting to be separated from you.

God bless my dear mother.

GEO. W. BETHUNE."

"*October* 30.

I was happy while studying for my last sermon. It was on Galatians iii. 19: The law in the hands of the mediator. If you will compare the 8th and 17th verses of the chapter, you will see how strongly the apostle argues to show that the law is actually under or part of the system of mercy. A most cheering and edifying thought.

(8th verse. And the scripture, foreseeing that God would justify the heathen through faith, preached before the gospel unto Abraham, saying, in thee shall all nations be blessed.

17th verse. And this I say, that the covenant that was confirmed before of God in Christ, the law, which was four hundred and thirty years after, cannot disannul, that it should make the promise of no effect.

19th verse. Wherefore then serveth the law? It was added because of transgressions, till the seed should come to whom the promise was made; and it was ordained by angels in the hand of a mediator.)

It seems to me that the reasoning of the apostles throughout the chapter, upsets the millenarian notions about the glory the Jews are to have in the latter days. The seed of Abraham to whom the promises are made, is the seed of faith, not of nature. The moment Jew and Gentile are in Christ, they are *one*, no difference.

I am quite well, though a little Mondayish, for I worked hard yesterday."

"*November* 5.

I was preaching this morning to a handful of my people (for the weather was stormy), on the first verse of the xc. Psalm: 'The Lord *our* dwelling-place in all generations.' *Our*, the plural pronoun, connects the believer with all God's people in the past and in the future, as one family, having one dwelling-place, *home* in God. The thoughts open beautifully.

I had a high compliment paid me the other day, and as it may gratify you, I may be pardoned the vanity of telling it. Professor Anthon (the learned Anthon of Columbia College) has dedicated his late edition of Xenophon's Memorabilia of Socrates to me. I have not even seen the Professor for many years, though he has been kind enough to write me twice in answer to some literary questions I put to him.

It runs: 'To Rev. George W. Bethune, D.D. the able theologian, the eloquent divine, the graceful and accomplished scholar, this work is respectfully dedicated by one who takes pride in claiming him as an early pupil and a steadfast friend.'

There is no interested motive that can be imagined for this."

All this writing had one inevitable effect, and we must alas! here chronicle that Dr. Bethune's hand-writing, once so neat and plain, had by this time become illegible altogether.

"You laugh at your hand-writing," says his friend Littell. "How beautiful it is *in general*, but how much *in general* it is! I take great credit to myself for making it out, and as it looks like some of the Arabic MSS., which are copied into some of your Commentaries, I may have too readily yielded to the notion that I could not read them."

Here is another whimsical jeremiade of later date.* It seems we little know how much we cause our brother to sin by careless calligraphy.

"MY DEAR MAJOR: Yours of the 23d reached me yesterday. I had previously received the Doctor's. It was one of his distinguished efforts, fairly *brilliant*.

I knew he must be going somewhere by the way the lines ran. I thought he must be going a fishing for there were lots of fins tails and fish-hooks. But where, O Roberto! that was the question. I followed the lines in hopes they might terminate at the destined place. But no, they did not terminate at all. Instinctively I turned over the leaf; they were running still, sliding down into the very south-east corner of the sheet, and the doctor still paying out.

In despair I took the back track. In other words tried to read the letter backwards. Tracing my way slowly back, I found about the middle of the letter the word 'river'. This confirmed me in the notion that

* From Dr. I. Wheaton Smith.

the Dr. *was* going a fishing, for it seemed to me a river would be a very appropriate place for it. But what river? Here I was hung up again, till glancing on I made out with difficulty the word 'Lake.' I conjectured that the river must empty into this lake, which seemed a very proper thing for a river to do. I now felt tolerably certain the Dr. was going a fishing in a river emptying into a lake, and as the fishing would naturally be somewhere about the outlet, I was pretty sure of finding him. But *what* lake, I could not divine. The best I could make of it was 'Jimco'. I had never heard of such a lake, and wondered where it could be; when to complete my wonderment I found the word preceding river was Seven. Now, thought I, if there are seven of these rivers emptying into Lake 'Jimco', the Lord only knows which of them the Dr. is going to fish, and for all I know he may fish Lake 'Jimco' itself.

In this dilemma your letter arrived, and with aid from it I have been able to translate a large portion of the Doctor's. Now, I beg of you, don't tell the Dr. that I criticize his writing, for, just as likely as not, in attempting any sudden change he will spoil his hand."

In the early part of September, 1848, the "Union Magazine" was purchased by John Sartain. Dr. Bethune was offered one hundred dollars per month to edit it. This offer he was under the necessity of declining, and contented himself with undertaking to supply nine articles per year at $50 per article. The enterprising purchasers of the Magazine would fain have bound him wholly to their interests by a promise not to write for other periodicals, but they did not succeed in so doing. He was, however, glad to have it to say that he was writing for one Monthly, in order to resist the importunities of others.

Aunt Betsey's fireside lectures began to appear in the latter part of the year 1849. These lectures which appeared in the "Union Magazine" were amusing and popular. Aunt Betsey was a real personage, a favorite aunt of Mrs. Bethune, whom he knew and loved right well.

"The advice of the Laird of Dumbiedykes' father may be applied" writes the author to his mother, "with a little change to a book intended to do good. 'Be aye preparing to print such books, for they do good while you are sleeping; far away from your immediate sphere, and even after you are dead.' I am, it is true, by no means great at authorship, but have the consolation of knowing that my books have done some good."

We present a specimen of Aunt Betsey's circle as talking from Sartain.

"We are a quiet family of a half dozen; my excellent sister and her excellent husband, the one a steady, sensible notable housewife, the other a zealous gentleman farmer, whose purse suffers occsaionally from his promising experiments; their daughter Kate, in the bloom of seventeen, light-hearted and bright-minded, not the less winning for being not a little mischievous, as Kates always are; their son Tom, two years older, somewhat of a coxcomb, but a good fellow at bottom, who is dubbed a law-student, from spending a few hours a week in 'Squire Lackbrief's office; Aunt Betsey, my mother's older and only sister; and myself, familiarly called Uncle Tom, of whom the less said the better, a confirmed bachelor, and less fond of talking than using my pen, though it is of little use, except in recording such scraps of second-hand wisdom as I hear from others.

Nov. 10, 18—. This afternoon Tom returned from town, bringing Kate a letter, crossed and recrossed in a minute, faint-inked chirography, from a quondam schoolmate of hers, now a dashing belle. Kate's brow flushed, and her hands trembled with excitement as she read the epistle under the lamp; 'What is it my child?' said her mother. Kate read on to the last word of the glossy, rose-colored sheet; and then, drawing her chair between my sister and Aunt Betsey, she began:

'Only think, Fanny Pryer says that old Miss Meddler told her that'— Here she sunk her voice so low that Tom and I (his father was deep in the account of a cattle sale) could only catch — 'Mrs. . . . . you know Miss . . . . that married the rich brewer's son only two years ago . . . . Major . . . . used to be her lover. . . . father broke off the match . . . .

came back from Europe . . . . constantly walking together . . . . family consultation . · . . likely to be a duel . . . . everybody talking about it . . . . hushed up . . . . must not say anything to any one, at least that she told me . . . .'

'Fie! Fie! my dearie, what does thee fash thy bonny head with such bletherin' malice. It's no becoming a lassie like thee, or any lady, to file her tongue with tales like that. The evilest sign of a woman, I know, is being given to scandal.'

(Aunt Betsey was regularly set in for a fireside lecture.)

'Old Dr. McCrecchie of the Tollbooth-kirk, never said a truer word, than that a "scandalous tongue always showed a licentious heart"; for "out of the fulness of the heart the mouth speaketh", and it is only out of an evil heart that evil things can come. Charity, which is a complete name for all goodness, just as Love is the name of God — "thinketh no evil."

'But aunt, dear aunty,' put in the blushing Kate, 'when people expose themselves, surely charity' —

'Is not easily provoked, dearie, which, though I don't know the oreeginal, means, I suppose, is not easily suspicious of evil, sees everything in the best light, makes every possible allowance, and even imagines excuses it cannot see, because "it rejoiceth not in iniquity", — hates the very sight and thought of crime, and if it cannot discover innocence, turns its bonny eye away up to heaven with a tear in it, as a prayer for the sinner's pardon to our heavenly Father, who "pitieth our infirmities, and remembereth that we are but dust". So should thee do, my darling. If our good God looked at our evil, "who could stand?" and it aye seems to me like a defying Him who is ever hearing what we say, to speak of our neighbour's faults, because the Saviour has told us we shall be measured by our own stoup. I have heard ministers say that the name of the devil is *accuser*, and we know that he was a liar from the beginning, so that wickedness, lying and scandal make up his character; and your scandalizers are just like the little devils that the muckle de'il uses to do his mischief with.

'But when our Lord came to destroy the works of the devil, and set us a pattern of a good man, he became the friend of sinners, because he pitied them, and interceded for their pardon. How much must God hate to hear us talking scandal, like the devil! How much must He love to hear us talking kindly, and gently, and meekly, like his well-beloved

Son! When the Blessed One was upon earth, his words were all merciful, except to those who thought themselves better than others, and spoke evil of them; that was enough to prove that they were desperately wicked themselves, because it was so unlike our Father in Heaven. They made a great pretence of goodness, but they were hypocrites, just white-washed sepulchres. Do you no mind when they brought to him the poor fallen misdoer, and she lay silent in the dust at his holy feet, without a word to say, in the sorrows of her shame, how he bid the one without sin to cast the first stone? There was but One without sin among that company, and He just bid her "go and sin no more."

Indeed, and indeed Dr. McCreechie was right, there is always a licentious heart where there is a scandalous tongue; it is they who love the sin that love to talk about it, and they, who know they would not resist temptation, that are most ready to think another has not. Their imaginations are just like the black corbie that Noah sent out of the ark, scenting the dead and the loathsome, and flying to glut themselves with what is vile; but let yours, lassie, be like the sweet silver-winged dove that came back with the green branch of hope in her bill. The world is bad enow, but God loves it, and his Son died for it, and it is yet to be like another heaven; and there's many a green branch for the dove, if there be many a dead thing for the corbie. It was like a dove that the Spirit came down to the Saviour, and without the spirit of a dove we can never fly up to him.

'Never be like a corbie, Katie dear, except it be to those that God changed from their nature, and sent to carry bread to his hungry saint. Mistress Wheatfield (Aunt Betsey is scrupulous in giving my sister her matronly title, as honour due to the female head of the family), if I am a wee bit hard on the lassie its no' in unkindness. But, 'deed, our Katie is just like the rest of us, the descendant of old Adam, and, what for should I not say, a daughter of old Eve? for she it was that the devil threw his glamour over, and the pleasant voice of his bonny bride led the man astray.

'The Apostle calls woman the weaker vessel, but he himself tells us that God puts strength into weak things, and women are strong for good, but may be also, as all know, strong for evil. As you train the lassie, you make the wife and mother; and the hand that rocks the cradle rules the world, as some one says.

'We are over-fond of talking about the dignity of the sex, and unwilling to show that *woman* can do wrong, in the same breath that we condemn *women* for doing wrong. Let Katie wear the ornaments of a meek and quiet spirit, which are of more price in God's sight than pearlings or diamonds. It's more than folly to say out in the church that we are "miserable sinners", and that "there's no health in us" and after each commandment "Lord have mercy upon us, and incline our hearts to keep this law"; and then, at our firesides, draw ourselves up as if we could not fall into the sin which others have fallen into. Human nature is a poor frail thing, and the more we think so of it, the more charitable will we be toward our fellow-sinners, and the more humble ourselves. "The beginning of strife is like the letting out of water", and so is the beginning of an evil habit. If you do not stop it at the first, the tide will soon be too strong for you. Katie has never talked scandal in my hearing before, and I am fain to keep her from ever talking it again.'

'But dear, good, precious Aunt Betsey,' half-sobbed Katie, 'I only—'

'Yes, dearie, you *only* — Miss Meddler *only* told Fanny Pryer, and Fanny Pryer *only* wrote to you, and you *only* told us, and if we *only* went on telling others, and they others, the character of these people, who may be as innocent as lambs, would be ruined. Just bring it home, and think what it is to have one's fair character stained in such a way! We would not be thieves, yet we take away what no gold or silver could buy or redeem; we would not be murderers, yet we break the hearts of our fellow-beings with shame; and this by *only* repeating what malice dared first *only* whisper in a single ear—until every one hears of it, and, then we excuse ourselves by saying, "the thing is so public that it is the talk of the town"!

'Don't tell me that circumstances are so strong as to make the thing certain. Such is the time for Charity to plead; for she "hopeth all things". Tom there can tell — that many a man has been condemned on circumstantial evidence, whose innocence afterward was "brought forth as the light". Our good house-dog Faithful, that Tom shot, — because a sheep was killed, and the dumb beast, that could not speak for himself, came home bloody about the mouth, — had been but defending his master's flock from the strange mastiff that was found the next day dead behind the stone-dyke; and all our sorrow can never bring back to our ear the deep bark at midnight that told us the sleepless sentinel was on his round. How sorry should we be, when this story of the——'s turns out false, if we have allowed ourselves for a moment to think so ill of them, much more, if we have led others to do so. One, who knows men's hearts better than we can know them, has left a blessing for those, against whom "*all* men speak all *manner* of *evil falsely* for his sake"; so the world treated the prophets and apostles: and so they crucified the spotless Lamb of God. Never, then, think a scandal must be true because all the world tells it. One little tongue, that is "set on fire of hell," may set the world on fire.

'Even if the scandalized people are guilty, we are not called on to be their executioners. A hangman is always held infamous by the general prejudice; but they are worthy of infamy who perform that office as amateurs.

'The devil has not so cloven a foot, but he may wear a kid slipper; yes, and he can write letters on rose-coloured paper, Katie, though they smell of musk instead of brimstone. . . . . . . And now, Katie, my darling,' said Aunt Betsey as she rose up, and then bent her stately head to kiss our pet on her wet cheeks, 'go your ways; and when you repeat the Lord's Prayer to-night, pause to think what you mean as you say:

"Forgive us our trespasses, as we forgive those who trespass against us, and lead us not into temptation, but deliver us from evil!'"

Here Jonas came in with our little supper, which we are too fond of old-fashioned comforts to miss, and Aunt Betsey's lecture on scandal was finished."

We must again pass over cursorily nearly a year of time, and a vast mass of correspondence. The time is without incident, and the correspondence of the usual character.

If any man in a prominent position would take the trouble to keep a register of all the irrelevant, and impertinent letters which he receives, what an amazing list it would be. What a drain upon his pocket to pay the postage of the answers; what a heavy tax in stationery. What hours of precious time consumed in deciphering their ignoble calligraphy, and consigning them to the waste-paper basket. How many scores of people to be gratified with an autograph and a sentiment, who have not the good breeding to enclose a stamp in the letter of application. How many whom he has never heard of desire introductions to those he has never seen. How many desire to be put in places which could by no possibility be in his gift. How many want his money on the simple pretext that he has it and they have not. How difficult, always, to say no, civilly, and how impossible in ninety-nine cases out of a hundred to say yes. Such letters and such annoyances, are the inevitable penalty of position. The careful wife of the subject of our memoirs, kept all her husband's letters, and filed them duly away. We are, therefore, admitted to the privilege of contemplating a small mountain of epistolary matter; each letter of which is amply done justice to, with a single glance, if "fair writ," or certainly consigned to oblivion, when ten minutes' strain upon the optic nerve has been given to illegible incoherence. One sensitive creature has been startled, in the stillness of his room, by a white dove that "perched above the chamber door"; immediately thereafter, he fell into an illness, and, on convalescing, wrote to Dr. Bethune for a piece of poetry suited to this interesting and inscrutable circumstance. Another, more importunate, has a country parish, must drive about, and is so afraid of a horse that his life is a burden to him. He pathetically prays our Doctor to procure him a post where he will not have to ride or drive. A third coolly asks him to revise a work for the press, but makes no mention of a cheque in payment. There are many letters anent the Thousand Island Church. There are outpourings of the heart on matters personal and religious; there are invitations to preach, and announcements of honorary elections; and, by the time we reach the missive which sets forth its writer's opinion, that "the yankees have thick epidermides," we shall have arrived at material for narrative.

We are now to chronicle another great change in our minister's life, in his departure from Philadelphia, the reasons for which are fully set forth in an elaborate paper of resignation, to the consistory of his church. It is dated Brooklyn, August 28, 1849.

The great cause for removal was the necessity of Mrs. Bethune's health, and his duty as a faithful husband. She had been compelled to remove to Brooklyn, and her frequent and painful attacks had constantly distracted the pastor's mind and heart:

"I have never been more sensible," he writes, "than I am at present, indeed, never have I felt so keenly the obligations under which I am, to you and your congregation. I recall, with hearty gratitude, the generous devotion of the little band, who began the enterprise of building the church under God for me. I recall, though I cannot sufficiently estimate, their devoted zeal, courage, perseverance and liberality, among the dark and difficult times of its earlier history. I recall the promptness with which they, and those in later times associated with them, have always met their engagements with me; and the very liberal manner in which they have ministered to my necessity and comfort beyond my claims upon them, especially when they enabled me to go abroad for my health, advancing me my salary when I was absent, and during the same time paying for the supply of the pulpit; and again more recently, in a munificent present as a token of their regard, on Christmas last. I recall the forbearance and earnest friendship shewn me during the bitterest trials of my ministerial life, when, on returning, sick and feeble from abroad, I found myself assailed by persecutions from those whom I would have died to serve. I recall the ever ready welcome which has met me on the threshhold of every household, from every individual of the congregation. Very fondly have I loved my people, and I know that I have been loved in return, notwithstanding my infirmities, my errors and my faults. I have ever felt as if my congregation was to me as a family. I am deeply sensible of my many deficiencies, but the more grateful for their affection, which has been granted to me notwithstanding them all.

In these circumstances, I feel, and I think you should feel, that nothing short of necessity could sever the bond between us. It is nothing less than the hand of God that dissolves our union, and to his Providence we should humbly submit, because what God does is wise and right. Neither ambition, nor avarice, nor love of ease, seduce me from you. Such motives I have more than once cheerfully resigned for your sake. I expect, on my separation from you, to take charge of a feeble, much dilapidated church, which has appealed to me for help, to save them from dissolution. I never expect to be so happy with another church, or to find such another people as that which my heart loves the more tenderly, as I must tear myself from it. As I have been writing, my mind's eye has been going from pew to pew, from person to person, seeing each familiar face, receiving the greeting of each familiar voice. Brethren and friends, I could not tear myself from you unless I were compelled to do so."

He then proceeds to show that no expedient will obviate the necessity of this separation, and considers its probable effect upon the congregation. Fears are entertained that the people will be scattered, but he says :

"Much will depend on the prompt action of the consistory and Board of Trustees, in supplying the vacant pulpit, by doing which, they may not merely prevent people from going away, but also induce others to join with you. For this reason, let me earnestly advise that as soon as possible, you decide upon calling some well-known and esteemed minister, without waiting until the congregation are distracted by various preferences, which would inevitably be the case, should you throw open your pulpit to candidates. Besides, such a minister as you should decide to have, would be far more likely to accept a call when promptly and unanimously given, than after a delay. It is also, believe me, a very poor way to judge of a preacher's qualifications, on hearing once or twice in the pulpit. It is far better to choose one whom you have never seen, if he has the high esteem of his brethren as a faithful and able minister of the New Testament. The intense anxiety I feel, and shall continue to feel in your future welfare, must be my excuse for not waiting until my advice is asked before I give it; and I dare to hope that if you act promptly, all, by the blessing of God, will be more than well. When the necessary formalities are gone through with, I shall, with the permission of Providence, go to Philadelphia, and attempt to utter my farewell. Commending you to God, and the bond of his grace, and assuring each of you of my grateful and undying affection, I am,

Your servant in the Gospel of Christ,

GEO. W. BETHUNE."

The receipt of this communication was bewailed, but its arguments could not be resisted. A crowd of letters from all sorts of people testify the golden opinions which had been won:

"Your letter and resignation," writes Captain G. D. Magruder, 6th of September, "was read to a crowded lecture-room on Monday night. Many tears were shed, and the deepest sorrow manifested by the people, but not a word of censure or blame did I hear from any quarter; there was a disposition not to receive your resignation, supposing a 'leave of absence for three or six months would answer your purpose,' but when told that this course had been proposed to you, there was a sorrowful acquiescence to the decrees of Providence, which seemed unendurable. That some small portion of the congregation will be induced to leave the church in her present distress, is more than probable, but that there will be anything like a general defection, I have no idea. The very circumstances of our trouble in parting from a pastor so justly cherished by us all, will draw more closely the bonds of union between those who love the cause of the Master, the great Head of the Church."

Another dear friend writes under the same date:

"MY DEAR DOMINIE: How shall I tell you of our grief? My thoughts come slowly and my words, also, when I attempt to give language to that which our hearts so deeply feel. We have for weeks been endeavoring to resign ourselves to the necessity of a separation which we knew to be inevitable, and thought we had in a measure succeeded; but when it was announced that you had actually determined upon it, we discovered how illy we were prepared. Whatever may have been our shortcomings and neglects of duty while you were still with us, whatever apparent coldness there may have been, all now is love and sorrow. I cannot bear to realize that your ministrations amongst us are at an end; and I fear, however much you may deprecate such a consequence, that the church will never recover from the effects of your loss. You cannot wonder that such should be the case, for your congregation is, in a peculiar manner, made up of members drawn together by personal attachment to you; admiration of your eloquence attracting them to the church, and love of yourself settling them there. Your endeavor has always been to make them good Christians, rather than sectarians. Is it strange then that, if any have previously had a preference for another form of worship, they should desire to return to it now that you have left?"

In 1848 he received an attractive invitation to a new Presbyterian enterprise in Baltimore, which was declined. In the same year he delivered the Oration before the Phi Beta Kappa of Dartmouth College. It may be well to add that, in each congregation, Dr. B's affectionate nature would lead him to take into closest counsel some sympathizing friend; and as Mrs. Peter R. Livingston was at Rhinebeck, so was Mrs. Langdon Elwyn in Philadelphia, a second mother. Thus we reach in this memoir, what mathematicians call a "special point;" we mean the removal to Brooklyn as stated supply to the Central Reformed Dutch Church.

Dr. Bethune had now attained the zenith of his fame, and it will not be rash to say stood foremost among our popular speakers. Facile princeps in his own denomination the whole body of Christians were ready to do him honor. Not only well known in various paths of literature, his influence was constantly sought by political aspirants. "For a bit of innocent mischief," as Thackeray says, we present an idea of the number and kind of communications which he received and answered. First comes a formula, terse and practical, to secure from a distinguished citizen his autograph.

REV. GEORGE BETHUNE, D.D. "NEW YORK, *Oct.* 29, 1849.

DEAR SIR: I employ all my leisure time in the collection of autographs. I am a clerk in a wholesale house in this city, and am consequently at work through the day. The evenings are mine own. Occasionally what is termed a dull day comes, when I may sit down and follow mine inclination. Then I endeavour to possess myself of the autographs of the great men of mine own and of other countries. I have been thus employed for three months only; during which time I have been very fortunate; since I have obtained communications from so great men as Pierpont, Tyng, Potts, Cone, Beecher, Magoun, Sprague, and many more of like caliber. I have, too, the autographs of Clay, of our own dear country; and of Lamartine of France. The former is, perhaps, one of the greatest men of our time. The latter, I think, is the greatest, because the best, man, that has lived in France since Lafayette. But this is a matter of opinion. I have the signatures of some twenty of the most celebrated clergymen, of all denominations, excepting one, in this country. I am sorry that I could not attend upon your anniversary address last evening. You will receive this communication from a member of your church with whom I am acquainted. If it shall be your pleasure to transmit your autograph to me, through him, or in any other way, I shall be much obliged.

Assuring you of my respect and esteem, I have the pleasure to be respectfully yours,

J. T. P——

My address is No. 1 Rutger's Street, in this city."

At the risk of wearying our readers we shall try to give some idea of the demands made upon a popular preacher's time, outside of the duties of his office. The following applications were made to Dr. Bethune in the course of a year. Nine literary societies of different colleges request addresses; two theological societies ask similar favors; the Church at Saugerties asks a sermon at the laying of corner-stone at Harlingen, and at its dedication; that of Southwark, a lecture to pay its debts; and that of Geason, a charge to its new pastor; and six other churches desire sermons upon various grounds; one person wishes him to come to Marbletown and preach for a church that is yet in the womb of the future; four Tract, two Bible, four Sunday school, one Sabbath, and three Colonization Associations put in their claims; fourteen Institutes, or Lyceums, demand lectures. Of more important claims, the New England Society, the Union Safety Committee, American Dramatic Fund Association, Demonstration of respect to Mr. J. Fennimore Cooper, and the Smithsonian Institute, each has a place. Only one Seamen's Friend Society calls for help, but the people at Biloxi, Miss., have devised a subscription plan which Dr. Bethune is to advance; one young minister would like instruction in the art of reading; Dr. K. wants a sermon printed; Mrs. O. appeals for the Orphan Asylum; the young ladies of Heidelberg Hall would be entertained; the steamer Lafayette needs a speech on its trial trip; the biographer of Rev. Walter Colton petitions for material; a stranger requests a copy of Fourth of July Address; Mr. R. heard Dr. Bethune lecture two years ago, and thinks that sufficient basis on which to demand an introduction to Hon. Daniel Webster; a disciple of Coke and Justinian, who quotes Latin freely, pleads for a copy of address; an illegible writer from Keokuk has something to say about his son George and West Point; a youth in the Navy wishes Dr. Bethune to have him ordered on shore; the Teachers and Friends of Education at Somerville, N. J., want to hear the Brooklyn pastor; Mr. B. wants Dr. B. to give a sermon, as the petitioner is unable to do it; Mr. Y. wishes to lecture before a Sunday school Association, for purposes of his own, and the Doctor is to help him; the Navy man appears again; a gentleman of Wilmington, Delaware, wishes aid in publishing a book that will enable him to support and educate two dear little boys; the Literary World defines its position and asks support; J. C. Guldin desires to know what is the date of Paraeus' lectures on Ursinus, owned by Dr. B.; a cautious architect would find the prevailing taste of a congregation for which he is to design a church; Rev. Dr. B. is introduced, a missionary whom Dr. Bethune is to entertain in the German tongue; Mr. H. leaves his MSS. for recommendation and criticisms, and the Minnesota Historical Society desire this overworked man to come and see them. The list might be continued up to one hundred and fifty requests for important aid in the space of a twelvemonth; and they come up from all parts of the land, from Maine to Georgia, and from the Atlantic far beyond the Mississippi.

CHAPTER X.

NEW CHURCH BROOKLYN.—GOES ABROAD.

THE middle of May, 1850, brought another change to Dr. Bethune, and one that has already been slightly mentioned. The steps towards this change are perfectly well described in the original papers :

J. H. BROWER AND OTHERS, TO DR. BETHUNE.

"BROOKLYN, *May* 15, 1850.

REVEREND AND DEAR SIR : After much reflection, and we trust under the guidance of the great Head of the Church, we have considered it our duty to lay before you in form the following suggestions and overtures.

You cannot but be aware of having a number of friends, who earnestly and sincerely desire your permanent settlement in this city. As a nucleus, and to make a basis of action, we have taken it upon ourselves to call upon you in this way, in the hope you may consider our overtures, and that the Supreme Director may guide your steps hitherward.

While the city of Brooklyn is proverbial for the many and well-supported churches of several denominations, it must be manifest to you that those of our denomination have not been conspicuous, nor eminently successful among them. It may not be well to venture upon any reasons for this ; but, seeing the fact, rather to seek the path of duty, to the end, with God's blessing upon our efforts, that our church may find a more elevated position, and larger sphere of usefulness in the cause of the Redeemer.

We cannot but feel it was through God's merciful interposition you came to Brooklyn, and for several months past have so faithfully ministered in spiritual things to all of us, and many others, whereby an expiring lamp has begun to burn brightly, and to give promise of still better days. It is true we cannot yet present ourselves to you in the matured strength we could wish, but remembering that the Saviour took little children in his arms and blessed them, we rely in faith upon a blessing in store for us, if we prayerfully seek it, and for His glory combine our works with our faith.

Our already large, and still rapidly increasing population, its marked church-going character, and highly creditable observance of the Sabbath and the sanctuary, seem to lay before us an ample field for our success; therefore, while we aim to include the congregation of the Central church, we propose, for obvious reasons, to take up an entirely new enterprise and church organization, under your pastoral charge (if you will authorize it) and without any unnecessary delay, purchase a proper location, procure the necessary plans to be adopted, (all with your good counsel and approval) and erect a church edifice. Towards the cost of all this, we are prepared to guarantee, by our own subscriptions, and of such others as we may be enabled to associate with us, a sum of not less than twenty-five thousand dollars; and, we may add, as the result of our deliberations, we have strong confidence that any debt which may remain upon the property, will be paid off within a reasonable time after it shall be ready for occupation.

We have also deliberated upon the necessary provision to be made for your own support in the settlement proposed, and feel ourselves justified in naming the sum of four thousand dollars per annum. If this latter suggestion may seem to you as abruptly approached, or out of place at this early stage of our overtures, we pray you will excuse it, when we say, we have felt it to be a connecting link in the chain of our duty, to assure you of our disposition and determination to provide a comfortable and cheerful fire-side for our spiritual teacher, while a bountiful Providence affords such to ourselves.

Having now laid the desires of our hearts and purposes of our hands before you, we cheerfully leave ourselves to your prayers, and the answer you shall receive from on high, and subscribe ourselves, Reverend and Dear Sir,

Very faithfully, your friends and servants,

J. H. Brower.
A. L. Reid.
John T. Moore.
Gerrit Smith.
B. B. Blydenburgh."

A favorable reply was sent, and now that a new church was to be erected involving large responsibilities, it seemed a good occasion for another tour to Europe, which would benefit his health, and strengthen him for future toil. On the 28th of June, he sailed in the Atlantic, and we have the following record of his progress :

"EDINBURGH, *Aug.* 14, 1850.

On leaving Liverpool, I went almost immediately to Ashbourne, near Dovedale, the scene of the Second (Cotton's) part of the Complete Angler. You will see by reading it over, that he (Cotton) comes across Viator and brings him to his house. Places on the road there are described, or at least named; there also is Dovedale, so called from the river Dove (*i. e.* in Saxon white, whence our word for the bird), which flows between high hills or mountains lying close together; it is a strikingly beautiful and, in places, sublime, ravine. Towards the head of Dovedale stands Beresford House, the residence of Cotton the Angler, where he entertained Father Walton, and put him to sleep in a bedroom, the chimney-piece of which was carved on each side, with the initials of his and Walton's name. Now, over this, to me, classic ground, I went step by step, and, strange to say, found that I knew much more about the olden times of the country than the people themselves. I fortunately fell in with Shipley, the Angler, whom I knew by his book, which I have had for several years. He is a barber, who has just got £300 a year by the will of his uncle, the late Vicar of Ashbourne. I found Beresford Hall in a most shocking condition, all, in fact, in ruins, except a few rooms; I looked for the chimney-piece (spoken of above), but it cannot be found; I did find, however, the fragments bearing date 1656, and have got enough wood from each of them for a landing net handle. Shipley promises that he can get for me the *tobacco box* of Izaak Walton, which he says has been in a family he knows of for two generations. He may be mistaken, but if I acquire it, what a relic it will be.

From Ashbourne I came through Derby to York, a most interesting old city; old walls, old churches, old houses, on every side. The Minster far exceeded all my imagination of it. Could we have such Gothic buildings, I should no longer oppose the task. From York I came to New

Castle on Tyne, where I lingered for a day, rummaging Grant's old book-shop; he is a fine example of an enthusiastic biblio-maniac. Last night I came here, and to-morrow go to Glasgow."

"BRISTOL, *Aug.* 28, 1850.

Winchester, where old Izaak Walton is buried, is like an old romance, with its Cathedral, very beautiful, and presenting the different styles of the different periods in which its several parts were built, and its college cloisters, and other ecclesiastical buildings hid away in labyrinths of green, and under avenues of old trees, while the city is built around them. I have never seen anything so full of past times; Salisbury in a great measure partakes of the same characteristics. The Cathedral is fine; the spire, I believe, is thought to be the finest in England, but I do not like it so well as Winchester."

"AMSTERDAM, *Sept.* 4, 1850.

Sunday I spent in Rotterdam, and had the pleasure of attending Divine Service, without understanding more than a thousandth part of what was said; but it would have done your heart good to hear the Dutchmen sing, with the noble, though not well-played, organ accompanying them. It was really like the voice of many waters.

I am very glad that I have set out on this tour through Holland, for it is very interesting to me. The only drawback to my satisfaction (besides my not being able to understand Dutch) is the expense; it is quite as dear as England, and, to one not knowing the language, perhaps more so.

On Monday I went up the lower branch of the Rhine to Arnheim, which is really a Dutch paradise. The place is not large, perhaps 15,000 inhabitants, and it was formerly fortified so as to be one of the strongest towns in the Low Countries, but now all these ramparts are turned into public walks, which are delightfully arranged and kept with the utmost skill. I saw one or two country-houses, the grounds of which were quite as well cared for as any in England. From Arnheim I came to Utrecht so famous in the history of these extraordinary people; saw a small but good collection of paintings; the place, now a college hall, in which the union of Utrecht was signed, that union was the pattern of our union of the states, looked over the Cathedral which has been shaken by storms and spoiled by modern improvements so-called; wandered through the streets amusing myself with the people's queer costumes some of them seemed quite as much amused with mine, and spent hours in the delicious, public pleasure-grounds, extending like those of Arnheim all round the city, — woods, water and rich green grass. Amsterdam is so much larger than any other of the cities of Holland that it presents of course far more objects of interest."

"Among other things that I have seen, is the famous bull painting by Paul Potter in the collections at the Hague. It ranks in pecuniary estimate as the fourth picture in the world. It is very large and the figures the size of life. The bull stands in the foreground of a Dutch meadow, the distance of which is admirably given; an old man, the herd, stands beside a tree; a placid looking cow is chewing her cud, with her broad, honest face towards you; two or three sheep are in different positions, and the young bull stands easily out, looking calmly in your eyes; but in the cow, the sheep, and particularly the bull, the imitation is so complete that it seems as if every hair was painted separately, this, too, without sacrificing the main effect to the detail. It were worth a voyage to Europe to see that picture alone. There are other fine pictures in the same gallery, but, with the exception of a Virgin and child by Murillo, and a somewhat shocking school of anatomy, representing a professor dissecting a dead body, I can remember only the bull.

I have also seen and heard the famous organ at Haarlaem, and truly it is a wonderful instrument, though not well played by the present organist, who gets five dollars every time it is exhibited. The *vox humana* stop, so called from its being meant to resemble the human voice, from the highest treble to the deepest bass, startles you with its life-like tones. The organ is now flourishing much, on its former claims to be the largest and best in the world; but the one at York Minster is now the largest, and the organ at Fribourg excels in the *vox humana.* Both are upon the whole better instruments. By the way, the ladies of Haarlaem are eminent for beauty. Haarlaem is throughout a beautiful city; and the environs, more than most of the towns of Holland, are delightfully arranged with woods and water where the people make their promenades on foot or in carriages during the summer, and in sleighs and on skates during the winter. In one of Washington Irving's books (the 'Tales of a Traveller, I think) you will find a description of the village of Broek, the cleanest place in the world; no carriages can enter its streets, no one is allowed to ride a horse, to smoke at nights or during the day without a cover to his pipe to prevent the ashes from falling. The houses have each one grand parlor which is never open but for a marriage, a christening, a burial or some great family festival; if the last, the front door is not opened, but only for the three former. It is wholly a dairy village, and the cows' stables are as clean as the cleanest house; they are scrubbed with the greatest care, the cows themselves are rubbed down and their tails tied up. It being only September the cows are now in the fields, and the inhabitants make their summer quarters in the stables. I saw one family eating their dinner in a stall. The multitude of round Dutch cheeses, looked like a store of cannon-balls in an arsenal. The road to Broek is along the great ship canal cut by Napoleon from the Texel to Amstel, the river on which Amsterdam is situated. The canal is considerably lower than the sea, the road lower than the bank of the canal, and the farms lower than the road: a single burst of the dyke would flood the whole country. The churches, as to their appearance during service, are very strange. The Dominie preaches without a gown, but wears bands, in some cases a band, or rather the two sewed together. During the prayers and the singing the men put off their hats, but when the sermon begins they generally put them on.

The collection is taken during the sermon, and in one instance they came round twice in succession. The prayers are extemporaneous, and the sermons terribly long. The ministers preach with earnestness, but in a pompous, heavy tone. All that I could distinctly make out from one of them was 'Baul and Paanabaas.'

The great churches (like cathedrals) have a separate division for marriages, and one day, in Amsterdam, I had the luck of seeing a grand wedding. About a hundred spectators seated themselves in the pews along the outer pannelling encasing the marriage chapel; within was a separate space enclosed, a sofa placed at one end, with perhaps fifteen chairs on each side forming a semi-circle where the friends of the bride and groom took their places with most studied solemnity;

the organ played beautiful variations on *dolce concento.* The minister ascended the pulpit, immediately in front of which was an inclined plane rising towards it, covered with a rich carpet; and under the pulpit a piece of embroidery with flowers in the centre and two most ominous looking dogs, not billing, but turning their heads from one another, as if in a sort of Dutch pet. The Dominie then made a long speech to the bride and groom still sitting on the sofa. Then a very long prayer, and then he told them to 'stand oop,' and they came to the part of the plane where there were two crimson ottomans to kneel on. Here they read from the book for some time, and exchanged vows without a ring. Then he bade them kneel, and the groom, who had been standing on the left of the bride, changed places with her, and knelt on her right, she kneeling also; then a long prayer again, and the benediction, after which the two sextons, who had been standing on each side under the pulpit, each advanced with a huge tin box, looking like half of a small mill-stone, and presented it to the bride and groom for their presents, then to the friends, and then took their station at the door to try from all the company, getting from me the magnificent sum of 'ein stuyver,' almost two and a half cents.

During the whole service there was neither a smile nor a tear, and the Dominie appeared to be going through a burial service, his tones expressive of sorrow rather than joy, and the organ wound up with 'old Hundred.' The groom was a Count something, perhaps fifty years old, and the bride an old maid of forty, so that 'old Hundred' was very much in place. She was dressed with a white lace hat, a splendid cashmere shawl of a white ground, a richly-figured pearl-colored silk with a flounce of lace a foot broad. My man told me that there was a breakfast set out in a room adjoining the church, and that the groom must have spent on the organist, the Dominie, the attendants, and the breakfast at least a thousand guilders ($ 415); but added he, 'la dame a beaucoup d'argent.' He says that the Dominie was so long about it because he was well paid, but that he would marry thirty poor couple in a quarter of the time. It is certainly a formidable business to get married in Holland.

You would be much amused with the costume and habits of the working women. They all wear short gowns and petticoats, and white cap with a broad frill, and most of them adorn their heads with plates of silver, and more often of gold, with a variety of chains and pendents. These ornaments are handed down as heirlooms, and are sometimes of great value. The women in this city carry burdens in baskets suspended from their shoulders, by such yokes as the milkmen in New York used to carry their cans, and when a little hurried they have the most funny swing from one side to the other, for all the world like a fashionable lady's wriggle. You cannot tell, from behind, a young girl from an old woman, for they are as alike in waists as they are in dress, and often when you think you are passing some overgrown grandmother, the fair, rosy face, and laughing eyes of sixteen, turn upon you. Their childhood certainly runs to *waist*, and the multitude of their balloon-like petticoats, put to shame all the exaggeration of abustling world."

"BREMEN, *Sept.* 11, 1850.

I have visited the only curiosity in this place worth seeing. On the market-place stands an old and beautiful building, the *Rathhaus* or Senate House, the freizes of which, in front, are sculptured with emblematical devices of Christian and Pagan Mythology strangely intermingled, and at the side there are statues of princes, and an emperor. In the market-place, front of it, stands a statue of Roland, eighteen feet high, the date of which I could not ascertain, but it is emblematical of the power which the senate of this little state of Bremen (about 60,000 souls) once claimed as a free city, and still professes to claim in a considerable degree.

It has been the pride of the senate to preserve, in a deep cellar under the Rathhaus, quantities of Rhine wine, some of which has attained a great age; huge casks full are ranged throughout the cellar, but in one chamber there are twelve casks marked with the name of the twelve Apostles, the wine of Judas being the best, because wine is treacherous. Another chamber is called the Rose, from a huge rose being painted on the ceiling, with an inscription in Latin, to the effect, that 'as without love the joys of wine were imperfect, and without wine Venus herself would grow cold, so the Rose of Venus should preside over the treasures of Bacchus.' I drank from curiosity a glass of the wine (Rudesheimer) which bore the most ancient date 1625, 224 years old, but the wine of 1846 pleases my palate better."

"HAMBURG *Sept.* 22, 1850.

In the afternoon I came to Hanover by the railroad. It is a pretty town, but without much to attract a stranger, but I had the great satisfaction of seeing and hearing the people mob Haynau, the Austrian butcher of the Hungarians. You will have seen in the papers an account of his being mobbed in London, when he went to see Barclay's brewery; he had been in Hanover two weeks before and was not disturbed, but received attentions from the King; after his affair in London, he fled to Hanover, and the people, excited by the news from London, rose in a crowd, drove him from the theatre and endangered his life, so that, escorted by the police at five o'clock this morning, he fled to Hesse Cassel, where he will probably have no better fate. It serves him right, the wretch that *flogged women!*

Hamburg, in the quarter where I am lodging is very beautiful. The Alster, a small river, is led into a large basin perhaps five hundred yards wide, forming a square, along the sides of which are many handsome houses built after the great fire in 1842. As I look out from my high window I see the clear water, brilliant with the reflection of a thousand lights, and with boats on the surface, freighted with gay parties, music from the pavilion on the further side sweeping down on the gentle wind, and such music as only a German band or orchestra can make. It is also very amusing to see the pretty Vrieland girls in a picturesque costume, a round hat turned up broadly at the sides, so as to make them higher than the crown, a laced boddice of some gay color, and very short petticoats setting off their trim legs in deep red stockings to great advantage: they are the Vrielanders, the market-people of Hamburgh. The servant-maids are also objects of curiosity, for it is a pride of theirs, and of the families with whom they live, to dress very showily; and they carry a box under their arms to contain the articles sent by them, which is always covered by a neat shawl."

"Dresden.

I went to Leipsic. Half a day was enough to exhaust all that was really curious in that town, which has its celebrity from its trade, and a great battle once fought near it, and yesterday, at four P. M., I arrived here. Last evening the moon shone brightly, and I made the best of it in rambling over the town. To-day I have spent entirely in the palace, which is crowded with precious curiosities, and in the glorious picture-gallery. In the last I hope to spend to-morrow, perhaps part of Monday. It far exceeds the gallery at Berlin, excellent as that is. I promised myself to give you some account of what is to be seen in Berlin, yet scarcely know where to begin or where to end. There is no describing a picture — how can the words of a pen give the exquisite sentiment of Carlo Dolci, the serene holiness of Raphael, the coloring of Rubens, the shadows of Rembrandt, the grace of Correggio, or the natural truth of Gerard?

Yet upon all these and many other very eminent masters, with some admirable Murillos and Claudes, I feasted myself until I was delirious with delight, intoxicated to confusion with enjoyment. Of course I shall remember comparatively few, but those few can never be forgotten. Among those noted, I was particularly struck by 'The angel opening the door of Peter's dungeon.' It is large, the figures the size of life; light streams in from the opened door upon the form and face of Peter, who is awaking with a mixed expression of surprise and confusion, yet no timidity; a holy joy in his mission beams from the angel's countenance as he beckons the apostle forth. It is by Gerardo del Notti. There is also a large landscape by Salvator Rosa, finer than anything I have ever seen of that artist. But I am out of patience with myself for attempting to describe my impressions in that gallery, and I shall cease. There is however, a monument by a modern sculptor, Rauch, at Charlottenburgh which alone is worth going a thousand miles to see. It is of the late Queen of Prussia and her husband the King. It is placed within a little Doric temple, in a retired part of the gardens about the little palace at Charlottenburgh. The light is most admirably managed, being let in from windows near the roof; some blue panes in the porch soften the light from the interior, so as to give the sculpture the very best advantage. The King and Queen each recline upon a Grecian couch, the couches being perhaps six feet apart. He is clothed in his uniform, his cloak thrown loosely around him, hiding the stiffness of our modern costume, his head is bare, and he lies as tranquilly as if reposing after fatigue. His countenance is most life-like and serene; but the figure of the Queen so absorbed me that I had little time for the King's, fine as it is. She was in life eminently beautiful and eminently good. The sculptor (except that he has made both statues one foot larger than life,) has represented her as she was. She lies with her face upwards, a face of wonderful loveliness and, even in sleep, full of sweet, pious gentleness. Her form is exquisite in proportion, and is draped in a simple night-dress, the arms bare, but otherwise covered to the neck. Her lower limbs are crossed, and her hands laid meekly, but most naturally, upon her bosom. So naturally is the drapery wrought, that, at a little distance I could not distinguish (at first) between the marble and the white cloth which the attendant had removed on our coming in, and rolled up at the foot. On each side of the statues is a rich candelabrum with figures around the shaft, one representing the Graces, the other the Fates, the countenances of each expressive of grief. All around the freize of the temple are texts of Scripture (in German) very well chosen, and above a little altar-shaped table, is a fresco representing the Saviour on a throne, and the deceased King and Queen kneeling, and laying down their crowns at his feet, — the inscription — 'I am the Lord, and besides me, there is none else.' Rarely, I may say never, have I had a deeper impression made upon me than by the whole monument, especially the figure of the Queen. I was silent for an hour after I left the building, following my guide about the grounds almost unconsciously.

At Leipsic I saw the church from which Luther thundered. The church has been altered within a few years past, but the pulpit is sacredly preserved in a little closet by itself. It is nearly round in shape with some carving of a poor kind. I also drank a glass of Rhine wine in the cellar where Goethe laid part of the scene of his Faust, and where Faust and, afterwards, Goethe himself, had 'kept it up.'"

"Berlin.

At the great church here I attended service after the Lutheran method, and listened to an exceedingly eloquent man. Of course I could not make out all he said, but could see and feel that he was most eloquent. His delivery was so good as to be a perfect study. The congregation sung one or two German chorals extremely well, and a choir of men and boys chanted well, while the organ was magnificently played. On my way home I looked into another church and saw a baptism. I was too late for the service of the English Chapel, indeed, I prefer attending worship with the people of the town I am in. It widens one's heart to worship with strangers the God and Saviour we worship at home. The people have at least the appearance of devotion, and it is not for us to judge the heart. How could I doubt the earnest, solemn, rapt faces which were upturned to catch the preacher's words, or bowed down in prayer; afterwards beaming with fervor as they joined in a grand chorus of two thousand voices. The rest of the Sabbath is a holiday, as you know, on the Continent rather than a *holy* day, and it pained me to think that the impressions made by the sermon of the morning were to be effaced by the amusements of the evening. Far sweeter are our quiet Sabbath evenings at home, and far better for the people. I must however say for Berlin that externally it is one of the best-regulated cities I have ever seen. The hack carriages, porters, and even the hotels are under a very strict and just system, so that one who knows the rules need never be cheated. After ten o'clock at night the streets are almost deserted and no impropriety of any kind permitted. As yet I am unprepared to give you any description of what I have seen. Six hours were consumed at Potsdam, the summer residence of the king, where there are several palaces, among them the famous *San Souci*, built by Frederick the Great to shew that after all the cost of the Seven Years' War, he was still very well provided with money. The grounds were very extensive. I must have driven and walked miles upon miles through them. They are crowded with statues and fountains and parterres of rich flowers, showing that enormous wealth has been lavished upon them, though often in bad taste."

"PRAGUE.

I was greatly delighted with Dresden. As a city it is not well built, but beautifully situated, and after the monotonous flat countries I have been in for weeks, the hills which encircled it, the sides of which are mostly covered with vineyards, had quite a refreshing look. But the charm of Dresden is its picture-gallery. There is, to be sure, in a range of apartments connected with the palace (called the Green Vaults), an immense collection of precious things, gold plate, jewels, and articles of curious, costly workmanship; and in another palace a very precious and most extensive collection of porcelain, Chinese, Japanese and European; in fact, a complete history of earthen-ware in the ware itself, near which is a small collection of antique sculpture &c. All this I went through, besides looking at the curiosities of the Royal Library and the rooms of the palace, yet I consider the time spent among these as more than lost, as it diminished my time of enjoyment in the gallery. The gallery is an extensive but mean building, yet within it are rich treasures, perhaps the richest out of Italy. First among the foremost is the Madonna of Raphael, called the St. Sistine from the Pope, who is represented in it. It is very large and the figures of colossal size. The Virgin, holding in her arms the divine child, has descended upon a fleecy cloud, appearing to Pope Sixtus, who kneels on her right, and St. Barbara, who kneels on her left. The Pope, gazing up on his heavenly visitants, represents the adoration of high intellectual faith. St. Barbara, turning her head away, as it were, from the glory of the Presence, gives the ideal of humble reverence. The figures of the Pope and Barbara are wonderfully fine, and either alone would be a master-piece of art. At the foot of the picture are two little cherubims or angels looking up with beautiful rapture, and they are justly considered exquisite in character and glow, but the charm of the picture, besides its beautiful harmony, is the Virgin herself. Her feet scarcely rest even on the cloud. She floats in air; her position is upright, the child sitting upon her right arm. The child I do not entirely like. It is impossible for art to represent Deity incarnate as a child, even more so than as a man. Here Raphael in striving to give dignity has given rather sternness; but, oh! the face of the Virgin. There is nothing to my eye so lovely upon canvas; far before the Madonna of the chair at Florence. I have gazed upon it for hours, and shall carry it away upon my heart. That picture is really worth my whole journey. Besides the Madonna, there are many gems, five or six favourites. Here is the Magdalena of Correggio, a small picture, in which the Magdalen in a drapery of blue reclines on the ground reading, her head resting on her arm. You have often seen copies and engravings of it, but of course all fall short of the sweet reality. I must confess, however, some disappointment; delighted as I was, it did not come up to my expectations. Here is also the *Adoration of the Shepherds* by Correggio, a large picture, in which the light mainly comes from the child, though the morning has broke, and the early dawn with the supernatural light mingle together in a wonderful manner. You remember the same subject by Gerard at Florence; this is a finer picture in the judgment of artists, but the one at Florence comes very near to it in my judgment. Here are also two heads of our Saviour by Guido Reni; the one representing him breaking the bread, the other covered with thorns; both very, very admirable. There are several other Guidos, as well as Correggios; a St. Cecilia, and the girl with John the Baptist's head in a charger, both ranked very high.

Caracci has here a head of our Saviour which is most divine, and there is a capital Murillo, a Virgin and child, with that star-like character so peculiar to him. There is a profusion of Titians, Rembrandts, Rubens, Gerard, Douws, Synders and Potters, besides countless others of inferior note (the catalogue was over 1000!!). One of the Douws is the sweetest, if not the best, of all his I have seen. It is a sweet-faced girl holding a candle out of a window in a dark night to pluck a bunch of grapes. His famous cat is here, a grey pussy sitting on a window-sill so tranquilly that you can almost hear her purr. A landscape by Ruysdael struck me as particularly excellent. But were I to write a week I should not begin to finish the list of these glorious things.

I had also at Dresden a great musical treat. I attended the Lutheran church on Sunday morning, making one of a large congregation, of perhaps three thousand persons. And how they did sing with all their lungs the noble chorals in which the Germans delight; but on my way home I looked into *the* (only) Catholic Church (the royal family are Catholics, but nearly all the people Protestants) and there I heard a mass performed in a style so grand and beautiful as to be entrancing. The music is by the Chapel Master of the king. I have secured a MS. copy of it and hope (D. V.) to hear some of its airs in my own new church at Brooklyn.

This morning at five o'clock I left Dresden for this place and have been enchanted all day with the scenery. The *Elbe* passes the whole way between mountains, and the scene on both sides is by turns, and often together, magnificent and grand; in fact this part of Saxony is called Saxon Switzerland, so much does it resemble the true land of the Swiss. There is all along a constant succession or rather continuation of views which exhaust all the terms by which we express admiration. 'Sublime,' 'magnificent,' 'ravishing,' 'delicious,' were the exclamations from those on our little deck in all languages. The finest view is that near the Königsburg or Royal Citadel; but there is another nearly as striking where the mountains present the same sinuous appearance as the Palisades on the Hudson, but in this superior, as, about a hundred feet from the top which rises precipitately, the sides sloped to the shore covered with vines and verdure, studded also with neat houses. As a whole I like it nearly as well as the Rhine; and, but for the towering pinnacled Alps, quite as well as any part of Switzerland except the Lakes. The sun was setting as we took the rail; but an hour after the full moon rose in silvering splendor and shone upon the calm river and the mountains which line its shores. Here, too, for the first time in Europe, I found railway cars after our American fashion. Everywhere else that I have been they use the coach-body cars, such as we rode in from London to Liverpool."

"VIENNA.

I was greatly pleased with Prague as a city, though there is not much besides the city itself to see. There are a few pictures in the Wallenstein collection, but no great things. The city, however, is very finely situated in a basin surrounded by hills along which are old fortifications and walls; and the view from one of the hills which is named after Ziska, the great general of the Reformers in that section, is one of the best I have ever had. I am rather disappointed in Vienna, though it is undoubtedly a very fine city, and perhaps at this season I do not see it to advantage. The streets are narrow and the squares mean, the best houses being in the suburbs of the city. Then there are undoubtedly some good buildings. The picture-gallery (royal) and another private collection are large, and contain some very good things. There is an exquisite Madonna and child by Raphael; one of the best Cuyps I have yet seen, and very many Rubens, and some of the Dutch school, of which I am not so fond as I am of the Italian. By the way, in coming from Prague here I fell in with a Hungarian, who told me that he had wished to go to America after having been compromised by the insurrection. When he found that I was an American, of the North, as they call us, he told his little girl to kiss my hand."

"VIENNA.

I went by railroad to Presburg (perhaps sixty-miles) which I reached in the dark and where my first experience of a Hungarian Inn was far from agreeable; but the steam voyage down the swift Danube made up for my inconveniences. Not far from Presburg was the scene of a great battle between the Austrians and Hungarians in which the latter were victorious; and about half way to Pesth is the little city of Comoru whose fortress under Klapka held out to the last and was surrendered only upon the best terms, after the Hungarians had been everywhere else scattered. I had the good fortune to find several very agreeable fellow-passengers and my being an 'American of the North' secured me some attention, partly because we are rare birds here, partly because we showed some sympathy for the Hungarians, and partly because they were curious to know more of our country and its institutions. Comoru is not, as one might suppose, a fortress on a high rocky precipice, but on a plain, with the Danube on one side and extensive marshes on the other. The towns and villages and farms for many miles still show melancholy traces of war. Austria is now completely dominant and the Hungarians are made to feel it in various ways. They all spoke sadly of their country, and many said 'All is lost.'

Between Comoru and Pesth the river cuts its way through a fine range of mountains and some have thought that the scenery was equal to the best part of the Rhine; but it is not so, nor is it equal to the Elbe from Dresden to Lobositz, though it is very fine. My window at Pesth commanded the Danube, over which is thrown a magnificent suspension bridge, perhaps the finest in the world, and the old city of Buda with its mountains on the opposite sides. It so happened that, during the night, a large steam mill on the Pesth side was burned to the ground, and the glow upon Buda and its rocky hills made the scene very grand: indeed I do not remember anything that I have seen (at night) so much so. My return from Pesth was very uncomfortable. The current of the Danube is so rapid that it requires twice the time to ascend that it does to descend."

"MUNICH.

Notwithstanding the storm I really enjoyed the scenery up the Danube to Lintz; in some respects the storm improved it, giving a yet wilder grandeur to the mountain ridges, and old ruined castles along the shores. The environs of Passau, a little city at the junction of the Inn with the Danube can seldom be surpassed for beauty and variety; while the road, for miles after leaving Passau, runs along a ridge between the two rivers, giving a magnificent view on either side. The country reminded me sometimes of Switzerland, sometimes of home. The houses are Swiss, but the abundance of wood and rail-fences, with many other things, seem like America. All the way I was obliged to speak German, and my German is very ridiculous. My expectation was to reach here by midnight on Saturday, but the condition of the roads kept me back until late on Sunday morning much to my regret ; but it was impossible to stop as there was no place of refuge nearer than this, and our postillions compelled us to go on. As yet I have seen little of Munich, but enough to astonish me with the very great contributions to science and art made by the late king, who was two years ago compelled by the people to abdicate his throne in favor of his son, because, though an old man, he chose to play the fool with that famous harpy, Lola Montez. Every part of the city is crowded with monuments of his magnificent patronage of art. Besides two very large and splendid churches, one built in honor of his patron Saint Louis, the other to commemorate the fiftieth year of his marriage (called by the Germans, the golden wedding), he has caused to be erected a very large building for sculptures, another for pictures, another for an agricultural museum, another for the library, the second in size in the world, another for the University, another for a blind asylum, besides three palaces, triumphal arches, statues &c. &c., &c. No one of these buildings, except the Blind Asylum, could have cost less than a million of dollars, some of them must have cost much more. The Sculpture Gallery in its interior is the most beautiful building I have ever seen; paved throughout with tessellated marble, and each hall or room of a different pattern, adorned with fresco paintings and stored with most precious monuments of ancient and modern sculpture. The new palace contains a series of rooms decorated in the most lavish style with frescoes and guilt bronze statues and golden ornaments, and an entrance and staircase so splendid as to seem like a dream of Oriental romance; though scarcely so beautiful, and not so grand, as the staircase of his new library. Besides the churches he has built entirely, he has given the stained glass windows, nineteen in number, to a new church in the suburbs, which represent the history of the Virgin Mary, and I may safely say there are no windows in the world like them. To-morrow, should the weather prove fine, there will be inaugurated with appropriate ceremonies the statue of Bavaria in bronze, sixty-one feet high, the *head* of which contains seats for eight people: it is placed between two beautiful temples, each adorned with columns and sculpture in a lavish manner. All these edifices are in pure taste of different orders, but chiefly Greek. The entire expense must have been enormous. I have not yet been in the picture-gallery, having spent the day in the sculpture gallery, the palaces and the churches. To-morrow I devote to the paintings.

"CONSTANCE.

I wrote you that there had been erected a bronze statue of Bavaria at Munich, sixty-one feet high; on Wednesday (the ceremony having been several times postponed on account of the weather) the statue was displayed to the people, and it was the occasion of a great fête. As it was erected by the ci-devant King Louis, who was compelled to abdicate, the present king, his son, did not appear, but gave up the honor of the day to the old man. The ceremony took place on an immense parade ground outside the city, and at least 20,000 people were present. A gay pavilion was erected for the royal party, and I pushed through the crowd, until I got pretty near them. There was a long procession of the several trades, each bringing some appropriate contribution; the military and civil bands playing all the while as only a German band can play.

Before the statue there was a screen of boards completely hiding it from view; when, after a burst of delicious music from the band, at a signal given, the screen fell down and the beautiful creation of genius and taste stood before the multitude, who were silent in admiration perhaps half a minute before they broke out in thundering cheers. Then a short oration was pronounced, and several hundred men's voices sang, accompanied by the band, an ode in honor of the occasion. The whole affair lasted three hours, but was well worth the fatigue it cost me. The figure represents a young maiden, draped in a bear skin, with a wreath of vine leaves and wheat ears around her head, a sheathed sword in one hand and a wreath of victory held aloft in the other. Nowithstanding the immense size, the countenance is lovely, youthful and mild; perhaps the proportions of the form are a little too large, but the artist's design was to represent Bavaria strong, The artist, Swanthaler, did not live to see his work triumphant. His bust was borne in the procession with a guard of honor."

"LONDON.

It is at Antwerp that you see the very best works of Rubens, together with some capital specimens of other, and older, Flemish masters. There are especially, three pictures of Rubens, the Crucifixion, the Descent from the Cross, and another Crucifixion (called, Christ between the Thieves), which will remain in my memory as long as I live. The Cathedral at Antwerp disappointed me, after those I had seen elsewhere.

Ghent is full of historical associations, and the streets, in many parts, retain their antique appearance, so that it was not difficult to realize that you were moving about the scenes where once figured the Van Artevelds and the other brave men of Ghent. The same is true, though in a less degree, of Bruges and you may imagine what pleasure I had, fond as I am of Netherlandish history, in going over the ground already so familiar to me.

There are also some very nice old pictures by some Dutch, or rather Flemish masters, whom I know but little of. Then it is no wonder that I allowed one mail train after another to slip by, leaving me behind, especially, as I care very little for England."

Meanwhile, the new church edifice approached completion. It was a massive structure, very rich in interior adornment, admirably located, and will ever remain the best monument to its accomplished pastor. Erected by Lefevre, it was everything that could be desired in point of beauty, but its cost far exceeded the original estimates. A parsonage, according to Dr. Bethune's plan, was also erected by the aid of some friends; so connected with the church that Mrs. Bethune, from her invalid couch, might hear and take part in the service. The name assumed by the corporation was, The Church on the Heights. The regular call for Dr. Bethune is dated, Nov. 25, 1851. It must have been the triumph of ministeral success when this most beautiful temple was completed and he was permitted to dedicate it with the solemn service of his Liturgy to the Triune God. At once it took a front rank in the city of churches. Before this settlement was effected, another very inviting proposition had been made to him.

C. VAN RENSSELAER TO DR. BETHUNE.

"PHILADELPHIA, *April* 16, 1850.

MY DEAR DOCTOR: My views as to the man who ought to be Chancellor of the N. Y. University are unchanged, that is to say confirmed. Providence has now opened the way for his inauguration, which I have no doubt will take place about the time of 'Commencement.' If your friends bring forward your name, the appointment will be nearly if not quite, unanimous. No Episcopal layman will stand the shadow of a chance. Whatever influence, however diminutive, I may have with anybody, shall be cheerfully and dutifully given in the right direction.

I am, yours sincerely,
COURTLANDT VAN RENSSELAER."

This election, as Chancellor of the New York University, took place. The office was one of high honor, and affording a grand opportunity of cultivating his literary tastes. The students, hearing of the choice, had been in front of his hotel cheering him for some time ; but the same evening came the committee from the church in Brooklyn, and he who had promised to preach the Gospel had no difficulty in making his choice.

"NEW YORK, *April* 22, 1850.

CHARLES BUTLER, ESQ.,
President of the Council of the New York University.

MY DEAR SIR : Having learned that I have been named in connection with the vacant chancellorship of your Institution, by gentlemen for the honor and kindness of whose preference I am deeply grateful, it is due to the Council and myself that I should express my desire not to be considered as a candidate for this office. Yours very truly,
GEO. W. BETHUNE."

" HOTEL ST. DENIS, *Dec.* 4, 1852.

The Rev. Dr. Bethune's compliments to Mr. Ullman, and begs to say, that the enclosed tickets for Madame Sontag's concert of last evening, did not reach him until this morning.

Dr. Bethune has also to acknowledge a very courteous invitation, also enclosed, to Madame Sontag's rehearsal on Saturday morning last, with a polite offer of tickets for any of Madame Sontag's concerts.

In declining these invitations, Dr. Bethune only obeys a rule he has laid down for himself, never to accept gratuitous favors, which he cannot hope in any way to reciprocate.

Dr. Bethune has been delighted in listening to Madame Sontag, and hopes to have the same high gratification when the concerts come on his disengaged evenings; but he must be permitted to go in on the same footing with the vast multitude, and contribute his mite to the aggregate return of a grateful public for the very remarkable enjoyment Madam Sontag's visit has brought to us here; a return which he hopes may be, if possible, as great as the amiable talent which calls it forth. Mr. Ullman will, therefore, pardon the request that Dr. Bethune's name may be left off the free list altogether."

DR. BETHUNE TO MRS. J. BETHUNE. "BOSTON, *Feb.* 1, 1850.

MY BELOVED MOTHER: I have come here from Providence this morning, and have had my heart full of you, remembering that this is your birthday. Dearest mother, how thankful I am to God for sparing you to me, and to so much usefulness so long. Of all my blessings next to those of the Gospel, I have always reckoned your prayers and counsels and cares for me, among the chiefest. Repay you I never can. Would that I could do more towards it; but dear mother, you know the deep, grateful, devoted affection, of your ever affectionate son,

GEORGE."

The following is the last of Mrs. Joanna Bethune's letters to her son; the excellent and noble lady's hand has become very tremulous, but her love is as strong as ever:

"*Nov.* 15, 1852.

MY BELOVED SON: George McCartee mentioned at breakfast that you proposed returning to the city this week. Now, my dear, I think you had better delay it till the first of the week; you certainly could not preach, or ought not, and the first of the week will be time enough. I need not say how happy I will be to have you with me, but your health is most to be attended to. I am pretty well, and so is George. With love and respect to all with you, dear, dear son,

Your affectionate mother,

J. BETHUNE."

Soon after this time Mrs. Bethune's brain softened, but her son remained ever her faithful and tender guardian.

This seems a suitable place to say a few words of the lectures, which our pastor was so often called to deliver before learned bodies, or popular assemblages. His Philadelphia congregation had spoken with pride and satisfaction of their pastor, as one who not only faithfully ministered unto them, but went forth among all people, and was useful every where. This was true, and had he accepted all the invitations urged on him, he would soon have worn out his health. An emphatic warning from his friend and physician, Dr. Dunglison, caused him to be wise in time. On one occasion he was asked to abate his price in regard to the poor people of a country village. He writes in reply:

"MY DEAR SIR: I regret being obliged to explain my note of the 6th. The invitations to lecture which I refuse, are ten times as many as those I accept. Lecturing is disagreeable to me. I should greatly prefer not to lecture at all, as it often interferes with my more sacred duties, besides involving a very troublesome correspondence, and other not slight annoyances. I am therefore compelled to adopt fixed rules, to avoid affronting, by any partiality (as I have friends scattered here and there over the country), and to get rid of as many lectures as I can. I set my fee at $50, not so much with the purpose of getting it, as to avoid being asked to lecture anywhere. That ($50, with my expenses) is the fee, or rather the lowest fee I have asked in answer to every request, and is what I receive for every lecture I delivered this season, except *one*, which I considered myself bound to give, by a last year's promise. Besides, requests to lecture for charitable purposes, are sufficiently numerous to keep me doing nothing else in lecturing, did I comply with them all. It is sometimes the poor, sometimes a church, sometimes a parsonage, etc., so that were I to deviate from my rule for one, I must for all, and, therefore, I do it for none.

The fees I get for lecturing, enable me to do many acts of charity, such that I could not otherwise, and the demands on my purse by the poor of Brooklyn, are quite as heavy, I doubt not, as those of the poor at Belleville on yours.

Another thing: where I am known, nobody will suspect me of being under the pecuniary necessity, or of having the disposition, to drive a bargain in such matters; but I think it the more my duty, as I shall not be suspected of mercenary motives, to contend for the right of intellectual labour to its reward. You would not think it right to ask a trader or a mechanic, to give fifty per cent. off his price, to the poor of your place. You could make your poor very comfortable without going out of your town, at that rate. Now think of it, my dear sir, have you a right to ask Dr. D. or myself, or any one else, to do so, because our labour is intellectual, and not manual? I think of my brethren far more than of myself in this matter, for most cheerfully would I lecture at Belleville, for no other reward than the pleasure of obliging my friends, if I could do so, as I said in my former note, '*consistently.*' In town, where they have had any experience of lectures, in New England, especially, they have given over connecting charitable purposes with their causes, at least so far as the pay of the lecturer is concerned. If money is needed for any town purpose, it would be more easy for each one to pay double for his ticket, than to take half from the lecturer's fee.

I have been thus explicit, that you may see clearly the reasons of my former note. My lecture is not in any case worth what I ask; but the trouble it costs me is worth more at a fair rate.

And now my dear sir, having explained myself, I must ask you to relieve me from my contingent promise to lecture at Belleville this season. I cannot deviate from my rule, but, at the same time, I cannot think of burdening a charitable purpose by demands of money for myself.

At some other time, when my mind is clearer, and my friends desire it, I may have the opportunity of serving them at Belleville, but not now."

A friend of Dr. Bethune, who, like the rest, puts in his plea for a lecture or address, has the thoughtfulness to say, "It must be no small task upon you merely to reply to applications of a particular nature, especially at this season of preparing for the Anniversaries, when Dr. Bethune is always put down, 'to be had, if possible.'"

Dr. Bethune's own account of his lectures, is the best that can be given:

LETTER TO DR. DUNGLISON. "BROOKLYN, *Nov.* 14, 1854.

The lectures I have ready, are what are called popular, that is, separate lectures on miscellaneous topics; for all the world like our quondam Athenian Institute lectures. Thus I have one on 'Lectures and Lecturers' (an introductory), considering popular lectures and lecturers in an amusing, but I hope not unserviceable, light. Another on 'Common Sense,' which, by the way, is long enough for two, and a mixture of metaphysics and familiar illustrations. A third on 'Work and Labor; the moral uses of the distinction between them'; the best of my lectures. Another on 'The Orator of the Present Day,' originally a Phi Beta Kappa oration for Brown University, inquiring into the secrets of the orator's power, &c. Another on 'Oracles,' and another blocked out, but not written, on Divination; in both of which, I strike at the Spiritualisms (so-called) of the present day, while I give illustrations of the subject itself. I sball try to write another during the winter, but am not sure what on. Such are the lectures I have read, one or more in a season, here, in New York, New Haven, &c., &c."

These lectures were delivered all over the land, and as they did much to increase the reputation of the speaker, besides affording substantial gain, it may be interesting to know the subjects of those remaining unpublished: "The Moral Opinions of the Ancients"; "Socrates, Pythagoras, and Plato"; "Aristotle, Zeno, Epicurus"; "Holland and the Hollanders," two lectures, and very popular; "Divination"; two lectures on "Epidemics," and one on "False Estimates." It is hoped that a due selection will be made for publication, as it would constitute the most charming volume of Dr. Bethune's, that has seen the light of day.

CHAPTER XI.

PLATFORM ORATORY.

THIS chapter is devoted to another specialty of Dr. Bethune. If there was one point in which he outshone his compeers, it was in platform speaking; such as was called for at religious anniversaries, or in the discussion of important public questions. His fluent oratory and quickness of repartee would have made him an invaluable member of a political party, in either House of Congress. But he had more, he had a sound, practical common sense, which commanded the popular heart. Little justice can be done to this distinguished trait of our minister, in the short space allotted. We can only present specimens that may illustrate his power. The first that we offer is a speech made in behalf of his favorite Colonization scheme. His efforts in this cause were frequent; probably one speech was made every year after his entrance into public life; the key-note to them all is found in his expression "From the bottom of my heart I hate slavery", a feature that brought him early in his career into fierce conflict with a distinguished Southern agitator, Hon. Henry A. Wise. The speech quoted was made at Washington, before the American Colonization Society, February, 1850, Hon. Henry Clay being President.

"I am not in the habit of making apologies when I rise to speak, because I think when one sees reason for not speaking, he should hold his tongue. I should be lacking both in common sense and common modesty did I not feel the difficulty of speaking upon a question like this, at a time when everything relating to the black race, coming otherwise than from a Southern man, is looked upon with suspicion and jealousy. Not, sir, that I would hesitate to avow my own sentiments; I would never live where I may not speak my conscientious opinions, but, sir, we are upon, as you have very justly said, a common ground here to-night, where no advocate of this cause has a right to compromise the Society by the expression of any individual opinion which might clash with, or in any way seem to be antagonistic to the opinions of others. I had, however, this consolation, sir, in coming here. I knew, sir, if you will permit me to say, I knew that you would open this meeting with some remarks. I anticipated that they would be short, but falling from a mouth that never uttered a word without a meaning, and whose one sentence is worth, in expression and force, more than a hundred such as mine.

I was very sure that principles would be advanced and established, behind which I might venture to speak. I have no more fear of the collision of conflicting opinions, than I should fear the spray of the ocean after it had dashed against the adamantine rock. It has been well said, sir, by yourself and the gentleman who has preceded me, that this Society has suffered the most virulent opposition. It has been most truly opposed by the fanatics at the North, and the fanatics at the South. I call that man a fanatic, sir, who, under the influence of a perverted conscience, allows malignity to take the place of benevolence; who lets himself down to abuse without measure his honest and logical opponent; and is not willing to listen to reasons upon the question in which all are concerned. I care not where that man lives, whether at the North or in the South, in the East or in the West, he is a fanatic, and he is dangerous, just in proportion as he seems to himself to be conscientious, because his false conscience assumes the aspect, and to a certain extent, the force of right and duty. There is an opposite fanaticism, and the imitation of the fanatic by those who have not the excuse, which vents itself in loud words and earnest denunciations. That I fear not. The blusterer always has been a coward, and is not to be dreaded by the wise man. Like the bubble, he bursts with his own wind.

When we began this cause, sir, or at least some time after we began it, after it gained sufficient strength to provoke the opposition of him who moves the hearts of the children of evil, we find that the Society was charged with doing absolutely wrong, wrong it was said to the cause of the black man, because it took the free black away from the South instead of permitting him to remain like a thorn and a fester in the sides of those who were his brethren in bondage. This was charged against it. Another was that we took away the black man who had been born upon our soil, and who, by the arrangements of Providence who gave him a birth-place here, had as much right to rest himself here as you.

We were told again, it was preposterous to talk of Christianizing the continent of Africa, where such instruments were to be used; the refuse, as was said, of the black race of the United States. Now, sir, what has been the consequence? What have we seen but this very remarkable fact, that the same people who have opposed the Society, have adopted the very measures for which they impeach the Society? As to the taking away the black man of the South, it is notorious that they are doing it in various ways. It is notorious, also sir, that they have endeavored to establish colonies, not exactly within the limits of the United States, but through their assistance, and, to a certain extent, liberal assistance, within the limits of the British Possessions on the Continent; and, in their efforts to colonize, have moved the black man from the South, of which we were accused as a crime; taking him away from the soil he had a right to, and moving him away to the North, sir, whose frosts are as hurtful to his constitution as the heats of the South are to those of us who are born in the North. Nay sir—*nay* gentlemen, and as I see my friends with ready pens by me, I beg them to remember I speak of him with respect. I honor him for being actuated by the very best intentions, however I might differ with him in the manner in which he carries them out. I speak of Mr. Gerrit Smith. Would to God his large heart was with us still. He himself has offered his acres of wild land in the coldest section of the State of New York for a colonization scheme. It seems then, sir, that they have acknowledged the truth of the classic maxim, that 'it is lawful to learn from an enemy,' for they have taken the first leaf out of our book.

One thing, sir, we were told, we were reproached for endeavoring to persuade the people of the United States that Africa was the proper place for the black man; that this land of Christian privileges was the place to which Providence, who maketh the wrath of man to praise him, had brought him, and here he had remained. It has been said that we could not evangelize Africa through the instrumentality of such agents. What have they done, sir? Do you not remember the history of the Amistad? God in his Providence sent them to our shores, and these very people they sent back again to Africa. Our opponents have patterned after us, and so far as they have proceeded, their scheme is as much like ours as a badly managed scheme can be like a good one for the same purposes.

Now here, sir, is the demonstration of it in the very mouths, in the hands, of our most virulent opponents at the North in favor of our scheme, and, sir, no doubt all the honest men there among them, will be with us still. We were told on the other hand at the South, by the fanatics there, it was preposterous to think of elevating the black man; God had made him inferior; God intended him for a servant; it was flat flying in the face of Providence, to endeavor to make him anything else, and that he never could succeed; his whole history in all the past, from time immemorial, had been that of degradation, slavery, ignorance and misery: sir, the history is true; such has been the history of the black man, and I consider that amidst all the wonderful events of this remarkable century in which we live, there is none so remarkable as the present condition of the Republic of Liberia.

What has been the history of the black man! That everywhere it has been that of slavery, of degradation, of ignorance, even in Africa, in his own native land, is perfectly notorious to all who know anything of the subject. He is in the condition of a slave who holds his life and all that he can call dear to him, at the will of his savage, despot master; but, sir, go back to that book which Providence, after the lapse of thousands of years, has opened for us. We may read there the records of his past history.

Go to the monuments of Egypt and you will find there the black man a slave; emphatically a slave. I believe you can scarcely find an instance in which he appears upon those monuments, in which he does not bear with him tributes about his person, in token that the people from whom he comes are subject to the Pharaohs of Egypt.

It is supposed that no one can make a calculation other than that of a supposition. It is supposed, however, that over that vast continent there can be scattered not less than a hundred and fifty millions;

probably when we come to penetrate into its hitherto impenetrable depths we shall find them to be one quarter more, judging by the area, and by what we know of certain portions of it very recently explored.

What has Africa been? I speak not of that section of Africa that was inhabited by other races. I cannot go into the romance of speaking of Egypt and its people; its kings, its philosophers, and its saints. I know very well, sir, every one knows, they were under, I speak of that portion of Africa inhabited by the black man, the woolly-headed African, (laughter) and wherever he has these characteristics he is in the deepest degradation; at least so far as explored. He has been for thousands and thousands of years so, and so far back that history tells us no other tale. And that gentleman who has but recently returned from Liberia, that gentleman who knows Liberia from a long residence, will tell you that nowhere upon the face of the earth, nowhere in time past or present has there existed, or does there exist, a superstition so base, so cruel, so horrid, so revolting, as that which reigns over the minds and hearts of the native Africans.

It is true, sir, that the African has been always degraded; always been oppressed; always been in ignorance. It might be thought, sir, that one who had been crushed so long, could never rise, but like that giant of old, of whom we read in classic fable, upon whom Etna was put, his breast must be so bruised, his limbs so paralyzed by the long pressure of the superincumbent weight, that he cannot erect himself as a man, and take any place in the way of advancement and civilization. But, sir, there is a light brighter than that of reason; there is a happy spring from a nobler source than that of passion; there is the light of religion and the light of promise shedding their rays far in the future. What does that religion teach him? I know no one who has common sense will contend for the absolute equality of all men in physical strength, in intellectual, in ability to advance in the career of civilization. No one contends for this; I am speaking of those fundamental rights every man has, or should be acknowledged to have. God made the black man as well as you or me, and unless we give up the Bible, which is the charter of our hopes, and the ground of our faith, we must believe he came from the same original pair, and we are brethren, brethren by the fiat of the Creator.

We cannot divorce ourselves from this fraternity, except we fling off the devotion of our Father who is in Heaven; when He who spake as never man spoke, and who justified his sympathy with the poor and the rich, and gave himself to the poor, when He repeated from his divine lips the law of the ancient Israelites, and tells us we must love our neighbor as ourselves. He told you, sir, he told me, he tells all of us, that wherever a human heart beats, wherever a human heart glows, wherever a man stands in the image of God, there is our neighbor, whom we are bound to love as ourselves.

I care not where he is; whether in China, whether in Africa, or whether it be in America. I care not who claims rule over him; he is my brother; he is my neighbor; I am bound to love him, and God will hold me accursed if I do not do this. Nay, sir, through the teaching of God's Holy Spirit, I am taught my sins, and that there is but one fountain open for sin and uncleanness. When I follow the guiding of the Holy Spirit, and it leads me to the foot of the cross whence springs a living fountain of divine blood shed for the lost, the unworthy and the guilty, I find kneeling at the foot of that cross, washing himself in that same sacred stream, as welcome to my Master as myself, as readily admitted into the family of God as the highest among the children of men; I find the black man washed in the same blood with me, sanctified by the same Spirit; adopted by the same God, and made heir of the same happy immortality. How dare I refuse, how dare I refuse him all the strength of Christian sympathy and Christian benevolence? I know not how, sir; while that Bible lasts I must follow it; and, sir, it is upon this principle that the Society is acting.

We are, as you very justly observed, united by that simple article of our constitution which covers him, and doubtless does cover persons of different notions as a detail of its workings, and gives us a right to differ; makes us sovereigns in our own spheres; while we are united in the great object: but, sir, I do not go too far, I am sure you will not refuse me permission to say, that the Colonization Society is the combination of the true friends of the colored race in the United States. I mean the friends of the black man who desire to see him elevated.

Now, sir, what do we see in the year '93 and '94? I am not good at dates, sir, but, somewhere about there, the negroes of St. Domingo, the whole of the population of that island, or the greater part of it, rose in revolt, and have endeavored to establish one ever since; endeavored to form themselves into some sort of government. What do we see? Take that monkey empire (laughter) that has been the world's laughing stock; look at the result of their plans: Faustin I., with his cordon of dukes and nobles around him, so that there can be scarcely a private man left in his dominions (laughter). There is the result in one part. Compare it, sir, with the Liberian Republic. Compare it with the enlightened, free and intellectual exercise of every principle and right that man can claim, moderated and held from excess by the wisest restraints and the most salutary arrangement. Sir, I do not believe there exists upon earth a government whose constitution is more liberal, more enlightened, or more judicious, having in it, we believe, the elements of greater permanence than the Republic of Liberia. It is, sir, the black man; it is not the white man ruling over him as in Sierra Leone. It is not the white man forcing him on as in the British West Indies.

Nor is it the black man where the mixed race is flogging him and chaining him, as was done in the beginning of freedom in the West Indies. It is the black man governing himself, governing himself according to written statutes; governing himself with an enlightened view of his own worth, his own dignity, his relations to his fellow-man, and his confidence in the power and justice of God, who loves His children, it were impossible to doubt it, who loves his children all alike, and alike vindicates his mercy by the history of that race, as well as our own.

Now, sir, there is the reply that we make to the fanaticism of the South. Look at our Liberia, look at it, sir, we challenge investigation. The ships of almost every civilized nation have touched at its port; emissaries from our own country, or rather messengers, have gone to examine into the existing state of things, and if testimony has been unanimous to any nation, it is that in favor of the Republic of Liberia. Nay, sir, it has been more than hinted at by the eloquent gentleman who has preceded me. Great Britain has acknowledged the superiority of our scheme over her own.

Since that, Clarkson and, by implication, Wilberforce, have been actuated against us. These good men were brought into it, however, in the feebleness of their expiring years, at least Clarkson in his feebleness, to record a sentiment in opposition to our society. What has been the result? Great Britain, in one of her ablest periodicals, and by one of her ablest men, has declared that Sierra Leone must be abandoned; that it is a failure; and with the same voice they have pointed to the Republic of Liberia, and declared it to be successful. Nay, after all the money that has been spent upon that very coast by Great Britain, by this country and others, money, sir, is but the simplest portion of the tribute we have given. We have sent our gallant officers to die upon that plague-smitten coast; many, many a family in this land, more in England, have been clothed in the sackcloth of bitterness from the loss of life wasted in good intentions, but miserable failures, to suppress the slave trade; but now, sir, for seven hundred miles of the entire coast of that section of Africa, in a short time, from the further part of Liberia to Sierra Leone, this society will have destroyed the slave trade. What navies could not do, and what navies with millions of cartouches and hundreds of cannon and thousands of men, our little republic with its little army and its little treasury have accomplished.

It is probable if the white man had done it, as my friend remarked, we should have exulted over it, it would have been claimed as a triumph of the white man's superiority; but it has not. We have nursed him, sir, he was a child, but now the black man is erect, tall, and as strong as a man, but a child in intellect, in habit, and in foresight.

We had to nurse him; but he is now a man. I remember well, sir, you remember it well, and many of us here, with what fear and trembling we ventured upon the experiment. But holy and wise men believed it possible, especially after the career of that glorious man, that martyr to this cause, whose mind and heart had a strength rarely paralleled; I mean Buchanan, the last white governor of Liberia — the people who hear me may perhaps smile at it as an exaggeration—he was one of the greatest men that God ever made, in mind, in heart, or in appearance, — after his career, whom God sent, I am sure of it, God sent him to make the way for a black man to assume the reins of government.

He died, sir; and at last a colored man governs the colony, and he governs the colony better than it was ever governed before, not altogether in favor of his own credit, but also to the credit of the people, who have been nursed into self-government. What is a Republic without self-government? There is that colony, and that Republic, aye, sir, *Republics* are always longer lived than *Monarchies*. It is the history of the world, unless perhaps some of the great empires of whose history we know comparatively little. But, sir, that Republic of Liberia will outlive every kingdom of Europe, and may not live very long either to do that. (Applause.) Now, sir, I will discuss this point only for a moment; here is the demonstration given that the black man can govern himself. We have made the demonstration, sir, and it has been acknowledged sir, that he can govern himself. By whom, sir, have you stated that the Republic had been acknowledged; by whom, sir? would to God you had not been obliged to falter as your heart compels you to do. Acknowledged by Great Britain and not by us; and why, sir? I am willing to give Great Britain the credit of philanthropy. I do not forget she has other qualities besides philanthropy; trade, sir, she loves trade. What was it that gave to it its predominance? I can trace no characteristic in the Anglo-Saxon that gave them more force than their love of trade.

You can trace it, sir, in all the history of the Anglo-Saxon race, but it has been from the Republic of the Netherlands, we have learned the great lesson of trade, and from whose shores went the Anglo-Saxons who have given to England her great national characteristic, trade! trade! trade! This is what the Anglo-Saxon conquers by and conquers for. Find me a spot, sir, upon the face of the earth where they have not smuggled a piece of their goods and merchandise. You cannot find a British port, but there you will find the haunt of the smuggler who is protected by those very forts. The far-famed Gibraltar, with its battlements and garrison, is little better than a smuggling port to take advantage of the weaker people of the Mediterranean and its neighborhood. But, sir, what is the case now? there is a little chance of trade open upon a certain coast of our own continent. It looks small as a mosquito; but, sir, the hum of that mosquito has not been unheard across the broad Atlantic, and the queenly Victoria shakes hand by proxy, with the breechless young vagabond who is called the king. For what, sir? For trade, to make money. I do not blame them; it is right to make money if you can do it honestly; and I am sure we are the last people in this country, if we allow the Eastern States to belong to us, to say it is not right to make money. Sir, you have the motive for the acknowledgment of the independence of Liberia; I do not say that it is the only motive.

I know of no greater mistake in morals than to suppose a man's actions spring from one motive. The concurrence and concentration of different motives bear upon the man; some are less easily deducted than others, but still always a combination.

God forbid I should question her (Great Britain's) benevolence in the acknowledgment, but I fear it was done upon the chance of penetrating Africa through those rivers. I fear that her excellent Governor, Roberts, would have gone home without his acknowledgment. Now, sir, I believe that we are a philanthropic people, and I believe that we love to make money; but I say, sir, that the statesman who refuses to acknowledge the Republic of Liberia, misses greatly his duty to the United States and his country, as a commercial people.

But, sir, I am trespassing upon a point which will be handled far more ably by my friend who has just returned from the coast of Africa. Therefore, sir, I leave the subject, congratulating ourselves again upon the great success, and congratulating no one more than yourself, to whose presiding skill and energy and to whose high example we owe so much of our success in our scheme. You contributed the noblest donation of all when you gave your name. But, sir, we may all in our little spheres rejoice. The smallest star in the firmament rejoices in the light that God has given it. But, sir, there are those of us here, as we look back to hours of conflict, who cannot say we are scarred with a hundred fights, because fortunately, our armor was so proved, that the weapons struck upon us shivered in the grasp of the hand that struck with all the vehemence that malignity could give. Yes, sir, we can remember our hours of darkness; they were many; but how bright is the future! Happy to believe we have not simply planted a little shrub, but a mighty tree that has been sown like a grain of mustard seed, which yet shall wave its branches laden with celestial blessings over the Continent of Africa and the millions of the colored race. In this connection, we cannot but rejoice that the colored man was brought here.

Could he have been educated for this purpose, where, I ask you, sir, where could he have been educated for that career which he is now entering upon in Liberia, but in this land where constitutional rights are thoroughly understood, where the right of self-government is so clearly propagated, where the success of our blessed institutions has shown by an irresistible demonstration that freedom is the best heritage of man?"

To understand better Dr. Bethune's position on the question of Slavery, we must consider his course in the Synod of his own Church. In 1855 a large classis in North Carolina being dissatisfied with errors in the German Church, asked for admission into the Dutch body. Dr. Bethune opposed the proceeding.

"We should feel very kindly toward these brethren who have come to us. They are Christian men, who consider themselves to be suffering for the sake of truth—who sympathize with us in doctrine, and who have paid us the high respect of asking to be united with our interest. God forbid, therefore, that one word should fall from my lips, or from this Synod, which should in any way wound the feelings, or show disrespect to these estimable brethren.

If the proposition was to exclude a slave-holder from the communion, I would oppose such an uncharitable and un-Christian act. I would rather die than own a slave, unless it were that, in accepting the ownership, I did it for his own good; but I would rather die than allow a Christian brother to be unjustly cast out of the house of God, when our great Master paid the highest compliment he ever paid to a human being, in saying to one who was a slave-owner and a soldier, "I have not found so great faith, no, not in Israel." But we are not called upon to do this. In the providence of God we have been happily freed from this difficulty, and I think that we should remember what the wise man says, with a great deal of point: "He that passeth by and meddleth with strife belonging not to him, is like one who taketh a dog by the ears;" there would be a precious deal of howling. And so I feel in this case. Here we have not the strife among us. I know there has been an attempt to introduce it among us. I have seen with regret, movements made in some part of the Church to indorse the action of a body with whom we hold relations upon the subject. If there be an attempt to press this matter in this body, I for one am ready to swing clear of the American Board of Commissioners of Foreign Missions, rather than one word should be uttered upon Slavery. I do not agree with the action of that Board, but at the same time I am willing to let other people have consciences on that subject; but the thing is to keep it out of the house here. I believe that there is no man among us, unless he happens to be carried away by the spirit of fanaticism, that makes him forget the interests of the Church, who is willing to enter into a discussion of the subject on this floor, and I therefore hold my tongue, and do not say what I am prepared to say in other places, lest I do injustice to the feeling of some brethren, and thus create discussions.

I would not hold with a class of men who condemn every man at the South; but at the same time, I would not say that any one who has a conscience upon the subject, different from mine, should be forced to take action, which, if I were in his place, I would not be willing to be forced into. I would say, 'Come as near to us as possible,' without saying, 'Come in.' If they want funds for their Seminary, for their Church; if they want anything which we can do for them, let us do it. My idea, illustrated in other words, is this: Because our neighbor is a good man (for which we love him), if he has a slight taint of the small pox, I do not think he should be allowed to innoculate with it our whole Church."

Having presented a resolution expressive of courtesy and kindness towards the brethren from North Carolina, but declining the union, he continued:—

"That although he might be called a sneak and timid, yet he believed they were not called upon to discuss the slavery question. A serpent was a sneak, but he remembered the advice of one of high authority, 'Be ye wise as serpents.' Some gentlemen were very anxious to fight lions. Let them mount their hobbys, for his part he did not want to fight a cat."

The occasion was one of intense excitement, the claims of the Classis upon Christian sympathy were strong—it would have presented a grand mission field for the Dutch Church,—but their request was declined, and very much through the wise forecast of Dr. Bethune. Many who opposed him sharply then as a truckler to Northern fanaticism, lived to thank him for his wise counsels.

We next follow our debater to the exciting Tract Controversy, where he appears on the other side of the great argument. The discussion really begun in 1856, when proposals were made at the meeting of the American Tract Society, to print essays on the subject of slavery, a course which would at once stop the work of the Society in the Southern States; action was postponed by the appointment of a committee who should consider the subject and report next year.

In 1857 they suggested that tracts should be printed teaching masters their duties, and it was hoped that this course would satisfy all parties. But the Society found that even such tracts would incense the South, and, for the sake of their national position, delayed the publication. This inaction aroused new agitation. Parties began to array themselves in order; appeals were sent to all the New England members for their presence, which put the management of the Society on the defensive, and they rallied their strength. At the Anti-Slavery caucus, preceeding the meeting, Mr. Tappan said, "When my neighbor, Dr. Bethune, comes here to-morrow, and I believe he is coming, as he is a perfect cornucopia of fun you will have an abundance of it."

The great assembly convened in the church in Lafayette Place, and, though none but life-members and directors were admitted, yet the house was filled to its utmost capacity. Probably never in this country was there such a grand gathering of Christian men, absorbed in the question whether this great Society should be sustained or rent asunder, for such seemed the issue at stake.

Dr. Magee explained the course of the Society. Bishop Mc'Ilvaine, with great dignity, defended its interests. Dr. Tyng led the opposition, when a vote was demanded. It was taken amidst intense excitement. Those condemning the management being first called for, three hundred and forty-five rose; it seemed a large number, but when the other side voted, it seemed as if the whole house rose *en masse.* The victory was complete. Dr. Bacon, of New Haven, cried, "We give it up." Dr. Bethune replied, "Yes, but we want to know how much you give it up." There was much difficulty in the count, but it was finally agreed that it was about ten to one. But the opposition was not vanquished. Dr. Bacon pressed the resolution of last year, about tracts on slavery, saying, "I believe that God governs the world; and I don't believe, in the long run, the devil is to beat," and gave warning that, if defeated to-day, he would continue this agitation, and his children, and children's children, would follow it up. When Dr. Bethune arose it was as the mouth-piece of the house. It was quite certain that the Society was sustained, the great interest was safe; but the great majority needed an expression of their feeling, and for the intense emotion a great speaker was needed. Dr. B. ascended to the majesty of the occasion. He protested against the action of last year as being unaniomus.

"We are now called upon to publish tracts on slavery, though we thereby shut our tracts out of fifteen States of the Union! But the gentlemen come here to drive the Society into decisive and destructive measures, and Dr. Bacon tells us that he will never give it up; he will pursue us, with all the little Bacons after him, from generation to generation. (Great laughter.) Dr. Bacon also expresses his confidence that he and his friends will get the victory in the end, because he believes that the devil will be whipped at last! He classes us with the children of the devil. But we believe that we are on the side of the truth and of righteousness, that the Bible is with us, God is with us, and we intend to stand by the Society to the end. If Dr. Bacon is a *life*-member, so are we, and whenever he comes to agitate this subject he will find us here. And before this Society shall pervert its sacred trust to the publication of abolition tracts, we will carry the question through every Court in the land. (Great applause.) The gentleman from New Haven, Dr. Bacon, asks if the moral law is abrogated by slavery? if adultery is not adultery at the South? I answer by asking if adultery is any worse south of Mason and Dixon's line than it is north of it? Is sin any *worse* in a black man than a white man? And as to this particular sin, I say, 'let him that is without sin, cast the first stone.' No one can doubt about the evangelical origin of that sentiment. This exhibits the difference between the views of the gentlemen on the other side and ours. We wish to publish tracts against sin, all sin; to rebuke and oppose it; but we see no reason for treating covetousness, or licentiousness, or oppression, as worse in one part of the country than in another.

We are united as a Society, not merely in a charter, but in a trust; we have given our money, our fathers have given their money, and we have exerted our various talents for the upbuilding of this institution. Our money is between every brick. Yes, it is the very mortar which holds the bricks together. It is distributed through all the stereotype plates, in all the presses of the Society. It is in more than this; it is in the glorious system of evangelical operations which this Society has inaugurated, and still maintains. We stand where our fathers placed us; and it is my privilege to remember the day on which this Society was begun. I remember it well; and it has been dear to my heart ever since. It is yet sacred in my thoughts, that the life of my grandmother, Isabella Graham, the greatest treasure which our family ever had — one of the treasures which the church of God esteems the most precious — we committed to this Tract Society; we have given money, my father before me, all of us have given money; but what is money to a gift like that?

What are we to print but tracts for circulation, for the dissemination of evangelical religion and sound morals, that are 'calculated to meet the approbation of all evangelical Christians?' When, therefore, Christians who in the judgment of charity can be called evangelical, say that a tract must not be printed, I hold, according to the sacredness of the compact, according to the fidelity of the trust, that that tract ought not to be printed.

Sir, it is something to get funds, it is something to have auxiliaries and supporters; but I tell you what is better than funds, and better than auxiliaries, it is a *field* where we can work. Here, at the thickly settled North, abounding in churches, where every man lives within the sound of the Gospel, — in the free North, where are institutions cultivating religion and virtue by their various influences, — in the favored North, where we have so many institutions of learning, and so many religious advantages, this Tract Society is not so much needed. We have other powerful means to enlighten and evangelize; but we see at the South ten millions of immortal souls. What shall we do for them? We care not whether they are black or white persons who have these souls. I only know three things: that these souls are immortal; that they are sinful; and that Christ who died for me, died for them. And, sir, what I want to do through this Society is, to send the precious Gospel there, and I wish to clog its progress with no difficulties."

He believed in the certain emancipation of the slaves in the United States, not only from his confidence in the triumph of Christianity, but from his confidence in our political institutions and the predominance of free labor. These men are to be free, and he wanted to know in what moral condition they are to be free? He wanted to prepare them for that great advent of freedom. He wanted to prepare them to take their place where they ought to be, by the side of the white man.

"I go for sending the tract with the Gospel, and I go for it for this reason: because I believe that, according to the philosophy of our blessed religion, mankind must be changed from within; and that no external appliances are ever going to bring about the reformation of men. I do not believe the doctrine of the infidel 'Westminster,' that morals must precede missions which carry the Gospel. The evangelical method is, to send the doctrine of Jesus Christ and him crucified, first, that is, the Gospel. Preach it to black men, preach it to white men. This is what we want. There are slaves there suffering in body and soul; slaves who have none of the comforts that we have in this world. Sir, I wish to make them freemen of the Lord. I care not, comparatively, whether they be bond or free, whether they be Jew or Gentile, whether they be Barbarian or Greek; if they are saved by faith in the blood of Jesus, this world matters little. There is heaven, eternal heaven, when their brief sorrows are over; and it is because this Gospel is my comfort, that I want to send it to the poorest negro of the South.

I recognize no difference between my black brother and myself. Born of the same nature, drawing hope from the same Christ, lying down alike in the grave, and hoping for one home in heaven, he is my brother. None shall divorce him from me. I am his keeper; but the greatest blessing God bids me bestow upon my neighbor is to love my neighbor as myself, and of all things in this world — liberty, riches, learning, friends, — I would say, give me Christ, give me Christ. Take riches, honor, friends, liberty, life, but give me Christ; let me know that my Redeemer liveth; let Christ be in me the hope of glory everlasting. And because I love Christ best for myself, I would give Christ to the black man, and I would send a knowledge of Christ to the black man in the tracts of this Society. So do I turn away from every plan which shall hinder the full and free operation of this Society over that vast South. Hinder us not, hinder us not. The way is great, we have a mighty work to do. Souls, immortal souls, are going down to death, whom we are bound to rescue. Hinder us not. We cannot forsake the South. I do not mean the institutions of the South. I mean the slaves of the South, the masters of the South, all the sinners of the South. God, Jehovah, in whom we trust, has put the obligation upon our consciences. We cannot turn aside. 'God is our refuge, and our strength; therefore will we not fear, though the earth be removed, though the mountains thereof be carried into the midst of the sea.'"

His position on the slavery question is thus clearly defined: opposed to it with all his heart, holding that slavery was a "crime," desirous to avoid all connection with it, yet he would select the most prudent course to alleviate its sorrows and prepare the way for freedom.

We insert here, as bearing directly upon this point, a letter to Mr. John Brydon, Edinburgh, dated Newburgh-on-the-Hudson, July, 1853. The opinions entertained were of course modified, though not changed, by the political events of seven years later.

"MY DEAR SIR:—I cannot retract what I said of Mrs. Stowe, and as I am little accustomed to mould my opinions, except from my own convictions, you must believe, though I may lose somewhat of your favor, that they are from my own mind and not from without. Of the system of slavery, I think as badly as you can. Nothing would tempt me to share in its common evil; but I cannot approve of the gross misrepresentations of Mrs. Stowe's book, which show the clergy of this country in the worst possible light, and studiously avoid allusions to the many palliating circumstances which a Christian charity should duly consider. My observation of the South has been large. I have personally labored among the slaves as a preacher, and been an eye-witness of sacrifices and pains on the part of good people for those who, not by choice of theirs, had been put under them.

The evidence in Mrs. Stowe's second book is very shocking; but if a like attempt were made by a Socialist to exhibit the evils of marriage or even of parental authority or of the relations of landlord and tenant, &c., &c., a far worse show could be made. More wives are killed by their husbands, than slaves by their masters, a hundred times. The evil is here, and the question is how to get rid of it, and on that but little light has yet been thrown from any quarter. The Americans were not alone in finding difficulty resulting from disorders in society from a long growth of wrong. When England has cleared her skirts of evils within her own limits, it will be time enough for her to dictate to us.

But my quarrel with Mrs. Stowe is not for having written her book, malignant as some parts of it are. It is for consenting to be fêted by your people in reward for her book. We are not deceived, nor ought she to be, as to the cause of such honor being awarded her among you. The proof is too plain that it is a jealous hate of America, not a love of human happiness; a hate which grows without any occasion, but our increasing commercial and moral rivalry. At the very moment that Mrs. Stowe was received with acclamations, the British armies were carrying blood-shed and rapine into the Burman empire, and all British India is but a bloody monument of British rapacity, cruelty, and selfishness—yet what voice of mercy is heard from your pseudo-philanthropists on that subject? Slavery, far worse than our country knows, prevails in Russia, your monarchical ally, yet what voice has been heard in Britain against that? Does the fact that our slaves are black and the Russians white make the difference? No, my friend, your anti-slavery feeling against America is but the form of British hate, Britain's pet Pharisaism—which, while it declaims against the views of others, tolerates the most monstrous evils at home and abroad. If anything could make the unholy farce more transparent, it is the fact that the Duchess of Sutherland heads the movement. Sutherland is a name which her Grace's mother and father made infamous for the most horrid cruelties in driving their Highland clansmen from their homes of centuries in circumstances unrivalled for cruelty, except it be by more recent evictions in Ireland. The United States have freely given homes to the fugitive slaves who were driven out of Great Britain by tyrannies, such as no Southern planter ever dreamed of. Mrs. Stowe knows the reason of her British popularity, and I call it the conduct of a traitor to receive personal favors at the expense of one's country. As to your emancipation of the West India slaves (a pretty mess you have made of it) the parallel holds not good, as the owners of these slaves did not emancipate them, but were forced by a foreign parliament against all the votes which indirectly represented them to the measure. Our Northern States had long before,—New York in 1818—set their slaves free, and now the power to free those at the South lies in Southern hands, not ours. The people who voted the West India slaves free were 3000 miles away from any evils or dangers consequent upon the step; the more than three millions of blacks are within our own borders. The British West India slavery was so cruel that the number of the slaves decreased; in our Southern States they increase faster than any population in the world, a clear sign that physically at least they are not ill treated. Do you know, also, that the number of slaves voluntarily and without compensation set free in this country, considerably exceeds all that Great Britain has emancipated? These are the reasons why Mrs. Stowe, as an American woman, should have declined honors at the cost of her country's honor. I speak from my own heart. When I first went to Great Britain in 1836, I found myself assailed at every dinner-table in England and Scotland, from that of the peer downwards, with attacks on my country. I withdrew myself from all society, but those of my personal friends. I bore letters to some of the most eminent men of Glasgow, Drs. Wardlaw, Hugh, and others, but I presented none of them, for they had united in a meeting of pharisaical hate of America. When I have been in Great Britain, twice since, I have travelled as an unknown stranger, rather than break bread under roofs where my country was abused. This, depend upon it, is the feeling of the more thoughtful among Americans visiting Great Britain; Mrs. Stowe is a notorious exception. Fervently do I long and pray and labor for the emancipation of the slaves. I hate the system which oppresses them, and every system of oppression. But I cannot condemn my fellow sinner at the South for being placed in temptations I know nothing of, nor can I shut my eyes to any evil but *one*. When the beam is out of the eye of Great Britain, she may well see clearer. The times threaten a period not far off when Great Britain and the United States should stand shoulder to shoulder for the liberties of the world. The once harsh mother will need the arm of her sturdy child. All that can tend to bind us together should be carefully cherished, and we were tending to this when the devil assumed the form of charity and stirred up Uncle Tom's Cabin to distract and embitter.

Yours affectionately,

GEO. W. BETHUNE."

Desire to present Dr. Bethune's relation to this subject in connection has carried us, in time, beyond another of the grand occasions in his life; the meeting of sympathy with the Madiai, where he represented "the martyrs of Holland and the inflexible opponents of papal intolerance." A gentleman who has had large privileges of hearing distinguished men at home and abroad, has told us that he never listened to so fine a specimen of forensic eloquence.

"At Florence, Italy, several members of the Madiai family had been imprisoned at hard labor for the single crime of possessing a Bible ; and they were sentenced to suffer for several years ; this fact, published abroad, had excited the rebuke of the civilized world. Immense meetings had been held in London, Edinburgh and Dublin, to denounce the barbarism, and it was arranged that on the 7th January, 1853, the city of New York should utter its voice. Metropolitan Hall was engaged, the largest in the country and capable of holding about 6000 persons ; it was an assembly of the wit, beauty and religion of the city gathered together to hear their favorite orators, and to express Christian sympathy with the persecuted. Mr. Westervelt, the mayor of the city, presided, and addresses were made by representative men of different denominations ; but Dr. Bethune rose head and shoulders above them all. Never shall I forget the sensation as his clear, bell-like voice rang upon my ears. He came from the back part of the stage speaking as he advanced, his great body seeming to grow larger with emotion at every step he took.

'I feel as if I were called again into the presence of centuries long past. I seem to hear those sublime words ringing in my ears: I believe in the Holy Ghost, and in the holy Catholic church, and in the communion of Saints. There is but one head and one body ; and wherever there is one who believes in Jesus Christ, there is a member of that Church ; and if one member suffers, all the members suffer with it. If we have the Holy Ghost within us, if we have become vitally united to the body of our blessed Lord by a living faith, there is not one of us whose heart is not bleeding with those beloved Christians who are now crushed beneath the foot of the oppressor ; and we must, before God, who gave us hearts and faith, speak out. I am sure we must all feel it, and our sympathies must find relief; and if it reach no further than to give us relief from this pent-up emotion, this meeting is a blessing to the freemen and inhabitants of New York.

I said I felt as if I were called into centuries long past away. We read of the sufferings of the primitive Christians; we read of them who were stoned and sawn asunder, who sang amidst the smoke of their fires, who perished in dungeons with the long pain of fatal hunger; and, until a very short time ago, we had felt, as Christians, that those days had past. There were some prophecies that, interpreted in a particular light, seemed to tell that the days of that persecution might return; but we had long been in the habit of feeling that those days had gone.

It is not long since we had the privilege of welcoming the stranger among us, and it was a higher privilege to welcome the exiles from the island of Madeira. Then, for the first time, we were permitted to see the Confessors such as are now canonized by that same Church of Rome. And now we are told, that two obscure individuals, in the midst of that Church, are incarcerated and treated as felons, for no crime but reading the Bible. From my heart I sympathize with that brother and sister in Christ; but much remains yet behind to be filled up of the sufferings of Christ. There remains yet a necessity for the sufferings of the people of God to prove, in the first place, the evil of that spirit which exalts itself against the Scriptures; and in the second place, to prove the divinity of that faith which upholds the soul above torture, and imprisonment, and death.

This proves that the spirit of that power is unchanged. It is impossible for an American, brought up from his childhood amidst the light, and liberty and privileges which we enjoy in this land, it is impossible for him to conceive the tyranny and oppression which exist in the Old World; and when we tell him of it, he tells us that we are calumniating our brethren and that it is not right to bring such charges against men, because their ancestors in past centuries have been guilty of crimes, and that the growing light of science and the interchange of philanthropic feeling have wrought a great revolution in the spirit of that church which was formerly recognized as a church of persecution. Here is a fact rising up before us, which tells us that the spirit which persecuted the Albigenses is still there, not dead, but rampant and ready, so far as it has the power, to crush now, as it was ready to crush five hundred years ago. Am I wrong in this? I see a brother here upon the stage who told me once in preaching preparatory to the Sacrament, he took occasion to explain the fallacy of the doctrine of transubstantiation held by the Catholic Church, and that one of his parishioners complained of his slandering the Catholics; for we all know, said the man, that nobody can believe such nonsense. This was the light he took of it, and precisely in the same manner do we find people believing it impossible that the spirit of persecution can still exist as it existed in former years. The spirit of antichrist is the same at all times. The spirit of Christ says Search the Scriptures; and wherever there comes a spirit which forbids you to search the Scriptures, you may depend upon it that there is the spirit of antichrist, because it is opposed to it. (Applause.) And now we know that his oppression exists, does it not become us to aid the oppressed? Are we not a republic? and are we not the only nation on the face of the earth, except it be the little republic on the shores of Liberia, in which religious liberty is entire? (Applause). Since we in this country, as republicans, are bearing our testimony to the value of republican principles in the face of the whole earth, should we not believe that it is part of our mission not only to enjoy what God has sent us, but to diffuse it to others? This is the only country in which the principle of religious liberty has been permitted to work itself out; and as all our churches have flourished and grown strong, and been a blessing to us under the system, I say it is our duty, not as Protestants only, but as freemen, to lift up our voice against religious oppression wherever it may exist. (Loud applause.)

Now I wish to speak a few words in relation to the Romish Church. What is the meaning of the words Protestant Country, as applied to the United States? I read as follows: "I suppose that at last it will come down to signify nothing more than the majority of the inhabitants are Protestants; but has it never occurred to those who would make such an objection, that majorities and minorities are mere accidents, liable to change! whereas the constitution is a principle and not an accident; its great," and mark you this, "its great and unappreciable value is that it prescribes the duties of the majority, and protects with equal and impartial justice the rights of the minority. In this country the Constitution of the United States says the majority shall rule."

God grant it! "Now in pursuance of the constitution, this is neither a Protestant nor a Catholic country, but a broad land of civil and religious freedom and equality secured to all." This is the eulogium pronounced upon the Constitution of the United States by Archbishop Hughes. Now, I have not the honor of knowing that gentleman personally, but we are sufficiently well known to the public to warrant my not waiting for an introduction, and I call upon him, in the name of the liberties which his church has enjoyed — in the name of that freedom which every Protestant in this house, that is worthy the name of Protestant, is willing to accord to every Roman Catholic in the land — I call upon him in gratitude to the Baltimores and Williamses, and those whose spirits made that Constitution of ours free from every stain of religious restraint — I call upon him to join us in calling upon the Duke of Tuscany to set free these people. (Tremendous applause.) If this oppression be not the work of Roman Catholicism, he cannot, he will not, refuse to join in the extension of that principle over which he rejoices. (cheers.) If he does not join us we shall believe that such oppression is part and parcel of Roman Catholicism, and that if they had the power here, they would act like the Duke of Tuscany. This is the point to which we come. We have stronger sympathies in one cause than another, and it is possible that I may have them; but I verily believe, if I know my own heart, that if this were a case of religious oppression of a Jew or Turk, much more the oppression of a Roman Catholic, who yet I hold to be a fellow-Christian — I may say my indignation would be as strong as it is now; and I would lift up my feeble voice in advocacy of the great principle, that, let man be Jew, Turk, Papist, or Protestant, let him alone. (Loud applause) Let him talk with his God, and let his God talk with him; and therefore it is not as a Protestant, but as a Christian citizen of a free land that I am glad to see my Catholic fellow-citizens as free as myself — therefore it is that I desire to protest against this oppression, and I call upon my Catholic brethren to join me in the protest. (Applause.) It will not come; depend upon it, it will not.

Every one who knows anything about Italy for years since, is aware that this very Duke of Tuscany was so kind, so clement, and so lenient a prince, that he may be said to have been the best beloved of all European sovereigns, unless it may be perhaps the Emperor of Russia, who is regarded with a sort of a religious affection; and I will tell you more, that if that conspiracy which broke out some years ago to consolidate Italy into one kingdom had been successful, the leaders would have placed him at the head of the kingdom. And why? Because of his liberal sentiments and kind heart they wished to put him on the throne. I have seen, sir, this old man walking, with his hands behind his back, superintending the improvements of Leghorn and other parts of his dominions, patting the little children on the head, talking to the working people, and nodding familiarly to the market-women, the very picture of a good king. Has this man changed? Yes. At that very time, the minions of the Pope endeavoured to use him in oppressing the people; but he put them one side, and set his face against religious tyranny. But he has now grown old, his brain has become weak, his heart fearful, and he has changed. It is not the Grand Duke of Tuscany now, it is the priest. Am I wrong in charging this upon the priesthood? The Pope is a priest, and the Pope is supreme at Rome. Let the Pope decree religious liberty; let the Pope wash his hands of religious oppression, let religion be free in Rome, and then I shall believe that religious oppression is not the act of the priest, but of the government.

But this very night there is within the city of Rome, a narrow street, with a gate at each end, into which is crammed every night from seven to eight hundred human beings. Drive through that street in the daytime, and you need perfume to keep you from fainting, such is the consequence of this dense population. Who are these people? They are almost under the shadow of the Vatican. And this most Christian sovereign of the most Christian Church, has the power to set them free; but he closes the gates on them at eight o'clock every evening in the winter, and nine o'clock in the summer, and opens them in the morning at a corresponding hour. Why is this? Because they are Jews, and the Roman Catholic religion tolerates no religion but its own. If we are guilty of slander—if it seems like calumny to charge oppression upon those who profess in some respects the same faith as ourselves, let them wash their hands of these things. The Pope ought to be the champion of religious freedom. He should set the example to the world by allowing truth to come into contact with error.

If there be a city, next to Jerusalem itself, filled with consecrated recollections, it is Rome—Rome, whose grounds are honey-combed with the tombs of early martyrs. A little while since, when there was danger, what did you see? A sovereign prince, the representative of the Apostle—puts on a livery and gets behind a travelling-carriage and flies like a lackey! The coward fled! And he whose voice of authority had roared like a bull from the Vatican, roared from the palace of Gæta, like a petted calf!

Are you here to sympathize with a gentleman, a nobleman? This man, who is imprisoned, is what is called a lackey, a hired servant. This man, when called to give up his Bible, did he fly? fly like a Pope? No; superstition has made a Pope a coward, while the Bible has raised a lackey to the dignity of a nobleman.'

He now called upon the priests to join in maintaining civil liberty. But he believed if they controlled the municipal authorities of this city as they do the Duke or Tuscany, his head to-morrow morning would not be worth a sixpence. 'And yet, said he,' I here declare before God, that I hope I have the spirit of my country's history, and have drunk deeply enough of the spirit of religious liberty, to lay my head upon a block and have it chopped off, before a single hair of the head of the most bigoted Papist in this land should suffer the least harm by religious persecution.' (Tumultuous applause, and the speaker took his seat.) While he attacked the system, he cherished no undue prejudices against the people. When at a public meeting Gavazzi one night attacked Chief Justice Taney as a Romanist, the writer remembers that Dr. Bethune abruptly left the stage, saying, 'He is a most pure man. Gavazzi knows nothing about us.'"

The following extract from his speech before the Seamen's Friend Society, affords yet another evidence of his powers as an orator:

"Suppose," said he, "that every ship that sails from this port, every ship especially that stretches her course into those quarters of the world where 'the darkness of the shadow of death,' is still on the nations, were manned by Christian seamen, commanded by pious officers, and were followed by the prayers of pious merchants, as eager that those ships should be made tributary to the glory of God, that those men should be made instrumental in carrying light among the destitute, as that they should bring home the profits of commercial enterprise, what would be the consequence? How soon would this earth be blessed with the knowledge of the Lord, and all nations rejoice in the blessing of that light which shines over us! This is what the Christian world must come to. Our religion does not inculcate piety merely for one day in the week, to take one dollar out of a thousand and put it into the treasury of the Lord. It should be like leaven that leaveneth the whole lump, pervading our whole life, and making our daily occupation sacred to God. Consecrating every instrumentality of our worldly comfort and prosperity, by making it subservient to the great cause of salvation throughout the whole world.

And where, if this doctrine be true, is this instrumentality so full of promise, or so certain, under Divine blessing, of success, as in the opportunities offered by the Seamen's Friend Society? He did not propose to enter into all the romance thrown around the seaman's character. A great many reckless and jovial characteristics he possessed on land. They afforded opportunities for a display of rhetoric, but practically, the sailor was like other men, born with the same naked depravities, exposed to the same temptations, and needing precisely the same grace of God that converted Paul, Mary Magdalene, or any sinner on the face of the earth. It was no more difficult for that grace to convert the sailor than the landsman. Either, according to his faith, was miraculous; a work great as creation. But when we believe it is the power of God, we believe that that power is promised to earnest faith; and the word which says, 'That which we sow, we shall also reap,' is the only encouragement which leads us on in this great work of attempting to evangelize the men of the sea. But the sailor has claims on us, not from his peculiar generosity or characteristics, which make it better or worse.

The soul of one man, all other things being equal, is worth as much as another; but, when converted, it may be worth more than another, in the influence which it may bring to bear on the world. If the sailor is going to distant lands, to a nation resembling our own at one time, to the shores cursed by the superstitions of Rome at another; on one voyage to a part darkened by the faith of the False Prophet, or upon another, to one where demonism shrouds its people in the absurdities of a cruel feticism; the conversion of this wanderer of the seas, who comes as near ubiquity as any man can, is worth, in this light, more than the conversion of ten ordinary men that stay at home, every night sleeping in the same bed, and every Sabbath worshipping in the same church. God, in his providence made great use of common men, but the conversion of these was not equal, in its influence, in the world at large, to the conversion of one intelligent sailor who travels over the earth.

Again, the sailor claims especial care, not because of his aptness or unaptness to receive instruction. God, by his Spirit, makes that soil the least promising, the most fruitful. But God works by means. We have Christian churches everwhere; but it is not so for the sailor. He is a few days in port, and many days at sea; one Sabbath within reach of the Gospel, and three, four, five, perhaps a year or two, where no Sabbath bell is heard, no gospel preached, and no Christian influence brought to bear; and because the sailor has not a Sabbath in ten that we have, should we work ten times as hard to do the sailor good on that Sabbath, as we do to serve ordinary men any common Sabbath of the year.

We want to intensify our labor for the sailor, because when we catch him, it is only for a little time; while the minister can preach to the ordinary people, if they will keep awake to hear him, every Sunday in the year. This society provides for the sailor at home, every accommodation; and, not content to bless him at home, it follows him abroad; and it was the great purpose of the charity, next to giving the sailor an opportunity of instruction here, to send the gospel to meet him everywhere he goes. Funds alone were needed to carry out fully this object; for wherever there is a port which gathers together a sufficient number of American ships to make a congregation, there were they ready to offer the gospel, with all the instrumentalities that surround it, as an appointed means of blessing to the world.

No harbor in which ships bearing the American flag are crowded, should be without a due provision for the dissemination of religious truth. Think of the example our country recently set to the world, perhaps too long delayed, but not the less glorious since manifested. A man, not a native of this country, a fugitive from the land of his birth, where his struggles in the cause of freedom, giving them the best interpretation, compromised his safety, — passing, as it were, only under the shadow of the American flag, that shadow consecrates him as under the protection of a mighty nation; and there, one who wears the uniform of this country, declares, in the face of a triple force, that he is safe; that he must be delivered up into the hands of those representing the dignity of that country, whose protection he claimed. And what has been the result?

The dignity of our country has been elevated in the estimation of the world. The name of the gallant Captain Ingraham cannot be uttered without calling forth the acclamations of his countrymen. (Applause.)

But, while doing him honor, he (Rev. Dr. Bethune) was not the less certain that there was not an officer in our American navy that was not prepared to do the same for an American, wherever found. Now, they wanted the church to be as faithful to the sailor, as the country is to her citizen; that the sailor, wherever he goes, might know that there is a friend armed with the panoply of the gospel, to shield him from the dangers, worse, a thousand-fold, than a foreign dungeon, chains, or temporal death; a friend that could lash his soul safe, as it were, to the cross that should float him safely over the waters to Heaven.

Wherever we have a commerce, wherever the American flag is unfurled, there is truth, defence, and a nation pledged for the safety of its citizens, who had the right to worship God as conscience should dictate. And every administration that should not get the privilege for them, should be turned out one after another. But what we ask, is more than the right to worship God as we desire; the opportunity, the church, the preacher, the communion vessels, the Bible, the hymn book, all the associations of Christianity, all consolations when away from our dear America, wherever we go, under the combined flags of the Bethel, and of the American nation."

At the memorial service of J. Fennimore Cooper, held at City Hall, New York, Sept. 25th, 1851, W. Irving in the chair, Dr. Bethune said:

"The eloquent gentleman, who has just addressed you, said that we had met to celebrate the obsequies 'of him who has been in all our thoughts.' Pardon me for dissenting from the expression. We have met to congratulate his spirit on its immortality. We are not permitted to look within the mysterious veil which divides time from eternity, or follow him before the presence of God; but we know that he died in firm faith upon the Son of God, our Redeemer, the only 'way, and truth, and life,' by whom we can 'come unto the Father.' In those almighty, just, and merciful hands, we can leave him; but while we mourn the departure of his generous worth on earth, it is our comfort and joy to know that his mind lives for as, and for all posterity, in his imperishable pages. If we may not hear fresh oracles of wisdom and truth from his once indefatigable pen, those which he has uttered remain with us, ever precious and affectionately cherished. It is now our desire to erect a memorial of our gratitude for so rich a legacy. The fame of our Cooper needs no artificial monument; with his own hand has he engraved it on the magic scenery of our country, and interwoven it with the legends of our history.

He was not a poet in the melody of rhythm or the responses of rhyme, but eminently one in the faculty of throwing the charms of imagination around rugged realities, and of elevating the soul with noble sentiments. Who, with any sense of poetry could read the 'Prairie' and not feel entranced by a poet's spell! He was a true poet, and, if we had the spiritual perception or the vivid imagination of a true poet, we should be conscious of a mournful moan,from out the rocky cliffs of the Hudson, answered by the sighing of its sad waves along the shores illustrated by his genius.

There is scarcely a portion of our land, or scene of our best history, or field of the ocean cut by an American keel, which does not bear testimony to his graphic truth. But, sir, how dare I attempt his eulogy, after his memory has been crowned this night by the classic hand of him, whom all of us acknowledge the foremost representative of American poetry; before an assembly of our citizens unparalleled for its combination of numbers, intelligence and moral worth, presided over—pardon me, sir, I would fain avoid the excuses of unnecessary compliment, but when I use the briefest term must pay the greatest — presided over by yourself!

My friend Mr. Bancroft has said (I cannot repeat his happy language, but will reach his thought) that we are not here to honor 'other men of letters,' the worthy compeers of their deceased brother; but I come out from this assembled senate of authors (among whom I have lawfully no place) to speak as one of the people, and say that we are assembled for their honor as well as his.

We are met to assure those eminent men, who give us the wise lessons of our history, ennoble our thoughts by the highest flights of song, and charm us with ethics in the pure strength of our Saxon tongue, made graceful and tender through the inspiration of an exquisite sensibility, that we are not ungrateful for the high benefits which the Father of lights confers upon us in their devoted services. This is the occasion for a precedent of admiring justice to our men of commanding and generous intellect. It is a sad thought, which can be relieved only by the faith that the records of genius are imperishable—but the present reality forces it upon us—the men whom we are this night happy to look upon, whose voice and pen are even now contributing their efforts for our delight and profit, must soon pass away.

We must have the satisfaction of assuring them by the honour we pay to the memory of their first-born, first-departed brother, that, when they are gone they shall not be forgotten. No, gentlemen, (bowing to Messrs Bryant, Bancroft, and Irving) go on in the noble career for which Providence has fitted you,—add hourly to the inestimable treasures already bestowed by your hands upon your countrymen and the world ; and if you need a motive beyond your own self-gratifying love of doing good, be assured that when you *vos quoque morituri* have left us, we, who now cover with tributary laurels the brow of Cooper, will follow your ashes with fond and loyal recollections.

Yet our thanks should not be expended in ' winged words', but, for the sake of posterity and the mass of our compatriot people, embodied in some enduring, public shape. Arts are kindred ; and among the best uses to which those who imitate the visible works of the Creator can be devoted, is the preservation of their form and features who have been benefactors of their country and mankind. Therefore would we, and our purpose shall not fail, erect such a monument to the honor of this great and good man, the first, I trust, of a long series, which shall commemorate his cotemporaries and successors in like dignity.

We could not fail to note,—as the orator of the evening in simple and elegant panegyric traced the long catalogue of our Cooper's writings,—that those which most concerned the history and scenes of his native land and ours, were most appreciated and efficient. The classical nations of antiquity deemed the fame of a hero or a sage not complete until they had inaugurated his statue. The capitals of modern Europe are crowded with such enduring presentments of those whom kings delight to honor as instruments of despotism, or for whom the people are permitted to testify esteem as friends of humanity. There is scarcely a town, however small, without one or more statues of the dead in its open squares. But, many as are the illustrious of our annals, you might look throughout our whole land, and (with some insignificant exceptions) discover no proofs that we can appreciate public services.

Let us, then, invoke the Genius of Sculpture, whose presence among us is so amply certified, to pourtray for the eyes of our people and their children, the lineaments of that face and form which, when living, were animated by the patriotic and zealous spirit of Cooper. Let it be placed, not in a hall of learning, or in a retreat of the few, but in the free common air and sunlight, where all may look upon it, and learn fresh gratitude, and gain fresh incentives to pursuits so honorable and so honored. We have been told that his voice is now heard in every civilized tongue, and we know, wherever it speaks, it tells the story of our national dignity and teaches the maxims of political wisdom and honesty which have raised us to our unexampled prosperity. Such are the best contributions we can make to the freedom of oppressed countries; because they show that without a popular love of justice and union, arms and blood are powerless to achieve liberty. The world has admired our Cooper as a man of genius; let them see that his countrymen love him as a wise champion of political truth, and a faithful citizen.

Without love, which our God has ordained to be the sole sufficient spring of all duty, virtue is but a name; and without patriotism (the scoff of knaves, but the admiration of the good) our citizenship will be hypocrisy. Let us cherish this grand virtue; let us teach it to posterity; and by public respect to the memory of those, who, like Cooper, have served earnestly under the institutions which educated them, conserve our self-respect and show our thankfulness for our wide, rich land, our unequalled constitution, and the union of those States, the bond of their security."

We conclude these specimens with a speech before the American Bible Society, perhaps the most elaborate effort of the kind that he ever prepared. He began by offering the following Resolution:

"As the Providence of God is bringing great numbers from foreign countries to reside among us, many of them without the Bible,

Resolved, That it is among our first duties to furnish them with that Sacred Book, that they may thus become a blessing and not an evil to our population.

I am thankful to the committee of arrangements for putting in my hands, a theme which will greatly assist me to redeem my speech from want of interest, because of the absolute want of time to prepare for it. Here is a theme which appeals to the heart of every man not only as a Christian, but also as a citizen of the United States. There was a great and sublime truth couched in the Neo-Platonic doctrine; that 'God is unity,' and that as we depart from God we run into multiplicity, and in proportion as we go away from God, do we become not only multiplicitous and conflicting, but even chaotic.

God in the beginning spoke to our first parents, and to their immediate offspring; but when men in the pride of their wicked hearts were not willing to retain him in their imagination, they went out from Him, and they 'changed the glory of the incorruptible God into an image made like unto corruptible man, and to birds and four-footed beasts, and creeping things,' and thence came all that horrible catalogue of vices which are included under the awful name of heathenism. Without God in the world, the nations became not only without religion, but without *virtue;* that bond, which out of the many, constitutes society, was lost when the centralizing, harmonizing, and comprehending doctrine of God was taken from the common soul of humanity; and sir, out of this came the separation of mankind. It was not only from the judgment of God but a moral necessity, that when the people erected a temple to the false god, Bel, there should have been a dispersion with a confusion of languages. They set up idolatry in the place of the true God; and so declared themselves traitorous rebels against the unity of the race, and God left them to their own devices, and their very speech became warped and strange to each other. They could not talk in one tongue, because they had lost the teaching of their common Father. Out of this came the multitude of languages which, much more, perhaps, than geographical position, separates our race into so many distinct and often conflicting nations. But, sir, under the influence of that same religion from which man departed at the rise of idolatry — that blessed religion which is taught in our Bible — we return to the unity from which we have departed.

We find the type of this in our own souls. How sweet to us, how sweet in the experience of every Christian agitated by the cares and the anxieties of life — how sweet to the Christian, when in his intellectual pursuits he finds himself troubled amidst the varieties and oppositions of human philosophy, when, like the messenger of Noah, he can find no rest as he pursues his weary and wandering way over the dark and storm-tossed sea; how sweet it is, sir, to come home to God, and have our Noah put forth his hand and take us into the ark of the blessed Bible! Then do we say with him of old, 'In the multitude of my thoughts within me' — in the chaos of these errors, doubts and anxieties, when human wisdom can give me no clue, when human teachers trouble me more by their contrarieties and differences — 'in the multitude of my thoughts within me, thy comforts delight my soul.' There is our comfort. We come home to God; he is our Noah, our *Rest*. Our reason bows herself and looks up in the face of a smiling Father; and as he speaks to us by his Spirit of life, and says, 'Peace, my child,' the peace of God, not merely the peace which God gives, but the peace which God has — the infinite, profound serenity, the infinite sublime calm which dwells in the mind of God, far above the conflicts of the storms that hang around this little world — 'the peace of God which passeth all understanding,' comes into our own hearts, and as far as our little finite can hold the infinite, it fills us with God himself, and our happiness is like his.

One of the heathern philosophers, and the wisest of them, tells us that 'virtue is the harmony of the soul;' when every thought, affection, desire, and motive are in perfect harmony, then is our virtue perfect. And another, copying from him, says, in language I have not good English enough properly to translate, that when it shall please the Divinity to take from our eyes the mists, as they were taken from the eyes of Diomed, we shall then see what to us is now invisible, we shall have the perfect mind, that is, the finished reason, which is all the same as virtue. It must be so; intellectual truth and moral rectitude must come together when they are perfect. *Perfecta mens, id est absoluta ratio, quod est idem virtus.*

Now, sir, this is the unity of God's blessed religion. It takes the human heart of the individual, which is but the type of the whole race; it pervades it with the love of God, which is the perfection of the law, and instantly all passion, all desires, all thoughts, all motives, come into perfect harmony, and the virtue of man is godliness, and all true righteousness is peace. This is the type of what will be the effect of our holy religion upon the whole world. Do we see, when we take up our precious Bible, where it leads us from its very beginning? There are philosophers of the world, your cosmogonists, or whatever you please to term them, that are boring down to the deepest stratum to frame their hypotheses, their ideas. God forbid that I should hold, for a moment, true science to be in quarrel with revelation. That can never be. No, sir, the God who made nature wrote the Bible; and I am not prepared to be an infidel as regards the one principle any more than an infidel as regards the other. My natural philosophy and my moral philosophy are in harmony with my religion; but we have here, as elsewhere, a multitude of thoughts in this human mind of ours.

The cosmogonist of fifty years since was as positive that he was right as the cosmogonist of this day is positive that his predecessor was utterly wrong. Men were as wise in their own conceits, before they found out the simple law upon which every child acts; the law of gravitation. It took them from the creation to Newton to find out the law which lies upon the very surface, open to every eye; yet were they very positive in those days. Wise were they, also, before the discovery was made of that wonderful element which pervades all the physical economy of this lower earth, and whose mysteries we have but begun to penetrate, — I mean that element called electricity, which enters into every physical change we have the ability to observe; which is found in light, life, in everything that has movement and increase. Yet the world, before they discovered electricity, were as wise in their own conceit as they are now; and may I ask, by way of parenthesis, who can tell that to-morrow there may not be discovered a principle which has been hidden from the world until now; which shall work as great changes in the theories of your cosmogonists, as the discovery of gravitation or of electricity?

But, sir, whatever may be our philosophical reasonings, the comfort of God delights our souls, and fills us with a peace that passeth all understanding, when, as we read, 'In the beginning God created the heaven and the earth.' There is where we begin; and when we go back there, there is no conflict; we have returned to peace. 'God created the heavens and the earth.' It is my opinion that the best proof, and the proof that is irresistible, of the being of God, is, that we know his being, and may contemplate him, as he is presented to us in the Scriptures. God alone could reveal God. Were there no God, the thought of the Infinite One could never have entered our minds. But, sir, when we have that thought, how does it lead us down from the original Cause, to the possible changes and results of the world's history. 'God created the heavens and the earth;' God laid these foundations; God planned the superstructure; God gave it its beauty and symmetry; and will the Architect, looking complacently upon His beautiful work, abandon it? Can that go to chance which came from Infinite Mind? We go with the Bible up to God. When we take a step farther on, what do we find but the race in the one man and the one woman whom God gave him? and whatever differences or distances may, in the process of time, have come between man and man, and nations and nations, there we all meet. All, from the noble, proud of his genealogy, to the most lowly servant of our necessity, meet in the one man; no matter what tongue is spoken, no matter what be the hue of the skin, no matter what be the form of government, or the degree of civilization in which he lives. The man that looks to the first man who came from the hand of God, must recognize every other man, on the face of the whole earth, as his brother. Then again, when, from the wickedness of men, there came to be the necessity of the washing out of sin from the whole world, and the second father came, in Noah, we are again united in the ark of typical promise.

Let me, sir, pass on to a yet more interesting point of union, when God called out from the idolaters of that ancient superstition, from the very fires of Baal, his friend, His chosen instrument of good and blessing, the one he named Abraham, to go forth, not knowing whither he went, gave him that promise which the apostle Paul emphatically terms the Gospel, and said, 'In thy seed shall all nations be blessed.' There is no division there, no foreigner there, no division of human language or of human relationship there. 'In thy seed' not thy seeds, as of many, but as of one 'in thy seed, — which is Christ, the seed that succeeded in the promise, the seed of the covenant, 'in thy seed,' — in the seed of the woman, — 'in thy seed shall all nations be blessed.'

And then passing on through the intermediate Scriptures, when we hear the multitudinous voices of angels rejoicing over Bethlehem, the same voices, I doubt not, that swelled the diapason of their hallelujahs, when 'the morning stars sang together, and all the sons of God shouted for joy,' when they returned to sing again over the earth their adoring joy, because of the 'good news which shall be to all the people.' No division of language, no division of territory, no division of government there; 'for all people,' before the majesty of that Gospel, every system of human legislation, goes down; and, while we submit ourselves 'to the powers that be,' in obedience to the blessed example of him who counted it his chiefest honor, as an example of human virtue, to be the servant of all, and the servant of law; I say, while in obedience to his example we submit to the laws of human government, we hold to a far higher sentiment, 'we have another King, one Jesus.'

Wherever that name goes in its power it reigns; and Jesus shall reign until the whole world is his. Pardon me if I again return to this history. As we come on in the history of God's providence, the miraculous portion of which was finished, as we suppose, with the completion of the Sacred Canon, we see other indications alike springing from, and confirming the promise of, the Divine Word of God. We behold the nations still separate and conflicting. The philanthropist looks over the stormy sea, and his heart sickens, and he asks himself, Shall there never be peace? Shall these human brethren always bite and devour one another? Is there no method of purifying the human heart, the source whence come 'these wars and fightings amongst' us all? How shall we speak to them? They speak different languages; we cannot begin to tell them, though our hearts prompt us to utter the 'glad tidings of great joy.' We cannot begin to tell them the wonderful works of God, because we cannot speak in their various tongues. Yet here is the blessing of the Pentecost repeated. Yes, sir, tenfold is the blessing that rests upon your Society.

I do not remember how many languages were known, and reduced to system, at the time of the Pentecost; but you may count them all as they are given in the catalogue, by the sacred historian, and though they appear many, how few they are to the number of languages upon the face of the earth, at the present day! But what has the Bible

Society done? I say the Bible Society, because there will be no question here of my claiming, for the Bible Society, a share in the philological triumphs of missionaries and students under the influence of the Bible. What has the Bible Society done? At the beginning of this century, if I mistake not, the languages of men that had been reduced to system, to grammar, or dictionary, or even vocabulary, did not amount to more than some forty or fifty. What is the case now? Your Secretary can give the more exact number; I cannot be exact to a unit or so; but in your own library, — certainly, if not there, in the combined libraries of the American and the British and Foreign Bible Societies, — you will find the Word of God in one hundred and seventy languages. I call upon men of learning, I call upon the philosophers of the world, I call upon all the Universities which are claimed to be fountains of light and knowledge, I challenge the whole earth, in all its breadth and all its history, to give me an equal triumph to this; a triumph of science, and triumph of learning, and triumph of philanthropy, like that which has trebled, more than trebled, the common speech of the world, in less than sixty years; gives us access, literally so, where we had it to but fifty peoples, to one hundred and seventy; so that we and all of us who wish to talk can talk, or may soon talk, to the heart of our brother, wherever he lives, or whatever tongue he speaks, and make your Bible Society our own interpreter to all our kindred flesh. Ah, sir, I am not so weaned from the love of the world as not to rejoice over the triumphs of learning, and it is my delight to see how the triumphs of religion take the triumphs of learning into the most sacred fellowship.

When that great land, that mysterious nation, where there has been a civilization more ancient far than our own, that people whose records go back to the period when the ruins of the deluge were yet visible upon the face of their country, and which is locked up from the rest of the world because of its peculiar systems of governmental policy and its peculiarly difficult language, was to be treated with, when it was necessary that we, the commercial nations of the earth, England, France, and America, should talk to China, the many hundred millions of China, who was the interpreter? Did we go to Oxford? Could we find him in Paris? Had we him in our own Princeton, Yale, or Harvard? Sir, it was the missionary that talked for England, the son of Morrison, who translated the Bible; and the missionary that talked for America, our own noble Parker, at the mention of whose name, if this place were not sacred, you would burst forth in applause. It was a missionary, though unhappily not of our own pure Protestant creed, that talked for France. Were it not for a despised missionary, taught, animated, and inspired by the Word of God, which he loved, we could have made no treaty with China, because China could not have understood us, or we China. This is an illustrative fact, to my mind, of the greatest importance. It shows that it is not philanthropy, it is not learning, it is not commercial enterprise, but it is religion, the religion of the Bible, the religion of the Bible Society, if you will, which is to bring all nations together, to make them speak one language, and to sing in perfect harmony, at no distant day, one song unto God and His Christ. There are thoughts connected with this of infinite interest to us all; but while I speak thus, let me briefly, — for I will not weary an audience who are listening to me so patiently and kindly, — let me illustrate the fact by a touching incident:

During the war of the Crimea, after one of the most sanguinary engagements, when the furious Frank and bearded Turk, and stalwart Briton and stolid Russ, had mingled in the fearful fray; when the battle-field was strewed with the dead and dying, and strange faces were passing before the swimming eyes of those whose thoughts were going back to their homes, perchance by the Don or the Volga, where their 'young barbarians were at play;' perhaps their home, around which rustled the leaves of the vine, in merry France; perchance the home in the village, with its green lattice and its Sabbath chime of old England; when, in this fearful hour, as the prowler was stealing from one to another to rob the dead, and hate was seeking out more victims to glut itself upon, and there, in mortal agony, lay a poor Russian, thirsting for water with the burning thirst which only gunshot wounds can cause, there came near him a French and an English soldier. As they met together, searching for their comrades, they looked into his face, and he looked eagerly into theirs, and said, 'Christos!' Ah! sir, God be thanked for that name, the name which is above every name, which in all varieties of language we recognize as the name of Him 'whose we are, and whom we serve.'

But, sir, you will pardon me for leaving so long the resolution which you committed to me, and yet I do not think I have wandered from the spirit of it. It is, that 'to this land the Providence of God is bringing great numbers from foreign countries to reside among us, many of them without the Bible.' Such is the preamble. Who is doing this? What is the reason that these people come from so many countries, that your Secretary, according to ordinary speech, but not according to the higher diction of Christian philanthropy, calls foreign countries? Why is it that they come here? It is 'the providence of God;' the same providence that of old laid the foundations of the earth; the providence of Him who walked amongst the trees of the garden of Eden, and talked with our first father; the providence of Him who gathered our second family into his ark, the same type of that ark which is to gather the saved out of all nations; the providence of him who said to Abraham, 'in thy seed, (not in thy seeds, as to many, but unto thy seed, as of one) 'in thy seed shall all nations be blessed;' the providence of Him who sent his only begotten Son with good tidings 'which shall be to all peoples;' *that* 'providence brought these people to our shores.'

Who are they whom you call *foreigners*? Are they not children of our first father, Adam? If we rejoice in the blessings of the gospel that was first preached to Abraham, in the blessings of that gospel heralded at our Saviour's birth, we must acknowledge them as those to whom the gospel was sent as unto us. We have no right to exclude them, they come here to their Father's land; they come here to the tents of their brethren; they come here to join that company. I trust, at least, that many, with God's blessing, will join that 'commonwealth,' in which 'there are no more strangers and foreigners, but citizens with the saints and of the household of God.'

Now to come to the approximate fact of the illustration by which I have been endeavoring to show the comprehending, coalescing principle of this blessed religion of ours, combining with the providence of God. How long did this continent lie sleeping in the darkness of oblivion? How long were the forests waving over the soil which the plough had never stirred? How long were these territories, now crowded with populous cities and smiling farms, the hunting-ground of the wild man, not less savage than the beast that he hunted? Almost as long as that law of gravitation was hidden from the knowledge of man; almost as long as that great principle or element of electricity was hidden in mystery; almost as long as man was ignorant of the art of printing or the impelling force of steam; but it is but a little distance in the history of centuries that these great discoveries are a part.

At this time God opens this continent; and here He says to all nations of the earth, Here is a land where, for the first time since the institutions of human government, religion has been free from legal patronage or legal oppression; here, where for the first time with intelligent institutions, man has a right, under God, to be his own ruler; here is an asylum, like the blessed gospel, for every one that is under trouble and ignominy in the old world, to flee to and be at rest.

I wish to say nothing severe of any one, but I am frank to say, I have no sympathy with the spirit which says that the foreigner has no claim to our sympathy because he is a foreigner. Good, ancient George Herbert tells us that 'Man is God's image, but a poor man is Christ's stamp to boot.' And so I say wherever I see a human form, and human intellect, and human affection beaming from the human countenance, There is my brother. But when I see a man that is a stranger, and hear the accents of a foreign tongue, I see the image of Him who for my sake was 'a stranger in the earth,' and 'had not where to lay his head.' This is the sentiment which, to my faith, our religion enjoins. This is the sentiment which, as I believe, is the grand doctrine of our noble democracy, for I love to use that word; men pervert it, as they do other good words, but I rejoice to avow myself, in the same sentence, a Christian and a democrat. I mean, by that term, a man who acknowledges his fellow-man as his equal, and is willing to give to every man the rights which God has given to him. Here we have in this land, by the providence of God, the nations coming together.

Look at the nations of the world that have been separated; look at India sleeping, or convulsed in a delirium of half sleep, half wakefulness; look at those nations which show something of a civilization that they have had in these former ages from the light of science — for next to Egypt, India was once the most enlightened, if indeed India were not the mother from whom Egypt learned her philosophy. But what has India become? What has the exclusive nation of China become? Shut up to themselves, with no minglement of foreign bloods, no minglement of foreign habits and manners, in their own sameness from day to day, without impulse, without variety, without stimulus, there they lie what they were, nay, more dead than they were, thousands of years ago. But, sir, you may take, as you very well know, Tacitus or Cæsar, and you shall read in their writings the description of the Gaul, the German, and the Spaniard, and they are *exceptis excipiendis*, and you can know them at this day by the same characteristics.

They have more learning, more science, more religion certainly, but the spirit of the people is one, and as peoples they have risen but little, or from their risings they have fallen back, and made comparatively little progress. I mean progress in those great arts of comprehensive civilization and philanthropic philosophy which elevate the soul above the jealousies of earth, and combine men in the unities of Love. But why is it? Because shut up, each family to itself, they have married with their own blood, and the curse of the incest is upon them. But cross that narrow channel and enter our own motherland, at least the grandmother land of most of us here, and what a different condition is presented there! We have *our* motherland, but we delight to think of the grandmother-land from which our fathers came. Cross, I say, to England, and if you choose — and I wish that you would — abide a little while in the states of the Low Countries; for the history of those Low Netherlands is, in the respects of which I am about to speak, almost identical with that of England.

If you look at the origin of these people, on their little sandbars, beginning to wrest from the ocean the patrimony which they have bequeathed to their children, building in the course of successive centuries those dykes which have cost more than if they had been erected of solid brass from their foundation to their top, you will find that it was the blood of a free people of different blood driven on the one hand by the encroachments of the Roman empire, and on the other by the tyranny of feudal oppressors; yes, you will find that it was the combination of the blood of free people that made the early cities of Holland what they were; that taught them the combination of mutual rights; and, above all, taught them that union of free independent sovereignties from which *our* fathers learned the best secrets of our own unparalleled prosperity. It may be more familiar, however, to the memory of those to whom I speak — for it is not every one that has the courage to penetrate within the comparative obscurity which is hung over the shores of the Dutch, and but for the recent brilliancies of genius which have been shed by Motley and Prescott upon their history, we should know comparatively little of them.

Pass into England, and see what you have there. There are the ancient Britons, and traces of a race, if not races, yet more ancient. There you have the blood of the Saxons and the Angles, of the Danes and the Normans, and the Flemings, and the fugitive Huguenots.

You have them mingled; their names, the names of foreigners, stand high in their annals; and while the genuine Saxon is yet the basis of the people, every contributor to a combined race has marked its honorable position high amidst the catalogue of the nobles and the clergy and the learned jurists.

But sir, what has made England what she is? Men are proud to talk of Anglo-Saxon blood; men are proud to talk of commercial enterprise, and all that sort of thing; but I go behind Anglo-Saxon blood; I go to that which inspires enterprise, commerce, to the minglement of bloods in the British people. That is what has made them what they are. And here sir, God in this land of ours is working out a far more majestic purpose. England may do very well for an experiment upon a small scale, as a sculptor would model the gigantic statue of his imagination in a lump of plaster; but England is too little, sir, for the outworking of God's providence in that respect. There is a necessity for a wide continent, for a more comprehensive system of government; and God has found it here — found it here, sir. He knew it from the foundation of the earth. He predestined it when he predestined the triumph of his Son over all nations. God has given us here the theatre for this stupendous development. Here they come from all lands — all the children of our father Adam — all objects of our Saviour's love — all brethren of the same humanity. Here they come, talking as they land more languages, tenfold, than the languages of Babel, but soon learn to coalesce in a common tongue our noble English, which is to be the language of the whole world. Yes, sir, here they come, the best bloods of all nations of men — men who would rather be poor than under an oppressive government; men who say, 'Let me suffer, let the wife of my bosom suffer, but let us find a home for our children where they can rise.'

These are the people that come to us, the more than noble army of martyrs, men and women who suffer for posterity; and as I believe, though they know it not, suffer for God in their coming across the sea and in encountering the difficulties of a new land. These are the people whom we are to meet upon our shores. These are the people who bring us elements of excellence from every race; that here we may see the vivacity of the Gaul, the staid independence of the German, the athletic character and determination of the Briton, and all the other varieties of human virtue combining to form, not many nations, but *one*; to make, as God in his grace made out of the Jew and Gentile, out of all nations 'one new man:' so making peace 'between all nations.'

Now, sir, how are we going to bring these men into this union? It is by the power of the Bible which you print, by the power of that blessed name 'Christos,' which brought tears to the eyes of every one of you a moment since, the gospel which never fails to melt under the force of Christian love and in the alembic of God's fervent truth, all elements into one amalgam, that it may adorn with the most precious richness the brow of Christ, the King of nations and the King of saints. We need the Bible to do this; and the Bible *will* do it. We *can* talk to them, sir. Go to Washington, go to your universities, and tell them to give you the selection of their proudest men and their most accomplished interpreters; and all Washington and all your universities combined cannot give us men that can talk to one-tenth part of these people; but your Society can talk to each of them, be he what he may. Find out his country and his tongue, and when he comes to your Society for his language, it is in your library; you have the Book of Life there for him; give it to him.

Let us speak plainly of the claims of these people upon us. There was, far back in the brief history of our beloved land, but not far back in the history of the world's ages, a band of determined men who cast the anchor of their little vessel near to a cold and barren rock. The December winds were howling through their shrouds, and scattering ice upon their decks, and they could scarcely hold their canvass, which was frozen stiff as sheets of iron. They looked upon a bleak shore; they saw no trace of human brotherhood; they heard no sound of a human voice, except it be the howl which they knew not whether it was a man or the wild beasts; they saw no trace of man, unless it might be some broken arrow whose barb was red with human blood. They landed there; and on that rude and barren shore they knelt as 'strangers and foreigners' unto the stranger's God; giving worship to him and to his kingdom, and trusting in his providence.

Their story has had the advantage of more eloquence, more poetical illustration; but not far from the same period there came those more prosaic in their character, but not a whit less generous in their noble virtues, to this very spot where we are met; men who loved their Bible; men, every one of whom had their Bible clasped and riveted, as though they were determined to keep the devil himself from depriving them of their comforts; men who before they had been here many days, set up the worship of God in its simplicity;—I mean the men of Holland, who, in many respects, deserve the credit of being as much the moral progenitors of this land, as the pilgrim fathers of New England, for whom such a monopoly of generation has been claimed.

And there also came at successive times the Presbyterians from England and Ireland, Scotland and France, with the church-loving Cavaliers. They were all strangers; but, O sir, what must have been the thoughts of those pilgrims kneeling by that desert rock! What must have been the thoughts of those Hollanders as they knelt on the shores of that narrow peninsula, which is now crowned with this majestic city! Alone, far from their native land, far from the churches in which their fathers worshipped, far from the familiar speech of neighbor and friend—alone, alone,—yet not alone, for the 'Universal Father' was with them, this was their consoling thought, that wherever they went, whatever soil they touched, they got no farther from God. They were as near Him on the shores of Plymouth, and the Bay of Massachusetts—or whatever the name was at that period—amidst the woods of Virginia, on the sea islands of Carolina, or among the mountains of Pennsylvania; they were as near God there as though they knelt in the cathedral, whose flags had been hallowed by the tread of the generations of a thousand years.

And this is what I ask you to do in my resolution for these people who come here: meet them upon the shores; meet them with that one Word of God, whieh they can all understand, and which speaks to all, and tells them they are not strangers, that God is here, that the blessing of God upon the strangers, our fathers, is ready to rest upon them, strangers though they seem, and upon their children for ever; and thus shall we call perfect a nation which shall present to the world such a spectacle as no Papal universalism, no Roman empire, has ever equalled.

One word more: This is but a type again of that grandest triumph of all, when God shall throw open the doors of his own House, with its many mansions, for all his children; when, in a peace more joyous than that which welcomed the long-wandering prodigal home, the wide hall shall be filled for the banquet and the festival; when there shall come those of all kindreds, and climes, and tongues, under the face of the whole heavens; when all ages of the past, meeting with all the ages of posterity, all time, all lands, all people, shall come together, no longer separated, no longer multiplicity, but one in Christ, one in the love of God, through the Redeemer. O sir, I love to think of that time! How my soul goes out beyond the pettiness of party strife! How I seem to rise even in my littleness, as the morning bird on its light wing rises above the turmoil and hurly-burly of men, to sing unto God! How my heart goes out, exults beyond all these restrictions of a sinful world, and rejoices, as I recognize myself no longer a citizen of a narrow province, no longer as confined in my nationality to a few brother tribesmen, but as one of the vast family of God, the universal family of faith in Christ Jesus. How I rejoice as I anticipate that day when I shall be welcomed as I come near my Father's threshold—for we shall not come unwelcomed there—when I shall be welcomed by all these people that the religion of Christ has taught me to love upon earth; nay, when not only these people, but when all the tribes of God's creation, when the inhabitants of distant worlds, that have looked upon us with interest like that of the angels, when these shall come in from every province of God's universal empire, his spiritual children, we shall be one, gathered together in Christ, the Son of God, and therefore heir of all things; the Son of Man, and therefore our Elder Brother—when we shall be all gathered together in one, and God be the Father, and his glory the joy of the universe for ever."

CHAPTER XII.

ANONYMOUS ATTACK.

OUR search among the papers of Dr. Bethune has brought us up to the beginning of the year 1855. He was a man like the rest of us, and did not escape calumny. During the holidays he had attended a dinner of the St. Nicholas Society, where, according to Mr. H. T. Pierrepont "his speech was of a much more serious order than was usual at our anniversaries ; he spoke as a true son of New York and gave many references to history to the credit of the Dutch Nation." Yet, because he attended a public dinner, a paragraph appeared in a Hartford paper in which the writer, under the secure cover of "anonymous," made insinuations against Dr. B. both gross and cruel. This attack called forth a storm of indignation from all quarters ; and perhaps the pastor would not have known how many true and appreciating friends he had, had it not been for this unjustifiable slander. But apart from his well-ordered and scholarly speech, the laborious and exemplary life of the Doctor is the best reply ; indeed it were scarcely worth while to make a record of it except as one of the sore trials to which his sensitive nature was exposed, and to get his view of such attacks. Probably no two men when made the object of such moral assassination behave in the same way. One, who was in the habit of finding such jets of venom among his morning letters, when he did not know the hand looked for the signature, and when he saw none, instantly dropped the paper into the fire, and that was the end of it. But not every one has this self-command, while many of these poisonous stabs are delivered through the medium of the daily press.

The editor who lends himself to the transaction is rarely worth powder and shot, and the intended victim cannot always obtain redress. It may, perhaps, not be uninteresting to our readers to see one of the ways in which a "venomed stab" is sometimes parried, and we insert a few paragraphs which were found in Dr. B's handwriting among his papers; although we have no certainty that it was written in reference to the present occasion, it carries its own commentary.

TO AMERICANUS(?).

"You have written an anonymous letter, a dishonorable act which none but a coward would be guilty of. I might well take no heed of a charge so silly, coming from a source so mean, and should not, but for charity to point out the injustice you have done, that you may be deterred from writing anonymously again.

You must be strangely ignorant to suppose that a speaker (unexpectedly called upon) toward the close of a long, excited meeting, is responsible for the very words into which a tired reporter condenses his remarks. Had you been present you would have known that I was the most reluctant speaker of the evening, and that a hoarseness compelled me to stop suddenly. This is stated in one, at least, of the newspapers. Had you heard me you would also have known that I levelled the charges of gross immorality against the *Continental despots* who are combining against the freedom of the people. The reporter of the Express has left out *Continental* but retained the sense. Is Victoria of Continental Europe, is she a despot? Is she one of the conspirators against the freedom of the people?

As for the conspiring despots, I excepted Nicholas, whose personal habits are chaste; but of which of the rest can it be said that they are not vile, murderous, or perjured! My charge did not include the reigning houses of Sweden, Spain, Portugal; but you know little of present history, if you consider them other than debauched persons. You might make a stand for the weak but obstinate King of Prussia, whose personal life is not impure, had I not spoken of families or dynasties rather than single individuals; yet he is 'steeped in perjuries' with the 'blood of thousands' on his deceitful soul.

Your last accusation is as ridiculous as it is false. Assuming (what is utterly untrue even according to the report in the Express) that I intended the Queen of Great Britain in my denunciation, you charge me with 'traducing the land of my forefathers.' Is the *Queen* of Great Britain or her court, the *land* of my ancestors? If I should say, as I might, that George IV., all the Georges except the III., were debauched, would that be calumniating *Scotland?* I am a Scotchman sir, a title I value next to that of an American, by birth. I have never spoken of Scotland but with affectionate praise. No deserving person with a Scotch accent has ever asked my help and been refused it. When Scotland was threatened with famine, I wrote the Pennsylvanian Address which brought in for her relief $28,000. Of that sum my immediate personal exertions raised $1,200; and now I am accused by a malicious anonymous green-horn with calumniating the land of my fathers!

You sign yourself Americanus; but I cannot believe that you are a native-born citizen, though, possibly, you may have been naturalized.

You will, perhaps, think my language to you uncharitably harsh and so, unbecoming; but you are beyond the pale of charity. You are not a *man*, but an *anonymous thing.* You have *no name*, and, therefore, no character, no conscience, no feelings. You excuse yourself by saying that a public speech is open to public comments; but you are not the public, your charges are not public, you could not make them public without assuming a responsibility from which you hide; while a public speaker stands out openly. Had you written to me over your own name as a gentleman, I would gladly have responded kindly and set you right.

Take my advice and never write another anonymous letter. It is a crime which nothing can justify, except it be in reply to what is anonymous. If you have anything which you feel bound to say, put your name to it, and it will have as much respect as your name is worth;

but if you say what you are ashamed or afraid to indorse with your credit, you make yourself either a coward, or a knave, or both."

However unjustifiable, however silly, still there is a wonderful power in an evil report; it will travel much farther and be more eagerly related than the consistent life of godliness.

In the middle of the year the pastoral relation with the "Church on the Heights" became disturbed. To external appearance that church was in the highest state of prosperity. Its services were well sustained, and the audiences crowded, its benevolence large, and Sunday schools expanding, but the anxious eye of the pastor beheld signs of alarm. Contrary to his advice, the edifice had been more costly than was intended, and a heavy debt rested upon it; this made it necessary to place a high rental upon the seats, and caused dissatisfaction. Perhaps the spiritual state of the congregation was not as high as the earnest soul of the minister, although in this respect it was not inferior to others equally surrounded with social temptations, and occupied with business cares. We are not then surprised to hear that a proposition from certain New York brethren to Dr. Bethune, praying him to come over and help them to build up a church in Ninth street, was early listened to with favor. There must have been a great attraction in New York as the metropolis of the nation, but more, he was her favorite son. When he was assailed by cynics in Philadelphia, he only appeared in New York, and an immense audience rose and greeted him with rounds of applause; and never had he come to his native city without finding responsive and loving hearts to welcome him. "Dear New York," he exclaimed, "Few of you can remember it as I do, when we ran down the Flattenberg on our little sleighs, or skated on Lispenard's meadows and Barr's pond, and through Leonard street, up town. It is my birthplace, the home of my youth, and the asylum of my earliest affections." The flattering invitation to his home was serious and business-like, quite sufficiently so as to necessitate immediate action. The first step was to prepare a communication for the consistory of his church—a paper very decided in tone, and which would imply that the pastor had made up his mind to sever the relation; but this paper being placed in the hands of a prudent friend, Mr. F. I. Hosford, was probably at his remonstrance withdrawn, and in the middle of September, the greatly modified letter, which we subjoin, was transmitted to his church officers :

TO THE CONSISTORY OF THE CHURCH ON THE HEIGHTS, BROOKLYN, L. I.

"DEAR BRETHREN : — It is not without pain that I address you on a subject which occasions my deep solicitude, and now requires your kind, candid consideration.

I inclose a communication laid before me by a number of gentlemen, friendly to the Dutch church, in New York, which sufficiently explains its object and importance as relating to the interests of our denomination, and to myself, as one of its ministers.

You will agree with me, that while our immediate connection may be with a particular congregation, we owe, under God, allegiance to the church at large, and that our personal convenience or preferences should not bias our judgment respecting the larger duty.

Our first question in all cases should be directed to Him whose we are, and whom we should serve: "Lord, what wilt thou have us to do?" Yet among the methods of ascertaining the answer of heavenly wisdom, not the least is taking Christian counsel of wise men, especially of those whose official position gives them ecclesiastical authority, and whose tried friendship assures their sincerity. In this spirit I ask your advice, and hope that you will give it.

The expediency of my attempting by divine help, the building up of a church in New York under the present auspices, is argued at length in the communication of our friends—and, as you are not ignorant of the circumstances, I need say nothing further on that point.

The effect, which such a transfer of my services would have on our church in Brooklyn, you are of all persons the best able to judge of; consequences are in the hands of God, and our part is to do our duty, leaving results to Him.

I may, however, and should speak frankly of myself, as the one whose action is to be determined.

There are reasons, which so far as I can allow my personal feelings and private relations to sway me, urge me to go to New York. The hope of being better able to watch over the comfort of my beloved mother, now very aged and infirm, is a consideration that bears strongly upon me. She will not come to me in Brooklyn (and she has reasons for this, the force of which I cannot deny,) and so, if we are to be near each other, I should go to her in New York.

I have also some warm and attached friends in my native city, whose society I am now almost wholly deprived of, among whom it would be very pleasant to spend my declining years.

I cannot but think,—I have long thought, that I am not adapted as a man or a minister, in the pulpit or out of it, to the community of Brooklyn, and that my usefulness suffers by the prejudices (to use a mild word) which surround me. Human nature is mainly everywhere the same, but a larger sphere would be likely to contain more of those who, for any reasons, might prefer to avail themselves of my ministry, and sympathize with the course which my conscience binds me to pursue. My residence in Brooklyn has not been a happy one, and neither my church nor my house there, free from painful associations.

When the enterprise of our church was begun, I entered into it with expectations which I supposed warranted, and with distinctly avowed plans concerning my views of duty, as well as of church policy. The disappointments that followed greatly embarrassed me, distracting my mind and heart, occupying my time, and (still worse) throwing me sometimes into opposition of views entertained by some, if not of all, of you brethren. As I had carefully and explicitly declared at the beginning the methods which I should feel bound to pursue, I have kept to them; and although you have had much consideration for my convictions, I fear that sometimes I may have been regarded as too persistent, if not unreasonable.

My position has, in consequence, been painful, liable to reproach, and disagreeable surmise, and is likely to continue so as long as I retain it. I should, perhaps it may be said, have acted in view of this at an earlier period; but our friend Mr. M. will tell you, that at the time alluded to, I put into his hands, for presentation to you, what was equivalent to a resignation, which at his dissuasion I did not press. I wish it, however, to be distinctly understood, that I was then, and have always been, ready myself to withdraw, rather than that any one of the congregation should consider my remaining inconsistent with their right.

Disappointment in the plans on which I felt myself warranted in uniting with the enterprise of a church at Brooklyn, has severely embarrassed me in various ways; and now, should I remain with you, will put me to the necessity of some severe toils, which I might avoid by a change of pulpit.

I am now fifty years old, and ministers at my time of life do not often receive calls from such churches as are adapted to their habits, and should I refuse the present opportunity, and, subsequently feel myself obliged to resign my present charge, I should be most probably obliged to retire from pastoral duty.

I cannot conceal from you, that the poor attendance in our lecture-room has given me much anxiety. It would seem that I have not the power to draw our people to their devotional services on week evenings. My remonstrances, varied in every way I could think of, have, as the result shows, been regarded with indifference; and that, not by the careless only, but those prominent in both church and congregation. I have been accustomed (and I think rightly) to consider such a state of things as indicative of a decay in the power of a pastor over the people, and that the cause of it lies in him, rather than in them. Without a revival in the devotional services of the church, we cannot hope for a blessing. Let me then go, brethren, rather than remain, if I am in the way of spiritual good to you and the people. I have done, in the lecture-room, as well as I could, and so cannot promise to do better.

Brethren, I have opened my heart to you frankly. Perhaps, you will think me unduly sensitive, on some points, at least. But we ministers are a sensitive race; some of us, it may be, more so than others. Our wealth lies in principles, affections and sentiments. There we are most vulnerable, and suffer most. My former pastoral history has been such as to unfit me for trials, before never encountered.

On the other hand, there are strong motives disinclining me to leave Brooklyn.

When I began with the pressure of an enormous debt, which, contrary to what I had supposed an understood agreement, had been put upon us, I did not do it otherwise than in a spirit of self-sacrifice, intending to try the desperate experiment, and afterwards seek comparative rest elsewhere. But as I pursued my work, my heart grew to it, and to the people who gathered under my care. The numbers guided into the fold by my pastoral hand, the unaffected kindness manifested to me by many, the scenes of joy and sorrow in which I have sympathized with them, the memories of the precious dead, whom living I had learned to love, the attention not unfrequently accorded to my Sabbath teachings, the faithful zeal of our young people in enterprises of religious charity, the prayers that have been put up for me, and the prayers I have put up for you all, the very pains, and sufferings, and reproaches, and labors I have gone through for your sake, all have endeared me to some of you, but far more have endeared you all to me.

The Sabbath school and missionary enterprises, recently begun and carried on by our people under your lead, brethren, have done more than anything else in our history, to soothe my anxieties. We can never despair of a church, which puts the cause of mercy first, and itself second. If such is to be your future policy, you will have the blessing, whatever else happens to you.

The recent, and, as I understand, (inform me if I am mistaken) successful effort to pay all the debt of the church, excepting that for the ground, puts us, financially, just where I was promised that we should be when the church was complete. Only now, is the church pecuniarily in the condition in which alone I engaged to be its minister. We have passed through sad trials to reach this point. But the character of the effort which has thrown off the *incubus* that lay so heavily and long on our strength, has deeply affected me. So many have united, and all of them contributed so liberally, so much more liberally than we could have hoped, that I regard your congregation as strong, harmonious, consolidated, and of a most generous spirit. I should be most insensible, did I not feel personally and warmly grateful for the satisfaction derived from the result, but especially from the persons and means by which it has been reached.

I am also most conveniently domesticated in the house provided by the kind care of many friends, for the comfort of my invalid wife and myself. I can never hope to find a dwelling better adapted to our peculiar necessities; and although, with all its attractions, it has been the occasion to me, in some respects, of pain, in other respects, of embarassment, yet it is very pleasant to us as a memorial of kindness, and has been hallowed by many an hour of domestic enjoyment and religious retirement.

Thus, you see, my brethren, how my feelings and preferences alternate. I wish to do my duty. I wish to forget, so far as I can, all but the kindness I have received and the happiness I have enjoyed. I can truly say that no ambitious motives tempt me. I wish to do my duty, and in circumstances where I shall be least hindered in acting out what are now to me inflexible rules of duty.

If it be my duty to go to the enterprise now proposed to me, and attempt to build up, before my work on earth is done, another church for my Master's honor, I am ready to go; but I shall not tear myself away from my present charge without a bleeding heart.

If it be my duty to remain with you, I am ready to do so with affectionate zeal; though it will be at a sacrifice of private relationships, and temporal interests—of the latter, more than appears on the surface.

Brethren, notwithstanding my errors and infirmities, you are my friends. You are the friends of the Dutch Church. You are the overseers of the flock dear to us all. Advise me as a man and as a minister. I shrink from doing anything that may provoke your censure; nay I am unwilling to do—I cannot do anything in this matter without your approval.

But I expect from you the conscientious exercise of large and liberal judgment. Whatever be the result, I trust that we shall ever be united in the best bonds!

Your brother and servant in the kingdom and patience of Jesus Christ,

George W. Bethune.

Claverack, *September* 13, 1855."

The answer was promptly as follows:

"CONSISTORY ROOM OF THE CHURCH ON THE HEIGHTS.

BROOKLYN, *Sept.* 17, 1855.

GEORGE W. BETHUNE. D. D.

REVEREND AND DEAR SIR: The Consistory of this church have received, and endeavored in the fear of God, and with love for his church, and for you their pastor, to give to your communication of the 13th inst., and the accompanying documents, that attention which the nature and importance of the subject demanded, and which you so candidly requested; and although, from the necessity that existed, imperious as it seemed to them of an early answer, they have been unable so fully to present their views and arguments as otherwise they might have done, yet, they feel a greater confidence in this expression of their views, from the fact that they are the unanimous conviction of the members of the Consistory.

We do indeed, in the language of your communication, feel ourselves your 'friends'. We trust the views we suggest for your adoption, are such as will, if acted upon, prove us your judicious advisers.

It is almost impossible for us on this subject—a matter so dear to our hearts—to lay aside all personal desires and influences, but we have endeavoured impartially, as the friends of the Church to which we belong, and as the 'overseers of the flock dear to us all', to meet the question, you so fairly and frankly present.

Candour compels us to admit that there is great force and weight in the arguments presented by the gentlemen who have invited you to the field of usefulness in New York: and we use no flattering words when we say that we cannot reasonably doubt that your abilities and eloquence would soon draw around you in that commercial metropolis, a congregation in which you would doubtless be happy and useful to a great degree, while your presence there, would, we feel well assured, be of great service to the interests of the Dutch Church. We are not then blind or deaf to the prospects in that communication opened, nor to the views by those gentlemen expressed. Nor are we unmindful, dear sir, of the peculiar temptations and trials that have befallen you while with us; temptations and trials, not easily to be borne we admit; but in which you have had our sympathies, and those of the whole congregation—and which we now fondly hope are removed, so that they will no more trouble you hereafter.

We feel persuaded, dear sir, that you do yourself, if not the inhabitants of this city, injustice in supposing them incapable or unwilling to appreciate your services in their midst; and we trust the reasons we shall presently urge, will eradicate effectually any such impressions from your mind. When first, dear sir, it was proposed to you to become a pastor of a church in this city, it was with hesitation, almost amounting to a conviction that you would not accept it, that the Henry street church sought for your aid; and never can we forget, (whatever may be the final result) how unselfishly you put from you, other honorable, pressing, responsible positions, that you might give your energies, and devote the talents with which God had so liberally endowed you, towards the upbuilding of a weak, nay almost wholly broken-down church. You remember, doubtless, as well as we, the position of that church as you found it; but you do not, cannot know, as do some of us, the labors and struggles and efforts and prayers that had been made and offered, before it reached that sad condition—and apparently all had been in vain. When, thanks be to God, (for it was He alone who inclined your heart to it,) you entered into that then almost forsaken church, and became a shepherd to that flock, then without a shepherd's care. But if such was the condition of that particular church, what was the condition of the Dutch Church at large in this city and vicinity, prior to your advent? This was, sir, or rather should have been, a strong-hold of the Dutch Church. But where was its strength?

To particularize, would be invidious; but we ask you, sir, frankly, where was there a flourishing Dutch church when you came among us? And now, what is its state? Can you not, sir, see its growth; new churches where there were none before, strong churches where before there were weak ones, increased liberality of the former churches to benevolent objects, and a respect for the denomination in the community at large? And all this, we cannot deny it, since you came. Shall we not say that, under God, you, dear sir, have been in a great measure the honoured means of infusing this spirit, and bringing about this result? We do not doubt it. And is all this nothing accomplished? Is this work quite done? We look in faith for greater things.

But all this, had our own church not prospered, might have been of little avail in this expression of our views. An attentive observer of men and manners, as you are, cannot have failed of noticing ere this, that the population of Brooklyn, as a whole, is composed of that class of society, who are of middle life, and who not having yet (as a general thing) attained to any considerable wealth, are active, prospering, and vigorous; they are of that class whose future is full of promise. More, too, than ordinarily are they attached to their churches and church-privileges, and but little do they look for those sources of public, united, and social pleasures, which are sought for in other cities.

As a consequence of this state of things, it has followed, as of course, that dependant so much upon, and devoted so much to their church-privileges, they have been gifted with a class of Divines of rarely equalled ability and worth. And it was needful that our denomination should, in this respect, be able to take a position with the other tribes. But this very fact, conjoined with a precedence that the other denominations had acquired over ours, by reason of our slothfulness and inactivity, rendered the undertaking by no means an easy one, of establishing a new church in the midst of a city already so thickly settled with churches. Nor could we, nor would we, do otherwise, God helping us, than erect a building, which, while it would be worthy of our position, should be a temple beautiful as it ought to be for the worship of our God, and the honor of His name.

In addition to all this, it should not be forgotten that, although the Henry Street Church had, by the time you came there, become very much scattered, yet your coming among them, while it united them all readily, also made them feel the need of a larger place of worship, where more could enjoy your ministrations. This brought with it the necessity of buying and building, with its attendant expenses; and the following necessity of gathering together from the community a surplus congregation, to fill a much larger than the old building.

The history of the enterprise it is unnecessary to relate; the liberality of the people was much more than in proportion to their means, and the building progressed. Nor were you, dear sir, with gratitude we remember it, ever wanting in your sympathy and co-operation. The subsequent serious failure of one of the artificers, the inadequate estimate of the cost, and the ever attendant contingent and unexpected expenses incidental to a building of this magnitude, presented, when it was completed, the unhappy truth to the minds of the people, that, while they had a beautiful place of worship, and a minister whose services they could not too highly appreciate, they were greatly, sadly indebted. This was doubtless a source of great evil to the church, of embarrassment to yourself (not the less so, because contrary to your well-founded expectations), and has, we cannot deny it, been the fountain from which have flowed the bitter waters that have seemed, at times, destined to destroy our prosperity. No doubt, many persons have been prevented by the fact of this debt alone, from forming a connection with us, and have gone to other churches, free or freer of embarrassment, who would have been, to us, of great service by their counsel and prayers.

But now, thanks be to God, this source of trouble, anxiety and vexation, is removed, blotted out, and will no more harass our minds, or stand as a beacon warning, those outside of our church to remain clear from us and free from our troubles.

It is not necessary to repeat to you, dear sir, how this has been effected. Suffice it to say, that, but for you, we believe it could not have been done. It were idle to deny that our church is, much of it, composed of your personal admirers; those who have no particular sympathy for the Dutch Church, but great affection and regard for you, and your ministrations. Those who, should you leave us, would speedily leave us, too; and who, but that they had supposed you intended to remain with us, would have left us, unaided and alone, in this our time of embarrassment. Indeed, sir, the moment that the late unauthorized rumor got abroad, that you intended removing, all efforts to progress in the liquidation of the debt were paralyzed; and it was not until an assurance that the rumor was false had restored confidence again, that the committee were finally enabled to accomplish their much-desired and zealously-pursued object.

And now, dear sir, with your efforts, with God's blessing, what may we not look for? If, in our weakness, our love and liberality have abounded, what may we not expect now that we are strong, and have every reason to look for a large accession to our church from outside sources.

You have doubtless observed, sir, as have we, the constant growth of our city, in the vicinity of our church; a growth that must result, as it progresses, for the filling up of our own and other churches. You likewise, in looking around the church, and seeing the few old persons and great numbers of young, middle-aged and children, cannot but have great and reasonable hopes for the prosperity of our church, from those who are now in early years, and who, as they attain to man's estate, will serve God, we trust, in their day and generation.

Nor should we, nor can we, pass by the spiritual welfare of our church, best known to you, but gladly acknowledged by us.

Dear pastor, can you look on those gathered into the fold through your ministrations, and not feel that you have been doing a work for God? and can you believe that he has yet called you from this vineyard, so needing your care, to untried fields?

And the liberality of our church, of which so gratefully you have spoken oftentimes. It is not, of course, such as that of wealthier congregations, but in the sight of God, we are judged in our gifts as to that we have, not as to that we have not. And is there anywhere, in any church, a greater *spirit* of liberality, than ours has shown? And who but you, dear sir, under God, has implanted and cultivated this spirit, and what future fruits may it not bring forth?

Then, too, sir, where will you find so faithful a band of the young men 'who are strong, and in whom the Word of God abideth,' as here? Some of them, indeed, the fruits of your own ministry, and all nourished and fed by you. Active in every good word and work, ready to communicate are they; apt to teach, and faithful in those good works in which we know your soul delights.

But, dear sir, they need your fostering care still, and the enterprises in which they are engaged need your voice and counsel, or we fear for their ultimate success.

And now, dear friend and pastor, with prosperity in our circumstances, with God's blessing resting upon us, as we believe, with efforts to do good successfully at work and multiplying, with great hopes and confidence for the future, with a home in which we hope you may have much of happiness, and with our great labor accomplished, (thanks once more to God for it, who has inclined the liberal hearts of his people) we, the trustees of this church, to whom its interests are committed, are to advise whether we shall voluntarily consent to break up all this, to surrender the instrument by whose aid all this, under God, has been accomplished, the leader with whom we have come through our dangers into this promised land, that he may go elsewhere to incur new labor, to enter into new and untried fields, and to assume new responsibilities.

Dear sir, can we with faithfulmess to this church, consent to allow you to leave us? Would we not in so doing, verily be guilty before God and this people? We cannot. We dare not. We pray you stay with us, we entreat you not to leave us. May our people be your people, may God himself be our God.

With sentiments of greatest affection, sympathy and esteem, We are,

Dear Sir,

Your friends and fellow laborers.

James Myers.
John T. Moore.
Peter Duryee.
T. J. Hosford.
S. B. Stewart.
J. A. Nixsen.
Oscar D. Dike.
Livingston K. Miller."

"To the consistory of the church on the heights. Brooklyn.

Dear Brethren: I received on Wednesday last, your answer to my communication, requesting your Christian and friendly counsel on the question whether I should or should not accede to the proposal from New York that I should co-operate with a number of gentlemen in undertaking to build up a new church there. You are entitled to my hearty thanks, which I beg you to receive, for the very kind and patient manner in which you have addressed me; and, on my part, I have given to your views my careful and prayerful consideration. The result is that I shall decline the invitation from New York, and send the good gentlemen from whom I received it, a reply to such effect this day.

It becomes me, however, to say in all candor, that I have not reached this conclusion without anxious fears lest I might mistake the path of duty, and that I have been determined mainly by your determination. You have, and I have, we trust, endeavored to act conscientiously, and we must pray God to forgive any error of judgment into which we may unwittingly have fallen. If you could have been prevailed on to allow of my removal, I am persuaded, that, with the blessing vouchsafed to Christian endeavors, a new congregation of our church would be gathered, which might not a little subserve the cause of truth, and of our denomination in that great city; nor can I deny that I turn from the opportunity of such enlarged usefulness with lingering regret. Our relations, official and personal, are of such a sacred and affectionate character, that I could not go without your approval, and since such approval has been (though in the kindest terms) withheld, you have taken from me the largest share of responsibility.

I am also sensible to a degree that you cannot be, of having, in compliance with your wishes, imposed on myself future labors, fitted neither to my years nor my circumstances; but I look for my compensation, to the pleasure of obeying you whom I love, and of continuing to serve a people, every one of whom is dear to me, for reasons which will never cease to live in my heart. Those reasons I detailed to you in my previous letter, and feel now more strongly even than before. Be assured, brethren, that I resume my pastoral care, for a little while suspended in thought, with an honest desire to do my duty hopefully and cheerfully.

I am obliged to add, that while I yield to the conclusion you have reached, I do not fully agree in all the views you have expressed; but retain most of the convictions stated in my letter. You will not believe me blind to the gratifying fact, that my ministrations are acceptable, far beyond their merit, to a large, perhaps increasing congregation; but I am not more than I was, persuaded of my adaptation to the community of Brooklyn. You have, in your reply, substituted 'appreciation,' for adaptation, the term used by me. I deserve little appreciation; but there are varieties in the character of communities, as in soils, requiring varieties of culture. My education, habits of thought and language, views of Christian policy, and methods of action, differ widely from those of the large majority of the community in which we live. The discrepancy exposes me to many an awkwardness, and to worse. Here, again, I shall need your support, and it may be, defence.

There are many things in the spirit and enterprise of a large part of our church, which call for thanksgiving and joy, particularly, as you say, the exemplary conduct of our younger Christians; but, oh! brethren, the thinness of our prayer-meetings, tells another and a sadder story. I do not speak of the attendance on my weekly lectures, though it has tried me sorely, since that may be the fault of the preacher, though God knows I have tried to do my best. It is the union of the people in social prayer, which gives to their minister the most cheering expectation of blessing. Let us ourselves set an example of greater engagedness, and we may hope for that of others.

You allude to the way in which our heavy debt was contracted, and I fully appreciate your honorable motive for speaking as you have done; nor would I offer a remark on a subject which has already given all of us too much pain, were it not that your letter and mine which it answers will be preserved, on file or record of your body so (unintentionally on your part) making my statements to appear like inconsiderate or immoderate complaints. Permit me, therefore, to remind you that '*the inadequate estimate of cost*,' did not occur without remonstrance and warning from me at the earliest moment (of which proof exists), and that nothing intervened to lessen, as I think, the obligation, of the promise (on which I relied and without which I should never have joined the enterprise) that no debt except for the land, should remain when the church was dedicated. I could not be held responsible for errors against which I remonstrated, or for mistakes when I was not consulted. Neither do I think that the pecuniary obligation was the worst part of the difficulties springing from the debt, but believe that a greater degree of mutual confidence would have enabled us long before this to have extricated ourselves from the trouble. I do not say this, brethren, so much for the present as for the future that when any eye in other years may glance over the documents of this crisis, I may suffer no wrong. I trust with you that no root of bitterness may spring up from the past to try us again.

Dear brethren, though I have written thus plainly, my heart assures you of its most affectionate response, to all your warm words. Trouble is inevitable, and often the narrow way is thickest strewn with thorn and thistle; but Christian love and truth like yours are among the richest consolations afforded us by our sympathizing Lord. I fully rely on your assurances of regard and coöperation, offering you mine without reserve. Let us pray for God's grace to sanctify past experiences, and, forgetting all that is behind except his goodness and our unworthiness, let us reach forward to things that are before, looking unto Jesus who is now seated at the right hand of the Majesty on high, whither all the articles of our faith lead us.

Brethren, my heart's prayer and desire for our people is that they may be saved!

Pray for me that out of my weakness strength may abound unto you and yours from God our Father, by Jesus Christ our Lord, through the Holy Spirit. Amen.

Your brother and servant in the kingdom
and patience of Jesus Christ,

GEO. W. BETHUNE.

BROOKLYN, *Sept.* 22, 1855."

This decision gave general satisfaction. The matter was not understood in its details by the public at large, but now that there was a thorough understanding between pastor and people, it seemed as if the connection between Dr. Bethune and his church would be inseparable. Brooklyn rejoiced over the result, and public feeling was displayed in various ways.

One evening the Doctor was crossing by the Fulton Ferry; upon entering the cabin he found all the seats occupied, when a thick, husky voice cried, "Dr. Bethune, Dr. Bethune." Turning in its direction he found a man standing, who said, "Doctor, take my seat; it is an honor to give such a man a seat; ever since I heard of that big church in New York trying to get you away by giving a call of five thousand dollars, and you said, you'd see 'em d—d first, I have had great respect for you, and I think it an honor to give you a seat." It is needless to say that the well-meaning man was not in a condition to judge of the terms most appropriate for such an interview.

The Church on the Heights now went steadily onward in a career of unwonted prosperity, God blessed the preaching of his servant to the salvation of many, and the edification of his saints. The Sunday schools increased, and soon a mission chapel was originated; in fact his influence was exerted vigorously in extending his denomination by a line of churches from Greenwood to Newton Creek.

Perhaps we shall find no more suitable place to introduce the following incidents :

DR. TAYLOR TO DR. BETHUNE. "PHILADELPHIA, *Jan.* 4, 1858.

MY DEAR DR. BETHUNE : Soon after my removal to this city, when my study was located in the church edifice, I found among some old books in a closet, a small edition of the Book of Common Prayer, on the fly leaf of which your name was written just seven months before my l ttle eye saw the light of this world, namely, Jan. 1st, 1823. For your sake, as well as its own, I have kept it in good company on shelf and table, and sometimes, I trust that the fragrance of its precious things has perfumed a spirit that needed some such refreshment. Although neither of us is an Episcopalian, I trust that we have both grace and taste enough to appreciate what is excellent and venerable in the fair old symbol."

Dr. Taylor was minister of the 3d Reformed Dutch Church in Philadelphia, and a passage from his funeral sermon for Dr. Bethune will be the best possible commentary upon the above letter.

"A little sentence," says the preacher, "I found inscribed by his own pen in 1823, in a small and almost worn-out copy of the Book of Common Prayer, which had been left by him on a quiet shelf in the study of this edifice. He thought it lost, but when informed of it, he wrote me that this volume, the gift of a dear relative, had been the sweet guide of his soul when first he found the Saviour. It was returned to him, and long afterwards was one of his precious treasures. Since his death, an intimate friend has furnished me the same short prayer, copied from the Doctor's pocket Bible. It comes to us, therefore, under the double sanction of his Bible and his Prayer Book, and confirms our impression of his stamp of piety. These are the words, proper words for any believing sinner in life and death—words which are emphasized to-night by his infirmities, his struggles, his labors, his hopes, and his passage into the sinless life :

'Lord pardon what I have been; sanctify what I am; and order what I shall be, that thine may be the glory, and mine the eternal salvation, through Christ our Lord."'

These words, from one of the ancient fathers, are inseparably connected with Dr. Bethune, in the memory of all who knew him, and of many who have only heard of him ; and although they were selected from another, still of two men who walk along the way, one will pick up a bit of rock crystal, because it is large, and the other will stoop for a precious stone, because his trained eye recognizes its nobility of lustre.

Our Doctor's speech, his discourses, lectures, sermons, and speeches, were thick with gems thus gathered, for his memory was not only retentive, but likewise well ordered, and the shelves accessible.

We would willingly hope that the quiet which evidently reigned within about the time that this little remembrancer of the past came safely back, enabled him the better to give the consolation, of which Mrs. Bethune stood in need, for the afflicting death of her father, Col. Williams, which took place in March of this year. The house in Brooklyn was a house of mourning. A short and emphatic letter goes from it to assure its good friend, Dr. Dunglison, that he is not included among those whose presence would be intrusive. These two of the original "five" lived very near each other in soul, if not in body and a succession of notes ; those from Brooklyn apparently in crucial characters, those from Philadelphia resembling the cuneiform, were the means of discussion, sometimes serious, sometimes facetious, upon questions of orthography, orthoepy, etymology, syntax and prosody.

Dr. Bethune was a very fine scholar, and did not hesitate to call even the great Dunglison in question, when there was any doubt of his soundness in orthoepy.

DR. B. TO DR. DUNGLISON. "*Dec.* 21, 1857.

DEAR DR. DUNGLISON: My inclination to ask you a question is so strong that I cannot resist it. Your accuracy as an orthoepist has always excited my admiration, and led me in most cases to follow your lead unhesitatingly.

This has been the case in words ending in iasis, Elephantiasis, Psoriasis, you put the stress on the antepenultimate Psoria′sis. The lexicographers put it on the penult, Psorı′asis. The rule is that derivatives from the future of verbs in ᾰω making ᾱσω follow that quantity ψωριᾰω—ᾱσω—ψωριᾱσις. Please tell me your reason for deviating from the rule."

DR. DUNGLISON TO DR. BETHUNE. "PHILADELPHIA, *Dec.* 23, 1857.

MY DEAR DOCTOR: I cheerfully, and at once, reply to the question you put to me; and beg you to believe that I highly appreciate the kind remark with which it is accompanied. I have been not a little puzzled in regard to some of the suffixes in technical terms of Greek origin, and confess that I am so in regard to the one on which you consult me, ìàsis.

At the present day, it is almost always appropriated to skin diseases of a chronic kind, as in Petyria′sis, Elephantia′sis, Psoria′sis: of old it had much the same application. I do not know of a case in which the *a* was not marked—when marking was used—as short. In the case of Elephanti′asis, if I had not so marked it, I should have preferred Elephant′iasis, because both the *i* and the *a* are by the lexicographers rendered short, *Elephantĭăsis*, and when the first edition of my '*Dictionary*' was published, I accented in the manuscript words, similarly situated, after that fashion—*Car′diacus, Syr′iacus, gyp′tiacus, grave′olens*, for example. Mr. Charles Folsom, however, who, at Cambridge, read the proofs *once* for me—I being in Virginia—changed the accent to the *ĭ*; and I did not always sufficiently attend to uniformity, so that I find, even now, one or two of these words accented one way; another, in another way; and another without any accent at all. I should *prefer*, in such cases, the accentuation used in the MS. copy of my '*Dictionary*;' but I find the custom so general to place the accent—where two vowels come together—on the first; that I have—even in these words—been disposed to fall in with the custom—I mean the custom of those who are acquainted with all the circumstances of the case; and I say *Cardi'acus*, &c.; yet I have not got to say *grav'eolens*; as I ought for uniformity's sake. The advantage of *car'-diacus*, *grav'eolens*, &c., is, that the accent shows you know the quantity of the vowels—that they are both short.

In regard, however, to the words mentioned by you particularly, I am not in possession of a single Lexicon, English, German or American, that gives any other pronunciation than Psoriásis, Elephantiásis, Poteyriásis, &c.; nor have I ever heard them so called, except by one or two medical gentlemen here, who have now, however, determined to abandon the accentuation on the a: yet I doubt not that amongst the medical gentlemen in this country, short is the prevalent accentuation, whilst it is, I believe, unknown in Europe amongst educated physicians."

DR. B. TO DR. DUNGLISON. "*December* 24, 1857.

Usage is on your side dear Doctor, but I am not satisfied. Elephantĭăsis is as you say—but it is hardly from ελεφαντιάω-ασω the cause from the effect. Psoriasis is evidently from the verb ψωριάω-ασω Liddell and Scott give ψωρίᾶσις Hedericus (?) ψωριασις I can't find it in Scapula.

Labbe (?) I see shortens the penultimate *et passim omnes*—but look what he says on Elephantiasis. I have turned to Athenæus iv. 17. The line is

Π δ' εστίασις ἰσχάδες καὶ στέμφυλα

If the word be from the future of αω I do not see how all the authority of the modern world can make the *α* short.

All the best wishes of the season to you and yours.

Affectionately, GEO. W. BETHUNE."

DR. B. TO DR. DUNGLISON. "N. Y, *March* 10, 1853.

MY VERY DEAR FRIEND: I have just heard of the overwhelming sorrow which has come upon you, and cannot restrain myself from expressing at once the grief and sympathy I feel. I had known that Mrs. Dunglison was ill, and anxiously, from time to time, without troubling you, procured information. It is but a few weeks since Mrs. Elwyn wrote me most cheerful news, congratulating me on the hope I might cherish cf Mrs. Dunglison's recovery. I thanked God for you both, and for your children's sakes. You know dear Doctor, how esteemed—the word is too cold—how beloved your admirable wife was by all who had the happiness of seeing her in the home which she made so pleasant to her friends, and where we saw her fulfilling every duty with such cheerful tact and consideration. You know too, that of those friends, no one could have been more attached to Mrs. Dunglison, as well for her own kindness as for the blessing she was to the life of my dear friend, the father of her children. I must rely on your knowledge of my heart for assurance of my deep sense of your desolation, and of my suffering for you. Words cannot express what you will believe that I feel. Never in all my observation of people, have I known man and wife so fitted to make each other happy, or more devoted to each other's happiness; and how you are to bear your bereavement God only knows. To God only can I go with my anxiety for you, and most devoutly have my poor prayers gone up, as they will often, that He who has smitten would sustain you. The world is valueless at such a moment, but He who made the heart and sees its inmost bitterness has commanded us through his Son Jesus Christ, the man of sorrows and the God of comfort, to cast ourselves upon Him that we may find support in his bosom.

Dear Doctor, we are passing away—our lives fail, we go gradually to the grave, let us look abroad and beyond the present scene, and assure ourselves through the grace of God, of a better inheritance, where death cannot reach us, and sorrow cannot come, because there, there will be no more sin. It was but a day or two ago that I was thinking of your dear daughter who left you for heaven, and remembering thankfully that I had been of some use to her in preparation for a better life. Mrs. Lawrence (Benj. Richards' daughter) came in, and some not unpleasant tears were shed by us both, while speaking of that dear child, whose face was so often upturned to mine as I preached the gospel to her willing ears. Now the mother and daughter are united. Let us try to follow them, my friend.

I am pained that I did not know soon enough to be among those who were near you when the precious dust was laid in its resting place. Had I known, nothing short of absolute inability could have prevented me from going on. Mrs. Bethune joins me in assurances of sympathy.

Your greatly attached and affectionate friend,

George W. Bethune.

Robley Dunglison, M. D."

On the 11th Sept. 1854 Dr. Bethune writes to Dr. Dunglison to aid him in procuring a good physiological account of "Laughter" or "Mirthfulness". He wished also to know if Dr. D. could remember a good treatise on Ridicule, its uses and abuses, as it came within a plan of writing he had just then.

DR. DUNGLISON TO G. W. B. "PHILADELPHIA, *Nov.* 27, 1854.

MY DEAR DOCTOR: I have in my library two books, which, I think would interest you in your researches. One of these is on the 'Epidemics of the Middle Ages'. It was written by Hecker, Professor at Frederick William's University, Berlin, and was translated by Dr. B. G. Babington, M. D. F. R. S. It formed one of the volumes of the Sydenham Society's works for 1844; and is I doubt not, to be seen in New York. It embraces the '*Black Death*' (not in your line); the *Dancing Mania*, which is. By all means, cast your discriminating eye over it. The chapters are, first, Dancing Mania in Germany and the Netherlands; second, Dancing Mania in Italy (Tarantism); third, Dancing Mania in Abyssinia; fourth, Sympathy, with an appendix on different varieties of the delusion.

Another work, in two volumes, small octavo, is 'The Cradle of the Twin Giants, Science and History', by Henry Christmas, M. A. F. R. S. F. S. A. Librarian and Secretary of Zion College, London, 1849.

Book 4 of the second volume treats of Pneumatology; and the preface to the first volume contains a full bibliography of the authorities cited, which includes many works you might wish to see.

I do not know any French work '*Sur la Folie*', which contains what you desire. The best are those of Esguizol and Jenget, which I have. The '*Dictionnaire des Sciences Ridicules*,' the large work in upwards of sixty volumes, contains articles *convulsionnaire* for example, which may be worth looking at, but the two works first mentioned by me, comprise enough perhaps for you."

The following anecdote is furnished by the Rev. D. M. L. Quackenbush, in a letter to Mrs. Bethune:

"*March* 25, 1863.

My entreaty that you should favor me by writing some of the circumstances of the counsels of your wise husband, is linked in my mind with this remembrance, which may not be without its value to you. I had entered the study one day, when the Doctor said to me, 'A young minister to-day asked me to explain to him my rules and habits of study. I told him that I could show him how I studied, and laid upon the table before him, these two books:' showing me his Bible and concordance, both partly worn out with use. He then added, that he never trusted himself, on writing his sermons, to quote any passage of Scripture, until he had first, by the help of the concordance turned to it, that he might both assure himself of his correct remembrance of its words, and also of the relation in which it stood to the context. He urged the greatest conscientiousness upon this subject, that no misrepresentation of the mind of the Spirit might be made by those who preach the Word.

It was Dr. Bethune's habit while settled in Philadelphia, to preach once a month in the morning, and again in the evening, and not in the afternoon.

One very warm day in July, 1840, he was waited upon, soon after his morning service, by a committee of Dr. Barnes' church, who stated to him that their pastor had been absent several Sabbaths; that they had made arrangements, as they supposed, to have the pulpit filled the previous Sabbath, and also *that* day, but in both cases they had been disappointed, and they had pledged themselves to the congregation to procure a preacher for that afternoon, and they made a strong appeal to Dr. Bethune for his services, to enable them to fulfil their promise. A good deal prostrated by the heat, and his forenoon duties, the good-natured Dr. nevertheless said, that if after they should have tried for some other minister, whom they mentioned, they failed to procure one, he would certainly preach for them. They left, but of course did not succeed, and soon returned to claim the services of Dr. Bethune.

About 3 o'clock the Dr. went to his study, and selected a sermon, and on coming down, Mrs. B. advised him to take a cup of tea before he went, and, concluding to do so, he laid down his manuscript, and sat down to the table. After tea, he proceeded to Dr. Barnes' church, and found the house crowded, many of his own flock being present. He had selected a sermon preached two years previously in the city of New York, on the commencement of the anniversaries; and, remembering the text and hymn, he proceeded with the preliminary services, read his text, and then opening his manuscript, saw at a glance that, instead of bringing the sermon he intended, he had brought the one he had preached in the morning to his own congregation, half of whom were present now!

Without any visible pause, the Doctor, thrown suddenly upon his mental powers, and thinking (as he afterwards said to a friend) that any fool could preach a sermon when it laid before him, determined to see if he could not preach one, with another one before him; and, although he could not remember a particle of the manuscript, he commenced at once a sermon, founded upon *that* text. He was listened to with deep interest, but, after finishing, he made an apology to the congregation, by stating the fact of bringing the wrong sermon.

After church, the Rev. Dr. V., who was present, asked the Dr. if that was not the same sermon he had preached at the anniversaries in New York, two years previously. Dr. Bethune replied that it was. Then, said his friend, never take your manuscript of a sermon into the desk with you again, for I heard the sermon *then*, and have heard it *now*, and the last one was far the best, in every particular."

At this point we may introduce a few specimens of Dr. Bethune's wit. This is a side of his life which should be made the most rich and spicy; but how little capable are we to reproduce that, the charms of which belonged so much to its surroundings and to the expression of the voice.

One marked characteristic was its playfulness, and freedom from all malice. When occasion required it, he could be severe enough, but his habitual humor was gentle and kind. It was brilliant but harmless sheet lightning, blazing but not forked, nor fatal in its stroke. It was the overflow of his own genial life, natural, spontaneous, impressible, and often full of his classic culture and sparkling spirit. It was, however, held in check by his dignity and sense of propriety. And while it shone in conversation, and on the platform, it never intruded upon the sacred precincts of the pulpit.

Representing the Knickerbocker interest, he would, as occasion offered, play his jokes upon the New Englanders. One point where he had them at an advantage, was in the disposition to leave their bleak homes for more congenial climes. "They reminded him," he said, "of a Scotchman, who was found shuddering all over with a fearful dream. And what was the matter, was your father dead? Waur than that. Perhaps your mother? Na, waur than that. But what frightened you so, did you see the devil? Far waur than that. Why, what was it? Hech, mon, I dreamed I wor bock in Scotland; and then he shivered with horror."

On another occasion the toast was given, "Boston, the place from which people go to all parts of the world." The Doctor was quickly on his feet with the retort, "New York, the place to which people come from all parts of the world."

Lecturing on a very stormy night, the Doctor observed, "Though the assembly is small, we have only to open the upper windows, and we shall have an overflowing house." "As I came round the corner, the wind having deranged my umbrella, I had a lively sensation of what is called, 'scudding under bare poles.'" A gentleman, smaller in stature, speaking before him at a public meeting, said he did not know on what principle he was asked to precede Dr. Bethune, except that little wheels always were before big ones. The reply of the ready orator was by a Scotch anecdote, in which the spokesman praising a lad cries, "Weel done, wee Willie, muckle ane hae ketch ye." On another occasion, when Admiral (then Captain) Foote addressed the meeting first, Dr. Bethune said, "You know that we had to put our best foot foremost to-night."

Conversing with a stout gentleman, whose face bore external evidence of good living, yet who spoke in feeble tones, complained of his health, and said that he "was as weak as a moth," "A Behemoth, I think," replied the laughing minister. Sometimes, however, his wit was fully matched by that of his subject. Thus, when Dr. Bethune was walking with a clergyman almost as full in person as himself, they spied another Brooklyn pastor, who presented a perfect contrast to their rotundity, and who, at the time, was suffering from a horrible attack of dyspepsia. As he approached, Bethune said to his companion, within hearing of the third party, "See there! anybody that looks so cadaverous as that, can't have a good conscience." The thin parson was wide awake, and rejoined, "Brethren, I don't know about the conscience, but I'd rather have the gizzard of one of you, than the brains of both." The good Doctor enjoyed the sharp reply, and after a hearty laughter, said, "Let us go, we can't make anything out of him to-day."

On another occasion, when introducing a lank clerical friend of the same denomination, (Baptist) to another intimate companion, with a twinkle of the eye, and in tones which none could more amusingly employ, he added, to the ceremonial announcement of his name and position, "But he's rather shrunk in the wetting."

In a synodical debate, Dr. Bethune, taking a one-sided view of a subject, was charged with being a jug with one handle; after a little while a man who got himself on two horns of a dilemma, was represented as a jug with two handles, but it was reserved for the Doctor to make the best use of the joke; for a brother having risen who was rather famous for non-committalism, and who, on this subject was no where, Dr. Bethune said, we have had jugs with one handle and jugs with two handles, but here we have a jug with no handle at all."

But it was his story-telling, whether at the dinner-table, or in the social circle, that made all about him radiant with smiles. He had a fund of anecdotes, that seemed never exhausted, and yet, as we try to write them, they seem to have lost all their power. It was the grace and tact of the narrator that gave them their lustre.

One of his Scotch stories ran as follows; it related to the times of Claverhouse, when the poor Covenanters were so fearfully persecuted by his dragoons: A Scotch lad was reading to his parents the Scripture in the book of Revelation, and came to that passage, "and lo! another wonder in Heaven, a great red dragon," which he pronounced drag*oon*; "Hoot awa', laddie," cried the father, "that's no' richt, for I'se aye sure that nane of Claverhouse's men gang to Heaven; read it ower again." So the boy repeated the sentence, spelling the word dragon as before, drag*oon*. "Sure enoo, it's dragoon, noo' try it again, an' if ye no' read it richt this time, I'll e'en gie ye a thrashing," said the enraged father. The youngster attempting the passage the third time with great care, still rendered it in the same manner. The father was about seizing his cudgel to correct the reader of heresy, when the mother interposed, saying, "Dinna' fash yersel', auld mon, dun ye no speer (see) it was a wunner in Heaven, thet ane o' Claverhouse's men happened to get in?"

A young friend, who had joined the Baptists, approached him timidly, lest the Doctor might censure his choice. After some hesitation, he broached the subject with the remark, "Well, Doctor; yesterday I joined the Army of Zion."

"Did you," was the reply, "in which church?" "In the Pierrepont Street Baptist," came the faltering answer. "Oh! I understand," said the Doctor, "but I should call that joining the Navy." The young man was thus placed at his ease, and perfect fellowship was established.

In closing this chapter we subjoin as specimens of his kindly playfulness, the following "rhyming letters" the first furnished us by Mr. L. G. Clarke; the second written to a young friend, daughter of the Rev. E. H. May.

The Mr. Cary, upon whose name he rings the verbal changes, was a most accomplished Christian gentleman; a successful New-York merchant, possessed of a benignant and happy fortune; a bank president; an elegant essayist (his *nom de plume* "John Waters"), and a true lover, acknowledged judge, and generous patron of art. That he understood the æsthetics of the table may be inferred from the doctor's "versides," as he termed them;

"It's quite extraordinary
In my friend Mr. Cary
To pretend unto so much amazement,
That another should think
Cold water good drink,
When he can't dine in John Waters' basement.

His own store of wine
Is so varied and fine,
(Some of it came from the East in the Argo,)
That he should have pity,
And not be so witty
On a bard who has no Chateau Margau.

Why the man's very name
In poetical fame
Is waterish e'en if his verse be not;
And all know how he raves

About fountains and waves,
Whether salt or fresh waters cares he not.

As for stocks — and all that —
I'm a good democrat;
Hating banks — I defy all that stock-broking;
But Waters himself
By them has lost pelf,
So I guess — from his lachrymose joking.

But this I tell thee,
That with good company
Like you both — (I pray you don't doubt it!)
Cold water would be
More grateful to me,
Than magnums of good wine without it.

I write as I'm able
At my late breakfast table,
Preserving my best philosophy,
And wish you both health,
Fame, comfort, and wealth
In a cup of good strong Mocha coffee.

From Philadelphia,
This twenty-third day
Of March (though my hand seems to vary,)
I assure you, in tune,
'Tis G. W. Bethune
Writes you this by a kind secretary,

Mr. Lewis G. Clarke,
Who cannot keep dark
Any rhyme that a rash friend may send him.
But my heart's not a hard one,
So I give him my pardon,
With the hope that good luck may attend him!"

"It gives me hearty pleasure, my dear Miss Caro May,
To use my earliest leisure, in answering your lay;
But you are, I'm sure you know it, modest as you may be,
So natural a poet, as quite to puzzle me.
For you will be insisting on rhyme to answer rhyme,
And it costs me such a twisting of words about, and time,
That what to you is easy, since you were born a bard,
(Howe'er I strive to please ye) to me is very hard.
Eager as I endeavor to echo back your wit,
You are so very clever, I must give over it.
So I'll not stay now for phrases, or nicely measured strain,
But tell you how the case is, in rapid words and plain.
And first as you desire, I'll tell you of my wife,
She's happy near her sire, with a new lease of her life.
When we left you it was raining, and it rained on through the night,
But we thought not of complaining, for all turned out just right;
Next morning about seven, the clouds 'gan break away,
And gave us from eleven, a dry and pleasant day;
So we left the canal basin without fear or annoy,
And in the boat "John Mason" went safely up to Troy;
My father-in-law's old carriage, was waiting for us there,
(We rode in't at our marriage, a young and happy pair,
Since then through changes plenty, our wedded life has been;
I was just over twenty, my wife past seventeen;)
Her bed of India-rubber, I put the seats across,
Did you e'er know such a lubber, for a rhyme I'm at a loss;
We laid her then upon it, for the coach is very large,
And when I'd safely done it, I left my precious charge.
Mary squeezed in beside her, John mounted on the box
With a brother's care to guard her, safe from the ruts and rocks.
I went then to a stable, and hired a horse and chair,
For as yet I was not able to banish all my care,
And followed them to German's, it may be six miles or more,
'Cross a hill as high as Hermon's, and saw them safely o'er.
Then sadly there we parted, I shed tears like a boy,
And slow and broken-hearted went straightway back to Troy.
They arrived quite safe at Salem, at an hour not very late,

As nothing seemed to fail 'em a half an hour past eight;
I had a letter from her, in which she cheerily says,
She's having a sweet summer in her home of early days;
I go from here next Monday, in haste, her then to see
Stopping at Goshen one day with my sister's family.

Give my love to all around you, I have no time to write more,
And let it not astound you that I did not write before;
For I've been very busy with many a hard affair,
About which a merry missy, like you has little care!
God bless your father, mother, your sisters twain, also,
With each kind-hearted brother; and I wish yourself to know,
As I bid good-by unto you, though my name in haste I sign,
That a friendly heart more true you will rarely know than mine.
'Mongst those who love you dearly, (please write to Salem soon,)
Always reckon most sincerely, George W. Bethune."

CHAPTER XIII.

PATRIOTISM — UNION SPEECH.

We should neglect a great feature in Dr. Bethune if we did not describe him as a patriot, and a patriot of the first water, whose love of country, like every grand sentiment, bordered on the extravagant; whatever he did, he did strongly, and so his devotion to the Constitution and Union of the States was a mighty devotion.

"During the Presidential campaign of 1856, when the Kansas trouble filled the land with unusual excitement, he was the victim of the deepest anxiety. After the vote had determined that Mr. Buchanan was to be the next President, he wrote a long, earnest, and eloquent letter to that gentleman, with whom he had personal friendship, imploring him, as he loved his country, and would prevent the calamity of a civil war, to use his great influence, when in the Presidential chair, to arrest the march of the slave power, and repress the violence of its reckless propagandism. That letter he read to me in the privacy of his study, his voice at times choking with emotion, and the tears running down from his eyes, saying as he closed, 'I love my country, and if there is a word in this letter that ought not to be said, tell me to strike it out.' I shall never forget that day. It was the beginning of a series of mental excitements which has at last ended in the quiet sleep."

The foregoing is quoted from the Ohio State Journal of May 20, 1862, and comes from the Rev. E. S. Porter, D. D., who was intimate with Dr. Bethune. The original letter we have not been able to obtain and rather wonder that no copy of it exists among our papers, but the answer to it is as follows:

"WHEATLANDS, PENN, *Nov.* 27, 1856.

MY DEAR DR. BETHUNE: I have perused your very kind letter of the 21st inst., with deep interest, and sincerely regret that my numerous and pressing engagements allow me no time to answer it as it well deserves. I feel proud of your good opinion and am happy to say that the friendly sentiments which you express for myself have been cordially reciprocated on my part ever since our first acquaintance.

I feel, as I ought to do, the high responsibility of my position; but placing my trust in God, and asking wisdom from on high, I shall proceed with a cheerful and unfaltering spirit to perform the task assigned to me by my countrymen. This was neither sought nor desired by myself.

In haste, I remain very respectfully,

Your friend,

JAMES BUCHANAN.

REV. DR. BETHUNE."

The following acknowledgement from Edward Everett shows that Dr. Bethune was diligent in the good cause:

"I am extremely obliged to you for the kind expressions contained in the latter portion of your letter. I have looked, and still look, with great anxiety, upon the condition and tendency of affairs. We seem to be borne, upon a rushing tide, toward a doubtful future; and much more of the intellectual power of the country is put forth to drive the bark onward, than to steer its course or ascertain its destination. We are piling rosin into the furnace, and leaving the helm to take care of itself. If, as you are kind enough to think, my voice, almost spent, has not been uttered wholly in vain in favor of more prudent counsels, I shall, so far, have performed the duty of a good citizen."

In December, 1859, a great opportunity for the display of his oratorical powers came. The United States were to be dismembered. There breathed no man with soul so dead as to look with coldness on the fateful struggle. The great Union Meeting in the New York Academy of Music, was called, and he attended as a private individual. The meeting had been prevised, and Bethune was not on the programme, but when discovered, he was enthusiastically called for, even before the appointed speakers of the evening had delivered themselves. At first he hesitated, having a desire to avoid violent excitement, but moved by the tremendous popular cries, he came forward and addressed the meeting; we reproduce the speech as a noble expression of patriotism, and as it gives Dr. Bethune's sentiments on the Great Question.

"I rise, sir, not because I have the presumption to think that I can preserve the attention of this vast assembly, after all the excellent things they have heard this evening, at this late hour. But, sir, I come before this audience to show myself. (Great cheering.) Insignificant as I, personally, may be among the millions of this land, and weak in influence as my voice may be, when that voice is called for, and there is a question where I stand, I wish to be reckoned with the Union now and forever. (Loud cheers.) Yes, sir, I love the Union, and when I say that, it is with the wish that if that Union is to perish, I may die first. And, sir, there are many things which have been said here this evening, with some of which I may frankly say I could not coincide. I am not going to read law to you, sir. It is not my province, and I must be excused from accepting the theology of some gentlemen who have invaded mine. (Laughter.) Sir, when I saw the call of this meeting, I said I must be there. Never have I attended a public meeting in any way political before in my life. (Cheers, and cries of 'Good.') And I can say, with a clear conscience, that no man has ever heard me utter in public a single word of party politics. I belong to a higher service. (Renewed cheering.) I am, by my calling and my vows, a minister of the Gospel of Peace, and it is as a minister of peace that I am among you to-night. (Applause.) It is high time, when the pulpit is desecrated by appeals to the wildest fanaticism, (Loud cheers, and a remark, 'The right man is in the right place this time!') — when men, by voice of ecclesiastics, are canonized because they have shown the pluck of a bull-dog, with the blood-thirstiness of the tiger (applause) — it is high time, I say, that one who, humble as myself, believes that the Gospel is 'Peace on earth and good-will toward man,' should act upon his principles. (Loud applause.) I will not enter into any of the disputed questions that have been foisted into our meeting to-night. I have seen a discussion about the call of this meeting, that there was first one call, then it was altered for another call, that the same people who signed one could not have signed the other. I never read either one call or the other through (laughter); all I saw in the call was the word 'Union,' (continued cheering), and that was enough. (Renewed cheering.) I remember an honest Governor of Pennsylvania, whose ancestry was traceable in his broken speech, was appealed to for the pardon of a man who had murdered his wife, but the honest old man said, 'What! pardon a man for such a crime as that, — a man who could take a woman, and promise to nourish and cherish, and den kill her? Vy, he ought to be 'shamed of himself.' (Uproarious laughter and cheers.) So I say here to-night, if any man, in getting up this meeting, or in coming to this meeting, has had a thought of Democrat or Republican, or Native American higher in his mind than Union, he ought to be ashamed of himself. Nor shall I have sympathy with him except he repent in sackcloth and ashes. You talk of the Union being dissolved. Sir, there has been deep feeling in most of the speeches I have heard this evening. They say *if* this Union is to be dissolved — *when* the Union is dissolved. Why that, sir, is what we logicians call an impossible hypothesis. The Union is not going to be dissolved. Do you remember, sir, that once, in old Rome, there was a gulf opened across the city; it was widening and widening until it threatened to engulf the whole of that splendid Capitol, when one, Marcus Curtius, mounted his steed, fully armed and equipped, and rode toward the chasm and leaped into it, a willing victim to save his Rome? Sir, should such a chasm happen in our Union, there is not one, but there are a hundred Curtii, — a hundred times ten thousand, — that are willing to leap into it. Divide the Union! Where are you going to divide the line? (A voice, Mason and Dixon's line.) Mason and Dixon's fiddlesticks. Do you want to go? Which side do you mean to go? I know where I should go. It would be with that section that holds fastest to the Constitution as it is. (Loud cheers.)

Sir, if any man has a right to be proud of his native place, perhaps it is the man who speaks to you, for I was born in New York. But, sir, what is New York? What is the North? What is the South? What is the East? What is the West? Take away this Union and we are nothing; worse than nothing; a conflicting, jostling chaos of rude, crumbling fragments. It is not for me to enter into this question. But I repeat, where will you draw a line? Will you split the Mississippi? Try it. Are you going to divide by the assumed or imputed evil of slavery? Where does slavery stop? They grow cotton at the South, but where do they manufacture it? (Tremendous cheering.) I beg your pardon, but I have not time to be cheered. I have read a story of Cook, the drunken player, who once, in Liverpool, came upon the stage to act, and his condition being evident when he approached the footlights, they hissed him. His indignation restored him for a moment, and he looked at the Liverpoolians, as he called them, saying, 'You hiss George Frederick Cook, you people of Liverpool, with the sweat and blood of the slave between every two bricks of your house?' It was so. There never was a slave in Liverpool, if I remember, but they profited by the slave. They bought and sold him. Yes, sir, there exists, if I mistake not, in the plate-room of Windsor Castle, a splendid service of gold, given to one of the royal dukes, by Liverpool merchants, for his efforts to prevent the abolition of the slave-trade. But I wander from my purpose, in recalling that historical reminiscence, which was to say, that, in some sections of our land, where the loudest cry is heard upon this question, men have grown rich by these slaves; that the blood and sweat of the slave is between every two bricks of their sumptuous palaces. Now people may call this what they please, I call it hypocrisy. (Tremendous cheers.) Where will you draw this line? I will tell you where you must draw it. If you draw it at all you must draw it across and through our dearest affections. We are one people. The man who lives on the Aroostook, has his brother on the Rio Grande. The Northern mother has given her child to the Southern planter, and the Southern planter bows in thankfulness to God for the daughter of the North to cheer his home. Will you dissolve *this* Union? (Cries of 'No, no,' and cheers.)

I tell you, you need not ask the question. You cannot. You cannot. It will be far better than the Sabines and the Romans. You have not taken violently the women of the South to be your wives. You have exchanged consanguinity, you cannot separate them. What God hath joined together, let no man put asunder. (Prolonged applause, the whole assembly, on the platform, floor and galleries, rising, waving hats, cheering and shouting, in wild enthusiasm.) A word or two more. I will not say that I have said all that I wish. There are many things which I could, and in another condition of circumstances might be glad to say, which I shall not inflict upon you now. This is not a time for dry metaphysics. But I believe, sir, that we inherit from our fathers some degree of that honesty and truth for which they were distinguished and for which their God and our God blessed them. Our fathers made the compact of this Union — our fathers made the Constitution as the mighty bond that should hold it together. And I have one belief that this gift has of itself proven with its checks, its balances, and its securities, so good that any alteration would be for the worse ('Good!') — that it contains within itself a perfect remedy for every evil, if our people will faithfully apply it and wait for the operation of the remedy. There is, therefore, no room for revolution in this country; and it may be said of all those who hesitate about its principles. He that doubteth, is worthy of condemnation. (Cheers.) But, sir, why should we not keep to this, our fathers' faith? We should know that we are bound by that deed. Has it not been in the faith of that compact that this country has grown to its present prosperity, and shall we, the inheritors of all the blessings, break the vows of even political baptism, which, as our sponsors, they made for us? No, No! Let us keep this. Let all our people learn that they are bound by ties which none can break. The bones which are now mouldering to kindred dust are sacred with the memories of their patriotism. We should be violaters of the vows they made if we suffer one stone of the Union reared by them to be pulled down. Sir, I agree in many respects with my good friend the Professor, who spoke before me, and I have great regard for him, but I can not help thinking that he got among the stars to-night. (Laughter.) I believe in a system of government which is maintained by working men, men who work in their primary meetings, and who are not afraid of getting their coats torn by a rowdy; men who are willing to take their places and scuffle if it be necessary, to see that the voice of the people is attained. (Cheers and applause.) Men who, if their countrymen call them to office, do not mistake cowardice for modesty, and refuse to serve. No matter where the man is, there he should be faithful to God, faithful to man, faithful to his country, faithful to the world. I am thankful that I can not be a candidate for office. I once held an office under the general government, and I was offered another. The other I did not like, (laughter) but the first I did. It kept me five hours, and I was allowed my expenses as emolument. But as there was no omnibus riding in that direction, I did not get a sixpence. I am no candidate for office, sir, I belong to a king. I am a monarchist. I belong to another king — one Jesus. (Applause.) But I know no greater recreant to the principles of his faith, and no more dangerous agitator than he, who, under the pretense of serving the religion of Christ, uses his sacred office to urge men into riot and sedition. I am no candidate for office, because I hold an office so high that no other on earth can approach it. I am content with my lot — content to be simply a preacher of the Gospel of Jesus, and ask no higher reward than to help men toward heaven when they die, and keep them in peace while they live on earth. But, sir, there is one thing I never neglect to do, and that is, I do not forget, because I am a Christian and a minister of the gospel, that I am an American citizen; I always vote; I prepare my ballot with the same conscientiousness, and for which my friends frequently laugh at me, as if I thought my ticket was to elect. This is the way, I think, we ought to work; and one thing is certain, that, if I retain my reason, which God grant I may, I will never vote for any man, be he Democrat, Whig, Native, or — or — or — what do you call him? (A voice — 'Republican.') I beg pardon, that class has had so many names that I can not recall it at once. (Loud laughter.) I say I never will vote for any man, no, not if he were my own brother, not if he lay with me in my mother's womb, as did Esau with Jacob, on whose history, or antecedents, or associations there is the slightest stain or suspicion of DISUNION. (Tumultuous cheering, long and enthusiastic, and repeated.) I know a man may make a mistake and repent. The drunkard may reform from drink. Very well, let him reform, but keep the brandy bottle out of his way. I would not give him a chance to relapse. I believe that this is a true rule. Vote for a man who loves his country, and who shows he has good sense and considers what his country's good is.

Talk of incendiary documents. The most incendiary document is a thing that wears a coat and breeches, writes 'Honorable' before his name, and 'M. C.' after it, (laughter,) and goes to Washington to do anything else than take care of the people and the whole people. Let us stick to this, sir.

And while the grass grows on the hill,
And the stream runs through the vale,
May they still keep their faith,
Nor in their covenant fail.
God keep the fairest, widest land
That lies beneath the sun,
Our country, our whole country,
Our country ever one." (Loud cheering.)

The great meeting then adjourned, about ten minutes before midnight, with a volley of cheers.

As a conclusion to these expressions of patriotism, we add the following spirited, national hymn, which was written and set to music by Dr. Bethune :

"God's blessing be upon
Our own, our native land!
The land our fathers won
By the strong heart and hand,
The keen axe and the brand,
When they felled the forest's pride,
And the tyrant foe defied,
The free, the rich, the wide,
God for our native land!

Up with the starry sign,
The red stripes and the white!
Where'er its glories shine,
In peace or in the fight,

We own its high command:
For the flag our fathers gave,
O'er our children's heads shall wave,
And their children's children's grave;
God for our native land!

Who doth that flag defy,
We challenge as our foe;
Who will not for it die,
Out from us he must go!
So let them understand,
Who that dear flag disclaim,
Which won their fathers' fame,
We brand with endless shame;
God for our native land!

Our native land, to thee,
In one united vow,
To keep thee strong and free
And glorious as now;
We pledge each heart and hand,
By the blood our fathers shed,
By the ashes of our dead,
By the sacred soil we tread;
God for our native land."

That there were men in the South to whom these sentiments were acceptable, the following letter from I. B. Pinney, to Dr. Bethune will show.

"COL. OFF. N. Y. *Feb.* 9, 1860.

REV. DR. BETHUNE: My dear sir, my daughter Agnes is passing the winter in Texas, teaching, and in her last letter has a paragraph which I extract for you. Allow me to salute the future *President*.

She writes, 'Of course the recent raid of the abolitionists, and its results in bringing out the conservative portion of the community, is the subject of interest here as everywhere. Fortunately I am surrounded by conservative, union, sensible people, though Southerners; I believe I

so informed you before. But I did not tell you how the Colonel (Owen) was taken with Dr. Bethune's remarks at that meeting in the Academy. He frequently exclaims, 'Well, if I had been there that night, I should have got up and nominated Bethune for President. His ideas just suit me, and I believe he would make a good President.' Your speech was not made in vain, if so accceptable at the farthest South.
Truly Yours."

His name was distinctly pronounced on the stage of that meeting as the right candidate for the Presidency.

But affairs rapidly approached a consummation. In April following, the news reached New York that Fort Sumter had been fired upon and after a heavy cannonading had been surrendered. The tidings that the flag of our country had been assailed by brethren filled every loyal heart with indignation, and a meeting assembled in the great city, immense in size, and of such a fierce and heroic spirit as probably the world had not often seen. Those who were well acquainted with Dr. Bethune, had seen how his ideas were preparing for this great crisis. An old-fashioned democrat, a strong party man, who would stand at the poll with good Dr. Ludlow for hours to deposit his vote; with warm friendships in the South: yet we have seen how he warned Mr. Buchanan against the aggressive spirit of the South, and a few weeks before the great outbreak he was found in sharp debate with an old friend, Dr Hoge of Richmond; only the concluding sentences of the interview were heard. Dr. Hoge said sadly "I never expected to hear such things from you;" "Ah!" replied Dr. Bethune, "you have pushed us too far, you have pushed us too far." Now, at this great Sumter meeting, he came out fully and bravely; although under strict orders to avoid mental excitement, at the compulsion of the people he addressed them several times with great fire and energy. The next day was the Sabbath, and an immense audience filled his church; the sermon was not carefully prepared, but was a remarkable effort. The speaker was several times overcome with emotion, and when he came to speak of our deluded brethren, audible sobs were heard through the congregation. Here was a complete change of opinion and action, and some say it involved a great inconsistency, but let us then recall Macaulay's illustrations in the Essay on Sir James Mackintosh.

"And why is one person to be singled out from among millions and arraigned before posterity as a traitor to his opinions only because events produced on him the effect which they produced on a whole generation? People, who like Mr. Brothers in the last generation, and Mr. Percival in this, have been favored with revelations from heaven may be quite independent of the vulgar sources of knowledge. But such poor creatures as Mackintosh, Dumont, and Bentham had nothing but observation and reason to guide them, and they obeyed the guidance of observation and of reason. How is it in physics? A traveller falls in with a berry which he has never before seen. He tastes it and finds it sweet and refreshing. He praises it and resolves to introduce it into his own country. But in a few minutes he is taken violently sick; he is convulsed; he is at the point of death; he of course changes his opinion, pronounces this delicious food a poison, blames his own folly in tasting it, and cautions his friends against it. After a long and violent struggle he recovers, and finds himself much exhausted by his sufferings, but free from some chronic complaints which had been the torment of his life. He then changes his opinion again and pronounces this fruit a very powerful remedy, which ought to be employed only in extreme cases and with great caution, but which ought not to be absolutely excluded from the Pharmacopœia. And would it not be the height of absurdity to call such a man fickle and inconsistent because he had repeatedly altered his judgment? If he had not altered his judgment would he have been a rational being?

Dr. Bethune to a correspondent unknown.

"N. Y. *Feb.* 7, 1861.

My Dear Sir: Your note without date reached me a few days ago. Your book has not come. I may however say at once that the question it treats of has now but little interest for me. My love for the Union was not based upon the belief that slavery is right. I stood up for the Constitutional rights of those whom the Union made my countrymen: when the same people repudiate the Union they are no longer my countrymen; I am for letting the responsibilities of slavery rest where they belong. If you like it I am not for interfering with you, against you, or for you. But as for ourselves, we have not got it, we do not want it, and do not believe in it. One thing is certain. If the preservation (?) of the Union depends upon the *Northern people being convinced that slavery is either desirable or right*, the Union cannot stand; for we did it away (in New York) forty years and more since, and we shall not stultify ourselves. I am perfectly willing that a line should be drawn across the continent dividing the free country from the slave, across which neither people shall have any power over the other.

Whatever may be your Scriptural or ethical argument, there yet remains the grand question of its political expediency (for you will hardly contend that Christians are bound to enslave people). On that point the very bad recent behaviour of the seceding States has convinced me of the negative. Slavery makes not good democrats or good fellow-citizens. Convince the Southern conscience if you will and can, but let ours alone. We want no argument to prove that we may do what we should hate to do. Our prosperous freedom does not rest upon the bondage of others, but upon the blessing of God, promised to our own sweat. The fact is, I am sick of the whole discussion, and am strongly tempted to doubt the value of a Union with such troublesome neighbors as slavery gives us. I cannot, therefore, borrow your *book*; though in Christian kindness I wish you well.

Very truly yours,

Geo. W. Bethune."

Dr. Bethune's answer to a Southern lady.

"*May*, 1861.

My Dear Madam: Your letter of the 4th has only just now come, and affects me deeply. I remember the kind hospitality to which I was welcomed under your roof, with a lively gratitude, and deplore the madness of men, and the business of politicians, and the folly of their dupes, which have brought our country to this terrible war, dividing those who love each other sincerely, into hostile bands. Would to God that some influence from on high would stay the tide of angry passions, and command peace. I continually pray to God that even now he would interfere—but none except God can do this, no human voice, however venerable, can prevail here to stay the determination of our people to vindicate the flag they so much love, so foully outraged by your Southern leaders, and defend the Capital so impudently threatened by such determined conspirators as Davis, and such insane braggarts as Wise, etc. Dr. Miner will tell you that no man after his ability exerted himself more zealously to keep our people at peace with the South — I was only one of countless numbers at the South so disgraced. But the first shot at Sumter, the first clearly hostile assault upon that symbol of our nation and our honor, changed this in an instant to a determination to defend our nation until death, at any cost, and by every means of honourable warfare. I have never seen such unanimity, such enthusiasm, such devotion, as the fall of Sumter awakened in all classes of our citizens—nor is it lessened by the lapse of time. Our Northern blood is not like the easily heated blood of the South. Our people rarely fight duels; no reputable person carries, in ordinary life, a mortal weapon. They have been reproached by southern Hotspurs, because so unwilling to fight with cowards; but when they are roused their determination is terrible, and, I may add, strong as arms accustomed to earn bread by having to toil, can make them. They feel, and all feel, that the fight is not only for our outraged flag, but our nation, our government, the principles of liberty, civil and religious, received from our fathers, and the just inheritance of posterity. I firmly believe that the very large majority of our people will fight or carry on the war till their last dollar, rather than continue liable to such outrages and threats and insults as Davis and his crew heap upon us. Great as the enthusiasm has been here, depend upon it, it has only begun. For one man who has gone to the seat of war, there are ten, yes a score, willing to go the moment they are called for by the government— and as for money it will be ready in any amount.

In conversing with my brother ministers, I, as well as they, am astonished at the number of pious men that are in the ranks. Out of my own congregation has gone a score or two of the finest men we have. When the ladies meet to sew, and do what they can in preparation for the hospitals, it is sad to hear them compare their sorrows; one has a son gone, another two, and then one a husband, another a son-in-law, another a nephew, another weeps in silence for one dearer than all, and yet I tell you, before God, I have never heard any harsh word against the Southern people, or, at least, any harsher than 'How foolish and mad they are to let their angry passions go so far;' and in our daily prayer-meetings, and Sunday services, we pray for you when we pray for ourselves. In some of the churches the Sunday-schools are nearly all bereft of teachers."

"NEW YORK, *April* 9, 1860.

MY DEAR MR. BRAYTON: I am obliged to you for your note, which has not been answered simply because I had, as yet, nothing to say. I am also a little discouraged from giving any counsel to your church, as, though my regard for it is very strong, my counsels, on former occasions, were not taken, when, if they had been, some mistakes would have been prevented. The fact is, Mr. Brayton, congregations, as a general thing, are not as good judges of what minister will suit them, as well-informed ministers are. We know how to judge of our ministerial brethren, professionally, and, we know also, the precedents of those brethren, and judge of them by the *long run*, not as congregations do, by a few spasmodic efforts to show off, in a trial sermon or two. He must be a preciously small body, who cannot, somehow, get up one or two good sermons; and then again, few really able men, who respect their office and themselves, are willing to humiliate themselves by candidating, as it is termed; that is, hawking about samples of their ware, and showing off what nice sort of persons they are. Choose a minister by his well-known character, and that of his career. A man who has done well in one place, is, all other things being equal, likely to do well in another. These remarks are, I know, perfectly gratuitous. I never expect any congregation to accept them as good advice. I cannot find the sort of man you graphically describe, that is, a sort of St. Paul, and a little more so. I hear, occasionally, of such a gentleman, but recently settled over a church, but you must wait for at least six months, until his now new people find that he is only a descendant of Adam, and have

'Seen an end of all things called
Perfection here below.'

When you may buy it second-hand, at reduced price, the sordid matter of salary is often a difficulty; not the worldliness of the preacher, whose affections should be set on things above, but the worldliness of such people as butchers, and bakers, and tailors, and shoemakers, who will insist on being paid in the current mammon, for such things as the pastor needs while yet in body. I will not insinuate any charge of worldliness against the congregations who, by each of them adding five or ten dollars to their pew rent, could add five hundred or one thousand dollars to the minister's salary. Why should a man pay so much rent for a short, narrow slip of a pew, which he occupies only three or four hours a week? No spiritual-minded minister should think of putting such a tax upon an affectionate, heavenly-minded people. No. He should get up early in the morning, then, like an Israelite indeed, scratch around for manna, and, if he can't find any, trust Providence, who feeds the ravens and will not neglect black-coats and their offspring. They ought to keep their bodies under, and if they faithfully persevere until they get them under the sod, they have the consolation of knowing that they will need no more butcher's meat, and such gross aliments as cannot be got without money.

Seriously, I did make the suggestion you speak of, to Mrs. T. W., and I tried hard to get the man I thought of, but some other people had thought of him, too, and so he had the temerity to reject my advice, and there was an end of it. I have since been diligent in making inquiries, but not successful. If you could procure Mr. J. Elmendorf, now of S., you would get such a man as you need, but the people of S. need him, too. Mr. Voorhies formerly of G., now of B. B., (I think) is a delightful preacher, but then he was unwell some years ago, from an overworked brain, and preaches, I am told, only once a day. If you could give Dr. Kennedy, now in Troy, a comfortable stipend, he might, I speak of a possibility, be induced to go where his wife's family live, but I could not assure you that he would. Dr. McElroy told me, the other day, of a very good man, and has promised to tell me more, when he knows more about him. If favorable, I will let you know. I am told, also, that Dr. Chester of Buffalo is uneasy where he is, and he is, in my estimation, a man of rare excellence. It is possible that he might listen, but naturally would not consider it a call in Providence, unless it provided for his necessities. One of my greatest favorites, among our middle-aged clergy, is Mr. A. T. Stewart of Tarrytown, but then he is not a Spurgeon or a Chalmers, or an Apollos. He is only a well-trained theologian, a faithful, sound expositor of God's Word, and a hard-working, unpretentious, Christian man, of spotless life and absorbed devotion to doing good. You might take some leisure time to write to some of these gentlemen; there is no knowing what might come of it. In the meantime, upon the wretched principle that 'misery loves company,' you may console yourselves with the fact that the Fifth Avenue Presbyterian Church (late Dr. Alexander's) is still searching for an untranslated Apostle Paul, or hitherto unrecognized Luther; that one great collegiate church has two vacancies, and is anxiously peering into the shadows under which lie two hypothetical sons of thunder (there is only one), and that, generally, the supply of immaculate, exquisite excellence is not quite equal to the demand. There are some good men afloat, but of them it may be said, as it was of an aboriginal beauty, 'She won't hab Indian, — white man won't hab her.' That is, nothing less than the first church in the land of Beulah would meet their expectations. My serious advice is to get a first-rate man, who may build you up, and so enable you to give him what he needs. Under God, in a church, nine-tenths of everything depends on the man who is in the pulpit. To take a weak man because you are feeble is not as wise as to take a strong man who can make you strong. But to quote another Indian, 'poor pay, poor preach.' In a remote contingency you might take a promising boy-baby, get his organs certified by a phrenologist, and bring him up to your hand by a spoon. Your sportive letter has led me, despite of several efforts to be serious, into a similar strain; but I am truly anxious to serve you, and will do, as I am doing, all I can for you. Your church is dear to me as a child of my own travail, but the difficulties are many; may God give us light. With great regard, my dear sir,

Yours, very faithfully,

GEO. W. BETHUNE.

My excellent colleague, Dr. Van Nest, recommends very highly Mr.

G. Tallmadge of Green Point near Brooklyn. He, Mr. T., is an excellent man, but Dr. Van Nest knows him better than I do."

DR. BETHUNE TO MR. PRIUST. "*Jan.* 15, 1860.

I cannot answer your question with regard to the manner in which the slavery question has been affected by the revival, as you good people in England do not properly understand the relations of that matter. Decidedly the anti-slavery portion of our people (I use the term anti-slavery in its technical sense, we are all of us at the North anti-slavery in its pure sense) is not the evangelical portion, but with many good people among them it is composed of many sorts, infidels like the Tom Paineists, Transcendentalists, Socialists, Women's rights people, &c., &c., &c. My impression is that the revival has made very little change in this respect. More recently the Harper's Ferry massacre has struck horror into the hearts of many, and there is less disposition to treat this to us most vital matter rashly or to trifle with the bonds of our great Confederacy, the strength of which lies under God in two things. 1. In our union upon certain specific matters and *ad extra.* 2. In our non interference with each other inside of the separate state lines. Be assured, my dear sir, that the high interests at stake will not allow us *for any reason* to risk a dissolution of our Union, and we see more than ever what madness it would be to precipitate changes by violence which the progress of the Gospel will bring about peacefully. The Gospel in its influence on the heart is the only reformer of vice, the only liberator of the oppressed. Willing as I am to accept good at the hand of the Lord in any way I cannot give in to the infidel *humanitarianism* which substitutes the reforming methods of men for the great power of God. I do not suppose that living as you do remote from the scene you will fully agree with me. Anti-slavery is the pet pharisaism of Great Britain; but I am sure that were you here you would find that the very large majority of persons with whom for their piety, their benevolence and purity of doctrine you would most love to associate, are not known as what you would call anti-slavery in their sentiments. On the contrary you would be horror-struck at the sentiments uttered by that class of men who, with the same breath that they denounce slavery, denounce Christian churches, the Sabbath, the very Bible itself; declaring John

Brown a greater benefactor than Jesus Christ, and his gallows more glorious than the cross.

But as I said before I cannot discuss this question with you, and I fear that it is one too vast in its subject and consequences for *us* to settle. I hate slavery. I pray every night for the freedom of all slaves, but I have no sympathies with abolitionists so-called, and put my whole trust in the grace of God through the Gospel. If that fail, surely no scheme begun and carried on in a spirit adverse to that of the Gospel can succeed.

Most affectionately your friend,

GEO. W. BETHUNE."

DR. BETHUNE TO REV. E. PRUST. "*Sept.* 19, 1861.

I am not desirous of being detained long in England under the present threatening aspect of affairs, as I consider war between England and this country imminent should there be any hostile interferance with our measures to put down Southern rebellion. Our people are fighting for their national existence, and if England takes advantage of our embarrassment in the rebellion to break our remaining strength, our people will be only the more desperately determined to put forth their whole strength. I regret the Machiavellian policy which England sees fit to pursue for the sake of cotton. There are but two great Protestant Constitutional governments in the world, and in the event of a Continental combination against England this nation should be her ally. That now can never be. England has now no friends in America except among the slave-holders. With these apprehensions and feelings you can readily see how naturally I desire to get from England into France, with whom our relations are much more likely to be peaceful, and where I shall find a more friendly climate."

DR. BETHUNE TO JOSHUA COOKE, ESQ. "*September*, 1861.

Notwithstanding all, I am far from despairing of our dear country. What fear I have had of England or France has passed away. Our finances are easy, our troops numerous; we have the best military talent and energy, and the nasty political intermeddlers dare not mutter nor peep since Bull Run. We are not well governed; in fact, outside of the War Authorities, it is at Washington the reign of vulgarism and ignorance. But our people still live. They will not desert themselves nor allow their public servants to ruin them. The enthusiasm has abated in our cities, but enthusiasm never has had longer strength. Now that the government has money there is good reason for putting steady, administrative power in the place of shouting enthusiasm, popular war committees, &c.

Depend upon it that we shall triumph, and come out with less bulk perhaps, but finer gold. Make it part of your religion to trust, and of your patriotism to believe that the Union must prevail. Where do you think are all the *Wide-awakes.* Asleep! 'Docthur,' said an old Irishman to me as he was sending off three of his 'byes' to fight, 'you'll remember what our old General said. Peaceably if we can, but ye see we can't.' I see no reason to change my political principles. My faith is strong in their power to save the country. Above all let us not lose our hope in God. He may chasten, but he will lead us."

When Dr. Bethune was abroad and our national affairs grew more gloomy he became almost beside himself with anxiety. Still he defended his country on all occasions. In Florence, talking with some Englishmen, they said, "that we would have to change our government. What we wanted was a king, that was the divine plan." "Yes," replied the Doctor, "God did give Israel a king, but do you know how he gave him? He gave him 'in his wrath.' And then gentlemen, did you ever notice what sort of a man was chosen to rule over them? 'A keeper of asses.'"

Dr. B's address at the funeral of Hon. Benjamin F. Butler, presents his idea of a patriot's duty, and those who loved him can now appropriate the touching allusions to the speaker himself:

"This was the character of him whom we mourn, yet, rather congratulate, for his testimony to the power of Christianity. He was a man. He put nothing away from him that was man. I do not, and, I am sure he would not, adopt the sentiment casually and but partially expressed by my dear and reverend friend (Dr. Sprague), who 'almost' regretted to find him fighting in the controversies of political life. My friends, I ask you—as he would have asked—why should a man, because he is a Christian, be unfaithful to his country? What is the use of his religion, as a citizen, if it does not consecrate him to his political duties? I do not know how it may strike you—some of you doubtless have agreed with him, some have differed from him, and others have at various times, agreed, or differed from him and with him, as I have, but this is true, that if we had more Benjamin F. Butlers in our political life, we should have a better government and a better State. It is because you, Christian men, do not do your duty as citizens at primary meetings, at the polls, and in more public offices, it is because you do not do your duty, that our land is given up so much to trading, office-seekers, and hired gladiators. We may not all think alike, but I should as soon think of excommunicating a man from my Christian sympathy, because he was a Baptist or an Episcopalian, as of denying a man's patriotism because his views of political expediency or doctrine were not the same as my own. It is preposterous to say that where a country, like ours, is divided so nearly into two great parties, that one or the other half of the nation must be either rogues or fools.

But when we have men of large and noble minds and sentiments, to discuss those questions of difference, when we have men whose hearts are controlled by responsibility to God, who in all the earnestness of working out their own salvation, cannot forget the interests of their country, as public servants, then may we hope for better things than now. The character of Mr. Butler was consistent throughout. Whatever might have been said of him in the hurly-burly of political strife, in the glow and heat of party contest, there is not one who can stand beside that coffin, and say of the sleeper within it, that he was not a true man.

I beg pardon for allowing myself to be led so far out on this subject, but I feel strongly what I say.

When the great Pompey was sick at Neapolis, and was supposed to be near death, the whole population put garlands on their heads, and went to the house in which he lay, to congratulate him upon so happy and easy a close of such an honoured life. He recovered, and he recovered to die at last, assassinated by a eunuch and a slave upon a desert shore.

My friends, I have more of congratulation for the spirit which animated this clay than I have of grief. He lived well; he died well; and now he lives forevermore! Not a shadow over his precious memory, except the softening light of that blessed evening, the precursor of a morning which shall never fade. No abatement of his natural strength, no failure of his strong mind, no chill of his ardent heart; nothing to regret; all to hope for. Did he not die well?

It was in a foreign land, — but those who were dearest to his heart brought home about his bed, — and Paris is as near to Heaven as New York. He died well. And he went to his heavenly home, not unwelcomed. There was one to meet him on the very threshold of his Father's house —one, after whom we may believe his heart, since he lost her for a brief season, never ceased to yearn. He died well! He lives forever!

He was a man whose piety was his life, and you will pardon me for recurring to that theme for a moment. My dear mother said to me once, of a person whose manner I had spoken well of, 'My son, he puts on his politeness as he does his best coat. Give me a man whose politeness is in his skin!' So it was in Mr. Butler's religion. It was part of himself. There was no affectation about it. No one ever supposed there was. It shone out of his bright eye, (can it be, that that bright eye will never shine on us again?) it beamed from his countenance, it came from his heart. It was a transfiguration from within, that made his life so beautiful in all the grace and kindness of a Christian gentleman.

Let me say one word more, as I look over this assembly. I am a younger man than Mr. Butler, though a difference of ten years is not what it was when we were boys. I see before me many, of every period of life, some older, some younger. But how many are absent? How many of those who were associated with us, whom we have loved, and honoured, and cherished, with whom we have walked together, how many have gone, and how rapidly is the number diminishing. We must all come to it, my friends. We, too, must die, and die soon. Are we ready?"

These selections from his intimate writings, if we may be allowed the expression, together with his published speeches, will suffice to show how thoroughly he loved his country and how well he would have satisfied even Dr. Johnson by the thorough way in which he hated those who wished her ill ; indeed, he said that he never so much felt the want of a son that he might consecrate him to the service of his country.

CHAPTER XIV.

DEPARTURE FROM BROOKLYN—RESIDENCE IN NEW YORK RETURN TO EUROPE.

We must now retrace our steps. In the year 1858 Dr. Bethune was elected Professor of Church History and Pastoral Theology in the Theological Seminary at New Brunswick; but he could not be drawn from his pastoral work. As it was thought that his name and services would give strength to the institution, he consented to give a course of lectures on "Pulpit Eloquence" during the next session. He wrote: "The arrangement is however a very laborious and trying one for me; it takes me away from 10, A. M. to 10, P. M., and adding the Monday's work to the Sabbath's, I am pretty well done over, and my Tuesdays are dreadfully Mondayish. I am trying to do what is in my power, but I have had no experience as a teacher, and fear that I shall not accomplish much during my brief term of duty."

He was mistaken about the success of his lectures; they were counted the charm of the Seminary.

In the spring, circumstances led him to arrange a series of those popular lectures which were so eagerly sought for, and he delivered ten in as many different places within two weeks. But the over-exertion and intense excitement of these labors were too great for his strength, and premonitory symptoms, of which he had been warned, culminated in an attack of apoplexy.

This great misfortune befell Dr. Bethune about the middle of February, 1859. He was seized in the night with stupor from which he did not recover for some hours and it is related that on his return to consciousness, beholding Drs. Rosman and McClelland at his bedside, he, with his abounding humor, exclaimed, "Have the North and South Poles came together? Allopathy and Homeopathy?" Upon being informed that he had been dangerously sick, the merry spirit left him and he exhibited the serious mien of a man on the border of eternity.

There was, it is true, no paralyis resulting from this attack, but it left him exposed to the danger of another at any moment. It forced him to abandon his occupations, to leave the country, and quit his parishioners with such precipitation that we can hardly wonder at the misunderstanding which seems to have taken place.

"Rest your mind," said all the physicians, "Take things more easily," "Cast away care," "Enjoy yourself." "No one," writes the discreet Dunglison, "can be more prudent in regard to diet than yourself; but attention is needed to all the *non-naturals*, as the older physicians termed them, and of these, the mental efforts are apt to be the most neglected, not, perhaps, that the mere exercise of the brain may be injurious, but it is too apt to lead to a neglect of the due precautions of exercise, regularity of meals, &c., &c."

A sailing vessel bound for Naples was engaged and our broken-down minister sought that repose which alone could restore his nervous energy. But the voyage was too full of anxiety, and the invalid was writing letters when he should have been resting his wearied faculties. Nothing could be finer, more affectionate, than his first message, breathing towards his flock the very spirit of an Apostle.

"NAPLES, SABBATH EVENING, *April*, 1859.

DEARLY BELOVED FRIENDS: The impulse of my heart was to address you as 'my dear people,' as I have for so many years loved to do, but I check my pen from the sore, sorrowful remembrance that that happy privilege is no longer mine. No change of circumstances can change the affection I bear to you, an affection which has continually increased with the length and closeness of our relations as people and pastor. I should be utterly unworthy of the regard, kindness and respect which you have ever shown me, if I could cease to be grateful to you for the many proofs of your love which I have received, or thankful to God for having given such a rich evidence of his favor as the friendship of such friends and the pastorship of such a flock, gathered and established as a Church of Christ, by his blessing on my unworthy instrumentality. You will not, you cannot believe me capable of any other feelings towards you. Yet weeks have passed away since I was obliged to leave you, and weeks must pass before these words will reach you from a heart overflowing with sorrow and love. The same painful and imperious circumstances, which compelled me to leave my once happy home in Brooklyn, (mine no longer) so suddenly, and in order to do so with propriety made it, as I supposed, *my duty* to resign my call into the hands of your Consistory, did not allow me to address you a word of farewell personally or by letter. My physicians, fearing a return in a more dangerous form of the ailment which had affected me so seriously, ordered me in a most peremptory manner to abstain from all excitements of mind or feeling. To obey them entirely in that respect was impossible. My heart yearned to see the friends who I knew were crowding around my door, and to speak to them that I might thank them for their sympathy as well as to take counsel with them. As I turned from side to side on my sleepless bed, my brain swam with the thoughts and words I would fain have uttered from the pulpit. But I was not permitted to speak, and I could not then keep up the continuous action of writing. I remonstrated with the doctors. I told them that the repression of my feelings was more dangerous to me than their utterance could be — that I must communicate with my friends, or they might, from ignorance of the circumstances misjudge — perhaps think hardly of me; and that if they would not allow me to speak, they (the physicians) must speak for me. This they readily consented to do, and as I have reason to believe they kept their word. One of them, my excellent and most faithful friend, Doctor Rosman, who for many years has been more familiar with me and my house than any other person, (not an inmate of my family,) and certainly, as a parishioner, with warm attachments to me, assured me that he had done so as widely and as decidedly as he could. In these circumstances I yielded, believing that I was under God in the physicians' hands, as the persons best qualified to judge of my duty; and also relying with confidence upon the candor and kindness of my people to secure me from any possible suspicion of any wilful neglect, much less any want of respect and regard for them. The hand of the Lord was upon me, what could I do but be still under his chastenings. I shall, indeed, have labored among you, sympathizing with your griefs and joys, and receiving the confidences of your hearts, for so many years, to little effect, if you could believe me indifferent to your peace, or disregardful of your feelings.

This is, therefore, the first moment that I could address you. The kindness of Providence brought us here in safety yesterday. Day after to-morrow is the first mail-day for England. I write thus, without reserve or delay, as the thoughts flow from my heart along my pen, to tell you, beloved friends, before the God whose presence is with us both, that nothing but what I believe a moral necessity led me to ask the Consistory to release me from my pastoral responsibility, that I might take the steps which I conscientiously believed were best adapted to the restoration of my health, or, rather, the preservation of my life. Thus far Providence has not frowned on me. The bracing air of the sea, the seclusion of the ship, and I trust a higher blessing, have done a great deal towards strengthening me — nay, so much so that I have strong hope of being restored to my country in the autumn with a new lease of life, which I pray for, if it be for my Master's glory and my eternal good. The Friend who sticketh closer than a brother, has not forsaken me, but was with me as I walked under the shadow of death. Never has that blessed gospel which you have loved to hear from my lips, appeared more true, more precious, more necessary to the soul's peace than since I have been afflicted. Pray for me, dear friends, that my faith fail not, and that I may lie passive in *his* hands whose will is best for you, and me, and all of us. The brevity of my time will not allow me to say more at present. There are many particulars into which I cannot now enter. If it please God to bring me again alive to my country (I have now no other name for home), I shall be glad to make any other explanations that may be desired, being sure that the more my conduct is scrutinized in all its bearings, the more I shall have of your sympathy, the less of your blame. I have endeavored to do what, from the light I had, appeared to be not merely right but necessary. Certain it is, that I have left you for no lucre or advantage of this world.

These, *on former occasions*, I did not suffer to persuade me from you. My illness was not my fault, yet it may very well have been that my judgment was erroneous, and that I might have acted more wisely. The character of my illness (whatever it was) might have shaken a stronger brain than mine. Pray that my sins and errors may be forgiven, and that the Chief Shepherd would overrule all for the good of the church, your good, my good, and the glory of his dear name. Men are nothing but instruments. They pass away, but the testimony of the Lord abideth forever, and that testimony is with his chosen. Stand fast in his faith, his love, and his service; and in the end it will be seen that he hath done all things well. The same Holy Spirit, who has so abundantly blessed you through my poor instrumentality, has perchance removed me to bless you yet more abundantly through the labors of others entering upon mine. It is my heart's desire and prayer that He will, until those of you now without are brought into the covenant, and the whole church be glorified.

Finally, my brethren, farewell; be perfect; be of one mind; live in peace; and the very God of love and of peace shall be with you all.

GEO. W. BETHUNE."

Thus terminated his relation to the "Church on the Heights." His ministry of about six years and a half had been a great success. Having commenced with a small nucleus, the people had erected a splendid church edifice; the congregation embraced more than 200 families and there were 445 members in communion, and the contributions during his pastorate reached the handsome amount of $154,945.87. Dr. Bethune wrote, "Our increase has at no one time been large, but has been steadily encouraging." We are indebted to his faithful friend, an elder of the church, Mr. Tenyck Sutphen, for the following account of his pastor's ministry. "The work accomplished during his ministry among us was immense. No sooner had he gotten fairly at work in the congregation of the Old Central Church, than he felt the great need of more enlarged church accomodations and the necessity of a new organization. The accomplishment of these objects was almost at once resolved upon. The new church edifice was completed within a little more than a year from the time of its commencement, and I think it may with truth be said that the interior beauty of this temple surpasses that of almost any other church in our great cities. The inscription, carved into the stone freize above the columns, 'To the Triune God,' as enduring as the Church itself, was placed there at his suggestion.

After the dedication, Dr. B. commenced a series of Sabbath evening discourses on the *Parables of our Saviour*, which were continued nearly through the following winter and which drew crowded houses. Great activity marked every department of the new enterprise, whether in large-hearted benevolence to almost every worthy object, or in the real work of church progress. Our home Sabbath school was brought into a most flourishing condition; then, a large and most interesting Bible class taught by the Doctor on a week day was quickly commenced and largely attended; next, the Bethesda mission school was gathered and carried on by our church. Next in order, was the establishment of the Summit Street Chapel and Sabbath school, a branch of the 'Church on the Heights,' placed under the care of the Rev. Dr. Quackenbush.

Dr. B's heart was in the work and here he often used to

preach of a Sabbath evening, after having preached twice the same day in his 'Church on the Heights.'

Next was the establishment of the Myrtle Avenue mission school, a most thrifty enterprise of some hundreds of scholars; these three mission Sabbath schools were all conducted by teachers from his church, numbering over eighty thus engaged. The whole number of scholars taught in all our schools was 695. Dr. Bethune had an extraordinary faculty of drawing the young people of his congregation about him, making them love him; and then he would set them at work, feeling that the good they would gain to themselves in the Sabbath school would be great. Thus, through his influence, the young men's Sabbath afternoon meetings to pray for a blessing upon his preaching of the word were established, and many used to flock into these meetings immediately after the sermon, the Doctor very frequently following; indeed, he leaned much upon the strength derived from answers to those prayers.

He sought the prayers of the older people at their Sabbath morning gatherings to aid him through the labors of the day, and then, when his work was ended, he looked for the blessing upon it through the prayers of the young.

Notwithstanding the constant pressure upon his time, he seemed to know, as by intuition, every sick and dying one among his congregation, and was sure to be at their bedsides in the hour of extremity. None knew better than he how to give comfort in the chamber of affliction. 'Let your tears flow; mourning is not murmuring,' said the Doctor, to a poor heart-broken widow, as we entered her abode; and those words were electrical to calm her troubled spirit, hushing that chamber of death to the stillness of silent sorrow. A friend writes:

'Oh! those Friday evening meetings for prayer, how *near* the Saviour seemed to be in those calm hours! Here and there among his congregation are those who were laid as a weight upon his soul, and he at times felt that he could have no peace, until they came to a knowledge of salvation. My friends, (this was his common form of addressing them) if you realized the importance of this change of heart as I do, you would give yourself no rest day or night until you had secured an interest in the great salvation.'

Few public speakers understood so perfectly as Dr. Bethune how to give the most telling effect to every gesture. 'My friends, it is cold! very cold!' said the Doctor, as he wrapped the folds of his robe about him, at the close of a Thanksgiving sermon, on a chill November day. '*Remember the poor;*' and he would set his hearers an example of most liberal giving, often thrusting $ 50 into the plate at any special collection.

The Doctor said, in relation to the same subject, "I would as soon try to cultivate a farm without rain, as a church without Benevolence." One night, at the close of his appeal for funds, in aid of the Brooklyn City Tract Society, (Doctor Cutler being in the chair) he sank down almost exhausted, with the remark, 'Oh! Dr. Cutler, I wish I had as many dollars for you as I have words.'"

One of the great features of this ministry was a course of Sermons, illustrative of the Heidelberg Catechism. These were preached, according to the order of his church, and the pastor clothed them with all the interest that his well-stored mind, and gifts of eloquence could bestow. They embrace a complete system of theology, and have been published in two crown octavo volumes.

From the Bible class mentioned before, we have delightful reminiscences :

"It was attended by forty or fifty ladies, and the Doctor took great pains always to meet his engagement with them. At times we appeared to approach so near the gates of the celestial city, we thought we could almost look within. Once in our class, he remarked, 'One of my favorite theories, with regard to our heavenly home, is, that we shall love best in Heaven, those who have been instrumental in leading us nearest the Saviour while on earth.' After the lesson was concluded, I said to him, 'Dear Doctor, if your favorite theory should prove true, I shall love *you* very much when I reach home.' 'Ah! my child,' said he, pressing my head, while the tears filled his eyes, 'that will make Heaven to me.'

I can hardly believe that any member of that Bible class can ever go very far astray in theology. To this day, when difficulties of a theological nature have arisen in my own mind, the instructions of Doctor Bethune come before me with such strength that every error vanishes instantly.

He was so courteous to us all. If a timid one gave an answer not quite correct, he made his ever ready excuse, 'I put the question so awkwardly, you could not understand,' and then the question so repeated, that the answer must be perceived. Indeed, he was a perfect pattern of a courteous, dignified, Christian gentleman.

Never can I forget his putting the question, whether it were ever right, under any circumstances, to tell a lie? He brought up Paley's arguments, and permitted us to discuss the subject as long as we would. Then came his own quiet answer, shewing his unfaltering trust in the God who cannot lie. 'Never, never, can it be right,' said he, 'no matter what are the circumstances; leave yourself, leave all you love to God, he can take care of you, no matter how great the danger, he can provide a way of escape, but rather, far rather, give up your life than tell an untruth.

The Doctor was one day reasoning with a friend on the subject of Apostolic succession, in which the gentleman was a strong believer, when the Doctor proposed to test the question; he said to his friend, 'You know the Apostles had the power to take up serpents without being injured, now if your convention of Bishops which are met in New York, will permit me to upset a box of rattlesnakes among them, and no one is injured, it might convince me.'

One day Doctor B. asked by what agency our progress in knowledge, sanctification and perfection was to be carried on in Heaven? The question caused some surprise. Miss C. said, 'Why, I thought our probation ended with this life.' 'So it does,' he replied, 'we shall sin no more, and be beyond the reach of temptation, but we shall progress for ever.' Finding no one answered him, I said, 'I suppose the Holy Spirit is the agent of our progress there, as he is here;' Doctor B. replied that those were his views.

I recollect one lecture on prayer, in which he said, 'Prayer is the golden conduit, through which our desires ascend to God, and His grace descends to us;' he remarked, 'My sweetest hour for communion with God, is at midnight, when I am secure from interruption. The heart must be poured out in prayer; do with it as you do with the upper drawer of your bureau, which seems to be a receptacle for stray articles; turn it upside down, that you may see what sins you have forgotten or overlooked.'"

But before leaving Brooklyn, a record should be made of a charming literary association, such as Dr. Bethune loved to gather about him. Dr. Vinton relates:

"Our club was styled, 'The Friends,' consisting of Dr. Bethune, Dr. Storrs, Dr. Vinton, of the clergy, and Messrs Pierrepont, Brevoort, Silliman, Whitehouse, Embury, Van Wagener, Minor, Humphreys, Congdon, and H. K. Brown, Huntington, artists, who had the privilege of inviting a guest, whenever the club met at their respective houses.

This meeting began informally, by a banquet given to the three clergymen, after their joint course of Public Lectures. The club flourished till death entered and thinned its numbers, and now is among 'the memories of joys that are past,' which, 'like the music of Carrol, are sweet and pleasant, yet mournful to the soul.'"

From Italy, Dr. and Mrs. Bethune passed to Switzerland, when a delightful intimacy was formed with Rev. Dr. Geo. L. Prentiss, and in the autumn Dr. Bethune reached New York, to be welcomed "by scores of parishioners, with great affection." But he wrote to Dr. Prentiss:

"The leadings of Providence seem to indicate that a change of sphere will be better for my usefulness and comfort. What that sphere will be, I cannot yet say, but there is no lack of opportunities offered to me. I leave myself in the hands where I love best to be. 'The Lord has been my help, therefore under the shadow of his wings will I rejoice.'"

And God did take good care of his faithful servant. Mrs. Anson G. Phelps opened the doors of her hospitable mansion at Tarrytown. Proposals were made by a church in Boston. The University of Pennsylvania offered its Provostship. The course which this negotiation took was peculiar, interesting and instructive. Dr. Dunglison was the interpreter:

DR. BETHUNE TO DR. DUNGLISON. "*October* 6, 1859.

The University movement towards me, is very flattering. I consider it a very high compliment, and am very grateful to my friends who have so gracefully honored me.

Nothing could have been more unexpected. I desire very much to see you, but could not before I came this way; when I return, which will be in about a fortnight, I shall try hard to run over and report myself to you. By that time the October meeting of the University Board will have met and —— we may talk it over."

DR. BETHUNE TO DR. DUNGLISON. "*October* 27, 1859.

I found that my affairs demanded my closest attention, proposals of different kinds demanding my regard. Neither would I have liked to be spoken of as canvassing more Philadelphians. As I have been nominated, and the nomination is known, I should of course prefer not to answer any questions as to whether I would or would not, until the proper time came. At the same time I could not trifle with my friends.

Much as I esteem the honor of being elected to such a post, it is not so necessary to me that I would run amuck to attain it, and I should prefer withdrawal to defeat, or a doubtful contest. I am therefore glad to know that I have friends whose discretion is equal to their zeal."

DR. BETHUNE TO DR. DUNGLISON. "*November* 1. 1859.

As regards the wish of the trustees to know what I would do in a certain event, it is quite natural, and had they asked the question before I was nominated and the nomination known to the public, it would have been very reasonable. It is true that, as regards the latter consideration, your movement with that of other friends in my favor softens the case. But there is another practical difficulty in the way of such a contingent answer. I am solicited in other quarters, and by some considerable attractions; other propositions are ripening, about which I may or may not (more probably *may*) decide before the Trustees talk plainly to me. I cannot therefore so tie myself as to refuse (in effect) every other proposition, present or future, in waiting on the University. If they press me for an answer, wisdom, such as I have, dictates one in the negative, for (as I am sure you will not be sorry to know) your friend is somewhat in demand, and likely to be more so after a certain event which will transpire to-morrow, is known to the community.

I have a high estimation of the Provostship as a post of honorable importance, and a still higher respect for the Board of Trustees, who were in my time, and doubtless are still, a body not excelled in character and dignity by any in the land; but, notwithstanding, I cannot see the necessity or the expediency of accepting or refusing what, through not a few accidents, may never be offered me."

DR. BETHUNE TO DR. DUNGLISON. "*November* 10, 1859.

DEAR DR. DUNGLISON: Since we parted on Sunday evening, I have endeavored to give due weight to the considerations you urged in favor of my accepting the Provostship of the University of Pennsylvania, at the same time assuring me that there was no reasonable doubt of my being elected to the chair, if I was disposed towards it.

I now fulfil my promise of writing to you in a few days.

It is, so far as my experience goes, not usual to ask a gentleman whether he will or will not accept an office, before it is distinctly tendered to him, and I believe that the rule for professional men in such circumstances is to give no answer, or if pressed, to answer in the negative. I appreciate the reasons why the Board would like a favorable expression from me, before they go to the length of putting the office to my option; but, strong as the reasons are for the Board's pursuit of such a course, there are reasons as strong why a nominee should decline to commit himself before the proper time.

However I am not inclined to be punctilious where the intention towards me is so generous, or to put the Board of the University to any unnecessary trouble on my account, and therefore, in the absence of any communication from them, I beg you to do me the favor of communicating to the Board what I shall now say in such manner as shall be most convenient to you.

I consider the offer which has been made me of the Provostship of the University of Pennsylvania, as a very high honor, and one of which I am sorry to say, I am not deserving. The importance of the office is great, and the position it gives, a very high one, but still more do I estimate the evidence I have had of the confidence and esteem entertained for me by the gentlemen comprising the Board of Trustees.

When I had the honor to be one of that Board, I heard one of my fellow members (Mr. Brock) say that he considered his place in that body one of the very highest distinctions of his life; a sentiment I was only too happy to share. Many of our associates there have passed away, but as I look over the list of the present members, I see that the Board has suffered no diminution of dignity, social influence, and large intelligence. Most grateful am I to Divine Providence and to the Board, that I have been deemed fit to receive such a distinction at their hands.

Had the appointment been given me immediately on my return to this country, I should have been strongly moved to accept it with pleasure, especially as it would have enabled me to resume my residence in Philadelphia, where I spent fifteen of my happiest years, and where I have many friends very dear to my heart.

But it cannot be. My conscientious reluctance to leave the pulpit as my sphere of usefulness has been increased by a call from a church in my native city, offering me strong inducements of every kind to accept it, and I have done so.

Nothing then remains for me but to thank the Board of the University for the honor they intended to do me, and to beg they will assign it to some one more fitted to receive it than,

Yours very faithfully,

GEO. W. BETHUNE.

ROBLEY DUNGLISON, M. D.
PHILADELPHIA."

This negotiation, if pursued with less cautiousness, might have terminated more to the advantage of the University. The man whom they preferred was not within their reach. He had received a call as Associate minister of the Twenty-First Street Church, N. Y., with a salary of $5,000 a year. This handsome offer was accepted, and, on November twentieth, he was installed to labor in conjunction with the writer of this memoir.

The original design in this union was to establish another church in the growing part of the city, but in view of Dr. Bethune's uncertain health, this was soon abandoned. Still the relation was most delightful and profitable. Every day brought to the junior pastor its pleasant interviews. The church, which had always met with fair success, was now crowded to overflowing. During the first year the Doctor sustained his part of the service. A course of evening lectures on the Divine names and perfections was very interesting. Later there came an occasional note requesting relief from duty, after the Fort Sumter meeting of 1861 ; and when afterwards the Doctor removed to Catskill, he almost ceased from preaching.

In July, 1860, Mrs. Joanna Bethune was taken to her rest. The grief had been borne long before, in seeing the decay of her faculties ; but the son whose youth had been guided by her wisdom, had the privilege of returning those bounties, and when he closed her eyes in death, his manly sorrow was not embittered by vain regrets over filial duty unfulfilled. He had commenced the memoir of this remarkable lady before leaving America for the last time ; the sheets were placed for completion, in the hands of Rev. Dr. Prime, of the New York Observer, and in due season the volume appeared.

The love between mother and son was wonderful. Is it not true that great men have almost always had great mothers?

Brief quotations from Dr. Bethune's correspondence with the writer, will show a remarkable progress in grace, and a loosening hold from earthly things. Speaking of a sick minister, he wrote:

"But that we know the Master has all things in his nail-scarred hands, it would be sad to see one like him wasting in the midst of his days."

"The daylight may soon come, but things look very dark now; still I am not unhappy, trusting, as I ought, to that blessed Providence which has all along been so good to me. However, the ways of Providence are not always those we have marked out for ourselves, and we must follow, not dictate to Him who orders all things well."

"It is rather sad to be so helpless as we two old people are, but the Lord, I trust, will think upon us the more we are obliged to lean upon him. It is a necessity not without its sweetness, which allows us nothing to lean upon between us and Him."

"I think that a Sabbath spent by one's self has its use; it allows us a time for self-examination which we seldom get, and makes us more intent on personal communion with God, for which no public service can be a substitute."

"I can do nothing to help you to-morrow, but pray for God's blessing on his own word which I know you will preach; you will not forget to pray for me in private as well as public, as a poor, sinful man, whose hope in bodily and spiritual infirmity is that he may have strength from God through Jesus Christ."

"I am up rather early on this lovely morning, and from the window near which I am writing, the river calm as a mirror and the green woods and hills beyond it, look very sweet and lovely, putting one in mind of

'Sweet fields beyond the swelling flood
All dressed in living green,'

only that to-day the flood does not swell, but is the image of repose."

"It is well thus to be weaned from this world, though the process is trying. I acknowledge that I am depressed in spirits, body, mind, and what is worse, heart; I suppose I might have more courage if I were *stronger*, but the difficulty is that *I am weak.*"

"I have not been well since I left Catskill, indeed I fear that you should place little reliance on my poor help, either for next Sunday or after, unless God in his mercy be pleased to give me more health."

"We cannot eradicate real disease by ignoring or forgetting it, and the conviction of our mortality is healthful for the soul; I try to put my mind in a proper frame, nor do I wish to be gloomy. Freedom from care, I mean anxious, haunting care, is what I need, at least at the present."

"My neuralgia in the head is very distressing and frequent, and my left leg is so weak that I cannot walk far, and totter unless I use extreme caution, or move very deliberately; the fact is, I am a used-up man. Both Dunglison (who has quite as favorable an opinion of me as Hosack,) and Hosack himself, whatever some one has told you that he said, charge me that I must be on my guard against excitement, particularly *emotional* excitement. A pretty preacher I shall make without excitement, or being continually engaged in repressing emotions, especially since people expect excitement and emotion from me: yet I must be so cautious on pain of an apoplexy or a paralysis! No, my dear friend, I am sorry that you are so hopeful, for you will be disappointed; I shall have to give up, I cannot go on with my work, but must bow to a will higher than yours or mine. *This is so.* I beg you to believe it."

"I desire and aim at submission to my Master's will, but need much more simple faith than I have. Undoubtedly my state of health affects my spiritual perceptions, but it is not all a matter of nerves, and my constant prayer is, God be merciful to me a sinner!"

"'We're poor critters,'" said the widow Bedott, and so say I, and so will say you, taking me as a specimen. It is only a few days ago that I was so chirpy and so thankful because my fever seemed to have left me, and now I am bowed down by a terrible, that word is not too strong, terrible old nervous headache, or rather a headache that I think and hope is neuralgic, at the back of the head. It goes and comes, but it comes a good deal more than it goes, for it stays with me longer than it stays away: I have been subject to it more or less for years past, but it is worse than ever before; taking advantage of my weakness. As it is, it unfits me for anything and tortures me, so that I do not see how I can go to help you this week.

I am thoroughly convinced that I ought to go abroad, and, unless prevented, wish to go at the latest between the 1st and 15th October. I ought to get leave from the Consistory. How shall that be done, and what shall I ask for? Leave of absence or separation? I had no idea, until you suggested otherwise, of anything else but resignation, in which case the action of Classis would be required. If however you desire that I should retain my association under any arrangements, I will do as you say, only it must not be in any way to embarrass you or the church."

These extracts, most of which were written from Catskill, show that God was ripening his saint for glory. This residence on the Hudson, which had been taken with such anticipations of pleasure, where he had bought land and was building castles in the air, was really a scene of great trial, a place of Babylonish captivity, where God taught his servant that this world was not his home.

For two years he had lived under the constant apprehension of death, and never retired at night without saying the prayer his mother had taught him:

"Now I lay me down to sleep
I pray the Lord my soul to keep.
If I should die before I wake
I pray the Lord my soul to take."

On the 20th of May he had received another warning; his arm (luckily not the writing arm) and leg were numbed and sleepy and there were symptoms of pressure on the brain. He had become acutely sensitive to every sign of his malady, and a trip to Europe was resolved upon as the only hope.

DR. BETHUNE TO DR. DUNGLISON. "30th *July*.

I am better on the whole, dear Doctor, my leg is weak but not so much so as it was, and now that I have little fever my spirits are better. I have not, however, courage for work, and get more worried over the troubles of the country. I feel strongly inclined to escape for a while to some distant spot where I can live cheaply in a milder climate. You say that I must avoid emotional excitement. I cannot preach without emotions and those of the strongest, often of the most insurgent (?) kind."

TO THE CONSISTORY OF THE REFORMED DUTCH CHURCH, TWENTY-FIRST ST. NEW YORK. "NEW YORK, *Aug*, 30th, 1861.

DEAR BRETHREN: It is not without great pain that I address to you this communication, the necessity for which I regard as a sore affliction from the hands of God.

The relation I have been permitted to sustain towards you and my beloved friend, your pastor, Dr. Van Nest, for nearly two years, has been to me a source of great enjoyment, and I trust of genuine profit; may I not also hope of usefulness in my ministry? Most gladly would I continue it while God permits me to live and labor, but if I read his Providence aright he wills it otherwise; my health which received a severe and sudden shock in the early spring of 1859, and which I fondly hoped had been in a good measure restored, has, since May last, shown some marked symptoms of decay. In truth, the excitement of the times and my various efforts to do what I thought was my duty in the perilous state of the country, have been too much for the plethoric tendency of my head, and my faithful physician earnestly forbids my exposing myself to those forms of excitement which spring from strong emotions or severe brain labor. He also as earnestly recommends a change of winter climate. The exigencies of Mrs. Bethune's health coincide with those of my own. In this state of things, I have determined, with your kind permission to follow Doctor Hosack's counsel and seek in a foreign land the change which we need, and some relief from the exciting events constantly agitating our unhappy country.

It is therefore my desire, and, with your consent, my purpose, to go to the south of Europe about the beginning of October, or before the cold and after the stormy season. My petition to you now is that you will grant me the required leave of absence. I do not fix any time for my return, considering the state of my health and other circumstances too precarious for such anticipations.

If, on consultation with my dear colleague, you shall deem it more proper or more expedient that the official relation between us should be dissolved, I will readily unite with you in steps necessary to that end; but in any event I shall consider you in no way restrained from making such arrangements for the church as you may see fit.

I am frank to say that nothing short of what appears the necessity of my case would induce me to leave my place among you. I have been very happy and very thankful as one of your pastors, and shall ever, while I live, be grateful to God and to you for the many enjoyments I have had in my ministry to your church. What God has in store for me I cannot tell; but I never expect to find on earth, more pleasant friends, more agreeable work, or kinder parishioners than I have had in the Twenty-first Street Church! God bless you! God bless all the dear people of the congregation! Pray God to take care of me and mine in what remains to me of the present life, but especially to bless me as your fellow-sinner with the pardon of my guilt and his eternal salvation and to grant us all a happy reunion in our Father's house, where there will be no more pain, or grief, or parting!

Your affectionate and sorrowing minister,

GEO. W. BETHUNE."

DR. BETHUNE TO DR. DUNGLISON. "*Sept.* 13, 1861.

DEAR DR. DUNGLISON: I have been silent for a much longer time than I considered it possible to be, but I have been flying up and down, and here and there, so much, besides having so much to do, that I could not get an easy half-hour. I have continued to be comfortable and in good spirits since that *febricule* left me, and took with it the neuralgia from the back part of the head. It was that fever which put me so deeply in low spirits. My stay at Long Branch was of great use to me.

Mrs. Bethune and myself have made up our minds to go abroad again. I had a combination of motives to press that decision. Her own comfort requires a milder climate than I can give her in the United States. My church affairs are not promising, from the state of the times, and New York is a most expensive place of residence, and I find that the endeavor to avoid emotion in the pulpit, kills my manner and unfits me for the control which my constitutional energy has hitherto given me over an audience. At any rate it is better, so far as I can see, for us physically, mentally, and pecuniarily, that we should be away for a time at least. My congregation have given me leave of absence and I shall retain my connection (official) with them for a time at least. I make no calculations about our return, leaving ourselves and all else in God's hands."

On the 23d of September Dr. Bethune paid a hurried visit to Philadelphia, and took a final leave of his friends there. Very few that knew him had any faith in the permanence of his restoration. At the parting with Dr. Dunglison, one can conceive the two noble Romans saying to each other like Brutus and Cassius, —

> "Forever and forever farewell.
> If we do meet again, why, we shall smile;
> If not, why then this parting was well made."

On the next Lord's Day he preached an affectionate farewell sermon to his people, from 2 Thess., iii.,16; "Now the Lord of peace himself give you peace always by all means. The Lord be with you all." The following Saturday we said our last greeting, but there were not many words. The long pressure of the hand and the tear in the eye told the sad story.

Dr. Bethune to Dr. Van Nest. "At Sea, *Oct.* 13, 1861.

The excitement of preparing to come away, and a little service I had on hand last Sunday, were together a little too much for me, and I suffered somewhat in the afternoon of that day, which depressed my spirits as indicating that I could not have the pleasure of preaching as I had hoped to in a quiet way; but I think that after a while I may be able to do more. My heart is pained at times to think of my separation from dear friends, from the pulpit in which I have been so happy, and from my dear country; but when I think of God's goodness and favors, his 'loving kindness' and 'tender mercy' (what sweet words are these!) my heart melts in thankfulness till my eyes run over with pleasant tears. I have had my trials and feel them now, but if ever a simple man was called to thankfulness I am. Should you never see me again, or hear from me before I am summoned from life, you may say of me, 'He loved to give thanks to God, through Christ his Saviour.'"

Dr. Bethune to Dr. Van Nest.

"Birkenhead, *Oct.* 18, 1861.

I think over the pleasant days I have had with you, in and out of the church itself, and as I cannot hope for the full renewal of such pleasure on earth, I comfort myself with looking upward to still brighter scenes in a sinless, sorrowless, shadowless land."

Dr. Bethune to Dr. Van Nest.

"St. Pierre, Guernsey, *Nov.* 17, 1861.

I think of you and the dear, pleasant sanctuary where we have had such sweet communion, in meditation and duty, and I yearn to know where you are, and what our people are doing, and contrast my best privileges

('Where'er his saints assemble now,
There is a house for God.')

as a stranger in a strange land, with my fellowship at home in heaven. However, God is teaching me, in various ways, that I am a pilgrim and sojourner in the earth, and should be longing for my Father's house where there are many mansions."

Dr. Bethune to Dr. Prime.

"St. Pierre, Island of Guernsey, *Nov.* 11, 1861

My Dear Dr. Prime: You may be surprised at my dating from this somewhat out-of-the-way place, but I had been recommended by a medical friend to take Guernsey in our route to the west of France, because, as he thought, its climate is the best he met with in Europe; and as we did not care to go to Paris, it was convenient for us to reach Brittany by the steamer plying to and fro between the group of Channel Islands.

I am not sorry that we came here, especially as we were obliged to linger somewhere that one of our party might overtake us; for although the climate (at least in this November) is not all my friend thought it to be, the winds having been high and the temperature at night lower than we had hoped, the atmosphere is pure, and all of us have, I think, been more or less benefited by our sojourn here. The Island is very beautiful — perhaps pretty were a better word — with varied scenery, dotted over by graceful residences and tasteful grounds. The climate, also, must be remarkable for its amenity. Tropical plants, which we carefully screen from the slightest chill, geraniums, fuchsias, myrtles, hydrangeas and camellias, here, bloom in the open air. The orange, lemon and fig, ripen without protection; the aloe and other species of the cactus, flourish luxuriantly, and it would seem that the torrid and temperate zones have combined their productions on this favored spot. Grapes of several varieties (with a little care) abound, and the pears are really superb, the d'Angoulême and Beaumanoir especially, the latter weighing from six ounces to thirty; one example of thirty-two. My taste for fruit (a main article of my diet, when I can get it) has, therefore, sufficient gratification.

This Island is also full of historical interest, from the time of Celtic predominance down to recent times. The Druidical remains are numerous and very curious. As these islands were, from an early date, connected with the dukedom of Normandy, and so, after the conquest, brought under the control of Great Britain, and even now retain many of their native laws and usages, we are not surprised to find the homes of the principal families indicating their continental antiquity; for here are still De Lisles, De Beauvoirs, Saumareys, and others of equally old blood, who hold themselves aloof from the Islanders of less chivalric descent. They are said, however, to be very simple and kindly in their manners with each other, and not inhospitable to strangers, although, personally, I have had little opportunity to judge.

The Reformed religion was introduced here principally by fugitive Huguenots, and the pulpits of their very ancient parishes were supplied by zealous and determined Presbyterians, until that saintly defender of the faith, Charles II., compelled the reluctant anti-prelatists to succumb to *uniformity*. Even now the ancient spirit so far lingers, that in several of the rural parishes the white surplices, or 'change of vestment,' has never been tolerated to this day. There were instances of heroic constancy among the Non-Conformists of Guernsey, worthy of admiration, but the annals of such martyr-like devotion have been so zealously suppressed that no native historiographer, who would tell the story, could escape ostracism from the ruling class. At present, the Church of England has it all her own way, with the exception of a Scotch Free Church chapel, feebly maintained, some Wesleyans, with other Methodist varieties, and a few chapels of the Brethren or Bible Christians. Expecting to be shut up to the Episcopal service for some months at least, I have availed myself of my opportunity to enjoy more freedom while lingering here, and sought my Sabbath refreshment among the Dissenting chapels; but with the exception of the Scotch chapel aforesaid, at present supplied by a young licentiate of little experience, the preaching of the ministers I heard indicated more sincerity and earnestness than education or Scriptural accuracy. The abuse and neglect of the aspirate by an illiterate English declaimer is peculiarly offensive, and, spite of one's desire to be serious, irresistibly ludicrous, so that edification under such a declaimer is not very possible. One of them said the other night, speaking of the mocking inquiry of the Pharisees respecting our Lord, and suiting his emphasis to the occasion: 'They hasked hinsultingly, *Oo his e?*' H meets with hard treatment in Guernsey.

My own health has certainly been improved by the fresh air of the sea, always friendly to me. My most unpleasant symptoms have either disappeared or become very favorably modified. Still, I do not flatter myself that I am safe, except with great care and attention to myself and the blessing of my heavenly Father. The quiet I have enjoyed here, during the past three weeks, has probably been the best thing that could have happened to me.

We shall, however, be on our way southwardly as soon as we can, and before a very great while I hope to write you from the South of France. In the meantime, believe me, with great regard, your

Very faithful friend,

GEO. W. BETHUNE."

Thence the party proceeded to the city of Tours; arriving

there about the end of November. Dr. B. made no more stay at Tours than was necessary for repose, and the fatiguing journey to Bagnères de Bigorre, Hautes Pyrenèes, was soon completed.* He wrote to Dr. Van Nest: —

"I have great reason to be thankful that I am as well as I am. I shall never recover my health. I do not murmur at my heavenly Father's will, but thank him for giving me such warning and proof of my being a pilgrim on earth. I pray him to grant me more and more grace to be ready when the moment comes at whatever hour that may be, and trust also that it is not too great importuning to ask that he would spare me so much mental and physical self-control as will prevent me being an annoyance and mortification to my friends.

The news of the San Jacinto affair reached me only the other day. Whatever may be thought of it at home, it looks ugly over here. John Bull is rearing and roaring like one of his namesakes in Bashan. For myself I cannot help thinking that we had so much on our hands before, as to make it imprudent to take him by the horns. I cannot think that the *game was worth the candle, i. e.*, that Slidell and Mason are worth the trouble we put ourselves in to catch them.

My attention has been turned with greater interest to the history of the Huguenots, and then very naturally to the present condition of evangelical Protestantism in France; we, in the United States, have been not a little misled on the subject, having been made to think that the evangelical cause here has been wholly or in part upheld by a comparatively small number of Congregationalists dissenting from the regular Reformed Church, which is like our own in Presbyterianism and some other important respects, while the fact is that the number of *non*-dissenting Christians is both increasing and influential. I think that whatever we do should be for the support and encouragement of piety *in* the church itself, and not for the uprearing of a new and foreign sect, whose whole ecclesiastical constitution is at variance with the Huguenot traditions and sacred glory.

I still hope to be of use in the cause of Evangelical Protestantism in Southern Europe, but it will be acting on my *own hook.*

* At this place he made a formal resignation of his pastoral charge in Twenty First Street, but it was never acted upon by the ecclesiastical authorities.

The French National Reformed Church is own sister to our Reformed Church; and I should be glad to see a closer sympathy between *our* people and the noble band of Confessors for the truth in that body.

Opposite stands the neat Protestant Chapel, of which the most excellent minister, the Rev. M. Frossard, (same name really as our old friend, *Sir John Froissart* of the Chronicles, who was a canon somewhere in this part of the country) is preacher. He is a capital preacher and my kind, good friend. He has another chapel at Tarbes, some fifteen miles off, whither he goes on Saturday afternoon, and preaches on Sunday morning, when he drives over here in time to preach in the afternoon at three. Mr. F. also preaches on Friday, at 3 P. M. There is also an Episcopal or Church of England Chapel (in a room at present, but the chapel is to be built when they get money for it, which, I fear, is in the paulo post future,) and I go to church, as our English neighbors call it, at 11 A.M., where I enjoy the Scriptural readings, the always excellent collect for the day (you must have observed how very good those collects are), say the Lord's prayer four or five times, hear prayers for the Queen half a dozen times, get up and down as often as is *rubrical* and listen to a sermon at least negatively good, pay a few francs at the door in answer to an announcement by the preacher that the service is maintained wholly by voluntary contributions. By the way, there is nothing I do more cheerfully than make contributions for such a purpose, whether it be for Church of England service or that of the French church. The Church of England deserves great praise for the zeal they show in having worship in English wherever they can. It is like springs in the desert, oftentimes one hears an excellent sermon, but always the Scriptures. Psalms, Gospel and Epistle are good for our learning, and the prayers, substantial and evangelical (of which by constant repetition we get a little tired), sound more fresh in a land of foreign speech. Mr. F. is indefatigable. On Tuesday he was off at 6 A.M. to Carterets, perhaps thirty miles distant, to see the rafters of another chapel raised. I believe that he preaches every day somewhere. I have great pleasure in his society, and as he speaks enough tolerable English to make up for my intolerable French (the only instance of insincerity about the man is his insisting that I express myself três, três, três bien), we get along very well together."

My religious privileges in the 'Reformed French Church' here are very great. The minister is one of the best men and best preachers I have ever met with, and the mode of worship, with some slight variation in the order of the several parts, is our own. 1. Invocation, 2. Singing, 3. Reading Commandments, 4. Confession of sins in the form written by Beza, 5. Scripture, 6. Prayer, 7. Sermon introduced by a salutation, 8. Prayer with Lord's Prayer and Creed, 9. Singing, 10. Benediction. 'The Lord bless you and keep you,' &c. &c., and at the door the Deacon holds out his black bag with '*Souvenez-vous des pauvres, au nom de Dieu.*'

On Christmas day we had the Lord's Supper after an admirable sermon on the Song of the Angels, Luke ii., 14.

The only changes from the ordinary service were the *reading of a form* or liturgical office for the Supper, and we went forward two by two to receive the Sacrament from the hands of the pastor, he addressing us at the time some comfortable words of Scripture. A solemn address out of the Liturgy followed, a brief thanksgiving, singing a version of the Song of Zacharias, a special remembrance of the poor, and the blessing."

In this connection we quote portions of a letter to the Christian Intelligencer, one of Dr. Bethune's last efforts, the writing of which tried his health. It will be perceived that he had passed into Italy.

"FLORENCE, ITALY, *April* 3, 1862.

MR. EDITOR: Since my last writing to you, we have, by God's blessing, been able to come from the Pyrenees here, passing through Provence and along the Riviera, some of the most charming portions of France and Italy. We traveled slowly by carriage, making from thirty-five to forty miles a day, and resting a day or more whenever our invalid needed respite from exertion. I was thus necessarily prevented from getting my letters or papers, and from writing myself.

For yourself, my friend, you do not deserve an apology, as you neglected to send me the number of the *Intelligencer* containing my letter, or that containing the communication it seems to have called forth from Dr. Baird. There is a characteristic 'oiliness' about everything that the Doctor says or writes, which saved my head from being hurt, although he may have been roused to such unusual exertion by my having intruded on his *specialité*. Bnt he must learn to consider that, in this age of fast steamers and railroads, there are many travellers who are neither blind nor deaf; and that monopolies of infallibility, even in religious matters, are no longer secure.

A word in a friend's letter suggests that Dr. Baird was 'replying' to me, which was not so obvious, as the Doctor does not touch at all the main point to which I directed my remarks, which was, that, as a *Reformed Church*, our *Church* should sympathize with the *Reformed Church* of France, and, if possible, aid our sister communion by aiding the treasury of its Evangelizing Society, *La Société Centrale d' Evangelisation*. The Doctor has confounded the *preface* with which you, Mr. Editor, introduced my letter, with the letter itself. It was you, sir, not I, who called 'The American and Foreign Christian Union,' (twelve syllables) Dr. Baird's Society (seven syllables). It was, nevertheless, a natural phrase for an editor's rapid pen, and one no one would doubt the meaning of. There may be some persons, who, amidst the multitudes of Christian Unions, would not at once distinguish *the* Society; but who does not know Dr. Baird? On this side of the sea, the Society's name is little known, or lost in translation; but Dr. Baird's name is far-famed and untranslatable. 'Oh! we all know Dr. Baird,' I frequently heard, though once it was 'Robin Baird.' The Society is his, as truly as Minerva was Jupiter's daughter, having sprung from his brain; and, with some imperfections (for that which is born of man is often as imperfect as that which is born of woman), a very good invention it is. I should know something of it, as I took part in the first large public meeting to aid the movement, which was held at Philadelphia, in the year 1835, (?) I think, in the Central (then Rev. Dr. McDowell's) church. Since then, I have spoken at a number of its anniversaries, and other public meetings, and preached one of its annual sermons. Indeed, I am quite sure that Dr. Baird never made a request of me on behalf of his Society (or for himself either, for that matter) which I did not comply with.

It is true, the Society has a President, the best-beloved of us Dutchmen, Vice-Presidents a score, and all the articulated anatomy of those religious bodies, whose government is not Episcopal, Congregationalist, or Presbyterian, but *Secretary-ism*; that is, they have a Board, which meets to do what the Secretary has predetermined shall be done. The Doctor, while he retains his name, cannot throw off his identity with the founder, the inspirer, and engineer of the Society, and must bear his consequent responsibility. Indeed, I once heard a distinguished lady (widow of an eminent Governor), on coming home from Europe, express her surprise that 'Paris was so irreligious, after all Dr. Baird had done for France.' Be this as it may, neither Dr. Baird's name nor that of his Society is in all my letter. Neither does the Doctor's communication impugn any statement I made, but, on the contrary, confirms nearly all that I said.

If I chose, I could show why I do not agree with his statements about the pure Presbyterianism of either the Free Church of France (which is as like the Free Church of Scotland, as a horse-chestnut is like a chestnut horse, and whose polity may be best described as *F. Monod-ism*,) or of the 'Free Synod of Geneva.' But as all that is irrelevant to my letter, I postpone any more words, until I can give you convincing proof that such Presbyterianism would scarcely pass muster with us. I can hardly regret that my letter called forth the long document of Dr. Baird, as it is a very able, and, some things excepted, a most instructive paper. No man knows the subject on which it treats so well as Dr. Baird, who has been some thirty years and more studying it, and has had (as every one knows who has listened to his conversational lectures) rare opportunities of intercourse with European celebrities, from crowned heads and philosophers down.

Neither was it I (it was you, Mr. Editor) who *found fault* with Dr. Baird's Society for appointing an undue number of Congregationalists as their agents in their work. I had no right to find fault with a Society made up of different denominations for acting as their name 'Union' required. If a Congregationalist was a good agent, they had no right to reject him because of his sect. What I meant to say was, that it is more consistent *for us as a Church* to employ agencies resembling our own, and to assist our sister Reformed Church to carry on their work, than to employ or act through agencies not in harmony with, but, in fact, at variance with, the Reformed Church, which every person well-informed on the subject, must be surprised to hear Dr. Baird say is inferior as a representative of Presbyterianism, to the so-called '*Union* of Evangelical Churches,' which he thinks is a *synod.* Why do not they *call* it a synod? Is the (Dr. Baird's) 'Christian *Union*' a synod? And why not a union of *Presbyterian* churches, if they be a union of Presbyterian churches only, *and none other?* But more of this anon.

Dr. Baird may have reasons for objecting to my letter, but he has no right to do so. There are scores of intelligent Christians at home, who will agree with me that they had been led to believe the corruption in the National French Church was greater than Dr. Baird unites with me in declaring it to be, and must rejoice with me in discovering the more agreeable truth. My views respecting an opening of usefulness for our own church, should circumstances in Divine Providence permit us to enlarge our present scheme of missionary operations, involves no opposition to Dr. Baird's Society; and my past course in reference to the Christian Union has been utterly the reverse of unfriendliness to it, or to Dr. Baird himself.

The fact is, Mr. Editor, Dr. Baird has happily confirmed every idea in my letter, except that our Dutch Church should sympathize with the French Church, and support its missionary society, rather than a schismatic, dividing few, whose principal method of begging consists in misrepresenting the National Church.

Why has not Dr. Baird's Society encouraged *that* Church to send to the United States a deputation to make a special appeal? I am sure that they would be met with welcome by our Reformed Churches, and that we would regard them as in most important particulars homogeneous with ourselves. I am indignant at Dr. Baird's impeachment of the orthodox sufficiency of their liturgy and catechism! He makes it under the indistinct non-committal phrase, '*it is said*,' etc. Does Dr. Baird say it? Will he say that the liturgy and catechism of the National Reformed Church of France have been altered in such a way 'as might be expected by heterodox or latitudinarian ministers,' or in other words, so as to teach errror or suppress truth? If Dr. Baird himself makes the accusation, I am ready, not in a wiggle-waggle style, but directly and responsibly to assert that, after close examination, I cannot discover anything unsound, equivocal, or defective. In fact, all the mode of worship is so strikingly like our own, that, with the exception of some variation in the mere order of the parts, I could have thought myself in the Middle Dutch Church of former days.

But you shall soon have the documents, as a young friend who leaves this for a slow journey home to-morrow, has promised to take a package for me to New York.

Your friend and brother,

GEO. W. BETHUNE."

"My desire was to bring before our Reformed Church such facts as might awaken our sympathy for the Reformed Church of France, and possibly secure some help for their propagandist society, *la société centrale.*' The true men in that church are struggling manfully but Christianly with the remnant of errorists within their body, with their hindrances from the State law, and with popery and infidelity all around them. I think that they know best how to carry on their proper work under God, and that what we intend for evangelization in France, we had better send immediately to that society which is really the Domestic Missionary Board of the French Reformed Church, instead of sending it by other hands. My plan would be to get Synod to address a letter of Christian salutation and counsel to the French Reformed Church; and if it can be, to get *our* Foreign Board to take charge of any money good Christians among us may be willing to give for evangelization in France, and send it directly to '*la société centrale.*' I think such a letter expressing our faith in the divinity and atonement of Christ, and work of his Spirit, would be most welcome to the pious portion of that body, and greatly strengthen their hands and hearts."

Thus was he in that foreign land working for Christ's cause. Oh! what a great heart of love filled his bosom. Read his last letter to us, written two weeks before his death:

"It made me not a little sad to think of the actual termination to our colleague-ship, not long, but running through two pleasant years, during which I learned to know you so well, and to love you more, the more I knew you. What nice times we have had together, at least I hope you think so, the perfect homishness and *abandon* with which I sank down into that old chair, and smoked the pipe which you or your brother John had filled and handed to me. I almost blush to think how egotistically I presumed on being welcome at all times, and to everything; although it was 'the woman' tempted me, your inestimable Mrs. Van Nest, blessings on her! Then our more solemn moments, when we alternated prayer and sermon, never, I think, differing from one another, always sympathizing; only you a little too deferential to the older man, who nevertheless enjoyed it as coming from an honest and kind affection.

I sincerely enjoyed also my share of the work; sometimes, it is true, not quite sure that I kept my mind in unison with the people, or that they gave themselves up to my guidance in thought; but, nevertheless, bent upon preaching the simple and entire gospel to do them good, and discharging my duty so far as I might be enabled. I never knew the people as well as I wished, but the faces of most of those not too remote in their sittings in pulpit and lecture-room, rise to my mind's eye with photographic distinctness. I hope that by God's blessing I did some of them some good. My last regular work was done by your side, and I, who, in former years had held up so many, leaned upon your strong friendship, 'Very pleasant hast thou been to me! thy love to me was wonderful!' Pray for me still, I need your prayers, all your pr. yers."

What grace, what love, what modesty, what gratitude, what holy purpose shine in that letter. The man who wrote it was at the gate of Heaven. His epistles at this time remind us much of good Mr. Rutherford. The last letter in our possession was addressed to Dr. Dunglison :

"FLORENCE, *April* 18, 1862.

MY DEAR DOCTOR: It is a long time since I wrote to you, and in the meantime my indebtedness has been increased by your pleasant and very welcome letter, in which you roast me for being in a stew about my boils, although they were also accompanied by considerable *fri*cation (oh! Dr. B.). They had gradually become beautifully less since my leeching, and now have disappeared altogether. I am rather sorry for it, as I thought they might serve to draw off attention from my head. So that though there was no fun in having so many excrescences, I rather regret to tell you they are gone. *Quis talia fando temperet a lachry-*

mis? Who can help missing a lack of them. However, dear doctor, I have not had any ill turn since I wrote you, but have been very comfortable in most respects. I have not written sooner because we had a long journey from Bagnères here, during which I was too much hurried, or too tired, or both, to use my pen. It was a more difficult and fatiguing voyage for Mrs. Bethune, than even I had feared; for the rest, we escaped accident or serious injury, and our route was through a pleasant country.

It is so difficult for Mrs. Bethune to get on board a steamer, that we came by land, railway or carriage, the whole way, being nearly a month about it, and reaching here on the 15th of March. My nephew left us on the 24th, so that, in some respects, we are more lonely, but are compensated by there being quite a number of American friends all around us. We are still at a hotel but go to lodgings next week for a couple of months, after which we shall probably take ourselves to the Baths of Lucca for the summer.

As for the climate, what can you say for any climate in April? When the sun shines it is delicious; when it rains, or when there is snow on the Appenines it is trying to the nerves. However, I have liked it on the whole. Mrs. B. does not, although I hope the summer will make it more pleasing in her eyes. Though the prices of things have increased, the charms of Florence have not been diminished. The same treasures of art, the same loveliness of surrounding scenery, attract the voyager from all parts of the world, giving the resident from abroad an excellent society of whatever character he prefers; so that I know no place more eligible for a sojourn or a more protracted stay. There are just now so many pleasant American people here that with the addition of a few Scotch and English my visiting list is a little too large for convenience. We have also valuable and extensive libraries and collections, but I have little time for study. I was very tranquil (so far as news about our country throughout the Trent excitement would allow me to be) at Bagnères. I am more interested and amused here. I brooded too much at Bagnères. I am more active at Florence. The good news from home has brightened the world for me, and I have courage respecting the progress of events but we await with some excitement of anxiety the issue at No. 10, Corinth, Richmond, New Orleans, Savannah, and other places.

I have no disagreeable symptoms of late. I endeavor to obey your directions in every thing, although I cannot entirely suppress the apprehensiveness which is so natural to one in my physical condition."

Dr. Bethune's plan in coming to Italy involved the idea of Christian activity. He had been encouraged with the hope that he might find a sphere of usefulness in the little American Chapel at Florence, but the ground was well occupied by Rev. E. Hall. Then it was suggested that he should go to Rome, but "the American and Foreign Union had no chapel there. Gov. Randall, who was appointed ambassador to the papal city had not remained, and Cardinal Antonelli will not allow the Protestant Americans to have a place of worship. An American ambassador, whose house is America, could have it if he choose; a consul cannot." Probably it was a kind Providence that kept him from assuming this responsibility.

CHAPTER XV.

CLOSING SCENES.

It remains to chronicle the death of this good man and faithful soldier of Jesus Christ. Although the body had given some symptoms of failure, yet the lively letters quoted, the genial converse, and continued preaching, prove that his intellectual powers remained undimmed to the last.

On the 23rd of March he preached in the American Chapel on the "Transfiguration." His manner was earnest, and his sermon deeply interesting and impressive. He attended a prayer-meeting held in the English Church in behalf of Matamoras and his persecuted companions in Spain, where his address produced a marked effect. He also offered prayer; and his first thought when he came out of the meeting was that a similar meeting for prayer, uniting the Italians of the different congregations, should be held every day at twelve o'clock. He saw in such a service a means of promoting Christian fellowship which might accomplish much good.

He preached again in the American Chapel, April 20th, Easter Sunday. His subject was the "Resurrection." It was a most eloquent, edifying, and comforting discourse. Contrary to the solicitations of Mrs. Bethune he preached extempore. He had the idea that an extempore sermon would excite him less than a written one. Though his discourse awakened strong emotion both in himself and his hearers, yet no serious consequences appeared to follow the effort. Thursday, the 24th, Mrs. Hall accompanied the Doctor to the Baths of Lucca in search of a house, as it was his desire to pass the summer there.

He had also preached for the Scotch minister several times, and on the 27th of April he agreed to assist him again. In the morning, Mrs. Bethune heard him singing in his bedroom, "Keep me from fainting in my prayers." He was depressed, but insisted upon meeting his engagement on account of Mr. McDougall's domestic affliction. The text of the sermon was singularly appropriate to the event which followed; Matt. ix., 2. "And behold they brought unto him a man sick of the palsy, lying on a bed; and Jesus seeing their faith said unto the sick of the palsy, Son, be of good cheer; thy sins be forgiven thee." Mr. McDougall thought he saw an unwonted slowness in speaking, slight incorrectness in reading the Psalms and Scriptures, but others observed no sign of failure. After service, Dr. Bethune did not feel well, and requested Dr. Hazlett his physician to go with him to the vestry. The medical man accompanied him to his lodgings, where he soon fell asleep upon his chair while talking with Miss Hazlett. He was awakened to be placed upon a bed, while leeches were applied, but the fatal stroke of apoplexy had come. He attempted to speak but could not; he recognized his beloved wife for a moment, and pressed her hand, after which he became unconscious, and continued so till near midnight, when with little suffering, only a shivering of the body, he departed this life to a blessed immortality.

On the last evening of his life, while watching the setting sun, he said to Mrs. Bethune,

"Oh! Mary, how I wish that you loved Florence as I do. It is beautiful to live in and pleasant to die in."

It was much against her will that he preached on the following morning; for she had noticed a restlessness in his eye and manner, which, ever watchful and apprehensive as she was, she did not like; and was much relieved when, after the service, she heard his cheerful voice in the adjoining apartment. He begged her not to scold him for having been preaching extemporaneously. She looked sorrowfully, and said, "How could you? You must be tired." He answered, "A little."

The following was found in Dr. Bethune's portfolio, and was evidently written on the Saturday before his death.

"When time seems short and death is near,
And I am prest by doubt and fear,
And sins, an overflowing tide,
Assail my peace on every side,
This thought my refuge still shall be,
I know the Saviour died for me.

His name is *Jesus*, and he died
For guilty sinners crucified;
Content to die that he might win
Their ransom from the death of sin,
No sinner worse than I can be,
Therefore I know he died for me.

If grace were bought, I could not buy;
If grace were coined, no wealth have I;
By grace alone I draw my breath,
Held up from everlasting death,
Yet since I know his grace is free
I know the Saviour died for me.

I read God's holy word, and find
Great truths which far transcend my mind,
And little do I know beside
Of thoughts so high, so deep and wide;
This is my best theology,
I know the Saviour died for me.

My faith is weak, but 'tis thy gift;
Thou canst my helpless soul uplift,
And say 'Thy bonds of death are riven,
Thy sins by me are all forgiven,
And thou shalt live from guilt set free
For I, thy Saviour, died for thee.'"

We present the notes of his last sermon, but as he had preached on the same topic in New York, they may not have been prepared for the occasion. These however were not read, as the notes were forgotten, or left behind by the speaker.

"'Behold they brought to him a man sick of the palsy, lying on a bed; and Jesus, seeing their faith, said unto the sick of the palsy, Son, be of good cheer, thy sins be forgiven thee.' Matthew ix., 2.

To a careless reader, there might appear but little difference between one of our Lord's curative miracles and another. Yet when we come to observe them closely, each, while they all unite in setting forth his mightiness and willingness to save, has some peculiar lesson or tender encouragement, so that there is not a variety of spiritual need or distress, which cannot find in some particular ministration of the Saviour's mercy to bodily infirmity, a parable of his grace to the sinners and the penitent.

Sometimes to heal with a word, sometimes with a touch, sometimes he touching them, sometimes they touching him. Sometimes the afflicted came to him, sometimes he goes to them, sometimes, as in the case before us, the sufferer is brought by his believing friends— but if the application be only made, and the sick one be fairly brought to his notice, he heals him, no matter what the disease be, or how desperate its degree. It is for this reason that the Holy Ghost has caused the evangelists, especially Matthew and Luke, to record with so much simplicity and often particularity, his wonderful acts of tenderness and relief. He himself tells us, that while we are to listen to the gracious words of salvation which proceeded out of his mouth, we are to believe him for his 'works' sake.'

Sin brought in death; and the accompaniments, precursors and consequences of death and the effects of sin—the decay, the death, the corruption of the body, show us the greater decay, the more fearful death, the eternal condemnation of the sinful soul so that none but He who could forgive sin could heal the body, and He who could and was willing to heal the body, could and was willing to forgive sin.

Let us, my fellow-sinners, take the case before us and see what encouragement there is for us to hope in the mercy of Christ. The simple words of the verse present us with the scene. The palsied man lying on a bed gazing beseechingly up to Jesus, the friends who had brought him standing around him in silent yet confident expectation of his cure, and the blessed Master regarding their faith with affectionate sympathy because of their kindness to their helpless friend, and then turning with divine pity to the sufferer himself, delighting himself with the change which his merciful and mighty words work in his feelings and in his soul. No painter could group them better, but no pencil could give the expression of their countenances, especially the Godlike compassion and power of Him who delighted to save.

First. Consider the man's need. He was sick of the *palsy*. A disease peculiarly prostrating. Taking away, often in a moment without warning—all the control which the will has over the muscles, so that the part of the system affected—is, so far as the power of voluntary motion is concerned, dead.

The consciousness of impotence is humiliating. The paralytic has nothing of his own to rely upon. He is dependent upon the help of others.

He has no hope of a cure. This man was very bad. He is so helpless that he lies supine and passive, and must be carried.

Second. Consider the comfort he received. Be of good cheer.

No other living man had a right so to address him, for it was mockery to tell a man who was to lie in such helplessness, to be of good cheer. Still it was true that God could help him, and it was as clear that since God had come in human likeness to stand by his side and tell him to be of good cheer, that God would help him, as we find the Immanuel did. Our Lord always required faith of those who sought his help; and there could be no faith where there was not hope—nor hope where there was not good cheer.

Third. The method of comfort. Thy sins be forgiven thee.

It was radical—it must abound to the root and cause of the evil—the faith of his Saviour, whatever suffering or trouble we have in this life after our sins are forgiven us, there is nothing that should distress us, because God is our friend. Suffering and trouble are blessings because they work out our good. We are no longer guilty convicts given over to death, but children of the heavenly Father. *Son* be of good cheer.

It was sovereign.

The Son of man had a right to forgive sin. God has a right to forgive sin; because it is against him that we have sinned. God must be just in justifying the sinner, and therefore has he appointed and accepted the meritorious righteousness of Christ, and given him power on earth to forgive sins.

It was free.

No condition, no price, no reward, no works. The blessing is simply conferred and enjoyed. It was the duty as well as the privilege of the sufferer to be of good cheer and believe that his sins are forgiven him.

LESSONS:

First; our utter ruin, helplessness, hopelessness.

Second; Christ's power to save, willingness, delight.

Third; faith, looking to, reliance upon, expectation from, Christ.

Fourth; encouragement to attempt the salvation of sinners; Christ approves our faith, sympathizes with our zeal, rewards our efforts to aid him in his work.

Fifth; duty of friends to the unconverted, value of religious friends, improvement of the advantage of having religious friends.

He concluded thus, "Do you pray that the weak and stumbling sermon this morning may receive the Divine blessing, and it will."

Suitable services were held in Forence on the following Sunday. Rev. Henry O'Neile of the English church stood in the Scotch pulpit, and chose for his text, Numbers, x., 29. "We are journeying unto the place of which the Lord said, I will give it you: come thou with us, and we will do thee good: for the Lord hath spoken good concerning Israel."

"These words strike at the root of all our deep-laid plans, all our distant prospects, all our notions of happiness, which have only the world for their place or its direction for their limits. Since the last Sabbath when we assembled within these walls, we have seen the minister of God, still in the prime of his usefulness and mental vigor, coming from the pulpit where for the last time he delivered the message of salvation, which he loved to speak of, and which he knew how to announce with such power, just returning to his chamber to resign his spirit into his Saviour's hands. But

> "It matters little what hour o' the day
> The righteous falls asleep; death cannot come
> To him untimely, who is fit to die;
> The less of the cold earth; the more of Heaven,
> The briefer life, the longer immortality!'"

Soon the sad news was wafted across the Atlantic, and the Christian community of America bemoaned their leader. The churches in which he had ministered, at Rhinebeck, Philadelphia, Brooklyn and Twenty-First Street, clothed themselves in mourning. Funeral sermons were preached in these and other churches, and the discourses of Drs. W. J. R. Taylor in Philadelphia, Isaac Ferris in Brooklyn, and A. R. Thompson in New York, were afterwards published. The Christian Intelligencer, the organ of the Dutch church, shaded its columns with black. When the event was announced in the General Assembly of the Presbyterian Church, (O. S.), it adjourned in token of respect to the illustrious dead. The Historical Society of New York held a special meeting to commemorate him, when Mr. Bancroft and Rev. Dr. Osgood spoke in his praise. The American

Philosophical Society directed an Obituary notice to be prepared by Dr. Robley Dunglison. It was read before the Society and printed in pamphlet form. The testimonies of respect in the secular as well as religious press, expressed the general feeling that "a prince and a great man had fallen in Israel."

The remains of Dr. Bethune were embalmed and sent to the United States by the British bark, Undine ; the funeral services were held at the Reformed Dutch Church, corner of Fifth Avenue and Twenty-Ninth Street. It was a remarkable circumstance that he had given particular directions as to his funeral.

"Put on me my pulpit gown and bands, with my own pocket Bible in my right hand. Bury me with my mother, my father and my grandmother, in the family vault at Greenwood. I have had pleasant Christian fellowship with all evangelical denominations, so let my pall-bearers be taken from them all. Thus: Drs. Hutton, Cutler, Storrs, Mr. Van Dyke, Dr. Prentiss, or, if he cannot be had, Dr. William Adams, Rev. Mr. Davie of Flatlands, Rev. Mr. Wheaton Smith of Philadelphia, Dr. Kennedy or some like-minded Methodist, as Dr. McClintock or Mr. Milburn. Let a scarf be sent to Dr. Vinton of Trinity, New York, and Rev. Dr. Smith Pyne, of Washington.

Dr. Hutton and Mr. Willets to speak not in eulogy but in such terms of affection as they may choose, testifying to my love of preaching the simple gospel, and that for my Master's honor, not mine. Mr. Quackenbush and Dr. Taylor of Philadelphia to pray. Dr. Ferris to read the sentences from the funeral service prepared by me in the Reformed Dutch Liturgy. Braun's funeral chant from 1st Corinthians, xv., by the Twenty-First Street choir, to be sung, asking the Millers of Brooklyn to join them, and Mr. Johnson if he can. Our own young organist Harrison will play; sing also my own hymn, 'It is not death, to die," to a cheerful tune, and at the close (if it can be done,) Hommann's great Doxology, 'Now unto Him that loved us.' I should like also that my dear friends Mr. J. B. Stewart, Mr. Sutphen, Mr. James N. Prentice, and Mr. Trott, if they have no objection, would take their place among the mourners, for they will be true mourners I know. The above may be modified in any way by my beloved wife who always does what pleases me, but I have written the above to save her trouble at a time when I know her sorrow will be great. God bless her till we meet in bliss for Christ's sake. Amen." *

Death and other causes led to changes in the pall-bearers, but the programme was carried out as far as possible.

His beautiful hymn runs thus :

"It is not death to die
To leave this weary road,
And midst the brotherhood on high,
To be at home with God.

It is not death to close
The eye long dimmed with tears,
And wake in glorious repose,
To spend eternal years.

It is not death to bear
The wrench that sets us free
From dungeon-chain, to breathe the air
Of boundless liberty.

It is not death to fling
Aside this sinful dust,
And rise, on strong exulting wing,
To live among the just.

Jesus, thou Prince of Life!
Thy chosen cannot die;
Like thee, they conquer in the strife,
To reign with thee on high.

* These directions were committed to his wife's faithful attendant, Annie Dunbar, directly after the funeral of his mother.

The choir objected that the music was unsuited to the mournfulness of the occasion, and wished that it should be stated that it was not of their selection; but it was evident that Dr. Bethune did not wish his funeral to be over sad. He who had led such a life of joyful thanksgiving would have his death brightened by the sunshine of the resurrection.

Nature also smiled cheerily. The closing scene was briefly sketched by "Irenæus," Rev. Dr. Prime, of the N. Y. Observer:

"You will remember that when his gentle and noble heart was still, they embalmed his form and sent it home to us, that we might lay it with his sainted parents' dust. For three long months it was on the sea, and we feared the bark that bore it had been lost, and our friend had found his tomb in the unfathomed caves of ocean, there to rest till the sea gives up its dead. But the winds and waves had been charged with their errand, and they brought their burden safely here. And now devout men were bearing him to his burial.

It was at the close of a lovely September day when the procession reached Greenwood Cemetery. The tomb, to which it pursued its mournful way, was in the most picturesque portion of the grounds. On a hillside that slopes to a lake in the middle of which a fountain leaps and falls, surrounded by lofty forest trees, and among them white marble monuments marking the repose of the dead, here on this hlll-side the procession rested, and found the open tomb. At the head of it stood Chancellor Ferris, and on either side of him the officiating ministers and the bearers, many of them the most venerable and distinguished of the clergy, in their pulpit gowns with white scarfs, their gray heads uncovered and reverently bowed as the Chancellor read the words of Holy Writ, and the body of our departed brother was lowered into the tomb, and laid with his parents, and his grandmother Isabella Graham. The sun was just setting. Italy rarely if ever sees a more glorious sunset. Its last rays lingered in sympathy with us as we wept that the light of our friend's face, and voice, and love, like the sun, was going out in the darkness of the grave; but when we heard the rapturous words, 'this mortal shall put on immortality,' 'I am the resurrection and the life,' we saw him rising and soaring, not on the wings of seraphic eloquence, but clothed in white raiment, with palms of triumph in his hand before the throne of God and the Lamb, a glorified body and soul, rejoicing with the Redeemer and the redeemed in his Father's house.

O blessed are the dead who die in Christ. Why stand we here weeping when our brother and friend is blessed in the full enjoyment of God. One, far away, receives the sympathy of our hearts; for her, bereaved and desolate, unable to follow her beloved to his grave, and detained below while he has gone above, for her we weep, but why for him? We hear the voice of the prophet, 'Weep ye not for the dead, neither bemoan him, but weep sore for him that goeth away; for he shall return no more, nor see his native country.' So wept we when BETHUNE went away; sorrowing that we should see his face no more. But now we will thank God that his brow is covered with heavenly glory, and he is among the stars with those who turned many to righteousness.

Too soon for us, too soon for thy poor bleeding land, too soon for the struggling Church, but not too soon for thee, wast thou borne away from this world of conflict to thy serene abode on high. Would I were with thee, or even within sight of thy radiant crown!"

"Call no man happy till he dies," was the ancient saying. Not until the record is complete can we pronounce life a success. But Dr. Bethune's work was now finished and what could we desire to change for the better? His last days were undoubtedly very pleasant days. Spent in that charming Florence, his favorite city, surrounded by delightful society, for he wrote that if he had a chapel there it would be full of people; his last occupation preaching the gospel and speaking from that text which he felt appropriate to his own condition; saved from that incapacity which he so much dreaded; taken almost in a moment of time from the services of the church militant to the church tri umphant; dying on the Lord's day and on that part of the day which he always considered his own Sabbath, when, the toil of the sanctuary ended, he might repose in sweet communion with God, with his dear wife by his side, on the Sabbath evening this blessed saint fell asleep in Jesus. If we had studied to arrange the circumstances could any conclusion of life be made more grand, more beautiful, more merciful?

What addition would we make to his professional success! From his first preaching to the slaves and sailors at Savannah to his last efforts in Twenty First Street, New York, he was welcomed with the same enthusiasm. His public life was a continued ovation. The New York audience which cheered his appearance for several minutes expressed the general sentiment. The denomination with which he was connected offered him everything she had to give. She offered her best churches, and more than once elected him as Professor of Theology.

When any important charity was to be advocated, when any new temple was to be set apart for the service of God, when any great interest was be promoted, when any fundamental principle affecting the church of Christ was to be settled, he was the man to whom we all looked. Thus honored at home he gained us honor abroad. Each of the great catholic Societies invited him to be its orator. Before the American Board of Foreign Missions, the American and Foreign Christian Union, the Sabbath Association, and the American Sunday School Union, he preached the accustomed sermon. He was almost an annual speaker at the Seamen's Friend and Colonization Societies, while he appeared over and over again at the Anniversaries of the Bible and Tract Societies. Academical favors were lavished richly upon him; Harvard, Yale, Dartmouth, Brown University, Columbia, Andover, Union, and many other colleges were charmed with his eloquence. In fact, on all great public occasions, when a statue of Washington was to be inaugurated, when the Brooklyn water-works were to be opened, when the Historical Society was to erect a building, when honor was to be paid to some great name, when the Union was to be preserved, or war to be proclaimed against traitors to the Constitution, Dr. Bethune was the man for the hour.

But all this success, this applause of the world, never diverted him from the great duties of his office. Nay, he employed all these occasions as so many instruments of drawing men to his church and his Saviour. Thirty years before, he had declared his solemn purpose: "'My son,' said my dying father, the accents of parental and Christian affection struggling with the weakness of approaching death, 'tell dying sinners of a Saviour; all the rest is folly.' The command is safe in my heart, and the cross of Christ shall be the ever welcome and exhaustless burden of my addresses; and whether, O God, I die in my pulpit or on my bed, may my last words be, 'the cross of Christ! the cross of Christ! Jesus Christ and him crucified!'" Never did he fail from the promise then made, preaching always the simple, sincere gospel, and with his dying breath telling of Christ's power to comfort and heal.

It was moreover a merciful Providence that gave him a season of preparation for death. The prostration at Brooklyn, the anxiety at New York, might be considered misfortunes, but these were God's messengers of warning and were well improved. Dr. Bethune knew not the day, the hour of his death, but he felt that it might come instantly and made all his arrangements with perfect composure.

Then there was a wonderful preaching from his death itself. Before Elijah ascended to heaven he was led through the country, to visit the schools of the prophets going from Gilgal to Bethel, from Bethel to Jericho, from Jericho to the Jordan; everywhere bearing high testimony to his Master. So it happened with Dr. Bethune; God led him round about to confirm the churches. We must count it a singular Providence that, having attained great eminence as a minister, he should be brought from Brooklyn to New York, there to preach his sweet discourses and win affection; then he was taken to Catskill to leave a holy impression; afterwards he was led to foreign lands to hold sweet counsel with our Reformed brethren in France; finally he reached Florence to die, but he lived long enough to speak for Jesus and show the beauty of Christian grace. Thus did this man of God journey in a holy progress, feeling that death was seated at his elbow, living all the while on the very borders of the promised land. How could circumstances have been arranged to produce a wider impression by his death? The Christian heart of Florence was saddened. The French brethren felt the loss, and several churches in this country put on sackcloth, while the universal body of Christ felt that "the chariot of Israel and the horsemen thereof" had departed.

As to the event itself it was more like a translation than an ordinary end of life. True his body remained on earth but the change was so rapid, there was such freedom from sickness and pain, such close connection between his pulpit and his crown, there was such a short step from preaching the gospel of Christ on earth and joining the great multitude

BROWN'S STATUE OF Dr. BETHUNE.

who sing the praises of Christ in heaven, his end was so peaceful and so beautiful that the horror of death was almost taken away. The chariot of fire and horses of fire were not visible, but there were ministering angels to bear his ransomed spirit home.

Then there was the direction to place his Greek Testament in his right hand, in his coffin. What did it mean? It was a suitable companion to a minister, but did not the order discover more of his faith? How gloriously he used to preach about the resurrection! If ever there was a time when he was "exalted above measure" it was in the discussion of this grand doctrine. Perhaps he thought of this; perhaps faith gave the idea. He believed in the day of Christ, as coming soon, and when awakened at the sound of the last trump he would have this precious gift of the Spirit in hand, all ready for service. His was a happy life, few better, more useful, more successful; and it was blessed, glorious dying.

Not long since certain prominent citizens of New York assembled to lay plans for the erection of a statue of Dr. Bethune. H. K. Browne, Esq., was engaged as artist, and has produced a graceful figure in plaster, which it is designed to put in enduring marble, and to place either in the hall of the Historical Society or in some suitable position in the Central Park, to commemorate one of the most eloquent and gifted sons of the emporium.

A rare marble monument, inlaid with richest mosaics of different colors, and containing a striking likeness of Rev. Dr. Bethune, is the work of the Venetian, Salviati, who has discovered the ancient Byzantine mosaic arts. The work was done at the order of Mrs. Bethune, and is probably the only specimen of the kind in this country. It is placed in the Third Reformed Dutch Church, Philadelphia, where her husband was so loved and honored. This is the inscription:

REV. GEORGE W. BETHUNE, D. D.,
Founder of this Church,
Was born in New York, March 18, 1805.
For 37 years
He rejoiced to preach the Gospel.
After his sermon,
On the Lord's Day, April 27, 1862,
God took him.

We cannot more appropriately close this chapter than with this delightful hymn of its sainted author, — which is copied from his own manuscript:—

HYMN FOR RESURRECTION DAY.

'I SEE JESUS.'

"O JESUS, when I think of thee,
Thy manger, cross and throne,
My spirit trusts exultingly
In thee, and thee alone.

I see thee in thy weakness first;
Then, glorious from thy shame,
I see thee death's strong fetters burst
And reach heaven's mightiest name.

In each a brother's love I trace
By power divine exprest,
One, in thy Father God's embrace,
As on thy mother's breast.

For me thou didst become a man,
For me didst weep and die,

For me achieve thy wondrous plan,
For me ascend on high.

O let me share thy holy birth,
Thy faith, thy death to sin,
And, strong amidst the toils of earth,
My heavenly life begin.

Then shall I know what means the strain
Triumphant of St. Paul;
'To live is Christ, to die is gain!'
'Christ is my ALL IN ALL.'"

CHAPTER XVI.

PERSONAL REMINISCENCES.

Rev. Dr. Hutton, who knew Dr. Bethune from school-days, being requested to describe his *personnel,* writes:

"You have given me a pleasant but very difficult task; one from which I shrink and which I could refuse, were it not that the mere effort enables me to gratify the love which I felt, and still feel, for one whom I rejoice to have been allowed to call 'my friend,' and who has left the touching expression of his regard for myself by selecting me, from his many and dear friends, to deliver an address at his funeral.

I shrink from the task, therefore, only because I feel that the man was larger and broader than any description which I can give of him. I am certain that I cannot present even my own ideal of him.

As to his personal appearance, I think that no one would especially admire it, unless he were personally and intimately acquainted with him. He was in every respect a large man, mentally and physically. He was above the ordinary height, but from the shortness of his neck and the breadth and rotundity of his person, this was not generally observed. The high, broad and smooth brow, and the bright, clear, blue, Scotch eye, which softened, smiled or gleamed, under his varied emotions, redeemed his face from any fault which might be found with particular features. I loved to watch the play of his face under almost any circumstances in which I was privileged to see him. To me it was always interesting, often beautiful, and sometimes grand and eloquent.

As I thus recall his appearance, there rises before me a picture which memory has embalmed, and which fills my eyes with tears. It is of his face, when I unexpectedly entered his study and found him engaged at his table, his head raised to see who was the intruder. The brow corrugated with thought, the eye stern and slightly indignant, and then to see the sudden change, like the sun breaking through the cloud, the whole face lighting up, the genial smile, and the peculiar heave of the huge shoulders as he laid aside book or pen and grasped me by the hand, is a picture not to be described, but enjoyed forever.

His features in their combination, whatever else may be said of them, were expressive of thought, humour, courage; and I am sure that were the Doctor seen in a crowd of men, he would be singled out with the inquiry' who is he?' Surrounded from his infancy with all the advantages which wealth and culture could bestow, he was in the true sense of the word a gentleman, polished and graceful in all his movements, especially in his action as a speaker. I cannot recall an ungraceful action on any occasion, and as a platform speaker he had few equals.

His voice was singularly melodious ; strong, yet soft, and of great compass, filling the largest building, and when on the platform, where the whole man could be seen, his looks, the pose of his head, every muscle of his strong marked face, the glance of his eye, the tread of his foot, and every movement of his body, were instinct with power and emotion. For these occasions, he once informed me, he only prepared himself by a general train of thought, leaving language, and, in many respects, arrangement, to the occasion ; but his mind moved so rapidly and clearly, and his thoughts arranged themselves so naturally and promptly, that they never became confused or failed to be effective. Many who remember the contest between Abolitionism and the Colonization Society, and the part which Dr. Bethune took in it, will agree with me in my estimation of him as a platform speaker. They have seen him hold large audiences completely spell-bound, filled with pleasure or interest, laughing with mirth, or thrilling with indignation, as he willed.

As a preacher I never heard him without pleasure and profit, and in many important respects I consider him to have been a glorious model. He was so in the principles which guided him as a preacher of the Gospel. He never forgot when in the pulpit, that he was the ambassador of God; and all the powers of the man were subordinated to this exalted view of his work. Dr. Bethune was poet as well as orator, he had a fine and cultivated imagination, but he never allowed it to play in the pulpit, save only in aid of the truth. The fruit was never hidden by flower or foliage. He had been a student of the Greek and Latin classics, and admired them much, but they never were allowed to appear intrusively in his sermons. His style was simple, plain, neat and direct. He was full of humour, with a vivid sense of the ridiculous; but no one who only heard him in the pulpit would imagine it; there the solemnity of his work seemed to have entirely subdued every thought and feeling inconsistent with the duties owed to his Divine Master. Were I not afraid that I might be understood to intimate that there was something artificial in his pulpit performances (which there was not), I should say that there was something *reverential* in the very tones of his voice.

This perhaps is the very word which will express my idea of his pulpit performances. The whole seemed enveloped in an atmosphere which made you remark 'That man feels that he is in the presence of God, and never forgets it'. But after all, I am not satisfied with what my pen is recording. You cannot take Dr. Bethune apart and submit his peculiarities to analysis. Dr. Bethune was just Dr. Bethune; the whole genial man modified his peculiarities and qualifications. Much as he was to be admired and esteemed in his public life, much as we may commend him as scholar, orator, poet and preacher, it was to the single friend, in the retirement of social intercourse, that the whole lovable, genial man, the brother, the childlike heart were developed. Then you were made to feel that the great and admired orator had all the simplicity of a little child, that the man whom the world delighted to honour, was an humble self-distrustful Christian; that the eloquence which delighted the large public audiences that loved to hang on his lips, was the glow of his own quiet emotions, and the natural thought of his mind. I loved Bethune, but I learned to love and admire him, not in the forum, but in the study, at the midnight hour, in the quiet scenes which were hidden from the public gaze."

In reference to his appearance Dr. Bethune told with much spirit a story which reflected upon himself. When he was pastor in New York, passing through Twenty Second street an Irish servant addressed him: "Please, Misther, will you come into the house? the Mistress would like to spake with you." The polite divine acceded to the invitation, and soon a well dressed lady appeared, expressing great pleasure in making his acquaintance ; after conversing a few moments, the Doctor said, "You wished to see me, I understand." "Indeed," replied the lady with a little confusion, "I am most happy to know Dr. Bethune ;" and then proceeded to talk volubly. "Excuse me madam," said the Doctor returning to the charge, "the servant informed me that you wished to see me particularly." "Well," confessed the lady much abashed, "if I must tell you the truth, I directed the servant that if the *fat man* came along to-day she must stop him for I wanted to speak with him."

His powers of conversation were well known, and, perhaps, in no gift did he shine more pre-eminently than in the ability to entertain a social circle. Seldom did he appear more happy than when some chosen spirits had gathered round his festive board; as for instance, "the Five," in Philadelphia; "the Friends," in Brooklyn, or the "Alpha Delta," which was the name of his ministerial club in New York.

An incident is related of a young lady who against her will was beguiled by his honeyed tongue. She had taken her seat in a car going to New York when a stout gentleman passed through, apparently looking for a place. Soon he returned and, although there were many vacant seats, he came and crowded himself by her side. His size made this intrusion the less agreeable and the lady was much displeased. He made some attempts at conversation but she resolutely looked out of the window and answered all questions in monosyllables. Still, in a few minutes, her resolution was broken and she found herself charmed with her companion. Arrived at Dr. Wainwright's house, where she had been invited to dine, what was her astonishment to find this same stout gentleman taking his seat by the side of Mrs. Wainwright, and to learn that he was one of the lights of the American pulpit, Rev. Dr. Bethune. The recognition was mutual and explanations ensued. The doctor told her that he passed through the car to select an agreeable travelling companion, that he choose a seat by her side as most promising. He noticed her aversion and determined according to his ability to overcome it. The effort had been crowned with equal success.

Dr. Bethune's beneficence has been freqnently mentioned; but an anecdote will illustrate the freedom of his gifts.

"Money in his view had no value except as it contributed to make some body happy or advanced the cause of his Master. In this view he required more salary as a minister, and a heavier purse for giving, than most men in his station in life. A debt was a burden to him, but he would not hesitate a moment to incur it when he wanted the means to fulfil the promptings of his generous heart. A friend called upon him one day in New York, a few months before he left that city for his last voyage across the Atlantic. After sitting a few minutes together in the study, Dr. Bethune was summoned to the parlor by a 'call.' It was for a charity, and he soon returned, with that pleasant look, which proves that 'it is more blessed to give than to receive.' In a short time another 'call' and he paid his five dollars, (he seldom gave less) with alacrity, but was a little annoyed at the interruptions. In less than half an hour he was again summoned to the parlor, and this time it was a lady,— a subscription to some 'to-be-published' religious work of the applicant. He returned a moment to ask if his friend could change a ten dollar gold piece; he could not, and shortly the Doctor came back once more laughing and said, 'There, they've got all the money I had in the house, and now we'll go on quietly with our talk.' He had given thirty-four dollars away in twice as many minutes, and seemed perfectly satisfied."

Mrs. Bethune remembers that on the last Christmas day spent in New York, her husband came in to dinner with an unusually happy face. She asked, "What pleases you so much?"

He replied, "I am so glad I met with the old Scotchwoman as I came through the market to buy your fruits and flowers. I saw a person, poor but neat looking, anxiously examining some chickens and said to her, 'These are poor, those are better.' She looked at me sharply and spoke in broad Scotch. 'Ah! but they are too dear for a puir body.' I told the man to put one with vegetables into her basket and turned away hastily, but she followed me with such a look of joy and surprise that I cannot help feeling happy." Probably nothing could create for Dr. Bethune such a merry Christmas as the incident above. Benevolent himself, he delighted to teach others the happiness of doing good. The invitations to preach charity sermons were numerous and he possessed a happy faculty in persuading people thus to lend unto the Lord. His mother suggested that he should keep a list of the monies thus secured for religious interests, and if it had been done the sum would have been very large.

He seemed quite destitute of the sense of fear. Mr. Trott relates that on a certain occasion the Doctor fell from a dam by which they were attempting to cross a rapid stream. The Major was greatly alarmed, expecting to see his companion borne away by the waters; but, directly afterwards, the good clergyman's head emerged from some still water, and with great composure, he handed up his watch, requesting Mr. Trott to take care of it.

But his calling was the ministry and to this he devoted his best energies. The following impression is related by that prince of pulpit description, Rev. Dr. Sprague:

"When I heard Dr. Bethune in his own pulpit the subject of his discourse was the resurrection of the dead, and I believe this was regarded as one of his finest efforts, as he had delivered the same discourse a week or two before, and repeated it then by special request.

Besides containing a luminous scriptural view of the doctrine, if my memory serves me, he indulged himself in a part of the discourse in a somewhat philosophical vein, showing that he was capable of abstruse metaphysical disquisition, though there was not so much of this as to materially diminish the effect upon a popular assembly. He exhibited his subject in its consolatory bearings with inimitable pathos, and uttered himself with a fervent sublimity that bore his audience onward and upward by an impulse that seemed quite irresistible. His manner was strikingly simple, dignified, earnest and energetic; and though there was nothing that derogated in the least from its naturalness, yet it was manifiestly the result of the highest culture and made me feel that I was in contact with not only a highly gifted, but thoroughly accomplished mind. He held his audience, for I think fully an hour, in breathless silence; a fact which I thought more noticeable, as it was in his own church and the larger part of his congregation were his stated hearers, who were familiar with his attractive peculiarities."

One of his hearers used to say that Dr. Bethune when in the height of many of his perorations in the pulpit, reminded him of the majesty of the lion when he shook his mane and showed himself the monarch of the forest.

Another, most capable of judging, writes thus of his preaching:

"I think that he excelled in the gift of leading poor sinners to Christ, because he would show them their need of salvation and leave them no other hope. He set forth God's controversy with souls which were out of Christ, more plainly than any other preacher I ever heard. It was not alone that we had fallen in Adam and were totally corrupt by nature; it was not that we are wholly unable to turn from our sinful wanderings and choose a better service; but it was because we would not come to Christ and receive life, that we were justly condemned and without excuse. He would so unfold the heart of the sinner to himself that without one descriptive epithet, he would see how destitute it was of any natural holiness or likeness to God; he would show how vainly that heart might struggle to redeem itself; he would then remove one after another of the vain reliances at which men grasp to avoid the humbling doctrines of the Cross, and leave this needy trembling soul, like Peter, sinking in the treacherous waves, with no hope except in the agonizing cry 'Lord, save me.'

But I took my pen to sketch, not the preacher, but the friend. As I recall scene after scene of social life, in which his presence not only fills the foreground, but, like a special brightness, lights up all the picture, I strive to sum in one word the secret of that radiating glory. What was the charm, always potent, which he carried to every circle? His presence was an inspiration of joy, alike to each individual and to the social group. Vast resources of learning, without pedantry; varied accomplishments, without ostentation; a fund of ready wit, which had no taint of satirical bitterness; a keener vision in discerning the secret springs of human action, with no censoriousness of spirit; an innate sense of propriety never at fault; great conversational powers, with a delicacy of taste which gave a new and graceful drapery even to familiar thoughts: — these were gifts which made it easy for him to shine in any circle. But the charm was universal, and it needed more than this to account for the never-ceasing radiance. It must have been that, beneath all these gifts and accomplishments he had, sanctified by grace, a great heart of love that was ever welling up in blessing to all around him. The genial influence which went with him like an atmosphere, could have had no other source. It was never put on: it was not in the manner, but controlled it; it was not in the speech, but dictated it; it was not in the effort to bless others, but prompted it. It was a perennial spring, full of natural overflow, but turned from nature's bitterness, like Marah's waters, by the Branch of Healing; and thenceforth a fountain of perpetual blessing to all who tasted. Those that have sat by him in his library, while the swift-winged hours went by; or have visited with him in the family, where the face of the youngest child glowed with delight at his coming, or have seen him in larger social gatherings, where no shadows came between him and the hearts about him, — will readily accept the explanation I have given of the secret of his personal influence.

But the memories that have deepest root and the most enduring fragrance, are those which associate this loving friend with the sick room or the scenes of mourning. If his presence brought such brightness to the house of joy, what a blessing came with it to the home shadowed by affliction. By the bed of pain he had that sympathizing tenderness learned only of the Master. Here he was as gentle as a ministering angel. There was soothing in the tone of his voice; there was relief in the touch of his hand; he seemed to lift the weight of anguish from the sufferer and bear part of it himself. These chords of his loving heart had been touched so often, and with such rare skill beneath his own roof, that a deeper than ordinary experience had fitted him to minister unto others. And while soothing the bodily anguish, how skillfully would he lead the soul to lay its sicknesses at the feet of One who alone could restore it.

And when the shadow deepened and bereavement came, what a clasping hand was his for that bitter hour. How near he would bring the Heavenly Home to which the loved one had been translated! And how tenderly he would gather up, one by one, the ties which seemed all broken by this visible separation, and bind them into a three-fold cord to draw the heart heavenward, not only for comfort during the hours of grief, but for strength and hope in all the future pilgrimage."

The Rev. Dr. Taylor has furnished the following reminiscences of Dr. Bethune's services and influence in the highest court of the Church.

"Dr. Bethune's bearing in *Ecclesiastical assemblies* was peculiarly dignified and impressive. His reports on important subjects, as the minutes of the General Synod attest, were full and exhaustive. In debate he was a master of logic, repartee, courtesy and strength. He watched the proceedings closely, was keenly alive to the weak points of opponents and equally sensitive to his own position and influence. Some of his most powerful speeches were delivered in these assemblies of the Church, when great questions were at issue, and able opponents stirred him up to use his whole strength. Multitudes will attest how well he could employ his native wit or his classic culture, how choice and accurate he was in his Scriptural quotations and illustrations, and how liberal and yet conservative upon all important matters of doctrine and discipline; while those who unfortunately provoked his overwhelming replies will not soon forget them.

On one occasion he produced a report respecting the State of

Religion, which embraced a censure of a class of ministers who, for their own reasons, had secularized themselves more or less, and this at a time when the lack of ministers was the greatest trial of the Church. A member of the Synod, who felt aggrieved by the report, had prepared himself as he thought to demolish its author at the next morning session.

The Doctor was at the clerk's table, ready to proceed with his own remarks, when this member in stentorian tones, called for the reading of the report. 'What part of it does the brother wish to hear?' the chairman calmly asked. 'That part which contains slanders upon the ministry,' said the member. The Doctor looked at him for a moment, then cast the report upon the table, and with withering power merely answered, 'Mr. President, I have *nothing* to read for that brother!' The charge was drawn in an instant, and the defeated assailant sank quietly into his seat, while the report was discussed and adopted.

One of the Doctor's most memorable speeches was made at a synod held in Brooklyn, in which an appeal was being heard against action of a consistory, in excluding an elder-elect from office on the ground of his being a member of an *Odd Fellows'* lodge. The debate covered the whole ground of expediency, not only respecting secret societies, but dancing and other fashionable amusements; and it gave full play to the wit, learning, and ethical skill of our eloquent friend.

The writer has a most vivid remembrance of the great debate, extending over several days in the General Synod at New Brunswick in 1855, upon the question of the erection of a new Theological Hall for the Seminary in that city. It was a critical time for the Institution, and a complication of difficulties and disappointments embarrassed it with much excitement of feeling, and awakened profound interest in and out of the Synod. The church edifice was thronged, and each party girded itself for the conflict. Dr. Bethune, as chairman of the committee on education, made an elaborate report favoring the erection of a Theological Hall and proposing plans to secure the requisite funds. The debate developed his wonderful power as a 'master of assemblies' with great tact, and with an eloquence which stamped him as one of the greatest of ecclesiastical orators. He has left nothing in print superior to some of the magnificent passages of his chief speech on this subject. But his 'winged words' were not reported, and they live only in the memories of his enchanted hearers, and in the triumphant success of the plan of which he was the principal advocate and defender in that Synod. It is a remarkable coincidence that the entire sum (about $32,000) necessary for erecting the building, was given by a former Philadelphia parishioner of the Doctor, the late Mrs. Anna Hertzog. It bears the name of her deceased husband, the 'Peter Hertzog Theological Hall'. Hundreds of young men have found in it a home and a blessing. In 1853, Dr. Bethune was appointed a member of the Committee of the General Synod for the revision of the Liturgy of the Reformed Dutch Church. The Rev. Dr. E. S. Porter, one of the Committee, says of Dr. Bethune's labors in this arduous and protracted service—for which his studies and tastes had peculiarly fitted him: First, the alteration and improvement of the prayer before sermon were by him exclusively. He also went over all the prayers, and with the incidental aid of the Committee, amended their phraseology in some places where the translator or printer had been at fault. The Burial Service was furnished by Dr. B. as it now stands. He also submitted a Marriage form, but it was not adopted entire.

From first to last, Dr. Bethune gave his constant attention to all the subject matter submitted to the Committee, and felt a sincere desire to place before the Synod a revised copy of the Liturgy, which, when adopted might secure uniformity in our public usages. But we were all obliged to bear a disappointment. The Synod fell into an interminable debate about colons, semi-colons, commas and stops of one kind and another; and at length this only was gained, that the Revised Liturgy was permitted to be published. Still, I think, it is every year growing in favor and they who use it approve the results of the Committee's honest and hopeful labors."

"Dr. Bethune was accustomed" says a writer in the Independent, probably Dr. Storrs, "to speak of his early academical training as imperfect; not however through the want of the amplest opportunities which love and wealth could furnish him, but only through the want of any purpose on his part to improve himself by means of them. But in later years he was a fond and faithful student, not of philosophy and theology only, but of the best English literature, and of the classics. Few men were more familiar with the whole circle of English eloquence and poetry; and very few certainly, outside of the professional students and teachers of the languages, were so conversant as he with the Greek and Latin letters.

On his working night, the lights rarely left his windows until long after midnight, and the large and various library he had collected, showed the breadth and variety of his mental tastes, and scholarly culture."

When he was in London Dr. Bethune gratified his taste in this direction.

"I have now got among books. There you know my chief passion lies—for, next to my sweet wife, I think I love those inanimate but ever faithful friends, who are always ready to hold communion with you, and make the heart forget its troubles in the pleasures of the soul. Of course I do not mean to say I have been reading much, that is out of the question; but there is a pleasure which the student finds in but the sight and handling of volumes with which he has long been acquainted by report, but which he has never seen before; we come to think of books as living creatures, and love to look upon their faces, as it were. Yet I have not been buying more than a very few volumes—I know I cannot afford it, and am determined to deny myself."

As to the library itself, the scene of labor where so many of his great works were prepared, it had been accumulated at large expense and with much care. In the purchase he was constantly aided by his mother. "I cannot deny myself books," he wrote to her, "it would be like muzzling the ox that treadeth out the corn."

In the year 1857, in a list of the noted private libraries of New York, that of Dr. Bethune was included, and a description of it given by Dr. Wynne:

"Dr. Bethune has but a poor opinion of his own library. Having gathered it slowly for the studies incident to his own profession, and for the gratification of such tastes as may be allowed to relieve his more severe pursuits, he regards it more as a collection of instruments of work. Every volume in it being familiar to him from use, he has never catalogued it, and scarcely suspected it of being half its real extent until, by actual count, we convinced him that it numbered at least six thousand volumes. Its rough boards and broken bindings, betray more handling than care. His excuse is that the cost of binding one book, will buy another, and the inside of two volumes is worth more than one with a neat outside ; and that a clergyman has too many calls for his money to spend it in show, and that those who get it after him may dress it as they please. A large portion of the collection is of course theological, embracing nearly all of the standard divines, Church of England, Presbyterian, Puritan and others. Among them we notice an excellent and somewhat numerous and rare group of French Protestant preachers, whom the Dr. holds in high esteem for their logical eloquence; and near them all the French Catholic preachers of celebrity. There are also several shelves occupied with the more noted Catholic writers of systems and controversy, among which stand conspicuous, the Catena Amea Summa of Aquinas ; Sanchez, the fountain-head of Jesuitical Casuistry, De Sacramento Matrimonii,—and his several followers, down to Archbishop Kendrick, besides others which furnish a ready armory to turn against the Church of Rome. Systems, critical works, ecclesiastical histories, geographies, ancient and modern and of all classes; with most of the infidel oppugnators, whose sophisms a thorough divine should understand to refute on sufficient occasions. The Fathers are far from complete, but the Doctor has secured good editions of his favourites, Gregory Nazianzen, St. Bernard, Ambrose the glorious bishop of Milan, &c, &c.

There are also many of the greater and minor Reformers, some in full, others in part, and also some rare books of curiosity, bearing on the profession. The classical portion of the library is good. Scarcely any Greek or Latin Classic from Homer to Proclus, if the Hermaic Mystic deserved the rank of a Classic. The editions are all good, most of them the best. Among them we observe all the Byzantine historians, and Kuhn's voluminous edition of the Greek medical writers, with their Latin brethren of the pill-box. The ancient geographers, writers *de re rustica*, various works on customs and art, in fact, whatever bears on classical research and gossip, like Gallius and Apulcius, are ready at hand. The student is not obliged to take anything at second hand. There is, also, a choice and curious collection of works on ancient mythologies and mysteries from modern hands, such investigations having an especial charm for the inmate of this library. Indeed, there are few subjects connected with ancient religious, or moral opinion, on which there is not one or more trustworthy volumes. The portion devoted to general literature is not full, though many good, and some very curious works are in it. Among the rest, a collection of works on Scotch and English lyrical poetry, and a shelf or so of rare books, and tracts illustrating Scotch History and literature. There are also not a few curiosities which would be eagerly coveted by a bibliomaniac. Indeed, it has been the Doctor's rule, not to buy books which can be readily obtained, but to seize on the rare, the moment an opportunity offers. Perhaps the most peculiar distinction of the library is its Waltonion department, consisting of more than *four* hundred volumes,* of all sizes and dates.

Whatever illustrates Walton or his favorite art has been carefully and perseveringly gathered from European sales and catalogues, and pains taken to have, not only the best editions, but the several editions. All the Waltons, Cottons, and Venables are there, except the second and fourth of Walton, with one or two exceptions. All the books referred to by Walton, and those which illustrate his favorite rambles by the sea, or along the Dove. Every scrap of Walton's writing, and every compliment paid him, have been gathered. With the older writers are some of the best modern on Ichthyology. Nearly every book that bears on Angling, in English, German, French, Italian, Latin and Greek is there. With some of these, particular pains have been taken, thus *Oppian*, the *editio princeps*, the *Optima*, the *Aldine*, &c., &c., &c., the English translation, French, Italian, with his several commentators. *Ausonius*, the *princeps Optima*, *Aldine* and others, with all the translations. Some of these books are very rare, a passion for angling books having been a weakness of antiquarian collectors. The collection of Sale Catalogues, marked with prices and names, is of itself a curiosity. Many of the volumes are rich in autographs, MS. notes, and rare plates; some of the volumes are elegantly published, and of no mean literary merit. A catalogue of this library was appended to the American edition of Walton's Angler, and it may be said to be the most numerous, though, perhaps, from the lack of some five or six rare books or editions, not the most valuable, in the world. Since the publication of the catalogue, it has been considerably increased, though we suspect that the owner, from the press of more serious occupations, does not allow himself so much relaxation in the gratification of his mania, as he did formerly. The department of modern

* This actually counted seven hundred volumes.

literature can find little room in the Doctor's library, and occupies a place in another apartment. It comprises many valuable works, but is not worthy of special mention here."

Dr. Bethune gave all his property by will to Mrs. Bethune; but in case she should not survive him, made the following bequest:

"All my books on theological and classical learning, or bearing upon these subjects, I give to the General Synod of the Reformed Protestant Dutch Church, for the sole, unrestricted, and perpetual use of the Theological Seminary of said Church; on condition that they put and always keep them in good order, with the name of Bethune printed on the back, and on the inside of the front cover; which shall be done to the entire satisfaction and approval of my dear friend, the Rev. Abraham R. Van Nest, Doctor in Divinity, in the first instance, the Professor of Sacred Languages, and the Professor of Theology for the time being in the said Seminary, and to the approval of them and their successors in the office afterwards."

Mrs. Bethune has carried out the intention of her husband, and a large portion of the books fill an alcove of the Library at Hertsog Hall, New Brunswick, N. J. The same room is graced with a marble bust of Dr. Bethune, executed by J. A. Jackson, Esq., an American artist, resident at Florence, Italy, who was employed by Mrs. Bethune. These valuable gifts have been handsomely acknowledged by the representatives of the church and Seminary, and the Theological Professors, considering themselves as heirs-at-law of the illustrious departed, desire to make the following record of gratitude in this memoir:

"NEW BRUNSWICK, *March* 4, 1863.

REV. DR. VAN NEST.

DEAR BROTHER: My colleagues, in the Theological Seminary, have requested me to address a few lines to you, indicating our grateful appreciation of the services rendered to the Institution, by our revered and cherished friend, the Rev. Dr. Bethune.

In his death, we feel not only a personal bereavement, but are painfully sensible also, that the Seminary, with whose prosperity and trials we are identified, has lost a tried and faithful friend, who proved his devotion to its interests, by a consistent and zealous advocacy of every measure, calculated to enlarge its sphere of usefulness. It is a great comfort to us, to be able to point to the record of a man whom Christians of every name were ready to honor, and who was justly admired and beloved in the Church which claimed him as her own; and throughout his whole ministry, to trace the evidences of a love that never wavered, and a zeal that faltered not, when danger and embarassment threatened the Theological Seminary, and when fainter hearts might have succumbed to the pressure. We can never forget that, in a great degree, we are indebted to his influence for the munificent endowment, by which Hertzog Hall, in the good Providence of God, stands this day, as the happy home of a large number of young men, who are preparing for the glorious work of the gospel ministry. Probably one of the finest efforts ever made by Dr. Bethune, in a Synodical assembly, was on a memorable occasion, when the Theological Seminary was struggling with embarrassment, and the Church was raised by his eloquent words, from despondency to the exercise of faith in her covenant God, and it is noteworthy how soon the answer came, in the liberal gift, securing the home which the Seminary so much needed."

Allusions are then made to Dr. Bethune's relations with the Institution which have been already mentioned:

"Dr. Bethune, though not a graduate of our Theological Seminary, proved his devotion to its welfare through his whole ministerial life, and gave touching evidence of his love, by bequeathing, in case he should survive Mrs. Bethune, the greater part of his costly, and well-selected library, to the Seminary. (Although this provision of his will became nugatory by reason of his decease before Mrs. Bethune's, yet it was as a law to her, and she promptly gave to it practical force by sending to us a large selection from the volumes which had been so precious to her husband.) We need scarcely say, that he could not have given to us a more acceptable token of his good will, than we find in his purpose to transfer to our charge and to our enjoyment, the scholarly companions of his hours of study and of leisure, and to bid us and our successors cherish the friends who were the solace of his own cultivated mind. They occupy their appropriate place in the alcoves of the library in Hertzog Hall, which is adorned with the marble bust of the generous friend.

We trust it will be some consolation to Mrs. Bethune to know that our sympathy in her bereavement is all the more earnest and heartfelt, from an appreciation of the character of the friend whom our Heavenly Father has taken to himself.

With kind regards, yours truly,

J. F. Berg."

We have many evidences that the night was Dr. Bethune's favorite time for work. He has left a charming poem, on "Night Study," and his friend Mr. Hillard, writes from Boston:

"Mr. Bancroft, who recalls with real pleasure the hours he spent under your hospitable roof, tells me that you work late, and that the stars of midnight look down upon you at your books, or over your manuscripts. Beware of this, it is a most seductive habit, as I well know, for I hold with him who says, 'the dead of midnight is the hour of thought,' but it is a great consumer of the oil of life."

The impression that he made upon a stranger is thus given by the Rev. Mr. Stallybrass of London:

"Rome, *December* 2, 1862.

I saw Dr. Bethune now for the first time in the vestry at Casa Schneider where I had been preaching, and the spontaneous and irresistible impression which he produced on my mind, as he entered the door was, — 'Whoever you are, you are a man of vast power.' Real greatness has no hiding-place where it may conceal itself, and the mind rises instinctively to pay it homage, as the senate on the capitol yonder was wont to rise at the entrance of an emperor. Strength sat enthroned right naturally on that noble brow of Dr. Bethune; and enforced a recognition of his dignity; and that beautiful voice, but withal so firm in its mellow tones, did not belie the presentiment I had of the masculine vigor of his intellect. The evening which I had the pleasure of passing with him at the house of Mr. Duncan, convinced me that the native robustness of his faculties was greatly enhanced by their wide, catholic and generous culture; that he had intermeddled with all knowledge and that he had thoroughly appropriated and assimilated the stores which he had gathered. He appeared to me to put a rein on this fancy and humor, but from one or two specimens of it which I witnessed, I felt sure that the hiding of their power was in him. What Dr. Bethune was in his palmy days in America, I of course do not know, but if he was a wreck in Florence, I for one should envy such a wreck. That clearness of thought uttering itself in corresponding clearness of language, that judicial quietness and authority with which he was wont to utter his opinions, the authority which is not assumed and which is the opposite of dogmatism; surely betokened no relaxation in the native tension of his powers. His general information was remarkable. I remember at one time hearing him talk to several gentlemen upon the history of Africa, and he discoursed almost without interruption for the space of an hour, detailing the most interesting facts. At another time he entertained us with an off-hand lecture on architecture, showing the origin of the different orders, and concluding thus: 'Now if you would have the principles in short compass try and remember these ten lines;' which were then recited. He was in fact a full man, well informed on most subjects."

But the most pleasing topic for the conclusion of our memoir, and that which is most important, was his sincere life of faith. Rev. Mr. Cooke who was brought into the closest relation by the communion of forest life, thus discourses of the simplicity of his piety:

"Dr. Bethune's theological sentiments were undoubtedly in hearty accordance with the venerable symbol which expresses the faith of his communion, yet of all the parts and supports of this noble temple of faith, the humiliation, sacrifice and resurrection of the Lord Jesus Christ were plainly to him the main pillar. We might be many days with him and hear no allusion to the abstruse features of his belief; but he could never be many hours with him, without the most tender allusion to or recognition of, Christ's love to the sinner; to himself the sinner. And this characteristic of his mere religious faith, was equally such of his practical piety. This sinner, this Saviour, were plainly his uppermost religious thoughts. How much they predominated in his public discourses, is known to others more fully than to me; but how full his conversation was of these themes, I can largely testify. In the house, on the steamer, under the tent, on the mossy slope in the wilderness, the name and the offering of the Saviour came as readily and frequently to his lips, as the literary quotation, the reminiscence of travel, the anecdote or burst of humor. Subjection to the Redeemer was evidently a leaven, pervading his whole character; all other qualities were to be controlled by, or be in unison with it.

I remember a conversation with a gentleman in the backwoods of Canada, in which he remarked with the deepest feeling on this trait in Dr. Bethune.

The Doctor had spent the previous night in his family; a family of unusual cultivation, for those regions. His devotions with them at the family altar, were so simple, earnest, and childlike, that they were overpowered; and the gentleman owned that he had new lustre shed on religious character and living, by the scenes of the past night and morning at his house. In the conversation of their guest there had been everything to mark the man of gifts, the scholar, the traveller, the divine; and when they bent in prayer it was in expectation of devotion of the same character with his conversation. But no! their guest was at once a little child, pleading with his Father, in recognition, supplication, and praise: and they all rose from their knees in tears. This is perhaps as good an illustration as I could give of the point I am dwelling on.

On his last visit West, he spent a Sabbath at St. Katharine's, Canada West. One of the leading members of a church to which he preached spoke to me with delight of his ministration. He took the platform in front of and lower than the pulpit, and addressed his hearers familiarly on 'the great salvation.' 'I could have sat all day and all night and listened,' said this gentleman; 'it was like a father, or an elder brother, giving lessons drawn from a lifetime for the good of those younger or of lesser experience and knowledge than himself.

In a letter to me, written just as he set out on his last voyage from home, he writes: 'do pray for me, my dear C. as a sinner wholly dependent on the mercy of God through Jesus Christ, for salvation, and earnestly desirous of eternal life. I need special aid from the Holy Spirit to rise above the effect of nervous depression on my mind.' All is in these few words, illustrative of the nature of his piety."

Rev. G. F. Comfort was with Dr. Bethune frequently during his last visit to Florence, and his relation possesses interest.

"Long shall I remember the first long walk we took together. It was a beautiful morning in April; we passed down the Lungo d' Arno till we came to the Cascine, thence turning by the Villa Demidoff we walked along the dykes that every where intersect those fertile plains. The air was warm, clear, and balmy. The fields were fragrant with the flowers of early spring. The bright green of the vine leaves and of the mulberry trees under the brilliant light of the sun almost dazzled the eyes. Beyond, Florence with its domes, towers, and palaces rested in beautiful repose on the plains; Fiesole, San Miniato, and the Appenines filled up the background of the enchanting picture.

It was a scene to awaken the liveliest emotions of the heart, and most deeply did Dr. Bethune drink in its influence. His mind almost leaped with activity as he discoursed of classic literature, of religion, of art and of politics. The walk proved to be longer than we had expected, but Dr. Bethune did not appear to be wearied by it. Indeed, on that and several other occasions, he seemed able to endure more fatigue than I could, young and healthy as I was. Dr. Bethune often talked of our country (and you well know how deeply his heart was moved for our beloved land, in this its time of agony), but never have I heard him express himself with more clearness and feeling than on that morning. The course of the Scotch seemed to pain him the most deeply, of all those that have turned their influence against the American Union, especially that of the members of the Free Church. He spoke of the position he had taken on public occasions, years ago, concerning the necessity of our people's cultivating a more patriotic and national spirit, and of the opposition his views met with, especially at several college commencements. Then, turning to those very opposers, he showed where nearly every one of them had used, since this fearful rebellion broke out, almost the identical words that he used when we were in peace.

The best evidence that can be given of his religious experience was the calmness and Christian cheerfulness with which he looked forward to death. I remember particularly the impression made upon my mind by his quiet and untroubled manner of speaking of his probably near approaching death. It was while walking down the Arno, below the Cascine. He remarked, 'I do not expect ever to see America again, and I shall probably die here in Florence. For me, personally, it is all the same, and Florence is a beautiful place to die in. I should like to live some years longer, if I could do good, but my days are probably numbered and I believe I am ready to go.' These, I think, were his exact words. Without knowing, at the time, his disease, I asked him what it was; he replied, calmly, it was apoplexy or palsy.

I called upon Dr. Bethune the evening before the Sunday on which he so suddenly passed away. During the course of the conversation, he gave a short sketch of his life. He spoke of the time and circumstances under which he entered the ministry, of how near his calling lay to his heart, and of the changes he passed through in his ministerial labors at Rhinebeck, Utica, Philadelphia, Brooklyn and New York. I asked him in which place his labors had been most pleasant. 'I cannot tell,' was his reply; 'God has always been gracious to me, and the world has treated me kindly. God has always given me kind friends that have helped me in my labors, and I have tried to work in His fear.'

Speaking of his preaching on the coming Sabbath, I took the liberty to remark that it seemed to me that he ought to decline preaching as far as possible. He replied, 'I shall do so hereafter, as far as I can. My physical system is so liable now, to be broken down, that I feel the necessity of avoiding the excitement and the consequent relapse that is induced by preaching. I shall not preach very hard to-morrow. And still I love to preach when I can. My time is short here, and I desire to do what little may be in my power before I go hence.'

I remarked, before leaving, that I should, perhaps, go to hear

Father Gavazzi on the coming Sabbath. 'Do so,' was his reply; 'you can hear English preaching at home, at any time. Improve your opportunity of hearing the Italians in their efforts to evangelize this country. They are doing much good for Italy.' "

Perhaps the grandeur and frequent elevation of his manner led some to think him proud and lifted up, but we have shown that he walked very humbly before God. His taste for speculation and philosophic research might have seduced him from the simplicity of Christ, yet he was like a little child sitting at the feet of Jesus to receive instruction. Bred a strict Calvinist, he never departed from the faith of his fathers; yet he was most catholic in spirit and embraced all Christians in his arms of charity. Beaming with humor, imparting vivacity to every circle in which he mingled ; yet there was a tinge of melancholy about the man which softened the brightest smile. A sharp controversialist, mightily fierce for what he considered the path of duty, yet he never broke the rules of politeness, never forgot to be a gentleman. Everywhere he was recognized as a leader, and courted by all, yet none were too mean for his courtesy, and he was especially considerate of young men.

The clarion voice of that eloquent preacher of Christ and him crucified, is now silent. That valiant soldier of the cross, who rose victorious from a hundred battles fought for the cause of truth and righteousness, has now gone to receive the conqueror's reward. The true patriot, who loved his native land with a devotion strong as death, has become a citizen of the New Jerusalem. That ripe scholar, rich in varied stores of earthly knowledge, is now studying out the glories of that place where "there shall be no more death, neither sorrow, nor crying, neither shall there be any more pain." That earnest lover of Jesus now has his wish fully gratified, and beholds his Saviour face to face. Death has obtained this noble victim; nevertheless he lives, lives in our memories, lives in the churches which he reared to Immanuel's praise, lives in the charities which he advanced, lives in precious souls helped on to heaven. Nor can we conclude this record better than in his own words on the death of Washington Irving. "Let us honor his memory by following his example, if we cannot imitate the beauty of his power, for it is not given to every one to be great, to instruct all as a master; let us each in his sphere show in his life that he has not read in vain the lessons of that beautiful teacher, who, though dead, yet speaketh."

FINIS.

www.ingramcontent.com/pod-product-compliance
Lightning Source LLC
LaVergne TN
LVHW021123110826
845150LV00005B/932
9781425551490